Slow Cooker
Comfort Food

Slow Cooker Comfort Food

275 Soul-Satisfying Recipes

Judith Finlayson

Robert
ROSE

Slow Cooker Comfort Food
Text copyright © 2009 Judith Finlayson
Photographs copyright © 2009 Robert Rose Inc.
Cover and text design copyright © 2009 Robert Rose Inc.

For complete cataloguing information, see page 384.

Disclaimer
The recipes in this book have been carefully tested by our kitchen and our tasters. To the best of our knowledge, they are safe and nutritious for ordinary use and users. For those people with food or other allergies, or who have special food requirements or health issues, please read the suggested contents of each recipe carefully and determine whether or not they may create a problem for you. All recipes are used at the risk of the consumer.

We cannot be responsible for any hazards, loss or damage that may occur as a result of any recipe use.

For those with special needs, allergies, requirements or health problems, in the event of any doubt, please contact your medical adviser prior to the use of any recipe.

Design and Production: PageWave Graphics Inc.
Editor: Carol Sherman
Recipe Editor: Jennifer MacKenzie
Proofreader: Gillian Watts
Photography: Colin Erricson
Food Styling: Kathryn Robertson
Prop Styling: Charlene Erricson

Cover image: Braised Veal with Pearl Onions and Sweet Peas (page 232)

We acknowledge the financial support of the Government of Canada through the Book Publishing Industry Development Program (BPIDP) for our publishing activities.

Published by Robert Rose Inc.
120 Eglinton Avenue East, Suite 800, Toronto, Ontario, Canada M4P 1E2
Tel: (416) 322-6552 Fax: (416) 322-6936

Printed and bound in Canada

1 2 3 4 5 6 7 8 9 TCP 17 16 15 14 13 12 11 10 09

Contents

Introduction

"Stay me with flagons, comfort me with apples: for I am sick of love."
— Song of Solomon

Whether King Solomon actually wrote the poem that bears his name is hotly debated among biblical scholars, but there's little doubt the lovesick author recognized that food, as well as wine, has the power to ease emotional pain. Today we call this phenomenon comfort food — the home-style victuals we associate with emotional nourishment in addition to physical sustenance. It's the chicken soup prepared for an invalid or the hearty stew served as an antidote to inclement weather.

When the esteemed writer M.F.K. Fisher was asked why she chose food as her primary topic — rather than more obvious subjects such as power or love — she replied that in her mind these three basic needs were so deeply intertwined she couldn't think of them as separate entities. "So it happens that when I write of hunger, I am really writing about love and the hunger for it, and warmth and the love of it and the hunger for it . . . ," she commented, furthering the idea that consuming food is much more than an act of survival. It is also a way of obtaining spiritual satisfaction or providing a sense of security in unsettled times.

Consider annual holidays, a feature of many cultures. Some, such as Thanksgiving, Passover and Ramadan, are associated with foods in ritualistic ways that reference the past (turkey, matzo and harira, respectively). Food as a salve and historical connector is, perhaps, most evident in immigrant communities, where traditional dishes function as a link with the homeland and help people adjust to unfamiliar environments. If cherished recipes are all that people can bring with them, these dishes reverberate, providing a sense of continuity that may be lacking in daily life.

In 1977, Webster's Dictionary broke new ground when it added a definition of comfort food that included the notion "food prepared in a traditional style having a usually nostalgic or sentimental appeal." This idea is easy to grasp — most of us have a repertoire of cherished recollections involving food, from a favorite relative's home-baked cookies to the dishes served at special occasions and holiday meals.

In the first volume of his massive opus *À la recherche du temps perdu (Remembrance of Things Past)*, the French writer Marcel Proust explored the emotional connections between food and memory. In the process he elevated the madeleine, a tiny shell-shaped cake, to iconic status. Returning to his childhood home for a visit with his mother, the author felt very despondent. When she served him tea accompanied by a madeleine, one bite had a magical effect: the taste of the cake lifted his depression. At first Proust was puzzled by his reaction, but he pondered his experience and eventually made the connection. As a child, before leaving for church on Sundays, he would visit his beloved Aunt Léonie to share a madeleine dipped in tea. He realized that the taste of his mother's cake had resurrected these long-forgotten happy memories and cheered him up. So, not surprisingly, the aroma of chicken soup simmering on the stove evokes vivid images of my mother, and the kitchen in my childhood home where I spent many hours drawing, coloring or perhaps even helping out while she cooked. These are happy memories I associate with a sense of stability as well as physical and emotional well-being. In my mind they are linked with homegrown North American dishes such as pot roast, beef stew, chilies, fruit cobblers and creamy puddings.

But people are diverse, and the same foods don't resonate with everyone. For my friend Raghavan Iyer, who grew up in Bombay, comfort food is the rich curries, steamed cakes and sweet desserts of his lacto-vegetarian family and, later, the taboo street food he discovered on his own, all of which he has written about in his splendid memoir, *The Turmeric Trail*. Whenever I visit Vancouver and lunch with a Chinese-Canadian friend, we enjoy his preferred homey pleasures — congee, slurpy noodles in pork broth or steamed buns. Similarly, in England my British friends gravitate toward what they cheerfully call "nursery food," which includes steamed puddings such as spotted dick, not to mention tea heavily laced with milk and sugar. If you hail from Mexico, tacos and atole are likely to make your list, and German people are inclined to crave sausages and sauerkraut.

All of which is to say, although most people have a clear idea of what constitutes comfort food ("Don't forget lasagna," one friend suggested, and "There's nothing like a good goulash when it's cold outside," offered another), the concept is actually pretty open-ended. The list varies depending upon the individual. Moreover, in our globalized world, fresh ideas for unpretentious dishes with the potential for emotional resonance are likely to come from anywhere. For instance, nowadays a visitor to any major city is likely to feel overwhelmed by the number and diversity of ethnic restaurants. This culinary bazaar has dramatically increased the comfort-food pool from which we all can draw, and as a result many people have bonded with previously exotic offerings such as pho, polenta and risotto. In recent years my husband developed a comfortable-old-shoe fondness for a version of captain's curry that we often enjoy at a neighborhood café. It's not unusual for us to spend a chilly Sunday afternoon cooking up curry and dal, now traditional cold-weather dishes in our home. Neither of us is of French heritage, but when our daughter was a baby we adopted tourtière, a favorite meat pie from Quebec, as our traditional Christmas Eve meal. I have no doubt that it will rank high on our daughter's comfort-food hit parade.

International travel is another catalyst for expanding your gastronomic repertoire and integrating resonant discoveries into your culinary memory book. After a trip to Thailand several years ago, my family fell in love with mangos and sticky rice, which we now make in various forms and which inspired my recipe Black Sticky Rice

Congee with Coconut (see page 30). Chocolate Atole (see page 34) grew out of a visit to El Bajio, a wonderful restaurant in Mexico City where I first sipped this sumptuous drink. And my fondness for sauerkraut (see Choucroute Ragoût, page 245, Braised Canadian Bacon with Sauerkraut, page 258, and Braised Ribs with Sauerkraut, page 270), which I now make annually myself, emerged the year I graduated from university and spent a summer living in Munich. As you try the recipes in this book, I hope you'll be encouraged to create new food traditions of your own.

In other words, while comfort food is strongly linked with a person's past, certain comestibles have the potential to transcend time and place and work their way into our hearts. I've tried to capture these essentials in this book, building the recipes around wholesome, robust dishes, many of which have retro appeal: warm and soothing appetizers such as Cheddar-Onion Melt (see page 45), comforting soups such as Classic Cream of Mushroom (see page 62), hearty stews such as Wine-Soaked Beef Bourguignon (see page 180) and sumptuous desserts such as Chocolate Bread-and-Butter Pudding (see page 357). My concept of comfort food is strongly linked with cold-weather cooking. It is warm and welcoming and provides a sense of sustenance — a kind of culinary haven in a heartless world. But most of all it is delicious. When things seem grim, there is nothing like a mouth-watering bite of something delectable to set things right. Or, as the ever-elegant M.F.K. Fisher reflected, "At the end [of a good meal] you know that Fate cannot harm you, for you have dined."

Using Your Slow Cooker

An Effective Time Manager

In addition to producing great-tasting food, a slow cooker is one of the most effective time management tools any cook can have. Basically it allows you to be in the kitchen when it suits your schedule. If you prefer, you can do most of the prep work in advance, when it's most convenient for you, and once the appliance is turned on there is little or nothing left for you to do. The slow cooker performs unattended while you carry on with your workaday life. You can be away from the kitchen all day and return to a hot, delicious meal.

Slow Cooker Basics

A Low-Tech Appliance

Slow cookers are amazingly low-tech. The appliance usually consists of a metal casing and a stoneware insert with a tight-fitting lid. For convenience, you should be able to remove the insert from the metal casing. This makes it easier to clean and increases its versatility, not only as a vessel for refrigerating dishes that have been prepared to the Make Ahead stage, but also as a serving dish. The casing contains the heat source, electrical coils that usually surround the stoneware insert. These coils do their work using the energy it takes to power a 100-watt light bulb. Because the slow cooker operates on such a small amount of energy, you can safely leave it turned on while you are away from home.

Shapes, Sizes and Configurations

Slow cookers are generally round or oval in shape and range in size from 1 to 8 quarts. The small round ones are ideal for dips and fondues, as well as some soups, main courses and desserts. The smaller oval ones (approximately $1\frac{1}{2}$ to 4 quarts) are extremely versatile, as they are small enough to work well with smaller quantities but have enough volume to accommodate some full-batch recipes. The larger sizes, usually oval in shape, are necessary to cook big-batch dishes and those that need to be cooked in a dish or pan that can fit into the stoneware.

I have recommended slow cooker sizes for all my recipes. However, please be aware that so many new models are coming onto the market that I have not been able to test all the configurations myself. Use your common sense. The stoneware should be about one-third to three-quarters full. Pieces of meat that can feed a large number of people (such as pork butt cooked in a minimal amount of liquid) may fit quite nicely into some of the smaller oval shapes, but dishes that contain an abundance of vegetables and liquid will likely need a model that can accommodate greater volume. The smaller oval cookers are extremely versatile because the larger bottom surface can accommodate chunks of fish or larger pieces of meat such as half a brisket. Because I use my slow cookers a lot for entertaining, I feel there is a benefit to having at least two: a smaller (1 1/2 to 4 quart), which is ideal for preparing dips, roasting nuts or making recipes with smaller yields, and a larger (6 to 8 quart) oval one, which I use most of the time to cook recipes with larger yields as well as those calling for a baking dish or pan set inside the stoneware. Once you begin using your slow cooker, you will get a sense of what suits your needs.

Some manufacturers sell a "slow cooker" which is actually a multi-cooker. These have a heating element at the bottom, and in my experience they cook faster than traditional slow cookers. Also, since the heat source is at the bottom, the food is likely to scorch unless it is stirred.

Your slow cooker should come with a booklet that explains how to use the appliance. I recommend that you read this carefully and/or visit the manufacturer's website for specific information on the model you purchased. There are now so many models, shapes and sizes of slow cookers on the market that it is impossible to give one-size-fits-all instructions for using them.

Cooking Times

Over the years I've cooked in a wide variety of slow cookers and have found that cooking times can vary substantially from one to another. This is true even among different models sold under the same brand. The quality control on some of the lower-priced models may not be as rigorous as it should be, which accounts for some of the difference. That said, I've also found that some of the newer slow cookers tend to cook much more quickly than those that are a few years old. Please bear these discrepancies in mind if you follow my recipes and find that your food is overcooked. Although it may not seem particularly helpful if you're just starting out, the only firm advice I can give is *Know your slow cooker*. After trying a few of these recipes, you will get a sense of whether your slow cooker is faster or slower than the ones I use, and you will be able to adjust the cooking times accordingly. Other variables that can affect cooking time are extreme humidity, power fluctuations and high altitude. Be extra vigilant if any of these circumstances affect you.

Cooking Great-Tasting Food

The slow cooker's less-is-better approach is, in many ways, the secret of its success. The appliance does its work by cooking foods very slowly — from about 200°F (90°C) on the Low setting to 300°F (150°C) on High. This slow, moist cooking environment enables the appliance to produce mouth-watering pot roasts, briskets, chilies and many kinds of soups and stews. It also helps to ensure success with delicate puddings and custards, among other dishes. In fact, I'm so pleased with the slow cooker's strengths that there are many dishes I wouldn't cook any other way — for instance, pot roast, beef brisket or short ribs, beef, veal and lamb shanks, chilies and many kinds of stew. I also love to make cheesecakes in my slow cooker because they emerge from this damp cocoon perfectly cooked every time. They have a beautifully creamy texture and don't dry out or crack, which happens all too easily in the oven.

Some benefits of long, slow cooking:
- it breaks down the tough connective tissue of less tender cuts of meat;
- it allows the seasoning in complex sauces to intermingle without scorching;
- it makes succulent chilies and stews that don't dry out or stick to the bottom of the pot; and
- it ensures success with delicate dishes such as puddings and custards.

Entertaining Worthy

I often use my slow cookers to help prepare the meal when I entertain, and as you use this book you'll notice recipes that have been identified as "Entertaining Worthy." Some of these, such as Shrimp Bisque, Braised Halibut on a Bed of Creamy Leeks and Madame Saint-Ange's Peruvian Cream are clearly "special occasion" dishes, but many, including Paprikash Cobbler, Onion-Braised Brisket and Poached Quince, may strike you as pretty down-home, particularly if you're trying to impress guests. All of which is to say, my selections are entirely subjective and very much reflect my own approach to entertaining. While every now and again I like to pull out the stops and do a bang-up elegant dinner party, most of the time I prefer to have one or two couples over for a casual Friday night meal. And on those evenings the kinds of dishes everyone prefers tend to be classic low-key comfort foods, which in my opinion are truly "entertaining worthy."

Understanding Your Slow Cooker

Like all appliances, the slow cooker has its unique way of doing things, so you need to understand how it works and adapt your cooking style accordingly. Years ago, when friends learned I was writing my first slow cooker cookbook, many had the same response: "Oh, you mean that appliance that allows you to throw the ingredients in and return home to a cooked meal!"

"Well, sort of," was my response. Over the years I've learned to think of my slow cooker as an indispensable helpmate, and I can hardly imagine living without its assistance. But I also know that it can't work miracles. Off the top of my head, I can't think of any great dish that results when ingredients are merely "thrown together." Success in the slow cooker, like success in the oven or on top of the stove, depends upon using proper cooking techniques. The slow cooker saves you time because it allows you to forget about the food once it is in the stoneware. But you still must pay attention to the advance preparation. Here are a few tips that will help to ensure slow cooker success.

Brown Meat and Soften Vegetables

Although it requires an extra pan, I am committed to browning most meats and softening vegetables before adding them to the slow cooker. In my experience this is not the most time-consuming part of preparing a slow cooker dish — it usually takes longer to peel and chop the vegetables, which you have to do anyway. But it dramatically improves the quality of the dish for two reasons. Not only does browning add color, it begins the process of caramelization, which breaks down the natural sugars in foods and releases their flavor. It also extracts the fat-soluble components of foods, which further enriches the taste. Moreover, tossing herbs and spices in with the softened vegetables helps to produce a sauce in which the flavors are better integrated than they would be if this step were skipped.

Reduce the Quantity of Liquid

As you use your slow cooker, one of the first things you will notice is that it generates liquid. Because slow cookers cook at a low heat, tightly covered, liquid doesn't evaporate as it does in the oven or on top of the stove. As a result, food made from traditional recipes will be watery. So the second rule of successful slow cooking is to reduce the amount of liquid. Because I don't want to reduce the flavor, I prefer to cook with stock rather than water.

Cut Root Vegetables into Thin Slices or Small Pieces

Perhaps surprisingly, root vegetables — carrots, parsnips and particularly potatoes — cook even more slowly than meat in the slow cooker. Root vegetables should be thinly sliced or cut into small pieces: no larger than 1-inch (2.5 cm) cubes.

Pay Attention to Cooking Temperature

To achieve maximum results, less tender cuts of meat should be cooked as slowly as possible. Expect to cook whole cuts of meat such as brisket and roasts for 8 to 10 hours on Low to become truly succulent. If you're short of time and at home during the day, cook whole cuts of meat on High for 1 to 2 hours before switching the temperature to Low. As noted in Food Safety in the Slow Cooker (see page 18), if adding cold ingredients, particularly large cuts of meat, to the slow cooker, set it on High for an hour before lowering the temperature.

Many desserts such as those containing milk, cream or some leavening agents need to be cooked on High. In these recipes, a Low setting is not suggested as an option. For recipes that aren't dependent upon cooking at a particular temperature, the rule of thumb is that 1 hour of cooking on High equals 2 to $2\frac{1}{2}$ hours on Low.

Don't Overcook

Although slow cooking reduces your chances of overcooking food, it is still not a "one size fits all" solution to meal preparation. If you want your slow cooker to cook while you are away, you should plan your day carefully if you have more delicate meats such as chicken in the pot. It is very easy to overcook poultry, which shouldn't require more than 6 hours on Low. If cooking white meat, which dries out easily, reduce the cooking time to 5 hours. Because legs and thighs stand up well in the slow cooker, I remove the skin before cooking to reduce the fat content in the sauce.

Use Ingredients Appropriately

Some ingredients do not respond well to long, slow cooking and should be added during the last 30 minutes, after the temperature has been increased to High. These include peas, leafy greens, seafood, milk and cream (which will curdle if cooked too long). I love to cook with peppers, but I've learned that most become bitter if cooked for too long. The solution to this problem is to add peppers to recipes during the last 30 minutes of cooking. All the recipes in this book address these concerns in the instructions.

Whole-Leaf Herbs and Spices

For best results use whole rather than ground herbs and spices in the slow cooker. Whole spices such as cinnamon sticks, vanilla beans and whole-leaf herbs such as dried thyme and oregano leaves release their flavors slowly throughout the long cooking period, unlike ground spices and herbs, which tend to lose flavor during slow cooking. If you're using fresh herbs, add them finely chopped, during the last hour of cooking, unless you include the whole stem (this works best with thyme and rosemary).

I recommend the use of cracked black peppercorns rather than ground pepper in many of my recipes because they release flavor slowly during the long cooking process. "Cracked pepper" can be purchased in the spice sections of supermarkets, but I like to make my own with a mortar and pestle. A rolling pin or even a heavy can on its side will also break up the peppercorns for use in slow-cooked dishes. If you prefer to use ground black pepper, use one-quarter to one-half the amount of cracked black peppercorns called for in the recipe.

Using Dishes and Pans in the Slow Cooker

Some dishes, notably puddings and custards, need to be cooked in an extra dish that is placed in the slow cooker stoneware. Not only will you need a large oval slow cooker for this purpose, finding a dish or pan that fits into the stoneware can be a challenge. I've found that standard 7-inch (17.5 cm) square, 4-cup (1 L) and 6-cup (1.5 L) ovenproof baking dishes or soufflé dishes are the best all-round pans for this purpose, and I've used them to cook most of the custard-like recipes in this book. A 7-inch (17.5 cm) springform pan, which fits into a large oval slow cooker, is also a useful item for making cheesecakes.

Before you decide to make a recipe requiring a baking dish, ensure that you have a container that will fit into your stoneware. I've noted the size and dimensions of the containers used in all relevant recipes. Be aware that varying the size and shape of the dish is likely to affect cooking times.

Making Smaller Quantities

Over the years many people have asked me for slow cooker recipes that make smaller quantities, suitable for one or two people. Since most recipes reheat well or can be frozen for future use, making a big-batch recipe can be an efficient strategy for having a delicious, nutritious meal on hand for those nights when there is no time to cook. However, since more and more households comprise single people or couples who want to enjoy the benefits of using a slow cooker, I have noted those recipes that are suitable for being halved. Since slow cookers depend on volume to operate efficiently, it is important to use a small slow cooker (approximately $1\frac{1}{2}$ to $3\frac{1}{2}$ quarts) when cutting a recipe in half.

Making Ahead

Most of the recipes in this book can be partially prepared ahead of time and held for up to two days in the refrigerator, which is a great time saver for busy days. (Look for the Make Ahead instructions accompanying appropriate recipes.) If a recipe contains meat, for food safety reasons you cannot brown it ahead of time, nor can uncooked meat be combined with vegetables and held. For small pieces of meat, such as diced bacon, ground meat or sausage meat, that are fully cooked with vegetables before being placed in the stoneware, it is important to ensure that the mixture cools quickly to a safe temperature. Therefore I recommend placing these mixtures in a shallow container, then refrigerating them. This ensures that they are out of the danger zone within the preferred 30 minutes.

As a rule of thumb, I recommend refrigerating mixtures in a separate container, then transferring them to the stoneware. However, some vegetarian dishes can be preassembled in the stoneware and refrigerated, in which case be sure not to turn the slow cooker on before dropping the stoneware into the casing — the dramatic temperature change could crack it.

Maximize Slow Cooker Convenience

To get the most out of your slow cooker, consider the following:
- Prepare ingredients to the cooking stage the night before you intend to cook, to keep work to a minimum in the morning.
- Cook a recipe overnight and refrigerate until ready to serve.
- Make a big-batch recipe and freeze a portion for a second or even a third meal.

Food Safety in the Slow Cooker

Because it cooks at a very low temperature for long periods of time, cooking with a slow cooker requires a bit more vigilance about food safety than does cooking at higher temperatures. The slow cooker needs to strike a delicate balance between cooking slowly enough that it doesn't require your attention and fast enough to ensure that food reaches temperatures that are appropriate to inhibit bacterial growth. Bacteria grow rapidly at temperatures higher than 40°F (4°C) and lower than 140°F (60°C). Once the temperature reaches 165°F (74°C), bacteria are killed. That's why it is so important to leave the lid on when you're slow cooking, particularly during the early stages. This helps to ensure that bacteria-killing temperatures are reached in the appropriate amount of time.

Slow cooker manufacturers have designed the appliance to ensure that bacterial growth is not a concern. So long as the lid is left on and the food is cooked for the appropriate length of time, that crucial temperature will be reached quickly enough to ensure food safety. Unless you have made part of the recipe ahead and refrigerated it, most of the ingredients in my recipes are warm when added to the slow cooker (the meat has been browned and the sauce has been thickened on the stovetop), which adds a cushion of comfort to any potential concerns about food safety.

The following tips will help to ensure that utmost food safety standards are met:

- Keep food refrigerated until you are ready to cook. Bacteria multiply quickly at room temperature. Do not allow ingredients to rise to room temperature before cooking.
- Do not partially cook meat or poultry and refrigerate for subsequent cooking. If you're browning meat before adding it to the slow cooker, do so just before placing it in the slow cooker. When cooking meat, try to get it to a high temperature as quickly as possible.
- If cooking a large cut of meat, such as a pot roast, which has been added to the stoneware without being browned, set the temperature at High for at least an hour to accelerate the cooking process.
- Pay attention to the make-ahead instructions for recipes that can be partially prepared in advance of cooking, as they have been developed to address food safety issues.
- If you're making part of a recipe ahead and it contains cooked meat such as sausage or ground beef mixed with vegetables, cool the mixture to a safe temperature (less than 40°F/4°C) as quickly as possible. To ensure it doesn't stay in the danger zone any longer than 30 minutes, spread the mixture in a shallow container (use more than one, if necessary), cover and refrigerate immediately. Or (this works in some recipes) refrigerate precooked meat such as ground beef or sausage and vegetables in separate containers and assemble when ready to cook. Do not brown meat until you're ready to cook. Browning meat, then refrigerating it encourages the growth of harmful bacteria.

- Do not put frozen meat, fish or poultry into a slow cooker. Unless otherwise instructed, thaw frozen food before adding to the slow cooker. Frozen fruits and vegetables should usually be thawed under cold running water to separate them before being added to recipes.
- Limit the number of times you lift the lid while food is cooking. Each time the lid is removed it takes approximately 20 minutes to recover the lost heat. This increases the time it takes for the food to reach the "safe zone."
- If the power goes out while you are away, discard the food if it has not finished cooking. If the food has cooked completely, it should be safe for up to 2 hours.
- Refrigerate leftovers as quickly as possible.
- Do not reheat food in the slow cooker.

Testing for Safety

If you are concerned that your slow cooker isn't cooking quickly enough to ensure food safety, try this simple test. Fill the stoneware insert with 8 cups (2 L) of cold water. Set temperature to Low for 8 hours. Using an accurate thermometer and checking quickly (because the temperature drops when the lid is removed), check to ensure that the temperature is 185°F (85°C). If the slow cooker has not reached that temperature, it's not heating food fast enough to avoid food safety problems. If the temperature is significantly higher than that, the appliance is not cooking slowly enough to be used as a slow cooker.

Leftovers

Many slow cookers have a Warm setting, which holds the food at 165°F (74°C). Programmable models will automatically switch to Warm when the time is up. Cooked food can be kept warm in the slow cooker for up to 2 hours. At that point it should be transferred to small containers so it cools as rapidly as possible and then be refrigerated or frozen. Because the appliance heats up so slowly, food should never be reheated in a slow cooker.

Bread and Breakfast

Sticky Rhubarb Bread

Sticky Rhubarb Bread

I just love the sticky rhubarb topping on this tasty bread. I like to serve it as a dessert, warm from the slow cooker, and plated with forks. Leftovers are great, but to get the full benefit of the rhubarb topping, I recommend that you warm it in the microwave.

Tip

I prefer to use half whole wheat flour when making this bread as it adds a pleasing texture. If you don't have any on hand, feel free to substitute all-purpose flour.

Makes 1 loaf (10 slices)

- Large (minimum 5 quart) oval slow cooker
- Greased 8- by 4-inch (20 by 10 cm) approx. loaf pan or 6-cup (1.5 L) soufflé or baking dish (see Tip, page 23)

Topping

1 cup	diced rhubarb	250 mL
⅓ cup	packed brown sugar, preferably Demerara or other raw cane sugar	75 mL
¼ cup	melted butter	50 mL
2 tbsp	freshly squeezed orange juice	25 mL

Bread

¾ cup	whole wheat flour (see Tip, left)	175 mL
¾ cup	all-purpose flour	175 mL
½ cup	granulated sugar	125 mL
½ cup	chopped pecans, optional	125 mL
1 tsp	baking powder	5 mL
½ tsp	salt	2 mL
½ tsp	freshly grated nutmeg	2 mL
1	egg	1
1 tsp	vanilla extract	5 mL
	Finely grated zest of 1 orange	
½ cup	sour cream	125 mL
½ cup	freshly squeezed orange juice	125 mL
¼ cup	vegetable oil	50 mL

1. **Topping:** In a bowl, combine rhubarb, brown sugar, butter and orange juice. Spread evenly over bottom of prepared pan.

2. **Bread:** In another bowl, combine whole wheat and all-purpose flours, sugar, pecans, if using, baking powder, salt and nutmeg. Make a well in the middle.

3. In a separate bowl, beat egg, vanilla and orange zest. Add sour cream, orange juice and oil and mix well. Pour into well and mix with dry ingredients just until blended.

4. Spoon batter into prepared pan. Cover tightly with foil and secure with a string. Place in slow cooker stoneware and pour in enough boiling water to come 1 inch (2.5 cm) up the sides of the dish. Cover and cook on High for 4 hours, until a tester inserted in the center comes out clean. Unmold and serve warm or let cool.

Parsnip-Laced Oat Bread

When I came across a recipe for this bread in The Book of New New England Cookery *by Judith and Evan Jones, I was so intrigued I just had to try it. This adaptation provides real whole-grain goodness plus the convenience of the slow cooker. Serve it warm with soup for a satisfying light dinner and enjoy any leftovers toasted with your favorite jam for breakfast.*

Vegetarian Friendly

Makes 1 loaf (12 slices)

- Large (minimum 5 quart) oval slow cooker
- Greased 8- by 4-inch (20 by 10 cm) approx. loaf pan or 6-cup (1.5 L) soufflé or baking dish (see Tip, right)

1¼ cups	rolled oats	300 mL
½ cup	whole wheat flour (see Tip, page 22)	125 mL
½ cup	all-purpose flour	125 mL
1 tsp	baking soda	5 mL
½ tsp	salt	2 mL
¼ tsp	freshly grated nutmeg	1 mL
1	egg, beaten	1
1 cup	mashed cooked parsnips (about 2)	250 mL
¼ cup	liquid honey	50 mL
½ cup	buttermilk	125 mL

1. In a food processor, process rolled oats until floury. Add whole wheat and all-purpose flours, baking soda, salt and nutmeg and pulse to blend.

2. In a bowl, combine egg, parsnips, honey and buttermilk until combined. Add to dry ingredients and pulse just until blended.

3. Spoon batter into prepared pan. Cover tightly with foil and secure with a string. Place in slow cooker stoneware and pour in enough boiling water to come 1 inch (2.5 mL) up the sides of the dish. Cover and cook on High for 4 hours, until a tester inserted in the center comes out clean. Unmold and serve warm or let cool.

Tip

This bread, like the others in this book, can be made in almost any kind of baking dish that will fit into your slow cooker. I have a variety of baking pans that work well: a small loaf pan, about 8 by 4 inches (20 by 10 cm), makes a traditionally shaped bread; a round 6-cup (1.5 L) soufflé dish or a square 7-inch (17.5 cm) baking dish produces slices of different shapes. All taste equally good.

Vegan Friendly

Can Be Halved
see Tips, below

Creamy Rice with Barley

This dense, nutritious cereal is just the thing to take the edge off a chilly morning. Topped with yogurt and drizzled with maple syrup, it will set you up for even the most stressful day.

Serves 6

- Small (2 to 3½ quart) slow cooker, lightly greased

½ cup	brown or red rice (see Tips, left)	125 mL
½ cup	barley (see Tips, left)	125 mL
2 tbsp	brown sugar, preferably Demerara or other raw cane sugar	25 mL
4 cups	vanilla-flavored rice milk	1 L
	Yogurt or non-dairy alternative	
	Maple syrup or liquid honey	

1. In prepared slow cooker stoneware, combine rice, barley, brown sugar and rice milk.
2. Cover and cook on Low for 8 hours or overnight, or on High for 4 hours. Stir well before serving.

Tips

If you are halving this recipe, be sure to use a small (1½ to 2 quart) slow cooker.

Use long-cooking red rice, such as Wehani, Thai or Camargue, or, if you prefer, use a blend of brown and wild rice.

I use whole (hulled) barley, which is the most nutritious version of the grain, but pot or pearled barley work well, too.

Refrigerate any leftovers. They reheat beautifully on the stovetop or in a microwave. Just add a little water and cover.

Hot Mixed Grains

Multigrain breakfasts allow you to enjoy a range of whole grains, providing a wider variety of nutrients than a single grain. I like to eat this with raw cane sugar and milk or with plain yogurt drizzled with maple syrup. For added nutrition, sprinkle with wheat germ or chopped toasted nuts.

Vegan Friendly

Can Be Halved
see Tips, below

Serves 4 to 6

- Small (2 to 3½ quart) slow cooker, lightly greased

¼ cup	oat groats or steel-cut oats	50 mL
¼ cup	brown, red or wild rice or any combination thereof	50 mL
¼ cup	wheat, spelt or rye berries	50 mL
Pinch	salt	Pinch
2½ cups	water	625 mL

1. In prepared slow cooker stoneware, combine oats, rice, wheat berries, salt and water.

2. Cover and cook on Low for 8 hours or overnight, or on High for 4 hours. Stir before serving.

Tips

If you are halving this recipe, be sure to use a small (1½ to 2 quart) slow cooker.

Refrigerate any leftovers. They reheat beautifully on the stovetop or in a microwave. Just add a little water and cover.

Oatmeal Banana Pecan Bread

This bread is loaded with whole-grain wholesomeness and it's delicious to boot! I love eating it for dessert while it is still warm, but it also makes a great snack when cooled.

Makes 1 loaf (12 slices)

Tip

If you don't have buttermilk, substitute your own soured milk. Stir 1 tsp (5 mL) lemon juice into ½ cup (125 mL) milk and let stand for 10 minutes.

- Large (minimum 5 quart) oval slow cooker
- Greased 8- by 4-inch (20 by 10 cm) approx. loaf pan or 6-cup (1.5 L) soufflé or baking dish (see Tip, page 27)

1¼ cups	rolled oats	300 mL
½ cup	whole wheat flour	125 mL
½ cup	all-purpose flour	125 mL
1 tsp	baking powder	5 mL
1 tsp	ground cinnamon	5 mL
½ tsp	salt	2 mL
1	egg, beaten	1
¾ cup	ripe bananas, mashed (about 2 bananas)	175 mL
½ cup	packed brown sugar, preferably Demerara or other raw cane sugar	125 mL
½ cup	buttermilk (see Tip, left)	125 mL
3 tbsp	vegetable oil	45 mL
1 tsp	vanilla extract	5 mL
¾ cup	chopped pecans	175 mL

1. In a food processor, process rolled oats until floury. Add whole wheat and all-purpose flours, baking powder, cinnamon and salt and pulse to blend.

2. In a bowl, combine egg, bananas, brown sugar, buttermilk, oil and vanilla. Mix well. Add to dry ingredients and pulse just until blended. Add pecans and pulse once or twice to distribute.

3. Spoon batter into prepared pan. Cover tightly with foil and secure with a string. Place in slow cooker stoneware and pour in enough boiling water to come 1 inch (2.5 mL) up the sides of the dish. Cover and cook on High for 4 hours, until a tester inserted in the center comes out clean. Unmold and serve warm or let cool.

Cranberry Orange Bread

This wholesome bread has great flavor that can be enjoyed any time of the day. It makes a great snack, substitutes for dessert and works as breakfast-on-the-run.

Makes 1 loaf (12 slices)

- Large (minimum 5 quart) oval slow cooker
- Greased 8- by 4-inch (20 by 10 cm) approx. loaf pan or 6-cup (1.5 L) soufflé or baking dish (see Tip, right)

2 cups	fresh or frozen cranberries	500 mL
2 tbsp	finely grated orange zest (2 oranges)	25 mL
1 cup	whole wheat pastry flour	250 mL
1 cup	all-purpose flour	250 mL
¾ cup	coarsely chopped pecans	175 mL
2 tsp	baking powder	10 mL
½ tsp	baking soda	2 mL
½ tsp	salt	2 mL
½ tsp	ground cinnamon	2 mL
1 cup	packed brown sugar, preferably Demerara or other raw cane sugar	250 mL
¾ cup	freshly squeezed orange juice (about 2 oranges)	175 mL
1	egg, beaten	1
⅓ cup	vegetable oil	75 mL

1. In a food processor, coarsely chop cranberries. Add orange zest and pulse until blended. Set aside.

2. In a large bowl, combine whole wheat and all-purpose flours, pecans, baking powder, baking soda, salt and cinnamon. Make a well in the middle.

3. In a separate bowl, beat brown sugar, orange juice, egg and oil until blended. Pour into well and mix just until blended. Stir in cranberries.

4. Spoon batter into prepared pan. Cover tightly with foil and secure with a string. Place in slow cooker stoneware and pour in enough boiling water to come 1 inch (2.5 mL) up the sides of the dish. Cover and cook on High for 4 hours, until a tester inserted in the center comes out clean. Unmold and serve warm or let cool.

Tip

This bread, like the others in this book, can be made in almost any kind of baking dish that will fit into your slow cooker. I have a variety of baking pans that work well: a small loaf pan, about 8 by 4 inches (20 by 10 cm), makes a traditionally shaped bread; a round 6-cup (1.5 L) soufflé dish or a square 7-inch (17.5 cm) baking dish produces slices of different shapes. All taste equally good.

Carrot Cake Bread

I really like to serve this luscious cake-like bread for dessert with the Cream Cheese Frosting, but it also works well on its own as a quick bread. It's moist and delicious and loaded with nutritious ingredients — perfect for any time you need a quick pick-me-up that is not too decadent.

Tip

If you're frosting this bread, make sure it is cool first. Otherwise, the heat of the warm loaf will melt the frosting.

Makes 1 loaf (12 slices)

- Large (minimum 5 quart) oval slow cooker

1 cup	all-purpose flour	250 mL
1/2 cup	whole wheat pastry flour	125 mL
1 tsp	baking powder	5 mL
1 tsp	ground cinnamon	5 mL
1/2 tsp	freshly grated nutmeg	2 mL
1/4 tsp	ground cloves	1 mL
1 cup	shredded carrots	250 mL
1/2 cup	melted butter	125 mL
1/2 cup	packed brown sugar, preferably Demerara or other raw cane sugar	125 mL
2	eggs, beaten	2
1 tsp	vanilla extract	5 mL
1 cup	crushed pineapple with juice	250 mL
1/2 cup	shredded coconut or chopped walnuts	125 mL

Cream Cheese Frosting, optional

4 oz	cream cheese, softened (1/2 cup/125 mL)	125 g
1/4 cup	butter, softened	50 mL
1/2 tsp	vanilla extract	2 mL
1 cup	confectioner's (icing) sugar, sifted	250 mL

1. In a bowl, combine all-purpose and whole wheat flours, baking powder, cinnamon, nutmeg and cloves. Stir in carrots. Make a well in the middle.

2. In a separate bowl, beat butter, brown sugar, eggs and vanilla until combined. Stir in pineapple with juice. Pour mixture into well and mix just until combined. Stir in coconut.

3. Spoon batter into prepared pan. Cover tightly with foil and secure with a string. Place in slow cooker stoneware and pour in enough boiling water to come 1 inch (2.5 mL) up the sides of the dish. Cover and cook on High for 4 hours, until a tester inserted in the center comes out clean. Unmold and let cool on a rack.

4. **Cream Cheese Frosting,** optional (see Tip, left). In a bowl, using an electric mixer on medium speed, beat cream cheese, butter and vanilla until smooth and creamy. Gradually add sugar, beating until fluffy. Cover and refrigerate until ready to use.

Sweet Potato Date Bread

This tasty bread is also very versatile. I make it in the afternoon so it's ready to eat as a healthy dessert at dinner. It's also a great snacking cake — perfect with an afternoon cup of tea — and it makes an excellent breakfast-on-the-run.

Vegetarian Friendly

Makes 1 loaf (12 slices)

- Large (minimum 5 quart) oval slow cooker
- Greased 8- by 4-inch (20 by 10 cm) approx. loaf pan or 6-cup (1.5 L) soufflé or baking dish (see Tip, right)

1 cup	all-purpose flour	250 mL
½ cup	whole wheat flour	125 mL
½ cup	packed brown sugar, preferably Demerara or other raw cane sugar	125 mL
2 tsp	baking powder	10 mL
½ tsp	baking soda	2 mL
½ tsp	salt	2 mL
1 tsp	ground cinnamon	5 mL
½ tsp	ground allspice	2 mL
½ tsp	ground ginger	2 mL
1 cup	puréed sweet potato	250 mL
½ cup	milk	125 mL
¼ cup	melted butter	50 mL
1	egg	1
½ cup	chopped soft dates, such as Medjool	125 mL
½ cup	chopped pecans	125 mL

1. In a large bowl, combine all-purpose and whole wheat flours, brown sugar, baking powder, baking soda, salt, cinnamon, allspice and ginger. Stir well and make a well in the middle.

2. In a separate bowl, combine sweet potato, milk, butter and egg. Mix well and add all at once to dry ingredients. Stir just until moistened. Fold in dates and pecans.

3. Spoon batter into prepared pan. Cover tightly with foil and secure with a string. Place pan in slow cooker stoneware and pour in enough boiling water to come 1 inch (2.5 cm) up the sides. Cover and cook on High for 4 hours, until a tester inserted in the center of the loaf comes out clean. Unmold and serve warm or let cool.

Tip

This bread, like the others in this book, can be make in almost any kind of baking dish that will fit into your slow cooker. I have a variety of baking pans that work well: a small loaf pan, about 8 by 4 inches (20 by 10 cm), makes a traditionally shaped bread; a round 6-cup (1.5 L) soufflé dish or a square 7-inch (17.5 cm) baking dish produces slices of different shapes. All taste equally good.

Oat Groats or Steel-Cut Oats

Groats are the whole oat kernel that hasn't been cut or flattened in any way. Steel-cut oats, also known as Irish or Scottish oatmeal, are whole oat groats cut into smaller pieces. These are the most nutritious versions of the grain. They are flavorful and nicely chewy and can be eaten with your favorite finish — milk or a non-dairy alternative, sugar or honey, raisins, chopped bananas, toasted nuts or seeds — almost anything that strikes your fancy will work.

Tips

If you are halving this recipe, be sure to use a small (1½ to 2 quart) slow cooker.

If you have problems with gluten and have been told to avoid oats, look for gluten-free steel-cut oats, which are now available.

Refrigerate any leftovers (see Tips, below).

Serves 4 to 6

- Small (2 to 3½ quart) slow cooker, lightly greased

1 cup	oat groats or steel-cut oats (see Tips, left)	250 mL
½ tsp	salt	2 mL
4 cups	water	1 L

1. In slow cooker stoneware, combine oats, salt and water.
2. Cover and cook on Low for 8 hours or overnight, or on High for 4 hours. Stir well before serving.

Whole-Grain "Cream of Wheat"

Growing up, I enjoyed the taste and texture of the breakfast cereal Cream of Wheat, but it is made from farina, which is missing the bran and most of the germ — the most nutritious parts of the grain. This version, made from whole-grain wheat flakes, captures the spirit of the prepared cereal while providing the full range of nutrients that whole wheat contains. Whole wheat is particularly high in fiber (4.3 g per ½ cup/125 mL cooked wheat berries), so a bowl of this tasty cereal will keep you satisfied until it's time for lunch.

Tips

If you are halving this recipe, be sure to use a small (1½ to 2 quart) slow cooker.

Substitute spelt or Kamut flakes for the wheat.

Refrigerate any leftovers. They reheat beautifully on the stovetop or in a microwave. Just add a little water and cover.

Serves 4

- Small (2 to 3½ quart) slow cooker, lightly greased

½ cup	wheat flakes (see Tips, left)	125 mL
2 tbsp	brown sugar, preferably Demerara or other raw cane sugar	25 mL
2 cups	vanilla-flavored soy milk	500 mL

1. In prepared slow cooker stoneware, combine wheat flakes, brown sugar and soy milk. Stir well.
2. Cover and cook on Low for 8 hours or overnight, or on High for 4 hours. Stir well before serving.

Blueberry Corn Bread

Corn and blueberries may seem like an unusual combination, but this tasty loaf melds these ingredients nicely. This is a great snacking bread — not too sweet and loaded with nutrition. Enjoy it any time of the day, even for breakfast.

Makes 1 loaf (12 slices)

- Large (minimum 5 quart) oval slow cooker
- Greased 8- by 4-inch (20 by 10 cm) approx. loaf pan or 6-cup (1.5 L) soufflé or baking dish (see Tips, left)

1¼ cups	stone-ground cornmeal (see Tips, left)	300 mL
¾ cup	all-purpose flour	175 mL
½ cup	packed brown sugar, preferably Demerara or other raw cane sugar	125 mL
2 tsp	baking powder	10 mL
1 tsp	baking soda	5 mL
1 tsp	salt	5 mL
1 cup	corn kernels	250 mL
1 cup	milk	250 mL
¾ cup	sour cream	175 mL
3	eggs, beaten	3
1 tsp	vanilla extract	5 mL
1½ cups	fresh or frozen blueberries	375 mL

1. In a large bowl, combine cornmeal, flour, brown sugar, baking powder, baking soda and salt. Make a well in the middle.

2. In a separate bowl, combine corn, milk, sour cream, eggs and vanilla. Pour into well and mix just until blended. Stir in blueberries.

3. Spoon batter into prepared pan. Cover tightly with foil and secure with a string. Place in slow cooker stoneware and pour in enough boiling water to come 1 inch (2.5 cm) up the sides of the dish. Cover and cook on High for 4 hours, until a tester inserted in the center comes out clean. Unmold and serve warm or let cool.

Tips

This bread, like the others in this book, can be made in almost any kind of baking dish that will fit into your slow cooker. I have a variety of baking pans that work well: a small loaf pan, about 8 by 4 inches (20 by 10 cm), makes a traditionally shaped bread; a round 6-cup (1.5 L) soufflé dish or a square 7-inch (17.5 cm) baking dish produces slices of different shapes. All taste equally good.

Be sure to use stone-ground cornmeal when making this bread. Not only is it the most nutritious form of the grain, the quantities of liquid in the recipe won't work with refined cornmeal.

Jalapeño Corn Bread

This is a light, buttery cornbread. I love to serve it as a side with grilled pork chops, but it works well in any cornbread-friendly situation. Add the second chile if you really like heat.

Vegetarian Friendly

Makes 1 loaf (10 slices)

- Large (minimum 5 quart) oval slow cooker
- Greased 8- by 4-inch (20 by 10 cm) approx. loaf pan or 6-cup (1.5 L) soufflé or baking dish (see Tip, page 32)

1 cup	stone-ground cornmeal (see Tip, right)	250 mL
½ cup	all-purpose flour	125 mL
2 tsp	granulated sugar	10 mL
1 tsp	baking soda	5 mL
1 tsp	salt	5 mL
½ tsp	freshly ground black pepper	2 mL
2	eggs, separated	2
1 cup	full-fat yogurt	250 mL
1 cup	shredded Cheddar cheese	250 mL
1 to 2	jalapeño peppers, seeded and diced	1 to 2
½ cup	melted butter	125 mL

1. In a large bowl, combine cornmeal, flour, sugar, baking soda, salt and pepper. Mix well and make a well in the middle.

2. Beat egg whites until stiff peaks form, and set aside.

3. In a separate bowl, combine egg yolks, yogurt, cheese, jalapeños and butter. Mix well and add all at once to dry ingredients. Stir just until moistened. Fold in egg whites.

4. Spoon batter into prepared pan. Cover tightly with foil and secure with a string. Place in slow cooker stoneware and pour in enough boiling water to come 1 inch (2.5 mL) up the sides of the dish. Cover and cook on High for 4 hours, until a tester inserted in the center comes out clean. Unmold and serve warm or let cool.

Tip

Be sure to use stone-ground cornmeal when making this bread. Not only is it the most nutritious form of the grain, the quantities of liquid in the recipe won't work with refined cornmeal.

Corny Cheddar Cheese Bread

Serve this with your favorite chili or warm from the oven with a dollop of salsa. It has great flavor and the tiny kernels of corn lend a wonderfully rustic finish.

Tips

Be sure to use stone-ground cornmeal when making this bread. Not only is it the most nutritious form of the grain, the quantities of liquid in the recipe won't work with refined cornmeal.

Can sizes vary from region to region. If your creamed corn doesn't conform to this size, use 1 cup (250 mL).

Makes 1 loaf (12 slices)

- Large (minimum 5 quart) oval slow cooker
- Greased 8- by 4-inch (20 by 10 cm) approx. loaf pan or 6-cup (1.5 L) soufflé or baking dish (see Tips, page 32)

1 cup	stone-ground cornmeal (see Tips, left)	250 mL
1 cup	all-purpose flour	250 mL
2 tsp	baking soda	10 mL
1 tsp	salt	5 mL
1 tsp	dry mustard	5 mL
2	eggs, beaten	2
1	can (10 oz/284 mL) creamed corn (see Tips, left)	1
1½ cups	shredded Cheddar cheese	375 mL
¾ cup	milk	175 mL
¼ cup	vegetable oil	50 mL
1 tbsp	Worcestershire sauce	15 mL

1. In a large bowl, combine cornmeal, flour, baking soda, salt and mustard. Mix well and make a well in the middle.

2. In a separate bowl, combine eggs, corn, cheese, milk, oil and Worcestershire sauce. Pour into well and mix just until combined.

3. Spoon batter into prepared pan. Cover tightly with foil and secure with a string. Place in slow cooker stoneware and pour in enough boiling water to come 1 inch (2.5 mL) up the sides of the dish. Cover and cook on High for 4 hours, until a tester inserted in the center comes out clean. Unmold and serve warm or let cool.

Maple-Sweetened Congee

If you're having trouble getting your family to eat a healthy breakfast because they are bored with the traditional options, try this. It is absolutely yummy and delightfully different.

Vegan Friendly

Can Be Halved
see Tips, below

Serves 4

- Lightly greased slow cooker stoneware
- Small (2 to 3½ quart) slow cooker

⅓ cup	brown rice	75 mL
4 cups	vanilla-flavored rice milk, divided (see Tips, right)	1 L
¼ cup	maple syrup	50 mL
	Finely chopped soft dates and/or candied ginger	
	Toasted almonds or walnuts, optional	

1. In a small saucepan over medium heat, bring rice and 2 cups (500 mL) of the rice milk to a boil. Boil for 2 minutes. Transfer to slow cooker stoneware. Stir in remaining rice milk and maple syrup.

2. Cover and cook on Low for 8 hours or overnight, or on High for 4 hours. Stir in dates and/or ginger to taste and sprinkle with toasted almonds, if using.

Tips

If you are halving this recipe, be sure to use a small (1½ to 2 quart) slow cooker.

If you don't have vanilla-flavored rice milk, add 1 tsp (5 mL) vanilla extract to plain rice milk.

Refrigerate any leftovers. This reheats beautifully on the stovetop or in a microwave.

Vegan Friendly

Can Be Halved
see Tips, below

Black Sticky Rice Congee with Coconut

I just love black sticky rice in sweet dishes, particularly when it's combined with the flavor of coconut. Here's another delicious way of adding a nutritious whole grain to your breakfast repertoire. Congee is typically described as a "porridge" but it's actually more like soup.

Tips

If you are halving this recipe, be sure to use a small (1$\frac{1}{2}$ to 2 quart) slow cooker.

Refrigerate any leftovers. This reheats beautifully on the stovetop or in a microwave.

Serves 6

- Lightly greased slow cooker stoneware
- Small (2 to 3$\frac{1}{2}$ quart) slow cooker

3 cups	water	750 mL
$\frac{1}{3}$ cup	black sticky rice	75 mL
$\frac{1}{2}$ cup	packed Demerara or other raw cane sugar	125 mL
1 tsp	almond extract	5 mL
Pinch	salt	Pinch
1	can (14 oz/400 mL) coconut milk	1
	Chopped bananas, optional	
	Chopped toasted almonds, optional	

1. In a small saucepan over high heat, bring water and black sticky rice to a vigorous boil. Boil for 2 minutes. Stir in brown sugar, almond extract and salt, then transfer to slow cooker stoneware. Cover and cook on Low for 8 hours or overnight, or on High for 4 hours. Stir well, then stir in coconut milk.

2. To serve, ladle into bowls and add bananas and/or almonds, if using.

Chocolate Atole

Atole is a Mexican beverage made from corn flour and flavored with fruit or chocolate. I think it's delicious and love having it for breakfast. If you have chocoholics in the house, they'll think they've died and gone to heaven when you hand them a steaming cup of this version. Incidentally, atole is reputed to be good for curing hangovers.

Vegan Friendly

Can Be Halved
see Tips, below

Serves 4 to 6

- Lightly greased slow cooker stoneware
- Small (2 to 3½ quart) slow cooker

¼ cup	stone-ground cornmeal	50 mL
½ cup	packed brown sugar, preferably Demerara or other raw cane sugar	125 mL
¼ cup	unsweetened cocoa powder	50 mL
1 tsp	ground cinnamon	5 mL
4 cups	soy milk, divided	1 L
1 tsp	vanilla extract	5 mL

1. In a saucepan over medium heat, toast cornmeal, stirring, until fragrant, about 4 minutes. Transfer to a mortar and pestle or a clean coffee grinder, and pound or grind as finely as you can. Stir in sugar, cocoa powder and cinnamon.

2. In same saucepan over medium-high heat, bring soy milk to a boil. Gradually add cornmeal mixture in a steady stream, stirring constantly. Return to a boil and transfer to prepared stoneware. Stir in vanilla.

3. Cover and cook on Low for 8 hours or overnight, or on High for 4 hours. Stir well before serving.

Tips

If you are halving this recipe, be sure to use a small (1½ to 2 quart) slow cooker.

Refrigerate any leftovers. This reheats beautifully on the stovetop or in a microwave.

Hot Curried Crab

Starters and Snacks

Tip

If you are halving this recipe, be sure to use a small (1½ to 2 quart) slow cooker.

Hot Curried Crab

This is a great dish for a party. I like to serve it with pieces of warm naan, but sliced baguette or rice crackers work well, too.

Makes about 2 cups (500 mL)

- Small (2 to 3½ quart) slow cooker

8 oz	cooked crabmeat, chopped	250 g
2 tbsp	finely chopped cilantro	25 mL
1 tbsp	extra virgin olive oil	15 mL
½ tsp	grated lime zest	2 mL
1 tbsp	freshly squeezed lime juice	15 mL
1 tsp	Asian chile sauce, such as sambal oelek	5 mL
1	package (8 oz/250 g) cream cheese, cubed	1
2 tbsp	mayonnaise	25 mL
4	green onions, white part with just a hint of green, finely chopped	4
1 tsp	Thai red curry paste	5 mL

1. In a bowl, combine crabmeat, cilantro, olive oil, lime zest and juice and chile sauce. Stir well. Cover and refrigerate until ready to use.

2. In slow cooker stoneware, combine cream cheese, mayonnaise, green onions and curry paste. Cover and cook on Low for 2 hours or High for 1 hour, until cheese is melted. Stir in crab mixture. Cover and cook on High for 30 minutes, until hot and bubbly. Stir well.

Hot and Smoky Shrimp

This warm and oh-so-soothing mélange, with just an intriguing hint of spice, makes a perfect starter for any meal — from casual to elegant. I prefer it spread on thin slices of crusty baguette or celery sticks, but plain crackers work well, too.

Entertaining Worthy

Can Be Halved
see Tip, below

Makes about 2 cups (500 mL)

- Small (2 to 3½ quart) slow cooker

8 oz	cooked salad shrimp, chopped	250 g
2 tbsp	finely chopped parsley	25 mL
1 tbsp	freshly squeezed lemon juice	15 mL
1 tbsp	extra virgin olive oil	15 mL
	Freshly ground black pepper	
1	package (8 oz/250 g) cream cheese, cubed	1
¼ cup	mayonnaise	50 mL
2	green onions, white part with just a hint of green, finely chopped	2
1 tsp	smoked hot paprika	5 mL

1. In a bowl, combine shrimp, parsley, lemon juice, olive oil and pepper to taste. Stir well. Cover and refrigerate until ready to use.

2. In slow cooker stoneware, combine cream cheese, mayonnaise, green onions and paprika.

3. Cover and cook on Low for 2 hours or High for 1 hour, until cheese is melted. Stir in shrimp mixture. Cover and cook on High for 30 minutes, until hot and bubbly. Stir well.

Tip

If you are halving this recipe, be sure to use a small (1½ to 2 quart) slow cooker.

Make Ahead

Complete Steps 1 and 2. Cover and refrigerate shrimp and cheese mixtures separately overnight. When you're ready to cook, complete the recipe.

Cajun-Spiced Shrimp and Crab

Take my word for it — on a blustery night guests love nothing more than a hot, spicy dip to accompany their welcoming drink. Serve this with sliced baguette, celery sticks, spears of Belgian endive, crackers or Melba toast.

Tips

If you are halving this recipe, be sure to use a small (1½ to 2 quart) slow cooker.

You could use 2 cans (each about 6 oz/170 g) crab, drained, and 1 can (3¾ oz/106 g) shrimp, drained.

If you are a heat seeker, add ½ tsp (2 mL) minced chile pepper just before serving.

Make Ahead

Complete Step 1, combining ingredients in a mixing bowl. Refrigerate overnight. When you're ready to cook, transfer to the stoneware and complete the recipe.

Makes about 2 cups (500 mL)

• Small (2 to 3½ quart) slow cooker

1	package (8 oz/250 g) cream cheese, cubed	1
¼ cup	tomato-based chili sauce	50 mL
¼ cup	mayonnaise	50 mL
2 tsp	Cajun seasoning	10 mL
¼ tsp	salt	1 mL
¼ tsp	freshly ground black pepper	1 mL
1	green bell pepper, seeded and diced	1
4	green onions, finely chopped	4
1 cup	cooked crabmeat, chopped (see Tips, left)	250 mL
½ cup	cooked salad shrimp, chopped	125 mL
	Hot pepper sauce or seeded and minced fresh chile pepper (see Tips, left)	

1. In slow cooker stoneware, combine cream cheese, chili sauce, mayonnaise, Cajun seasoning, salt, pepper, bell pepper, green onions, crabmeat and shrimp.

2. Cover and cook on High for 1 hour. Stir well. Cover and cook on High for 30 minutes, until hot and bubbly. Season with hot pepper sauce to taste.

Black Bean Nachos

This dip is a perennial hit. The last time I made it — for my daughter's 23rd birthday party — guests practically licked the bowl. Use spicy or mild salsa to suit your taste. If you're using sweet peppers rather than poblano and want a zestier result, add an extra jalapeño or chipotle pepper.

Makes about 3 cups (750 mL)

- Small (2 to 3½ quart) slow cooker

1	can (14 to 19 oz/398 to 540 mL) black beans, drained, rinsed and mashed	1
1 cup	prepared salsa	250 mL
4	green onions, finely chopped	4
2	roasted peppers (poblanos or sweet), peeled and diced	2
1	roasted jalapeño, seeded and diced, or 1 chipotle pepper in adobo sauce	1
2 cups	shredded Cheddar or Monterey Jack cheese	500 mL
	Tortilla chips	

1. In slow cooker stoneware, combine beans, salsa, green onions, poblano and jalapeño peppers and cheese.
2. Stir well. Cover and cook on High for 1½ hours, until mixture is hot and bubbly. Serve with tortilla chips.

Vegan Alternative

Substitute an equal quantity of vegan Cheddar or Monterey Jack cheese.

Tips

If you are halving this recipe, be sure to use a small (1½ to 2 quart) slow cooker.

This makes a chunky dip. If you prefer a smoother version, purée the drained beans and salsa to desired consistency in a food processor before adding to the stoneware.

Make Ahead

Complete Step 1, combining the ingredients in a mixing bowl rather than the stoneware. Cover and refrigerate overnight. When you're ready to cook, transfer to the stoneware and complete the recipe.

Tips

If you are halving this recipe, be sure to use a small (1½ to 2 quart) slow cooker.

To make baked potato sticks: Cut a baked potato in half and cut each half into quarters. Brush cut sides with olive oil and run under preheated broiler until nicely browned. Sprinkle with sea salt, if desired. Place on a platter and cover with cheese mixture.

Make Ahead

You can make this up to 2 days ahead of serving it. Cover and refrigerate in an ovenproof ramekin. When you're ready to serve, uncover and place in a preheated 400°F (200°C) oven until bubbly and top is browning, about 10 minutes. If the mixture gets overheated, it might start to separate. No problem, just stir well before serving.

Pimento-Spiked Cheesy Ham Melt with Potato Dippers

Served on baked potato sticks, this makes a substantial starter, just the thing to greet active outdoorsy folks coming in from the cold. For a more conventional presentation, serve the melt with sliced baguette or spread over toast points and run it under the broiler just as your guests arrive.

Makes about 2 cups (500 mL)

- Small (2 to 3½ quart) slow cooker

2 cups	shredded Cheddar cheese (about 4 oz/125 g)	500 mL
2 tbsp	minced green onion	25 mL
2 tbsp	mayonnaise	25 mL
2 tbsp	sour cream	25 mL
1 tsp	Dijon mustard	5 mL
⅛ tsp	cayenne pepper	0.5 mL
½ cup	finely minced smoked ham (about 4 oz/125 g)	125 mL
1 tbsp	minced pimento	15 mL
	Freshly ground black pepper	
	Baked potato sticks (see Tips, left)	

1. In slow cooker stoneware, combine Cheddar cheese, green onion, mayonnaise, sour cream, mustard and cayenne.

2. Cover and cook on Low for 2 hours or on High for 1 hour, until cheese is melted. Stir in ham and pimento. Cover and cook on High for 30 minutes, until flavors meld. Serve with potato sticks for dipping.

Variation

If you prefer, omit the baked potato sticks and serve the melt with sliced baguette.

Cheddar-Onion Melt

This is one of those classics that absolutely everyone adores. Serve this with sliced baguette, flatbread or even celery sticks and watch it disappear right to the last drop.

Vegetarian Friendly

Can Be Halved
see Tip, below

Makes about 2 cups (500 mL)

- Small (2 to 3½ quart) slow cooker

3 cups	shredded medium or old Cheddar cheese	750 mL
2	onions, grated	2
½ cup	mayonnaise	125 mL
2 tbsp	sour cream	25 mL
½ tsp	dry mustard	2 mL
⅛ tsp	cayenne pepper, optional	0.5 mL

1. In slow cooker stoneware, combine Cheddar cheese, onions, mayonnaise, sour cream, mustard and cayenne, if using. Cover and cook on Low for 2 hours or on High for 1 hour, until cheese is melted. Stir well and serve.

Tip

If you are halving this recipe, see Tips, page 44.

Make Ahead

You can make this up to 2 days ahead. Cover and refrigerate in an ovenproof ramekin. When ready to serve, uncover and place in a preheated 400°F (200°C) oven until bubbly and browning, about 10 minutes. If mixture gets overheated, it might start to separate. Just stir well.

Entertaining Worthy

Vegan Friendly

Can Be Halved
see Tips, below

Eggplant Caviar

Although its origins are Mediterranean, this flavorful spread has become a favorite around the world. What's more, it's loaded with nutrition. Serve it well chilled with warm pita bread or sliced veggies.

Makes about 3 cups (750 mL)

- Small (2 to 3½ quart) slow cooker

1	medium eggplant (about 1 lb/500 g) peeled and cut into 2-inch (5 cm) cubes	1
1 tsp	salt	5 mL
1 tbsp	cumin seeds	15 mL
2 tbsp	extra virgin olive oil, divided (approx.)	25 mL
½ tsp	cracked black peppercorns	2 mL
4	cloves garlic, minced	4
½ cup	diced peeled tomatoes (see Tips, left)	125 mL
4	green onions, white part only with just a hint of green, chopped	4
1	roasted red bell pepper, seeded and chopped	1
2	sun-dried tomatoes packed in oil, drained and chopped	2
½ cup	coarsely chopped parsley leaves	125 mL
2 tbsp	red wine vinegar	25 mL
	Fine sea salt and freshly ground black pepper	

1. In a colander over a sink, combine eggplant and salt. Toss and let stand for 30 minutes. Rinse thoroughly under cold running water. Lay a clean tea towel on a work surface. Working in batches over the sink and using your hands, squeeze liquid out of eggplant. Transfer to tea towel. When batches are complete, roll the towel up and press down to remove remaining liquid.

2. In a large dry skillet over medium heat, toast cumin seeds, stirring, until fragrant, about 3 minutes. Transfer to a mortar and pestle or a spice grinder and pound or grind as finely as you can. Set aside.

3. In same skillet, heat 1 tbsp (15 mL) of the oil over medium heat. Add sweated eggplant in batches and cook until browned, adding more oil as necessary. Transfer to slow cooker stoneware. Add reserved cumin, peppercorns, garlic and tomatoes. Cover and cook on Low for 4 hours or High for 2 hours.

4. Transfer to a food processor and process until smooth. Add green onions, roasted pepper, sun-dried tomatoes, parsley and vinegar and pulse until blended. Taste and season with salt and pepper to taste. Chill thoroughly.

Tips

If you are halving this recipe, be sure to use a small (1½ to 2 quart) slow cooker.

For the diced peeled tomatoes you can use a fresh tomato or well-drained canned diced tomatoes.

Make Ahead

You can make Eggplant Caviar up to 2 days ahead. Cover and refrigerate until you're ready to serve.

Chile Artichoke Dip

This mild-tasting dip has just a hint of spice balanced by the tang of citrus. This very enjoyable combination of flavors marries well with tostadas or celery sticks.

Entertaining Worthy

Vegetarian Friendly

Can Be Halved see Tip, below

Makes about 3 cups (750 mL)

- Small (2 to 3½ quart) slow cooker

1	package (8 oz/250 g) cream cheese, cubed	1
1 cup	shredded mozzarella	250 mL
¼ cup	mayonnaise	50 mL
1	clove garlic, minced	1
2 tsp	finely grated lemon zest	10 mL
1	can (14 oz/398 mL) artichokes, drained and chopped	1
1	can (4½ oz/127 mL) minced green chiles, drained	1
	Freshly ground black pepper	
	Tostadas or tortilla chips	

1. In slow cooker stoneware, combine cream cheese, mozzarella, mayonnaise, garlic, lemon zest, artichokes and chiles.

2. Season with black pepper to taste. Cover and cook on High for 2 hours, until hot and bubbly. Stir well and serve. Serve with tostadas or tortilla chips

Vegan Alternative

Substitute an equal quantity of vegan cream cheese, vegan mozzarella and vegan mayonnaise for the non-vegan products.

Tip

If you are halving this recipe, be sure to use a small (1½ to 2 quart) slow cooker.

Make Ahead

Complete Step 1, combining ingredients in a mixing bowl rather than the stoneware. Cover and refrigerate overnight. When you're ready to cook, transfer to the stoneware and complete the recipe.

Cajun-Spiced Peanuts

Normally I'm not a fan of peanuts, but these aromatic treats challenge that perception. Eaten warm, they are positively luscious.

Entertaining Worthy

Vegan Friendly

Can Be Halved see Tip, below

Makes about 2 cups (500 mL)

- Small (2 to 3½ quart) slow cooker

2 cups	raw peanuts	500 mL
2 tbsp	unrefined peanut or extra virgin olive oil	25 mL
2 tsp	Cajun spice	10 mL
Pinch	cayenne pepper	Pinch
1 tsp	fine sea salt	5 mL

1. In slow cooker stoneware, combine peanuts, oil, Cajun spice and cayenne. Place a clean tea towel, folded in half (so you will have 2 layers), over top of stoneware to absorb moisture. Cover and cook on High for 2 to 2½ hours, stirring occasionally, until peanuts are nicely roasted. Drain on paper towel. Place in a serving bowl, sprinkle with salt and stir to combine. Serve warm or cool.

Tip

If you are halving this recipe, be sure to use a small (1½ to 2 quart) slow cooker.

Spicy Tamari Almonds

I love eating these tasty tidbits as pre-dinner nibbles with a glass of cold white wine. Tamari is a wheat-free soy sauce, so you can serve this snack to people who are unable to tolerate gluten.

Makes about 2 cups (500 mL)

- Small (2 to 3½ quart) slow cooker

2 cups	whole almonds	500 mL
¼ tsp	cayenne pepper	1 mL
2 tbsp	tamari sauce	25 mL
1 tbsp	extra virgin olive oil	15 mL
	Fine sea salt	

Tip

If you are halving this recipe, be sure to use a small (1½ to 2 quart) slow cooker.

1. In slow cooker stoneware, combine almonds and cayenne. Place a clean tea towel, folded in half (so you will have 2 layers), over top of stoneware to absorb moisture. Cover and cook on High for 45 minutes.

2. In a small bowl, combine tamari and olive oil. Add to hot almonds and stir thoroughly to combine. Replace tea towel. Cover and cook on High for 1½ hours, until nuts are hot and fragrant, stirring every 30 minutes and replacing towel each time. Sprinkle with salt to taste. Store in an airtight container.

Maple Orange Pecans

I love snacking on these sweet, flavorful nuts, and they also make a great addition to salads or a garnish for desserts.

Makes about 2 cups (500 mL)

- Small (2 to 3½ quart) slow cooker
- Baking sheet, lined with waxed paper

¼ cup	maple syrup	50 mL
1 tbsp	grated orange zest	15 mL
½ tsp	ground cinnamon	2 mL
Pinch	cayenne pepper, optional	Pinch
2 cups	pecan halves	500 mL
	Sweet paprika	

Tip

If you are halving this recipe, be sure to use a small (1½ to 2 quart) slow cooker.

1. In slow cooker stoneware, combine maple syrup, orange zest, cinnamon and cayenne, if using.

2. Cover and cook on High for 30 minutes to meld flavors. Add pecans and stir well. Place a clean tea towel, folded in half (so you will have 2 layers), over top of stoneware to absorb moisture. Cover and cook on High for 1 hour or until nuts release their aroma and are nicely toasted. Spread out on prepared baking sheet. Sprinkle with paprika to taste and let cool (coating will harden). Store in an airtight container.

Entertaining Worthy

Vegetarian Friendly

Can Be Halved
see Tips, below

Zesty Spinach and Mushroom Dip

Here's a tasty and nutritious dip with wide appeal. Mildly flavored, with just a hint of spice, it makes a perfect nibble to accompany a glass of cold white wine.

Tips

If you are halving this recipe, be sure to use a small (1½ to 2 quart) slow cooker.

If you are using fresh spinach leaves that have not been prewashed, take care to wash them thoroughly, as they can be quite gritty. *To wash spinach:* Fill a clean sink with lukewarm water. Remove tough stems and submerge leaves in the water, swishing to remove the grit. Rinse thoroughly in a colander under cold running water, checking carefully to ensure that no sand remains. If you are using frozen spinach, thaw and squeeze out the excess moisture before adding to the slow cooker.

Make Ahead

Complete Step 1. Cover and refrigerate overnight. When you're ready to cook, complete the recipe.

Makes about 2 cups (500 mL)

- Small (2 to 3½ quart) slow cooker

2 tbsp	butter	25 mL
4	cloves garlic, minced	4
½ tsp	freshly ground black pepper	2 mL
8 oz	shiitake mushrooms, stemmed and chopped	250 g
4	green onions, white part with just a hint of green, sliced	4
1 lb	fresh spinach, stems removed, or 1 package (10 oz/300 g) spinach leaves, thawed if frozen (see Tips, left)	500 g
1	package (8 oz/250 g) cream cheese, cubed	1
⅛ tsp	cayenne pepper	0.5 mL
	Tostadas or tortilla chips	

1. In a skillet over medium-high heat, melt butter. Add garlic, pepper and mushrooms and cook, stirring, until mushrooms start to wilt, about 5 minutes. Add green onions and toss. Transfer to a food processor. Add spinach and process until very finely chopped.

2. Transfer to slow cooker stoneware. Add cream cheese, sprinkle with cayenne and season to taste with black pepper. Cover and cook on High for 2 hours, until hot and bubbly. Stir well before serving. Serve with tostados or tortilla chips.

Vegan Alternative

Substitute vegetable oil for the butter and vegan cream cheese for the regular kind.

Country Terrine

This is a simple terrine, mildly flavored and nicely moist. Served with crusty bread and a spirited condiment such as Dijon mustard or some cornichons, it's a real treat. I can't think of a better companion for a leisurely glass of wine.

Makes about 2 lbs (1 kg)

- Loaf pan, earthenware terrine or soufflé dish, lightly greased (see Tips, right)
- Large (minimum 5 quart) oval slow cooker
- Instant-read thermometer

1½ lbs	boneless pork shoulder, including fat, coarsely chopped	750 g
8 oz	stewing veal, coarsely chopped	250 g
4 oz	smoked bacon, trimmed of rind, cubed	125 g
2 tsp	cracked black peppercorns	10 mL
1 tsp	salt	5 mL
3 tbsp	brandy or cognac	45 mL
1	onion, grated	1
2	cloves garlic, puréed (see Tips, right)	2
2 tbsp	fresh thyme leaves	25 mL

1. In a meat grinder (or food processor in batches), grind pork, veal and bacon, transferring to a bowl as completed. Mix well. Add peppercorns, salt, brandy, onion, garlic and thyme and mix well. Cover and refrigerate overnight.

2. When you're ready to cook, transfer mixture to prepared pan. Cover tightly with foil and secure with a string. Place in stoneware and add hot water to come about halfway up the sides of the pan. Cover and cook on High about 4 hours, until juices run clear or an instant-read thermometer inserted into the center of the terrine registers 160°F (71°C). Chill overnight, weighted down (see Tips, right) before serving.

Tips

This terrine can be made in almost any kind of baking dish that will fit into your slow cooker. I have a variety of baking pans that work well: a small loaf pan, approximately 8 by 5 inches (20 by 12.5 cm), makes a traditionally shaped terrine; a round 4-cup (1 L) soufflé dish or a square 7-inch (17.5 cm) baking dish produces slices of different shapes.

To purée garlic, use a fine-tooth grater such as Microplane.

Placing a weight on a terrine while it cools compacts the meat and ensures it has a uniform texture. I keep a brick wrapped in plastic wrap for this purpose. It fits nicely into my loaf pan.

Tips

If you are halving this recipe, be sure to use a small (1½ to 2 quart) slow cooker.

You may want to use a whisk while combining the flour mixture and hot stock, to minimize the possibility of lumps.

Oh-So-Retro Swedish Meatballs

These were a cocktail party standard when I was growing up, and they are firmly lodged in my food memory bank. I like to serve them in a shallow serving dish or a deep platter, speared with cocktail toothpicks. If my experience is any measure, they will disappear in a flash. Make sure your guests have napkins or a plate to catch any drips.

Makes about 30 meatballs

• Small to medium (2 to 3½ quart) slow cooker

1 lb	lean ground beef, preferably sirloin	500 g
1 cup	fine dry bread crumbs	250 mL
1	onion, grated	1
1	egg, beaten	1
2 tsp	finely grated lemon zest	10 mL
2 tbsp	freshly squeezed lemon juice	25 mL
½ tsp	salt	2 mL
½ tsp	allspice	2 mL
	Freshly ground black pepper	
2 tbsp	olive oil	25 mL
3 tbsp	all-purpose flour	45 mL
½ tsp	cracked black peppercorns	2 mL
2 cups	reduced-sodium beef stock, heated to the boiling point	500 mL
½ cup	sour cream	125 mL
½ cup	finely chopped dill	125 mL

1. In a bowl, combine ground beef, bread crumbs, onion, egg, lemon zest and juice, salt, allspice and pepper to taste. Mix well. Using your hands, shape into balls about ½ inch (1 cm) in diameter.

2. In a large skillet, heat oil over medium-high heat. Add meatballs in batches and cook, stirring, until nicely browned, about 4 minutes per batch. Transfer to slow cooker stoneware as completed. Add flour to pan and cook, stirring, until frothy but not browning, about 2 minutes. Stir in peppercorns. Add beef stock and cook, stirring, until mixture comes to a boil and thickens, about 2 minutes (see Tips, left). Pour over meatballs.

3. Cover and cook on Low for 6 hours or on High for 3 hours, until meatballs are cooked through. Using a slotted spoon, transfer meatballs to a serving dish. Add sour cream and dill to stoneware and stir well. Pour over meatballs and serve.

Balsamic-Spiked Caramelized Onions with Shaved Parmesan

This is an elegant and delicious starter. Serve it plated or as a topping for crostini.

Entertaining Worthy

Vegetarian Friendly

Can Be Halved
see Tip, below

Serves 6

- Small to medium (2 to 3½ quart) slow cooker

4	onions, thinly sliced on the vertical	4
2 tsp	dried thyme leaves	10 mL
1 tsp	cracked black peppercorns	5 mL
¼ cup	olive oil	50 mL
2 tbsp	balsamic vinegar	25 mL
1 tsp	Demerara or other raw cane sugar	5 mL
	Thinly sliced prosciutto, optional	
	Freshly grated Parmesan	
	Baguette, optional	

1. In slow cooker stoneware, combine onions, thyme, peppercorns and olive oil. Stir well. Place a clean tea towel, folded in half (so you will have 2 layers), over top of stoneware to absorb moisture. Cover and cook on High for 3 hours, stirring every hour and replacing the towel each time, until onions are nicely caramelized.

2. In a small bowl or measuring cup, combine vinegar and brown sugar. Stir until sugar dissolves. Add to onions and stir well. Transfer onions with juices to a small serving dish.

3. To serve, spoon onions with sauce onto small plates. Top with a piece of prosciutto, if using, and garnish with Parmesan. Or use crostini as a base and make smaller portions.

Vegan Alternative
Substitute vegan Parmesan cheese for the regular version.

Tip
If you are halving this recipe, be sure to use a small (1½ to 2 quart) slow cooker.

Make Ahead
After adding vinegar and sugar, refrigerate onions. Warm on the stovetop in a saucepan.

Leek and Green Pea Soup
with Mascarpone and Mint

Soups

Leek and Green Pea Soup with Mascarpone and Mint

This delicious soup has a mild flavor but is very substantial. Serve it as a light main course or the centerpiece of a soup-and-salad dinner, or serve smaller portions as a prelude to an elegant meal. If you're serving this soup to guests and want to dress it up, top with garlic croutons or bacon bits.

Tip

If you are halving this recipe, be sure to use a small (1½ to 3½ quart) slow cooker.

Make Ahead

Complete Step 1. Cover and refrigerate for up to 2 days. When you're ready to cook, complete the recipe.

Serves 6 to 8

- Medium to large (3½ to 5 quart) slow cooker

1 tbsp	olive oil	15 mL
3	leeks, white part only, with just a hint of green, thinly sliced	3
2	stalks celery, diced	2
2	cloves garlic, minced	2
1 tsp	dried thyme leaves	5 mL
1 tsp	salt or to taste	5 mL
½ tsp	cracked black peppercorns	2 mL
1 cup	dried split green peas	250 mL
6 cups	vegetable or chicken stock, divided	1.5 L
2 cups	sweet green peas	500 mL
6 tbsp	mascarpone	90 mL
3 tbsp	chopped fresh mint	45 mL
	Freshly ground black pepper	
	Garlic croutons or crumbed bacon bits, optional	

1. In a skillet, heat oil over medium heat. Add leeks and celery and cook, stirring, until softened, about 5 minutes. Add garlic, thyme, salt and peppercorns and cook, stirring, for 1 minute. Add split green peas and toss to coat. Add 2 cups (500 mL) of the stock, bring to a boil and boil for 2 minutes.

2. Transfer to slow cooker stoneware. Stir in remaining 4 cups (1 L) of stock. Cover and cook on Low for 8 hours or on High for 4 hours, until peas are very tender.

3. Stir in sweet green peas. Cover and cook on High until peas are tender, about 10 minutes. Stir in mascarpone and mint and purée using an immersion blender. (If you don't have an immersion blender, do this, in batches, in a stand blender or food processor.) Season with pepper to taste. Ladle into bowls and garnish with croutons, if using.

Shrimp Bisque

True to its definition, this bisque is decadently rich and luscious. Although the vegetables are put through a sieve, I depart from tradition by serving the shrimp finely chopped after marinating them in grappa and cayenne. This is a special occasion soup. Serve in small bowls prior to a meal that matters.

Entertaining Worthy

Can Be Halved
see Tips, below

Serves 6 to 8

- Medium to large (3½ to 5 quart) slow cooker

8 oz	shrimp, peeled and deveined, reserving shells	250 g
2 tbsp	grappa or brandy	25 mL
¼ tsp	cayenne pepper	1 mL
1 cup	white wine	250 mL
1 cup	water	250 mL
1 tbsp	olive oil	15 mL
2	onions, finely chopped	2
4	stalks celery, diced	4
2	cloves garlic, minced	2
2 tsp	dried tarragon	10 mL
1 tsp	each salt and cracked black peppercorns	5 mL
1	can (14 oz/398 mL) tomatoes with juice	1
2 cups	fish stock	500 mL
½ cup	whipping (35%) cream	125 mL
	Snipped chives	

1. In a small bowl, combine shrimp, grappa and cayenne. Stir well, cover and refrigerate until ready to use.

2. Meanwhile, make shrimp stock. In a saucepan, combine reserved shrimp shells, white wine and water. Bring to a boil, reduce heat and simmer for 15 minutes. Strain, pushing the shells against the sieve to extract as much flavor as possible. Measure 1 cup (250 mL) and set aside. Freeze excess.

3. In a skillet, heat oil over medium heat. Add onions and celery and cook, stirring, until softened, about 5 minutes. Add garlic, tarragon, salt and peppercorns and cook, stirring, for 1 minute. Stir in tomatoes with juice and bring to a boil, breaking up with a spoon.

4. Transfer to slow cooker stoneware. Add shrimp stock and fish stock. Cover and cook on Low for 6 hours or on High for 3 hours.

5. Place a sieve over a large bowl and add contents of slow cooker. Using a wooden spoon, push vegetables through. Discard excess solids. Return all but 1 cup (250 mL) of mixture to stoneware and set temperature on High.

6. In a saucepan over medium heat, bring reserved cup (250 mL) of soup to a boil. Add shrimp with marinade and return to a boil. Cook until shrimp turn pink, about 1 minute. Transfer to slow cooker stoneware. Add whipping cream and cook on High for 5 minutes to meld flavors. To serve, ladle into bowls and garnish with chives.

Tips

If you are halving this recipe, be sure to use a small (1½ to 3½ quart) slow cooker.

When making this recipe, I use Italian San Marzano tomatoes, which are particularly rich. If you are using domestic tomatoes, stir in 2 tsp (10 mL) tomato paste, just before adding the tomatoes.

Make Ahead

Complete Steps 1, 2 and 3. Cover and refrigerate shrimp and tomato mixtures separately overnight. Make the shrimp stock. Cover and refrigerate overnight. When you're ready to cook, complete the recipe.

Cheddar Cheese Soup with Broccoli

This rich, delicious soup makes a perfect meal-in-a-bowl for chilly nights or après-ski. If you're craving a hearty old-fashioned meal, a small portion is also the perfect prelude to a classic dinner of roast beef with Yorkshire pudding. Either way, this is a winner.

Tip

If you are halving this recipe, be sure to use a small (2 to 3½ quart) slow cooker.

Make Ahead

Complete Step 1. Cover and refrigerate for up to 2 days. When you're ready to cook, complete the recipe.

Serves 6 to 8

- Medium to large (3½ to 5 quart) slow cooker

1 tbsp	olive oil	15 mL
2	onions, finely chopped	2
3	carrots, diced	3
3	stalks celery, diced	3
1 tsp	dry mustard	5 mL
½ tsp	salt	2 mL
½ tsp	cracked black peppercorns	2 mL
2 tbsp	all-purpose flour	25 mL
1 tbsp	tomato paste	15 mL
6 cups	Enhanced Vegetable Stock (see right) or chicken stock, divided	1.5 L
2 cups	cooked broccoli florets	500 mL
½ cup	whipping (35%) cream	125 mL
3 cups	shredded Cheddar cheese, preferably old	750 mL
	Hot pepper sauce, optional	

1. In a large skillet, heat oil over medium heat. Add onions, carrots and celery and cook, stirring, until softened, about 7 minutes. Add mustard, salt, peppercorns and flour and cook, stirring, for 1 minute. Stir in tomato paste. Add 1 cup (250 mL) of the stock and bring to a boil. Cook, stirring, until slightly thickened, about 2 minutes.

2. Transfer mixture to slow cooker stoneware. Add remaining 5 cups (1.25 L) of stock and stir well. Cover and cook on Low for 8 hours or on High for 4 hours.

3. Add broccoli, whipping cream and Cheddar cheese. Cover and cook on High for 15 minutes, until cheese is melted and mixture is bubbly. Purée using an immersion blender. (If you don't have an immersion blender, do this, in batches, in a stand blender or food processor.) Ladle into individual serving bowls and pass the hot pepper sauce, if using.

Variation

Cheddar Cheese Soup with Cauliflower: Substitute an equal quantity of cooked cauliflower florets for the broccoli.

Vegetarian and Vegan Alternatives

Enhanced Vegetable Stock: If you're making this soup for vegetarians, substitute 6 cups (1.5 L) Enhanced Vegetable Stock for the chicken stock. To enhance 8 cups (2 L) prepared or basic vegetable stock, combine in a large saucepan over medium heat with 2 carrots, peeled and coarsely chopped, 1 tbsp (15 mL) tomato paste, 1 tsp (5 mL) celery seed, 1 tsp (5 mL) cracked black peppercorns, 1/2 tsp (2 mL) dried thyme leaves, 4 parsley sprigs, 1 bay leaf and 1 cup (250 mL) dry white wine. Reduce heat to low and simmer, covered, for 30 minutes, then strain and discard solids. If you are cooking for vegans, also substitute soy creamer for the whipping cream and vegan Cheddar cheese for the regular version.

Tip

While veal stock gives the soup a bit more flavor, chicken stock also works very well in this recipe.

Laurent's Onion Soup with Anchovy Butter Crostini

This is the onion soup that Chef Laurent Godbout serves at his charming restaurant Chez L'Épicier in Old Montreal. I've adapted this from the recipe that appears in his cookbook Laurent Godbout. *The sweetness of the onions and port balanced by the sharpness of the Cheddar and anchovies is an inspiring combination.*

Serves 4

• Small (2 to 3½ quart) slow cooker

6	onions, thinly sliced on the vertical (about 2 lbs/1 kg)	6
2 tbsp	melted butter	25 mL
⅓ cup	port wine	75 mL
2 cups	veal or chicken stock (see Tip, left)	500 mL
⅓ cup	whipping (35%) cream	75 mL
	Salt and freshly ground black pepper	

Crostini

2 tbsp	softened butter (approx.)	25 mL
4	anchovy fillets, finely minced	4
2 tsp	finely chopped parsley	10 mL
4	slices whole wheat baguette	4
	Shredded old Cheddar cheese	

1. In slow cooker stoneware, combine onions and butter. Toss well to ensure onions are thoroughly coated. Place a clean tea towel, folded in half (so you will have 2 layers), over top of stoneware to absorb moisture. Cover and cook on High for 3½ to 4 hours, stirring every hour and replacing the towel each time, until onions are nicely caramelized.

2. Add port and stock and stir well. Cover (do not replace the towel) and cook on High for 1 hour. Purée using an immersion blender, then pass the mixture through a sieve. Return to stoneware. Add whipping cream and season with salt and pepper to taste. Keep warm.

3. **Crostini:** Preheat oven to 400°F (200°C). In a bowl, combine butter, anchovies and parsley, mixing with a wooden spoon until well blended. Butter bread on both sides with mixture. Place on baking sheet and bake on middle rack until lightly browned, turning once, about 7 minutes.

4. To serve, ladle soup into bowls and sprinkle with Cheddar cheese. Top with crostini and serve.

Cream of Garlic Soup

I first tasted this intriguing soup about eight years ago in New Orleans, at Bayona, Susan Spicer's highly regarded restaurant. I thought it was delicious, so when I came across the recipe in her book Crescent City Cooking, *I was keen to adapt it for the slow cooker. Because this is a rich soup, offer small servings before a special meal. I can't imagine a better prelude to a roast of beef or a crisp brown chicken.*

Tip
This works best in a small slow cooker because the diameter of the stoneware ensures that enough heat reaches the onions and garlic to ensure proper caramelization.

Serves 4 to 6

- Small (maximum 3½ quart) slow cooker (see Tip, right)

3	onions, thinly sliced	3
¾ cup	garlic cloves (about 2 heads)	175 mL
1 tbsp	melted butter	15 mL
1 tbsp	olive oil	15 mL
2	sprigs fresh thyme	2
4 cups	vegetable or chicken stock	1 L
1½ cups	cubed (½ inch/1 cm) French bread	375 mL
½ cup	whipping (35%) cream	125 mL
	Salt and freshly ground black pepper	

1. In slow cooker stoneware, combine onions, garlic, butter and olive oil. Stir well. Place a clean tea towel, folded in half (so you will have 2 layers), over top of stoneware to absorb moisture. Cover and cook on High for 3 hours, stirring every hour and replacing the towel each time, until onions are nicely caramelized.

2. Add thyme, stock and bread cubes. Cover (do not replace the towel) and cook on High for 1 hour. Remove thyme sprig and purée using an immersion blender. (You can also do this in a food processor, in batches, and return to stoneware.) Add whipping cream, cover and cook on High for 20 minutes, until heated through. Season with salt and pepper to taste.

Vegan Alternative
Substitute vegetable oil for the butter and soy creamer for the whipping cream.

Entertaining Worthy

Vegetarian Friendly

Can Be Halved
see Tip, below

Tip

If you are halving this recipe, be sure to use a small (1½ to 3½ quart) slow cooker.

Make Ahead

Complete Step 1. Cover and refrigerate mixture for up to 2 days. When you're ready to cook, complete the recipe.

Classic Cream of Mushroom Soup

This old-fashioned favorite is quintessential comfort food. It makes a perfect prelude to any meal or a great light supper with the addition of a salad.

Serves 6

- Medium to large (3½ to 5 quart) slow cooker

2 tbsp	butter	25 mL
1	leek, white part only with just a hint of green, finely chopped	1
1	carrot, peeled and diced	1
½ cup	minced shallots	125 mL
1 tsp	salt	5 mL
½ tsp	dried tarragon leaves	2 mL
¼ tsp	cracked black peppercorns	1 mL
1	bay leaf	1
3 tbsp	all-purpose flour	45 mL
2 tbsp	sherry, optional	25 mL
4 cups	vegetable, chicken or mushroom stock	1 L
1½ lbs	white mushrooms, trimmed and quartered	750 g
½ cup	whipping (35%) cream	125 mL
¼ cup	snipped chives	50 mL
	Garlic croutons, optional	

1. In a large skillet over medium heat, melt butter. Add leek, carrot and shallots and cook, stirring, until softened, about 7 minutes. Add salt, tarragon, peppercorns and bay leaf and stir well. Add flour and cook, stirring, for 1 minute. Increase heat to medium-high. Add sherry, if using, and 2 cups (500 mL) of the stock and bring to a boil. Cook, stirring, until slightly thickened, about 3 minutes.

2. Transfer to slow cooker stoneware. Stir in mushrooms and remaining 2 cups (500 mL) of stock. Cover and cook on Low for 6 to 8 hours or on High for 3 to 4 hours, until mushrooms are tender. Remove and discard bay leaf. Stir in whipping cream. Working in batches, purée in a food processor or blender. (You can also do this in the stoneware using an immersion blender.) Ladle into bowls and garnish with chives and croutons, if using.

Vegan Alternative

Substitute vegetable oil for the butter and soy creamer for the whipping cream.

Classic Cream of Celery Soup

An old-fashioned favorite, this tasty soup, which relies on potato and just a bit of cream for its luscious finish, is the perfect way to begin a celebratory meal. It also makes a great lunch.

Entertaining Worthy

Vegetarian Friendly

Can Be Halved
see Tips, below

Serves 6

- Medium to large (3½ to 5 quart) slow cooker

1 tbsp	butter	15 mL
3	leeks, white part only with just a hint of green, cleaned and chopped	3
3 cups	diced celery (about 1 whole bunch)	750 mL
1 tsp	dried thyme leaves	5 mL
½ tsp	cracked black peppercorns	2 mL
2 tbsp	all-purpose flour	25 mL
4 cups	vegetable or chicken stock, divided	1 L
1	potato, peeled and diced	1
½ cup	whipping (35%) cream	125 mL
	Salt and freshly ground black pepper	
	Finely chopped celery leaves (see Tips, right)	

1. In a large skillet, melt butter over medium heat. Add leeks and celery and cook, stirring, until softened, about 5 minutes. Add thyme and peppercorns and cook, stirring, for 1 minute. Stir in flour and cook for 1 minute. Add 1 cup (250 mL) of the stock and bring to a boil. Cook, stirring, until mixture thickens, about 2 minutes.

2. Transfer to slow cooker stoneware. Add remaining 3 cups (750 mL) of stock and potato. Cover and cook on Low for 6 hours or on High for 3 hours, until potato is tender. Stir in whipping cream. Season with salt and pepper to taste. To serve, ladle into bowls and garnish with celery leaves.

Variations

Classic Cream of Chicken Soup: Reduce the quantity of celery to 4 stalks. Stir in 2 cups (500 mL) diced cooked chicken along with the whipping cream and cook on High until heated through, about 15 minutes. Substitute a liberal garnish of finely chopped parsley for the celery leaves.

Vegan Alternative

Substitute an equal quantity of vegetable oil for the butter and soy creamer for the whipping cream.

Tips

If you are halving this recipe, be sure to use a small (1½ to 3½ quart) slow cooker.

This is a great recipe because it allows you to use up the tough outer stalks of celery. Unless you want your soup to be fibrous, I recommend peeling these stalks with a vegetable peeler before dicing.

When you are chopping the celery, set aside the leaves. Chop finely, cover and refrigerate until the soup has finished cooking. They make an elegant and tasty garnish.

Make Ahead

Complete Step 1. Cover and refrigerate for up to 2 days. When you're ready to cook, complete the recipe.

Can Be Halved
see Tip, below

Mushroom and Wild Rice Chowder with Corn

This slightly different take on chowder highlights indigenous North American foods such as wild rice and corn. I like to serve this with salad and whole-grain bread for a light dinner. If you're cooking for vegetarians, substitute miso for the bacon (see Vegan Alternative, below). Add the paprika if you like heat and a bit of smoke.

Tip

If you are halving this recipe, be sure to use a small (2 to 3½ quart) slow cooker.

Make Ahead

Complete Steps 1 and 2. Cover and refrigerate mixture for up to 2 days. When you're ready to cook, complete the recipe.

Serves 6

- Large (approx. 5 quart) slow cooker

1 tbsp	olive oil	15 mL
2 oz	chunk bacon, diced, optional	60 g
2	onions, finely chopped	2
2	carrots, peeled and diced	2
2	stalks celery, diced	2
4	cloves garlic, minced	4
1 tsp	salt	5 mL
1 tsp	cracked black peppercorns	5 mL
1 tsp	dried thyme leaves	5 mL
½ cup	wild rice or brown and wild rice mixture	125 mL
6 cups	chicken stock, divided	1.5 L
8 oz	cremini mushrooms, trimmed and quartered	250 g
2 cups	corn kernels	500 mL
½ tsp	smoked hot paprika, optional	2 mL

1. In a skillet, heat oil over medium-high heat. Add bacon, if using, and cook, stirring, until browned, about 4 minutes. Using a slotted spoon, transfer to a paper towel to drain. Transfer to slow cooker stoneware.

2. Add onions, carrots and celery to pan and cook, stirring, until softened, about 7 minutes. Add garlic, salt, peppercorns and thyme and cook, stirring, for 1 minute. Add wild rice and toss until coated. Add 2 cups (500 mL) of the stock and bring to a boil. Boil for 2 minutes.

3. Transfer to slow cooker stoneware. Add mushrooms and remaining 4 cups (1 L) of stock and stir well. Cover and cook on Low for 6 hours or on High for 3 hours. Stir in corn and smoked paprika, if using. Cover and cook on High for 20 minutes, until corn is tender.

Vegan Alternative

Omit the bacon. Substitute vegetable stock for the chicken stock and stir in ½ cup (125 mL) white miso along with the corn.

Vegan Friendly

Can Be Halved
see Tip, below

Creamy Tomato Soup

When I was growing up, one of my favorite soups was my mother's "homemade" tomato soup, which she made using canned tomatoes and milk. When I wasn't feeling up to snuff, a comforting bowl, served with soda biscuits on the side, always improved my spirits. This soup is a facsimile of that homespun icon.

Serves 6

- Medium to large (3½ to 5 quart) slow cooker

1 tbsp	olive oil	15 mL
2	onions, finely chopped	2
2	stalks celery, diced	2
4	cloves garlic, minced	4
1 tsp	salt or to taste	5 mL
1 tsp	cracked black peppercorns	5 mL
½ tsp	ground allspice	2 mL
1	can (28 oz/796 mL) tomatoes with juice, coarsely chopped	1
4 cups	vegetable or chicken stock	1 L
½ cup	whipping (35%) cream or soy creamer	125 mL

Tip

If you are halving this recipe, be sure to use a small (1½ to 3½ quart) slow cooker.

Make Ahead

Complete Step 1. Cover and refrigerate for up to 2 days. When you're ready to cook, complete the recipe.

1. In a skillet, heat oil over medium heat. Add onions and celery and cook, stirring, until softened, about 5 minutes. Add garlic, salt, peppercorns and allspice and cook, stirring, for 1 minute. Add tomatoes with juice and bring to a boil.

2. Transfer to slow cooker stoneware. Stir in stock. Cover and cook on Low for 8 hours or on High for 4 hours. Purée using an immersion blender. (If you don't have an immersion blender, do this in a stand blender or food processor, in batches, and return to stoneware.) Stir in whipping cream and serve.

Variations

Creamy Tomato Broth: This is an elegant presentation, suitable for a special meal. Substitute 1 can (28 oz/796 mL) crushed tomatoes for the whole tomatoes. After the soup has finished cooking but before adding the cream, place a sieve over a large bowl and strain, using a wooden spoon to push solids through. Discard remaining solids. Return broth to stoneware, add cream and heat on High for 10 minutes to meld flavors.

Basil-Spiked Tomato Soup: Substitute ¼ cup (50 mL) basil pesto for the whipping cream. Drizzle over the soup just before serving. This works for the Creamy Tomato Broth as well.

Thai-Style Red Curry Tomato Soup

This luscious soup makes a delicious and unusual prelude to any meal. It is also very good as a light main course or for lunch.

Entertaining Worthy

Vegan Friendly

Can Be Halved
see Tips, below

Serves 6

- Medium to large (3½ to 5 quart) slow cooker

1 tbsp	olive or extra virgin coconut oil	15 mL
1	onion, chopped	1
4	cloves garlic, minced	4
2 tbsp	minced gingerroot	25 mL
½ tsp	salt	2 mL
½ tsp	cracked black peppercorns	2 mL
2	stalks lemongrass, trimmed, smashed and cut in half crosswise	2
1	can (28 oz/796 mL) tomatoes with juice, coarsely chopped	1
2 cups	vegetable or chicken stock	500 mL
1½ cups	coconut milk, divided	375 mL
1 to 2 tsp	Thai red curry paste (see Tips, right)	5 to 10 mL
	Finely chopped cilantro	

1. In a skillet, heat oil over medium heat. Add onion and cook, stirring, until softened, about 3 minutes. Add garlic, ginger, salt, peppercorns and lemongrass and cook, stirring, for 1 minute. Add tomatoes with juice and bring to a boil.

2. Transfer to slow cooker stoneware. Stir in stock. Cover and cook on Low for 8 hours or on High for 4 hours. Remove lemongrass and discard. Purée using an immersion blender. (If you don't have an immersion blender, do this in a stand blender or food processor, in batches, and return to stoneware.)

3. In a microwaveable bowl, combine ½ cup (125 mL) of the coconut milk and red curry paste. Stir well and microwave on High for 1 minute. Stir again. (The mixture should be thickened and fragrant; if not, microwave for another 30 seconds. If you don't have a microwave, do this in a saucepan on the stove for about 3 minutes.) Add to slow cooker stoneware along with remaining coconut milk. Cover and cook on High for 10 minutes, until flavors meld. Ladle into bowls and garnish with cilantro.

Tips

If you are halving this recipe, be sure to use a small (1½ to 3½ quart) slow cooker.

The quantity of curry paste you use depends upon your affinity for heat. One teaspoon (5 mL) is enough for me, but heat seekers may want to use as much as two.

Make Ahead

Compete Step 1. Cover and refrigerate for up to 2 days. When you're ready to cook, complete the recipe.

French-Style Pumpkin Soup with Leeks

In France there are many variations of this deliciously light and beautifully flavored soup. Here I have suggested a basic version that is simply perfect as is. If you're inclined to gild the lily, try adding the mussels (see Variation, below), my husband's favorite.

Tips

If you are halving this recipe, be sure to use a small (2 to 3½ quart) slow cooker.

Substitute an equal quantity of winter squash, such as butternut or acorn, for the pumpkin.

If you don't have an immersion blender, purée the soup, in batches, in a food processor.

Make Ahead

Complete Step 1. Cover and refrigerate for up to 2 days. When you're ready to cook, complete the recipe.

Serves 6

- Large (approx. 5 quart) slow cooker

2 tbsp	butter	25 mL
2	leeks, white part only with just a hint of green, thinly sliced	2
2	stalks celery, diced	2
2	carrots, peeled and diced	2
1 tsp	each salt and cracked black peppercorns	5 mL
4 cups	vegetable stock, divided	1 L
4 cups	cubed (1 inch/2.5 cm) peeled pumpkin (see Tips, left)	1 L
	Whipping (35%) cream, optional	
	Finely snipped chives	

1. In a skillet over medium heat, melt butter. Add leeks, celery and carrots and cook, stirring, until softened, about 7 minutes. Add salt and peppercorns and cook, stirring, for 1 minute. Add 2 cups (500 mL) of the stock and bring to a boil.

2. Transfer to slow cooker stoneware. Stir in pumpkin and remaining 2 cups (500 mL) of stock. Cover and cook on Low for 6 to 8 hours or on High for 3 to 4 hours, until pumpkin is tender. Purée using an immersion blender. Ladle into bowls, drizzle with whipping cream, if using, and garnish liberally with chives.

Variation

Pumpkin and Mussel Soup: In a large saucepan, bring ½ cup (125 mL) dry white wine and 1 tsp (5 mL) fennel seeds to a boil. Add 2 lbs (1 kg) cleaned mussels. Cover and cook until all the mussels have opened, about 5 minutes. Discard any that have not opened. Drain, reserving cooking liquid. Remove mussels from their shells. Strain cooking liquid through a fine sieve or paper coffee filter, discarding any sediment. About 20 minutes before the soup has finished cooking, add mussels and cooking liquid to stoneware and cook on High until heated through and flavors meld, about 10 minutes. If cooking ahead of time, combine shelled mussels with strained cooking liquid and refrigerate until ready to use.

Vegan Alternative

Substitute vegetable oil for the butter and soy creamer for the whipping cream.

Creamy Coconut Sweet Potato Soup

This is fusion-style comfort food that combines Southwestern sweet potatoes and chipotle pepper with coconut milk, an Asian staple. Regardless of its origins, it's delicious. Finish it with a garnish of cilantro or toasted pecans, depending on what strikes your fancy.

Vegan Friendly

Can Be Halved
see Tip, below

Serves 6

- Large (approx. 5 quart) slow cooker

1 tbsp	olive oil	15 mL
2	onions, finely chopped	2
4	stalks celery	4
4	cloves garlic, minced	4
2 tbsp	minced gingerroot	25 mL
2 tsp	ground cumin	10 mL
1 tsp	salt	5 mL
1 tsp	cracked black peppercorns	5 mL
5 cups	vegetable or chicken stock, divided	1.25 L
5 cups	cubed (1/2 inch/1 cm) peeled sweet potatoes (about 2 large)	1.25 L
1	can (14 oz/400 mL) coconut milk	1
1	chipotle pepper in abobo sauce, chopped	1
	Finely chopped cilantro, optional	
	Chopped toasted pecans, optional	

1. In a skillet, heat oil over medium heat. Add onions and celery and cook, stirring, until softened, about 5 minutes. Add garlic, ginger, cumin, salt and peppercorns and cook, stirring, for 1 minute. Add 2 cups (500 mL) of the stock and bring to a boil.

2. Transfer to slow cooker stoneware. Stir in sweet potatoes and remaining 3 cups (750 mL) of stock. Cover and cook on Low for 6 hours or on High for 3 hours, until sweet potato is tender.

3. Stir in coconut milk and chipotle pepper. Purée using an immersion blender. (You can also do this in a food processor, in batches, and return to stoneware.) Cover and cook on high for 15 minutes to meld flavors. Serve garnished with cilantro or toasted pecans, if desired.

Tip
If you are halving this recipe, be sure to use a small (2 to 3 1/2 quart) slow cooker.

Make Ahead
Complete Step 1. Cover and refrigerate for up to 2 days. When you're ready to cook, complete the recipe.

Entertaining Worthy

Vegan Friendly

Can Be Halved
see Tips, below

Ancho-Spiked Tortilla Soup

This zesty soup makes a great prelude to a Mexican-inspired meal or, with the addition of extra avocado or cooked chicken or turkey, a great main course. The crisp tortilla strips add a mild but very pleasant flavor and great texture.

Tips

If you are halving this recipe, be sure to use a small (2 to 3½ quart) slow cooker.

For the best flavor, toast and grind cumin seeds yourself. Place seeds in a dry skillet over medium heat and cook, stirring, until fragrant, about 3 minutes. Using a mortar and pestle or a spice grinder, pound or grind as finely as you can.

My favorite beans for this soup are pinto beans or small red Mexican beans, but red kidney or cranberry beans work well, too.

Make Ahead

Complete Step 1. Cover and refrigerate for up to 2 days. When you're ready to cook, complete the recipe.

Serves 6

• Medium to large (4 to 5 quart) slow cooker

1 tbsp	olive oil	15 mL
2	onions, finely chopped	2
4	stalks celery, diced	4
4	cloves garlic, minced	4
1 tbsp	dried oregano leaves, preferably Mexican	15 mL
2 tsp	ground cumin (see Tips, left)	10 mL
1 tsp	salt	5 mL
1 tsp	cracked black peppercorns	5 mL
2 cups	cooked pinto or red beans, rinsed and drained (see Tips, left)	500 mL
1	can (14 oz/398 mL) crushed tomatoes	1
6 cups	vegetable or chicken stock (see Tip, right)	1.5 L
2	dried ancho chiles	2
2 cups	boiling water	500 mL
1	can (4½ oz/127 mL) mild green chiles, drained	1
2 cups	corn kernels, thawed if frozen	500 mL
	Diced cooked chicken or turkey, optional	
3	6-inch (15 cm) corn tortillas, cut into 1-inch (2.5 cm) strips	3
	Oil for brushing	
1 to 2	avocados, cut into ½-inch (1 cm) cubes	1 to 2
	Finely chopped red or green onion	
	Sour cream or Mexican crema, optional	
	Finely chopped cilantro	

1. In a skillet, heat oil over medium heat. Add onions and celery and cook, stirring, until softened, about 5 minutes. Add garlic, oregano, cumin, salt and peppercorns and cook, stirring, for 1 minute. Add beans and crushed tomatoes and bring to a boil.

2. Transfer to slow cooker stoneware. Stir in stock. Cover and cook on Low for 8 hours or on High for 4 hours.

3. Half an hour before recipe has finished cooking, in a heatproof bowl, soak ancho chiles in boiling water for 20 minutes, weighing down with a cup to ensure they are submerged. Drain and discard stems and soaking water. Coarsely chop and add to slow cooker stoneware. Purée using an immersion blender. (If you don't have an immersion blender, do this in a stand blender or food processor, in batches, and return to stoneware.)

4. Add mild green chiles, corn and chicken, if using. Cover and cook on High about 20 minutes, until corn is tender.

5. Meanwhile, preheat oven to 400°F (200°C). Brush tortilla strips with oil. Place on a baking sheet and bake until crisp and golden, 4 minutes per side.

6. When ready to serve, ladle soup into bowls, lay tortilla strips across surface and top with chopped avocado, red onion, sour cream, if using, and cilantro.

Tip

For deeper flavor, if you're cooking for vegetarians, make this using Enhanced Vegetable Stock (see page 59).

Curried Cream of Parsnip Soup

The combination of sweet, slightly earthy parsnips with mild Indian spicing, finished with coconut milk and sweet green peas, is a marriage made in heaven. Serve this for lunch with some whole-grain bread, as a light dinner followed by salad or, in smaller portions, as a prelude to an elegant meal

Tips

If you are halving this recipe, be sure to use a small (2 to 3½ quart) slow cooker.

For best results, toast and grind the cumin yourself. Place seeds in a dry skillet over medium heat and cook, stirring, until fragrant, about 3 minutes. Using a mortar and pestle or a spice grinder, pound or grind as finely as you can.

If you are using very large parsnips, discard the woody core. The easiest way to do this is to cut parsnip into thirds horizontally and place flat surface on a cutting board. Using a sharp knife, cut around the core. Discard the core and cut the slices into 2-inch (5 cm) pieces.

Make Ahead

Complete Step 1. Cover and refrigerate for up to 2 days. When you're ready to cook, complete the recipe.

Serves 6 to 8

- Large (approx. 5 quart) slow cooker

1 tbsp	olive oil	15 mL
2	onions, chopped	2
4	cloves garlic, minced	4
2 tbsp	minced gingerroot	25 mL
2 tsp	ground coriander	10 mL
2 tsp	ground cumin (see Tips, left)	10 mL
1 tsp	salt	5 mL
½ tsp	cracked black peppercorns	2 mL
6 cups	vegetable or chicken stock, divided	1.5 L
6	parsnips, peeled and coarsely chopped (about 6 cups/1.5 L) (see Tips, left)	6
1 cup	coconut milk, divided	250 mL
2 tsp	curry powder	10 mL
2 cups	sweet green peas, thawed if frozen	500 mL

1. In a skillet, heat oil over medium heat. Add onions and cook, stirring, until softened, about 3 minutes. Add garlic, ginger, coriander, cumin, salt and peppercorns and cook, stirring, for 1 minute. Add 2 cups (500 mL) of the stock and bring to a boil.

2. Transfer to slow cooker stoneware. Add parsnips and remaining 4 cups (1 L) of stock. Cover and cook on Low for 6 to 8 hours or on High for 3 to 4 hours, until parsnips are tender.

3. Purée using an immersion blender. (You can also do this in a food processor, in batches, and return to the stoneware when completed.) In a small bowl, combine ¼ cup (50 mL) of the coconut milk and curry powder. Mix well. Add to slow cooker stoneware along with remaining coconut milk and peas. Cover and cook on High for 20 minutes, until peas are tender and flavors meld.

Cumin-Spiked Lentil Soup with Eggplant and Dill

Entertaining Worthy | Vegan Friendly | Can Be Halved see Tips, below

Although the combination of flavors in this soup is unusual, they work together like a charm. I like to serve this delicious concoction as a main course, followed by salad, for a light weekday dinner, but in smaller portions it's an ideal starter for a Mediterranean-themed dinner. Vary the quantity of yogurt to suit individual tastes.

Serves 6 to 8

- Medium to large (3½ to 5 quart) slow cooker

1	eggplant (about 1 lb/500 g), peeled and cut into 2-inch (5 cm) cubes	1
1 tsp	salt	5 mL
2 tbsp	olive oil, divided (approx.)	25 mL
2	onions, finely chopped	2
4	cloves garlic, minced	4
½ tsp	cracked black peppercorns	2 mL
1 tbsp	cumin seeds, toasted and ground (see Tips, right)	15 mL
1 cup	green or brown lentils, picked over and rinsed	250 mL
6 cups	vegetable or chicken stock	1.5 L
1 tbsp	freshly squeezed lemon juice	15 mL
½ cup	finely chopped dill	125 mL
	Plain yogurt or vegan sour cream	

1. In a colander over a sink, combine eggplant and salt. Toss and let stand for 30 minutes. Rinse thoroughly under cold running water. Lay a clean tea towel on a work surface. Working in batches over the sink and using your hands, squeeze liquid out of the eggplant. Transfer to the tea towel. When batches are complete, roll the towel up and press down to remove remaining liquid.

2. In a skillet, heat 1 tbsp (15 mL) of the oil over medium heat. Add sweated eggplant, in batches, and cook until browned, adding more oil as necessary. Transfer to slow cooker stoneware.

3. Add onions to pan, adding more oil if necessary, and cook, stirring, until softened, about 3 minutes. Add garlic, peppercorns and cumin and cook, stirring, for 1 minute. Add lentils and toss until coated. Add stock and bring to a boil.

4. Transfer to slow cooker stoneware. Cover and cook on Low for 8 hours or on High for 4 hours, until lentils are tender. Stir in lemon juice and dill. Purée using an immersion blender. (You can also do this, in batches, in a food processor or stand blender.) To serve, ladle into bowls and add a dollop of yogurt.

Tips

If you are halving this recipe, be sure to use a small (2 to 3½ quart) slow cooker.

I have not provided make ahead instructions for this soup because the partially cooked eggplant would become soggy if left to sit for any length of time.

For the best flavor, toast cumin seeds and grind them yourself. Place seeds in a dry skillet over medium heat and cook, stirring, until fragrant, about 3 minutes. Immediately transfer to a spice grinder or mortar and grind finely.

Can Be Halved
see Tips, below

Lentil and Smoked Sausage Soup with Parmesan Crostini

This stick-to-your-ribs soup is practically a meal in a bowl and the perfect antidote to the first blasts of cold weather. If you're serving it for dinner, all it needs is a simple green salad.

Tips

If you are halving this recipe, be sure to use a small (2 to 3½ quart) slow cooker.

Cayenne is very hot. If you prefer a milder result, use a less assertive ground pepper such as Aleppo.

Make Ahead

Complete Steps 1 and 2. Cover mixture, ensuring it cools promptly (see Making Ahead, page 17), and refrigerate for up to 2 days. When you're ready to cook, complete the recipe.

Serves 6 to 8

- Medium to large (4 to 5 quart) slow cooker

1 tbsp	olive oil	15 mL
2 oz	pancetta, diced	60 g
2	onions, finely chopped	2
2	stalks celery, diced	2
2	carrots, peeled and diced	2
4	cloves garlic, minced	4
1 tbsp	herbes de Provence	15 mL
1 tsp	salt	5 mL
1 tsp	cracked black peppercorns	5 mL
1 cup	green or brown lentils, picked over and rinsed	250 mL
6 cups	chicken stock, divided	1.5 L
8 oz	chopped smoked sausage, such as kielbasa	250 g
	Cayenne pepper (see Tips, left)	
6 to 8	slices baguette	6 to 8
	Olive oil	
	Freshly grated Parmesan	

1. In a skillet, heat oil over medium-high heat. Add pancetta and cook, stirring, until nicely browned. Using a slotted spoon, transfer to slow cooker stoneware. Reduce heat to medium.

2. Add onions, celery and carrots to pan and cook, stirring, until softened, about 7 minutes. Add garlic, herbes de Provence, salt and peppercorns and cook, stirring, for 1 minute. Add lentils and toss until coated. Add 2 cups (500 mL) of the stock and bring to a boil.

3. Transfer to slow cooker stoneware. Add remaining 4 cups (1 L) of stock. Cover and cook on Low for 6 hours or on High for 3 hours, until lentils are tender.

4. Add smoked sausage and cayenne to taste. Cover and cook on High for 10 minutes to meld flavors.

5. Meanwhile, make crostini. Preheat broiler. Brush baguette slices on both sides with olive oil and place under broiler until lightly browned on both sides, about 5 minutes. Sprinkle one side with Parmesan and place under broiler until cheese melts. To serve, ladle soup into bowls and float a crostini on top of each serving.

Spicy Lentil and Wild Rice Soup with Caramelized Onions

Here's a vegetarian soup so hearty and full of flavor that non-vegetarians will never miss the meat. The secret is caramelizing the onions, which adds depth to the broth. This makes a delicious lunch or, if followed by salad, a satisfying light supper. If you're feeling hungry, add some hearty whole-grain bread.

Serves 6 to 8

- Medium to large (3½ to 5 quart) slow cooker

2 tbsp	olive oil	2
3	onions, finely chopped	3
2 tbsp	packed brown sugar	25 mL
4	cloves garlic, minced	4
1 tbsp	ground cumin seeds (see Tips, right)	15 mL
1 tsp	ground turmeric	5 mL
1 tsp	cracked black peppercorns	5 mL
½ tsp	salt (see Tips, right)	5 mL
½ cup	green or brown lentils, picked over and rinsed	125 mL
½ cup	wild rice or brown and wild rice mixture	125 mL
6 cups	vegetable or chicken stock, divided	1.5 mL
¼ tsp	cayenne pepper	1 mL
2 tbsp	freshly squeezed lemon juice	25 mL
¼ cup	finely chopped parsley	50 mL

1. In a skillet, heat oil over medium-high heat. Add onions and cook, stirring, just until golden, about 5 minutes. Stir in brown sugar and cook, stirring, until onions caramelize, about 2 minutes. Reduce heat to medium.

2. Add garlic, cumin, turmeric, peppercorns and salt and cook, stirring, for 1 minute. Add lentils and wild rice and toss until coated. Add 2 cups (500 mL) of the stock, bring to a boil and boil for 2 minutes.

3. Transfer to slow cooker stoneware. Stir in remaining 4 cups (1 L) of stock. Cover and cook on Low for 6 to 8 hours or on High for 3 to 4 hours, until lentils are tender and wild rice is cooked. Dissolve cayenne in lemon juice and stir into soup. Cover and cook on High for 15 minutes to meld flavors. To serve, ladle soup into bowls and garnish with parsley.

Tips

If you are halving this recipe, be sure to use a small (2 to 3½ quart) slow cooker.

For the best flavor, toast cumin seeds and grind them yourself. Place seeds in a dry skillet over medium heat and cook, stirring, until fragrant, about 3 minutes. Immediately transfer to a spice grinder or mortar and grind finely.

This quantity of salt works well if you're using a commercial broth, which is likely to be high in sodium. If you're using homemade stock, you may want to increase the quantity.

Make Ahead

Complete Steps 1 and 2. Cover and refrigerate for up to 2 days. When you're ready to cook, complete the recipe.

Chicken Pho

There are few things more satisfying than a steaming bowl of pho, the noodle-based Vietnamese soup with a particularly flavorful broth.

Tips

If you are halving this recipe, be sure to use a small (1½ to 3½ quart) slow cooker.

For a more authentic flavor, substitute 1 piece (about 1 inch/2.5 cm) rock sugar for the granulated. It will provide a more caramelized flavor.

If you prefer, after stirring in the fish sauce (Step 3), refrigerate the soup for up to 2 days. Before reheating, skim off any fat that has risen to the surface. After the soup has reached a simmer, add noodles and heat gently until softened.

Make Ahead

Complete Step 1. Cover and refrigerate for up for 2 days. When you're ready to cook, complete the recipe.

Serves 6 to 8

- Medium to large (3½ to 5 quart) slow cooker

Broth

1 tbsp	oil	15 mL
2	onions, sliced	2
1	piece (2 inches/5 cm) gingerroot, peeled and quartered	1
2	stalks lemongrass, crushed	2
1 tbsp	coriander seeds	15 mL
2 tsp	salt	10 mL
6	black peppercorns	6
1	piece (2 inches/5 cm) cinnamon stick	1
1	whole star anise, optional	1
1 lb	skin-on bone-in chicken thighs	500 g
2 tsp	granulated sugar (see Tips, left)	10 mL
1 cup	coarsely chopped cilantro, leaves and stems	250 mL
4 cups	chicken stock	1 L

Pho

2 tbsp	fish sauce	25 mL
8 oz	dried rice noodles	250 g
4	green onions, finely chopped	4
2 cups	bean sprouts	500 mL
¼ cup	finely chopped cilantro	50 mL
	Minced Thai chiles, optional	
2	limes, cut in wedges	2

1. In a skillet, heat oil over medium heat. Add onions and cook, stirring, until softened. Add ginger, lemongrass, coriander seeds, salt, peppercorns, cinnamon stick and star anise, if using, and cook, stirring, for 1 minute. Add 2 cups (500 mL) water and bring to a boil.

2. Transfer to stoneware. Add chicken, sugar, cilantro and stock and stir well. Cover and cook on Low for 6 hours or on High for 3 hours, periodically skimming off impurities that float to the top.

3. **Pho:** Place a fine-mesh strainer over a large saucepan and strain, reserving broth. Set chicken aside and discard remaining solids. Remove skin from chicken and shred. Discard skin and bones. Return broth to stoneware along with chicken. Stir in fish sauce. Add rice noodles. Cover and cook on Low about 20 minutes, until softened.

4. To serve, ladle into bowls. Garnish with green onions, bean sprouts, cilantro and chiles, if using. Pass lime wedges at the table.

Winter Borscht

In naming this soup, I'm borrowing from my friend Margret Hovanec, who differentiates borscht made with beets that are stored from that made with beets fresh from the garden. The summer version often includes the vegetable's green leaves and is served chilled. This hearty version, which I love piping hot, is a meal in a bowl. Serve with dark rye bread and cold butter, and savor every mouthful.

Vegetarian Friendly

Can Be Halved
see Tip, below

Tip

If you are halving this recipe, be sure to use a small (2 to 3½ quart) slow cooker.

Make Ahead

Complete Step 1. Cover and refrigerate for up to 2 days. When you're ready to cook, complete the recipe.

Serves 6

- Medium to large (3½ to 5 quart) slow cooker

1 tbsp	oil	15 mL
2	onions, finely chopped	2
2	stalks celery, diced	2
2	cloves garlic, minced	2
2 tsp	ground allspice	10 mL
½ tsp	salt	2 mL
½ tsp	cracked black peppercorns	2 mL
3 tbsp	red wine vinegar	45 mL
1 tbsp	packed brown sugar	15 mL
1	can (14 oz/398 mL) diced tomatoes, with juice	1
4	large beets, peeled and diced	4
1	potato, peeled and shredded	1
6 cups	Enhanced Vegetable Stock (see page 59) or beef stock	1.5 L
1 cup	sour cream	250 mL
½ cup	finely chopped dill	125 mL

1. In a skillet, heat oil over medium heat. Add onions and celery and cook, stirring, until softened, about 5 minutes. Add garlic, allspice, salt and peppercorns and cook, stirring, for 1 minute. Add vinegar, brown sugar and tomatoes with juice and bring to a boil.

2. Transfer to slow cooker stoneware. Add beets, potato and stock. Cover and cook on Low for 8 hours or on High for 4 hours, until vegetables are tender. Purée using an immersion blender. (You can also do this, in batches, in a food processor.)

3. To serve, ladle into bowls, top with sour cream and garnish with dill.

Vegan Alternative

Substitute an equal quantity of vegan sour cream for the regular version.

Pasta e Fagioli

This is a particularly delicious version of a classic Italian soup. Add the cooked pasta at the last minute — otherwise it gets soggy.

Serves 6

Can Be Halved
see Tips, below

- Large (approx. 5 quart) slow cooker

1¼ cups	dried cannellini beans, soaked, drained and rinsed (see Tips, right)	300 mL
1 tbsp	olive oil	15 mL
4 oz	chunk pancetta or bacon, diced	125 g
2	onions, finely chopped	2
2	carrots, peeled and diced	2
2	stalks celery, diced	2
4	cloves garlic, minced	4
2	sprigs fresh rosemary or 1 tsp (5 mL) dried	2
1 tsp	dried oregano leaves	5 mL
½ tsp	cracked black peppercorns	2 mL
2	bay leaves	2
6 cups	chicken stock, divided	1.5 L
1	can (28 oz/796 mL) diced tomatoes with juice	1
3	dried red chile peppers (approx.) (see Tips, right)	3
1 cup	small pasta, such as elbow macaroni	250 mL
1 tbsp	butter, optional	15 mL
½ cup	finely chopped parsley	125 mL
	Freshly grated Parmesan	
	Extra virgin olive oil	

1. In a skillet, heat oil over medium-high heat. Add pancetta and cook, stirring, until it begins to crisp, about 4 minutes. Using a slotted spoon, transfer to slow cooker stoneware. Reduce heat to medium.

2. Add onions, carrots and celery to pan and cook, stirring, until softened, 7 minutes. Add garlic, rosemary, oregano, peppercorns and bay leaves and cook, stirring, for 1 minute. Add 2 cups (500 mL) stock and beans, bring to a boil and boil for 2 minutes.

3. Transfer to slow cooker stoneware. Add remaining 4 cups (1 L) of stock. Cover and cook on Low for 8 hours or on High for 4 hours, until beans are tender. Add tomatoes with juice and chile peppers. Cover and cook for 1 hour, until flavors meld.

4. Meanwhile, about 30 minutes before you are ready to serve the soup, cook pasta in a large pot of boiling salted water according to package directions. Drain well, toss with butter, if using, and stir into soup. Remove and discard bay leaves. To serve, ladle soup into bowls, garnish with parsley, Parmesan and a drizzle of oil.

Vegan Alternative

Omit pancetta, substitute vegetable stock for the chicken stock and vegan Parmesan for the regular version.

Tips

If you are halving this recipe, be sure to use a small (2 to 3½ quart) slow cooker.

Cannellini beans are also known as white kidney beans. The soaked dried beans cook in the broth, enhancing the flavor, but if you prefer, you may substitute 2½ cups (625 mL) canned white kidney beans, drained and rinsed, for this quantity.

If you have a leftover boot of Parmesan in the fridge (the tough outer rind), add it to the soup along with the stock. It will add pleasant creaminess.

Three chiles add a pleasant hint of heat to the soup. Use more if you are a heat seeker, increase the quantity to suit your taste.

Adding the tomatoes at the end is an extra step, but it allows you to cook the beans in the flavorful broth, which enhances their flavor. Otherwise, they would have to be cooked separately, as the acid in the tomatoes would cause them to be tough.

Can Be Halved
see Tips, below

Peppery Black Bean Soup with Cilantro and Lime

The first time I ever tasted a black bean soup was many years ago in an Argentine restaurant in New York. I just loved the combination of flavors and textures! This makes a delicious lunch or it can serve as the centerpiece of a soup-and-salad dinner.

Tips

If you are halving this recipe, be sure to use a small (2½ to 3½ quart) slow cooker.

For this quantity of black beans you can cook 3 cups (750 mL) dried beans yourself (see Basic Beans, page 341) or use 3 cans (each 14 to 19 oz/ 398 to 540 mL) of beans, thoroughly rinsed and drained.

This quantity of jalapeño produces a mildly spicy soup. If you are a heat seeker, add another jalapeño or two, or garnish the soup with extra-spicy salsa.

Make Ahead

Complete Steps 1 and 2. Cover and refrigerate bacon and onion mixture separately. When you're ready to cook, complete the recipe.

Serves 8

- Large (approx. 5 quart) slow cooker

1 tbsp	olive oil	15 mL
4 oz	chunk bacon, diced	125 g
2	onions, finely chopped	2
2	stalks celery, diced	2
2	carrots, peeled and diced	2
4	cloves garlic, minced	4
2 tbsp	cumin seeds, toasted and ground (see Tips, page 75)	25 mL
1 tbsp	dried oregano leaves	15 mL
1 tsp	salt	5 mL
1 tsp	cracked black peppercorns	5 mL
1	can (28 oz/796 mL) diced tomatoes with juice	1
6 cups	chicken stock	1.5 L
6 cups	cooked black beans (see Tips, left)	1.5 L
2	dried ancho or guajillo chile peppers	2
2 cups	boiling water	500 mL
2	green bell peppers, seeded and diced	2
1	jalapeño pepper, seeded and diced (see Tips, left)	1
½ cup	packed cilantro leaves	125 mL
¼ cup	freshly squeezed lime juice	50 mL
	Sour cream	
	Salsa	
	Lime wedges, optional	

1. In a skillet, heat oil over medium-high heat. Add bacon and cook, stirring, until crisp. Using a slotted spoon, transfer to a paper towel to drain. Set aside. Drain off all but 1 tbsp (15 mL) fat from pan, if necessary. Reduce heat to medium.

2. Add onions, celery and carrots to pan and cook, stirring, until vegetables are softened, about 7 minutes. Add garlic, cumin, oregano, salt and peppercorns and cook, stirring, for 1 minute. Add tomatoes with juice and bring to a boil.

3. Transfer to slow cooker stoneware. Stir in stock, beans and reserved bacon. Cover and cook on Low for 8 hours or on High for 4 hours.

4. One hour before you're ready to serve, in a heatproof bowl, soak ancho chiles in boiling water for 20 minutes, weighing down with a cup to ensure they remain submerged. Drain and discard stems and soaking water. Coarsely chop and add to soup along with bell peppers, jalapeño, cilantro and lime juice. Cover and cook on High for 20 minutes, until peppers are tender. Purée using an immersion blender. (You can also do this, in batches, in a food processor.) To serve, ladle into bowls and garnish with sour cream and/or salsa. Season with lime juice, if desired.

Vegan Alternative

Omit bacon, substitute vegetable stock or Enhanced Vegetable Stock (see page 59) for the chicken stock and vegan sour cream for the regular version.

Quebec-Style Split Pea Soup with Ham

This is the kind of pea soup I grew up eating, and I love it! Hearty and delicious, it makes a great light dinner accompanied by whole-grain bread and salad.

Can Be Halved
see Tips, below

Tips

If you are halving this recipe, be sure to use a small (2½ to 3½ quart) slow cooker.

Dried beans and peas can be tricky to cook. I find that giving the peas a good boil before adding them to the slow cooker helps to ensure they will be tender.

Smoked ham hocks can be found at butchers or in the meat department of well-stocked supermarkets. They are wonderful flavor enhancers, particularly for legumes.

Make Ahead

Complete Steps 1 and 2. Cover and refrigerate bacon and onion mixtures separately for up to 2 days. When you're ready to cook, complete the recipe.

Serves 6 to 8

- Large (approx. 5 quart) slow cooker

2	slices bacon	2
2	onions, finely chopped	2
2	cloves garlic, minced	2
1	bay leaf	1
1 tsp	salt	5 mL
½ tsp	cracked black peppercorns	2 mL
2 cups	yellow split peas (see Tips, left)	500 mL
12 cups	water	3 L
1	smoked ham hock or leftover ham bone (see Tips, left)	1

1. In a skillet over medium-high heat, fry bacon until crisp. Using a slotted spoon, transfer to a paper towel to drain. Crumble and refrigerate until ready to use. Drain all but 2 tbsp (25 mL) fat from pan.

2. Add onions and cook, stirring, until light golden, about 5 minutes. Add garlic, bay leaf, salt and peppercorns and cook, stirring, for 1 minute. Stir in peas and 2 cups (500 mL) of the water, bring to a boil and boil for 3 minutes.

3. Transfer to slow cooker stoneware. Add ham hock and remaining 10 cups (2.5 L) water. Cover and cook on Low for 8 to 10 hours or on High for 4 to 5 hours, until peas are very tender. Remove ham hock and shred meat from bone. Remove and discard bay leaf. Purée soup, if desired. Return meat to soup. To serve, ladle into bowls and garnish with crumbled bacon.

Soupe au Pistou

This hearty vegetable soup, finished with the French version of basil pesto, qualifies as Gallic comfort food. There are many variations. This version includes sweet potatoes and a pleasant hit of fennel in the herbes de Provence. Make it the centerpiece of a light dinner.

Vegan Friendly

Can Be Halved
see Tip, below

Serves 6

- Medium to large (3½ to 5 quart) slow cooker

Pistou

1 cup	loosely packed basil leaves	250 mL
¼ cup	toasted pine nuts	50 mL
4	cloves garlic, coarsely chopped	4
¼ cup	extra virgin olive oil	50 mL
½ cup	freshly grated Parmesan or vegan alternative	125 mL
	Salt and freshly ground pepper	
1 tbsp	olive oil	15 mL
2	medium leeks, white part with just a bit of green, thoroughly cleaned and thinly sliced	2
1	onion, finely chopped	1
2	carrots, peeled and diced	2
2	stalks celery, diced	2
1 tsp	herbes de Provence	5 mL
1 tsp	salt	5 mL
1 tsp	cracked black peppercorns	5 mL
1	can (14 oz/398 mL) diced tomatoes with juice	1
2	small sweet potatoes, peeled and diced	2
1	potato, peeled and diced	1
2 cups	cooked white kidney beans	500 mL
6 cups	vegetable stock	1.5 L
2 cups	sliced green beans	500 mL

1. **Pistou:** In a mini food processor, combine basil, pine nuts, garlic and olive oil and purée. Add Parmesan and pulse to blend. Season with salt and pepper to taste. Transfer to a serving bowl, cover and refrigerate until ready to use. Stir well before serving.

2. In a large saucepan, heat oil over medium heat. Add leeks, onion, carrots and celery and cook, stirring, until vegetables are softened, about 7 minutes. Add herbes de Provence, salt and peppercorns and cook, stirring, for 1 minute. Add tomatoes with juice and bring to a boil.

3. Transfer to slow cooker stoneware. Add sweet potatoes, potato, white beans and stock and stir well. Cover and cook on Low for 6 hours or on High for 3 hours, until vegetables are tender. Stir in green beans. Cover and cook on High for 20 minutes, until green beans are tender.

4. To serve, ladle hot soup into bowls. Pass the pistou and allow people to garnish for themselves.

Tip

If you are halving this recipe, be sure to use a small (2 to 3½ quart) slow cooker.

Make Ahead

Complete Steps 1 and 2. Cover and refrigerate pistou and leek mixture separately for up to 2 days. When you're ready to cook, complete the recipe.

Down-Home Chicken Gumbo

This is a much more delicious version of the chicken gumbo soup I enjoyed as a child, which, I'm sorry to say, came out of a can. Despite the difference in quality, it evokes an abundance of pleasant food memories — I could still enjoy it almost every day of the week.

Tips

If you are halving this recipe, be sure to use a small (2 to 3½ quart) slow cooker.

The quantity of Cajun seasoning and whether you add cayenne depend upon how hot your chorizo is. If you're in doubt, err on the side of caution. You can always pass hot pepper sauce at the table.

Andouille, a spicy smoked pork sausage used in Cajun cooking, is traditionally used in gumbo. If you can find uncooked andouille, by all means use it here. However, most andouille is precooked and heavily smoked, which wouldn't work in this recipe.

Okra is a great thickener for soups but becomes unpleasantly sticky when overcooked. Choose young okra pods 2 to 4 inches (5 to 10 cm) long that don't feel sticky to the touch, which means they are ripe. Gently scrub the pods, cut off the top and tail and slice.

Make Ahead

Complete Step 1. Cover and refrigerate for up to 2 days. When you're ready to cook, complete the recipe.

Serves 6

- Medium to large (4 to 5 quart) slow cooker

1 tbsp	olive oil	15 mL
8 oz	fresh chorizo sausage, removed from casings (see Tips, left)	250 g
2	onions, finely chopped	2
4	stalks celery, diced	4
4	cloves garlic, minced	4
1 to 2 tsp	Cajun seasoning (see Tips, left)	5 to 10 mL
1 tsp	salt	5 mL
1 tsp	cracked black peppercorns	5 mL
1	bay leaf	1
¼ cup	short-grain brown rice (see Tips, page 86)	50 mL
2 tbsp	tomato paste	25 mL
1	can (14 oz/398 mL) diced tomatoes, with juice	1
4 cups	chicken stock	1 L
1 lb	skinless boneless chicken thighs, cut into bite-size pieces	500 g
2 cups	sliced okra (¼ inch/0.5 cm) (see Tips, left)	500 mL
1	red bell pepper, seeded and diced	1
¼ tsp	cayenne pepper, optional (see Tips, left)	1 mL
	Finley chopped green onions, for garnish	

1. In a skillet, heat oil over medium heat. Add sausage, onions and celery and cook, stirring, until sausage is cooked through, about 7 minutes. Add garlic, Cajun seasoning to taste, salt, peppercorns and bay leaf and cook, stirring, for 1 minute. Add rice and toss until coated. Stir in tomato paste. Add tomatoes with juice and bring to a boil.

2. Transfer to slow cooker stoneware. Stir in stock and chicken. Cover and cook on Low for 5 hours or on High for 2½ hours, until hot and bubbly. Stir in okra, bell pepper and cayenne. Cover and cook on High for 20 minutes, until okra is tender. Remove and discard bay leaf. Garnish with green onions.

Can Be Halved
see Tips, below

Smoked Turkey Gumbo

If, like me, you periodically get cravings for smoked food, here's a recipe that will save you the trouble of heating up the smoker. I like to enjoy this for lunch with chunky whole-grain rolls.

Tips

If you are halving this recipe, be sure to use a small (2 to 3½ quart) slow cooker.

Cajun seasoning is a prepared blend and its spiciness varies from brand to brand. If yours is hot, use a smaller quantity.

Use any kind of chile pepper here, but taste the broth before adding and adjust the quantity to ensure the spiciness meets your taste. For instance, if you're using a habanero pepper, I'd recommend no more than half of one.

Short-grain brown rice is extremely glutinous and helps to thicken the gumbo.

Filé powder is ground sassafras leaves. It is a traditional Cajun seasoning used to thicken and add flavor to gumbo.

Make Ahead

Complete Steps 1 and 2. Cover and refrigerate bacon and onion mixture separately for up to 2 days. When you're ready to cook, complete the recipe.

Serves 6

- Medium to large (3½ to 5 quart) slow cooker

2 oz	chunk smoked bacon, diced	60 g
2	onions, finely chopped	2
4	stalks celery, diced	4
2	carrots, peeled and diced	2
4	cloves garlic, minced	4
1 to 2 tsp	Cajun seasoning (see Tips, left)	5 to 10 mL
1 tsp	salt	5 mL
1 tsp	cracked black peppercorns	5 mL
1 tsp	dried thyme leaves	5 mL
2	bay leaves	2
¼ cup	short-grain brown rice (see Tips, left)	50 mL
5 cups	chicken or turkey stock, divided	1.25 L
2 cups	cubed (½ inch/1 cm) smoked turkey	500 mL
1	red bell pepper, seeded and diced	1
1	fresh chile pepper, seeded and diced, optional	1
8 oz	smoked pork sausage, such as andouille, kielbasa or cured chorizo, cut into ½-inch (1 cm) slices	250 g
1 tsp	filé powder, optional	5 mL
	Finely chopped green onions	
	Hot pepper sauce	

1. In a skillet over medium-high heat, cook bacon until browned, about 4 minutes. Using a slotted spoon, transfer to a paper towel to drain. Cover and refrigerate until ready to use.

2. Add onions, celery and carrots to pan and cook, stirring, until vegetables are softened, about 7 minutes. Add garlic, Cajun seasoning to taste, salt, peppercorns, thyme and bay leaves and cook, stirring, for 1 minute. Add rice and toss to coat. Add 2 cups (500 mL) of the stock, bring to a boil and boil for 2 minutes.

3. Transfer to slow cooker stoneware. Add remaining 3 cups (750 mL) of stock. Cover and cook on Low for 6 hours or on High for 3 hours.

4. Add turkey, bell pepper, chile pepper, if using, and sausage. Cover and cook on High about 20 minutes, until pepper is tender and turkey is heated through. Remove and discard bay leaves. Stir in filé powder, if using, and serve. Garnish with green onions and pass the hot pepper sauce at the table.

Variation

Smoked Chicken Gumbo: Substitute smoked chicken for the turkey.

Harira with Chicken

Harira is a traditional Moroccan soup, often made with lamb. I find the meat-based version too heavy and prefer one made with vegetables, or this tasty version, which includes chicken.

Serves 8

Can Be
Halved
see Tips, below

- Medium to large (4 to 5 quart) slow cooker

1 tbsp	olive oil	15 mL
2	onions, finely chopped	2
2	stalks celery, diced	2
4	cloves garlic, minced	4
1 tbsp	minced gingerroot	15 mL
1 tbsp	ground cumin (see Tips, page 75)	15 mL
1	piece (2 inches/5 cm) cinnamon stick	1
1 tsp	salt	5 mL
1 tsp	cracked black peppercorns	5 mL
1/2 tsp	ground turmeric	2 mL
1/2 tsp	crumbled saffron threads	2 mL
1 cup	dried red lentils, rinsed	250 mL
2 cups	cooked chickpeas, drained and rinsed (see Tips, right)	500 mL
1	can (28 oz/796 mL) tomatoes, with juice, coarsely chopped	1
1 lb	skinless boneless chicken thighs, cut into bite-size pieces	500 g
4 cups	chicken stock	1 L
2 tsp	Aleppo pepper or 1/4 tsp (1 mL) cayenne pepper	10 mL
1 tbsp	freshly squeezed lemon juice	15 mL
1/2 cup	finely chopped parsley	125 mL

1. In a skillet, heat oil over medium heat. Add onions and celery and cook, stirring, until softened, about 3 minutes. Add garlic, ginger, cumin, cinnamon stick, salt, peppercorns, turmeric and saffron and cook, stirring, for 1 minute. Add lentils and toss until well coated with mixture. Add chickpeas and tomatoes with juice and bring to a boil.

2. Transfer to slow cooker stoneware. Stir in chicken and stock. Cover and cook on Low for 6 to 8 hours or on High for 3 to 4 hours, until lentils are tender. Dissolve Aleppo pepper in lemon juice and stir into soup. Cover and cook on High for 15 minutes to meld flavors. To serve, ladle into bowls and garnish with parsley.

Vegan Alternative

Omit chicken and substitute vegetable stock for the chicken stock.

Tips

If you are halving this recipe, be sure to use a small (2 to 3 1/2 quart) slow cooker.

For this quantity of chickpeas, cook 1 cup (250 mL) soaked dried chickpeas or use 1 can (14 to 19 oz/398 to 540 mL) rinsed drained chickpeas.

Make Ahead

Complete Step 1. Cover and refrigerate for up to 2 days. When you're ready to cook, complete the recipe.

Bean and Cabbage Soup with Smoked Sausage

This aromatic soup is really a meal in a bowl. You can make it a day ahead and the flavors will mellow. Instead of salad, follow this with robust whole-grain bread and some cheese with a bit of attitude, such as old Cheddar.

Tips

If you are halving this recipe, be sure to use a small (2 to 3½ quart) slow cooker.

If you prefer, substitute 1 can (14 to 19 oz/398 to 540 mL) rinsed drained white kidney or navy beans for the dried white beans. Add in Step 3 along with the remaining stock.

Make Ahead

Complete Steps 1 and 2. Cover and refrigerate for up to 2 days. When you're ready to cook, complete the recipe.

Serves 6

• Medium to large (3½ to 5 quart) slow cooker

1 cup	dried white beans, soaked and drained (see Tips, left)	250 mL
6	slices bacon (about 4 oz/125 g)	6
2	onions, chopped	2
2	stalks celery, diced	2
2	carrots, peeled and diced	2
4	cloves garlic, minced	4
1 tsp	dried thyme leaves	5 mL
½ tsp	salt	2 mL
½ tsp	cracked black peppercorns	2 mL
6 cups	chicken stock, divided	1.5 L
2 cups	shredded cabbage, preferably Savoy	500 mL
8 oz	kielbasa, diced	250 g

1. In a skillet over medium-high heat, cook bacon until crisp. Using a slotted spoon, transfer to a paper towel to drain. Cover and refrigerate until ready to use. Drain off all but 2 tbsp (25 mL) fat from the pan, if necessary. Reduce heat to medium.

2. Add onions, celery and carrots to pan and cook, stirring, until carrots are softened, about 7 minutes. Add garlic, thyme, salt and peppercorns and cook, stirring, for 1 minute. Add drained beans and 2 cups (500 mL) of the stock, bring to a boil and boil for 3 minutes.

3. Transfer to slow cooker stoneware. Add remaining 4 cups (1 L) of stock. Cover and cook on Low for 8 hours or on High for 4 hours, until beans are tender.

4. Stir in cabbage and kielbasa. Cover and cook on High about 20 minutes, until cabbage is tender. To serve, ladle into bowls and garnish with crumbled reserved bacon.

Mom's Chicken Noodle Soup

There really is nothing more comforting than a bowl of chicken soup. It's the culinary equivalent of a get-well card.

Serves 6

- Medium to large (3½ to 5 quart) slow cooker

1 tbsp	olive oil	15 mL
1 cup	shallots, coarsely chopped	250 mL
2	carrots, peeled and finely diced	2
4	cloves garlic	4
1	piece (1 inch/2.5 cm) gingerroot, peeled and quartered	1
½ tsp	salt	2 mL
½ tsp	cracked black peppercorns	2 mL
2 cups	water	500 mL
1 lb	skin-on bone-in chicken thighs	500 g
4 cups	chicken stock	1 L
4 oz	egg noodles	125 g

1. In a skillet, heat oil over medium heat. Add shallots and carrots and cook, stirring, until softened, about 7 minutes. Add garlic, ginger, salt and peppercorns and cook, stirring, for 1 minute. Add water and bring to a boil, scraping up brown bits from the bottom of the pan.

2. Transfer to slow cooker stoneware. Add chicken and stock. Cover and cook on Low for 6 hours or on High for 3 hours, periodically skimming off impurities that float to the top, until chicken is cooked through.

3. Place a fine-mesh strainer over a large saucepan and strain, reserving broth. Set chicken aside and discard remaining solids. Remove skin from chicken and shred. Discard skin and bones. Return broth to stoneware along with chicken and keep warm.

4. Meanwhile, in a large pot of boiling salted water, cook egg noodles according to package instructions. Drain and add to broth. Serve immediately.

Can Be Halved
see Tip, below

Tip
If you are halving this recipe, be sure to use a small (2 to 3½ quart) slow cooker.

Make Ahead
After completing Step 3, transfer soup to a large bowl, cover and refrigerate for up to 2 days. Skim off the fat and reheat in a large saucepan on the stovetop. After the soup has reached a simmer, add the noodles.

Poultry

Chicken Provençal

Entertaining Worthy

Can Be Halved
see Tips, below

Chicken Provençal

The secret ingredient in this easy-to-make dish is herbes de Provence, a pungent blend of dried herbs — such as thyme, savory, sage, lavender and fennel — that provides great flavor with virtually no effort on your part. The black olives add a pleasant bite. In keeping with the spirit of the dish I like to serve this with red rice from the Camargue region of France (look for it in specialty stores), but if that's not available, hot orzo is pretty good, too.

Tips

If you are halving this recipe, be sure to use a small (2 to 3 quart) slow cooker.

If you prefer, substitute 1 cup (250 mL) chicken stock plus 1 tbsp (15 mL) lemon juice for the white wine.

I like to use Italian San Marzano tomatoes, which are particularly rich. If you're using domestic tomatoes, add 1 tbsp (15 mL) tomato paste along with the wine.

Make Ahead

Complete Steps 2 and 3. Cover and refrigerate mixture for up to 2 days (see Making Ahead, page 17). When you're ready to cook, complete the recipe.

Serves 6

• Medium to large (3½ to 5 quart) slow cooker

3 lbs	skinless bone-in chicken thighs (12 thighs)	1.5 kg
1 tbsp	olive oil	15 mL
4 oz	chunk bacon, diced	125 g
2	onions, finely chopped	2
4	cloves garlic, minced	4
1½ tsp	herbes de Provence	7 mL
1 tsp	salt	5 mL
½ tsp	cracked black peppercorns	2 mL
1 cup	dry white wine (see Tips, left)	250 mL
1	can (14 oz/398 mL) tomatoes with juice, coarsely chopped (see Tips, left)	1
½ cup	chopped pitted black olives	125 mL

1. Arrange chicken evenly over bottom of slow cooker stoneware, overlapping as necessary.

2. In a skillet, heat oil over medium-high heat. Add bacon and cook, stirring, until nicely browned. Using a slotted spoon, transfer to slow cooker stoneware. Drain off all but 2 tbsp (25 mL) of the fat from the pan.

3. Add onions to pan and cook, stirring, until softened, about 3 minutes. Add garlic, herbes de Provence, salt and peppercorns and cook, stirring, for 1 minute. Add wine, bring to a boil and boil for 2 minutes. Add tomatoes with juice and bring to a boil.

4. Transfer to slow cooker stoneware. Cover and cook on Low for 6 hours or High for 3 hours, until juices run clear when chicken is pierced with a fork. Sprinkle olives evenly over top. Cover and cook on High about 5 minutes, until heated through.

Chicken 'n' Dumplings

When I was growing up, chicken and dumplings was often served for Sunday dinner. It's simple but delicious — with their soothingly supple texture, dumplings are a special treat. I love this dish as much today as I did when I was six years old.

Can Be Halved
see Tips, below

Serves 6

- Large (approx. 5 quart) slow cooker

1 tbsp	olive oil	15 mL
2	onions, finely chopped	2
2	carrots, peeled and diced	2
4	stalks celery, diced	4
4	cloves garlic, minced	4
1 tsp	each salt and cracked black peppercorns	5 mL
1 tsp	dried thyme leaves	5 mL
3 tbsp	all-purpose flour	45 mL
1 cup	dry white wine (see Tips, right)	250 mL
2 cups	hot chicken stock	500 mL
2 lbs	skinless boneless chicken thighs or breasts, cut into 1-inch (2.5 cm) cubes (see Tips, right)	1 kg
$\frac{1}{4}$ tsp	cayenne pepper, optional	1 mL
1 cup	green peas	250 mL

Dumplings

1	egg, beaten	1
$\frac{3}{4}$ cup	milk	175 mL
$\frac{1}{2}$ tsp	salt	2 mL
$\frac{1}{4}$ tsp	freshly ground black pepper	1 mL
$\frac{1}{4}$ cup	finely chopped parsley	50 mL
1 tbsp	baking powder	15 mL
1 cup	all-purpose flour	250 mL

1. In a skillet, heat oil over medium heat. Add onions, carrots and celery and cook, stirring, until softened, about 7 minutes. Add garlic, salt, peppercorns and thyme and cook, stirring, for 1 minute. Add flour and cook, stirring, for 1 minute. Add wine, bring to a boil and boil for 2 minutes. Stir in stock, return to a boil and cook, stirring, until mixture thickens, about 2 minutes.

2. Arrange chicken evenly over bottom of slow cooker and cover with sauce. Cover and cook on Low for 5 hours or on High for $2\frac{1}{2}$ hours, until juices run clear. Stir in cayenne, if using, and green peas and ensure slow cooker is set to High.

3. **Dumplings:** Meanwhile, in a bowl, whisk together egg, milk, salt, pepper and parsley. Whisk in baking powder. Add flour and mix well (batter will be thick). Drop batter by heaping tbsp (20 mL) into hot liquid. Cover and cook on High about 20 minutes, until dumplings are cooked through. Serve immediately.

Tips

If you are halving this recipe, be sure to use a small (2 to 3 quart) slow cooker.

If you don't want to use wine, add an extra cup (250 mL) of chicken stock plus 1 tbsp (15 mL) lemon juice.

If you are using chicken breasts, reduce the cooking time to 4 hours on Low or 2 hours on High before adding the dumplings.

Make Ahead

Complete Step 1. Cover and refrigerate mixture for up to 2 days. When you're ready to cook, complete the recipe.

Tips

If you are halving this recipe, be sure to use a small (2½ to 3 quart) slow cooker.

I recommend using either chicken breasts or legs and thighs in this recipe as, depending on your slow cooker, the cooking times may vary by as much as 1 hour for different parts. If overcooked, white meat will dry out and undermine results.

When measuring the butter for Steps 6 through 8, be sure to leave it at room temperature so the final 2 tbsp (25 mL) is softened for blending with the flour.

Coq au Vin

This is a special occasion dish — it's a fair bit of work, but the results are out of the ordinary. The advantage to making this in the slow cooker is that it will cook unattended while you do other things. I like to serve it over orzo, but potatoes or rice also makes a great accompaniment.

Serves 8

- Large (approx. 5 quart) slow cooker

2	onions, finely chopped	2
2	carrots, peeled and diced	2
2	stalks celery, diced	2
4	cloves garlic, minced	4
1 tsp	cracked black peppercorns	5 mL
3 cups	dry red wine	750 mL
5 lbs	skin-on bone-in chicken breasts or legs and thighs (see Tips, left)	2.5 kg
1 tbsp	olive oil	15 mL
4 oz	chunk bacon, diced	125 g
1 tsp	salt	5 mL
1 tsp	dried thyme leaves	5 mL
2	bay leaves	2
¼ cup	brandy or cognac	50 mL
¼ cup + 2 tbsp	all-purpose flour	50 mL + 25 mL
1 cup	chicken stock	250 mL
6 tbsp	butter, divided (see Tips, left)	90 mL
18	pearl onions, peeled	18
½ cup	water	125 mL
1 lb	mushrooms, trimmed and quartered	500 g
	Salt and freshly ground black pepper	
	Finely chopped parsley	

1. In a saucepan over medium heat, combine onions, carrots, celery, garlic, peppercorns and wine and bring to a boil. Boil for 2 minutes. Let cool to room temperature.

2. Place chicken in a large bowl and add cooled marinade. Cover and refrigerate at least overnight or for up to 2 days. When you're ready to cook, remove chicken from marinade and pat dry. Strain marinade through a sieve into a bowl and set aside; set vegetables aside separately.

3. In a skillet, heat oil over medium heat. Add bacon and cook, stirring, until browned. Using a slotted spoon, transfer to slow cooker stoneware. Add chicken, in batches, and cook until browned on all sides, about 4 minutes per batch. Transfer to stoneware as completed.

4. Add reserved vegetables to skillet and cook, stirring, until softened, about 7 minutes. Add salt, thyme and bay leaves and cook, stirring, for 1 minute. Add brandy and, standing well back, ignite, shaking the pan until the flames subside. Add $\frac{1}{4}$ cup (50 mL) of the flour and cook, stirring, for 2 minutes. Add reserved marinade and stock and bring to a boil. Cook, stirring, until mixture thickens, about 5 minutes.

5. Transfer to slow cooker stoneware. Cover and cook on Low for 4 to 6 hours or on High for 2 to 3 hours, until chicken is no longer pink. Remove and discard bay leaves.

6. Meanwhile, heat 2 tbsp (25 mL) of the butter in a skillet over medium heat. Add pearl onions and cook, stirring, until browned, about 10 minutes. Add water. Reduce heat to low. Cover and simmer about 30 minutes, until onions begin to caramelize. Set aside and keep warm.

7. In another skillet, heat 2 tbsp (25 mL) of butter over medium-high heat. Add mushrooms and cook, stirring, until they release their liquid, about 7 minutes. Season with salt and pepper to taste.

8. Transfer cooked chicken to a serving dish. Arrange onions and mushrooms over top and keep warm. Strain cooking liquid into a saucepan. Discard solids. In a small bowl, blend remaining 2 tbsp (25 mL) softened butter with remaining 2 tbsp (25 mL) of the flour and beat into sauce over low heat. Simmer, stirring, for about 1 minute. Pour over chicken and vegetables. Garnish with parsley.

Chicken with Chorizo

The flavors in this dish are Spanish but I like to serve it with a simple Italian-inspired risotto (made with just onions and chicken stock), perhaps because the combination reminds me of arroz con pollo, one of my favorite Spanish dishes. Plain rice or orzo works well, too. Finish the meal with a green vegetable or salad.

Tips

If you are halving this recipe, be sure to use a small (2 to 3 quart) slow cooker.

If you don't want to use wine, add an extra cup (250 mL) of chicken stock plus 1 tbsp (15 mL) lemon juice.

Add paprika if you like a bit of heat. Use smoked paprika for a smoky flavor.

Make Ahead

Complete Step 1. Cover and refrigerate mixture for up to 2 days. When you're ready to cook, complete the recipe.

Serves 6

- Large (approx. 5 quart) slow cooker

2 tbsp	olive oil	25 mL
2	onions, finely chopped	2
2	stalks celery, diced	2
4	cloves garlic, minced	4
1 tsp	salt	5 mL
1 tsp	cracked black peppercorns	5 mL
1 tsp	dried thyme leaves	5 mL
2 tbsp	sherry vinegar	25 mL
1 cup	dry white wine (see Tips, left)	250 mL
1	can (28 oz/796 mL) tomatoes with juice, coarsely chopped	1
3 lbs	skinless bone-in chicken thighs (about 12 thighs)	1.5 kg
1	green bell pepper, seeded and diced	1
4 oz	cured chorizo sausage, sliced	125 g
¼ tsp	hot paprika (see Tips, left) or pinch cayenne pepper, optional	1 mL

1. In a skillet, heat oil over medium heat. Add onions and celery and cook, stirring, until softened, about 5 minutes. Add garlic, salt, peppercorns and thyme and cook, stirring, for 1 minute. Add sherry vinegar and cook, stirring, until it evaporates, about 1 minute. Add wine, bring to a boil and boil for 2 minutes. Stir in tomatoes with juice.

2. Transfer to slow cooker stoneware. Add chicken and stir well. Cover and cook on Low for 6 hours or on High for 3 hours, until juices run clear when chicken is pierced with a fork. Add bell pepper, chorizo and paprika, if using. Cover and cook on High for 20 minutes, until pepper is tender.

Italian-Style Chicken with Potatoes

Nothing could be easier to make than this luscious Italian-inspired chicken dish. Add a tossed green salad and, if you're feeling celebratory, open some wine and enjoy!

Can Be Halved
see Tip, below

Tip
If you are halving this recipe, be sure to use a small (2½ to 3 quart) slow cooker.

Serves 6

- Large (approx. 5 quart) slow cooker
- Lightly greased slow cooker stoneware

3 lbs	skinless bone-in chicken thighs (about 12 thighs)	1.5 kg
3	potatoes (about 1½ lbs/750 g), peeled and diced	3
4	cloves garlic, minced	4
1 tsp	dried oregano leaves	5 mL
1 tsp	salt	5 mL
	Freshly ground black pepper	
1	can (28 oz/796 mL) tomatoes with juice, coarsely chopped	1
¼ cup	extra virgin olive oil	50 mL
¼ tsp	cayenne pepper, dissolved in 1 tbsp (15 mL) freshly squeezed lemon juice	1 mL
½ cup	chopped pitted black olives, optional	125 mL
½ cup	finely chopped parsley	125 mL

1. Arrange chicken evenly over bottom of prepared stoneware and scatter potatoes evenly over top. Sprinkle with garlic, oregano, salt and freshly ground pepper to taste. Add tomatoes with juice, then olive oil.

2. Cover and cook on Low for 6 hours or on High for 3 hours, until juices run clear when chicken is pierced with a fork. Stir in cayenne solution and olives, if using. Sprinkle parsley evenly over top. Cover and cook on High for 15 minutes, until flavors meld.

Entertaining Worthy

Can Be Halved
see Tips, below

Moroccan-Style Lemon Chicken with Olives

While some may think the flavors in this dish are a bit exotic to qualify as comfort food, I've included it here because I find it wonderfully soothing. It's a great dish for a Friday night dinner with friends. Serve the chicken over whole-grain couscous and accompany it with a green vegetable such as steamed beans or sautéed spinach.

Serves 6

• Medium to large (3½ to 5 quart) slow cooker

3 lbs	skinless bone-in chicken thighs (12 thighs)	1.5 kg
2	onions, quartered	2
4	cloves garlic, chopped	4
2 tbsp	coarsely chopped gingerroot	25 mL
½ tsp	saffron threads, crumbled	2 mL
½ tsp	ground cumin	2 mL
½ tsp	cracked black peppercorns	2 mL
2 tbsp	freshly squeezed lemon juice	25 mL
1 cup	chicken stock	250 mL
1	preserved lemon, flesh discarded, thoroughly rinsed and cut into thin strips (see Tips, left)	1
1 cup	pitted green olives	250 mL
	Salt	
	Cooked couscous, optional	
	Sweet paprika, optional	

1. Arrange chicken evenly over bottom of slow cooker stoneware.

2. In a food processor, combine onions, garlic and ginger and process until onions are almost puréed. Add saffron, cumin, peppercorns and lemon juice and process until blended. Add stock and pulse to mix.

3. Transfer to slow cooker stoneware. Mix well, ensuring all pieces of chicken are well coated with the mixture. Cover and cook on Low for 5½ hours or on High for 2½ hours. Add preserved lemon and olives. Cover and cook on High for 30 minutes, until juices run clear when chicken is pierced with a fork and flavors meld.

4. Using a slotted spoon, transfer chicken and solids to a deep platter. Cover and keep warm. Transfer sauce to a saucepan, bring to a boil over medium-high heat and cook until reduced by about one-third, about 5 minutes. Season to taste with salt. Serve immediately or, if desired, for a great presentation, spread cooked couscous in a ring around the edge of a deep platter. Arrange the chicken in the center and pour the reduced sauce over it. Dust with paprika.

Tips

If you are halving this recipe, be sure to use a small (2 to 3 quart) slow cooker.

Preserved lemons are a key ingredient in Moroccan cooking and are available in stores specializing in Middle Eastern foods. However, they are very easy to make — look for recipes in preserving books or Moroccan cookbooks. If all else fails, in his book *The Food Substitutions Bible*, David Joachim suggests cooking 1 sliced lemon, 1 tsp (5 mL) salt and a pinch of sugar in 2 tsp (10 mL) olive oil over medium-low heat until the lemon is very tender, 20 to 30 minutes.

Make Ahead

Complete Step 2. Cover and refrigerate mixture for up to 2 days. When you're ready to cook, complete the recipe.

Saffron-Braised Chicken

Superb flavor together with ease of preparation is a marriage made in heaven, which this dish provides. Don't balk at the generous hit of saffron — it really distinguishes the sauce. Add some steamed green beans and serve this over whole wheat couscous or hot bulgur (see Tips, left) for a delicious Mediterranean-themed dinner.

Tips

If you are halving this recipe, be sure to use a small (2 to 3 quart) slow cooker.

Bulgur is often overlooked as an accompaniment to dishes, but it is a whole grain with a delicious nutty flavor and is just as easy to cook as couscous. To cook bulgur to accompany this recipe, combine 1½ cups (375 mL) coarse or medium bulgur and 3 cups (750 mL) boiling water. Stir well, cover and set aside until water is absorbed and bulgur is tender to the bite, about 20 minutes.

Make Ahead

Complete Steps 1 and 2. Cover and refrigerate chicken and vegetable mixtures separately. When you're ready to cook, complete the recipe.

Serves 6

• Large (approx. 5 quart) slow cooker

Rub

2 tsp	finely grated garlic or garlic put through a press	10 mL
1 tsp	finely grated lemon zest	5 mL
1 tbsp	freshly squeezed lemon juice	15 mL
1 tsp	coarse sea salt	5 mL
½ tsp	saffron threads, crumbled	2 mL
1 tbsp	olive oil	15 mL
3 lbs	skinless bone-in chicken thighs (about 12 thighs)	1.5 kg
1 tbsp	olive oil, divided	15 mL
3	onions, thinly sliced on the vertical	3
1 tsp	dried oregano leaves	5 mL
½ tsp	cracked black peppercorns	2 mL
4	bay leaves	4
1	piece (2 inches/5 cm) cinnamon stick	1
2 tbsp	brandy or cognac	25 mL
2 cups	chicken stock	500 mL
	Couscous or bulgur	

1. **Rub:** In a bowl, combine garlic, lemon zest and juice, sea salt and saffron. Stir in olive oil. Spread evenly over chicken and rub mixture in. Cover and refrigerate for 2 hours or overnight. When you're ready to cook, arrange chicken evenly over bottom of slow cooker stoneware and drizzle with any residual juices.

2. In a skillet, heat olive oil over medium heat. Add onions and cook, stirring, until softened, about 3 minutes. Add oregano, peppercorns, bay leaves and cinnamon stick and cook, stirring, for 1 minute. Add brandy and cook until it evaporates, about 2 minutes. Stir in stock.

3. Transfer to slow cooker stoneware. Cover and cook on Low for 6 hours or on High for 3 hours, until juices run clear when chicken is pierced with a fork. Remove and discard bay leaves. Serve over couscous or bulgur.

Mediterranean-Style Chicken with White Beans

I see this dish as "Mediterranean fusion," a tasty mix of Italian and Spanish influences. It's a great one-pot meal. If you like a bit of heat and/or smoke, use hot or hot smoked paprika instead of sweet, or pass your favorite hot sauce at the table.

Serves 6

- Large (approx. 5 quart) slow cooker

1 tbsp	olive oil	15 mL
4 oz	chunk pancetta or bacon, diced	125 g
2	onions, diced	2
4	cloves garlic, minced	4
1 tsp	dried oregano leaves	5 mL
1 tsp	cracked black peppercorns	5 mL
½ tsp	salt	2 mL
2	bay leaves	2
2 tbsp	brandy or cognac, optional	25 mL
1	can (28 oz/796 mL) tomatoes with juice, coarsely chopped	1
1 cup	chicken stock	250 mL
4 cups	drained cooked white beans, such as cannellini (see Tips, right)	1 L
3 lbs	skinless bone-in chicken thighs (about 12 thighs)	1.5 kg
2 tsp	paprika, dissolved in 1 tbsp (15 mL) freshly squeezed lemon juice	10 mL
½ cup	finely chopped parsley	125 mL

1. In a skillet, heat oil over medium-high heat. Add pancetta and onions and cook, stirring, until pancetta is crispy and onions are golden, about 7 minutes. Drain off all but 1 tbsp (15 mL) fat from the pan, if necessary. Add garlic, oregano, peppercorns, salt and bay leaves and cook, stirring, for 1 minute. Add brandy, if using, and cook, stirring, until it evaporates, about 2 minutes. Add tomatoes with juice and stock and bring to a boil. Stir in beans.

2. Arrange chicken evenly over bottom of stoneware, then top with sauce. Cover and cook on Low for 6 hours or on High for 3 hours, until juices run clear when chicken is pierced with a fork. Stir in paprika solution and parsley. Cover and cook on High for 15 minutes, until flavors meld. Remove and discard bay leaves.

Tips

If you are halving this recipe, be sure to use a small (2½ to 3 quart) slow cooker.

For this quantity of cooked beans, use 2 cans (each 14 to 19 oz/398 to 540 mL), drained and rinsed, or soak and cook 2 cups (500 mL) dried white beans.

Make Ahead

Complete Step 1 but don't add the beans. Cover and refrigerate mixture for up to 2 days (see Making Ahead, page 17). When you're ready to cook, stir beans into mixture and complete the recipe.

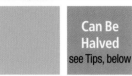
French-Style Chicken Avgolemono

Forget tradition and go for this unusual blend of flavors. The chicken, artichoke and potato combination is reminiscent of Provence, and the avgolemono finish is passionately Greek. This dish is on the rich side, so I'd recommend serving it over pasta such as orzo or plain rice. Finish the meal with a simple salad of mixed greens.

Tips

If you are halving this recipe, be sure to use a small (1½ to 3 quart) slow cooker.

To clean leeks: Fill a sink full of lukewarm water. Split the leeks in half lengthwise and submerge· in the water, swishing them around to remove all traces of dirt. Transfer to a colander and rinse thoroughly under cold water.

If you prefer, substitute an extra cup (250 mL) of chicken stock plus 1 tbsp (15 mL) lemon juice for the white wine.

Make Ahead

Complete Step 3, adding 1 tbsp (15 mL) of the oil to pan before softening leeks. Cover and refrigerate mixture for up to 2 days. When you're ready to cook, complete the recipe.

Serves 6

• Large (approx. 5 quart) slow cooker

3	large potatoes (each about 8 oz/250 g)	3
¼ cup	olive oil	50 mL
2	leeks, white and light green parts only, cleaned and sliced (see Tips, left)	2
4	cloves garlic, minced	4
2 tsp	dried Italian seasoning	10 mL
1 tsp	each salt and cracked black peppercorns	2 mL
1 cup	dry white wine (see Tips, left)	250 mL
1 cup	chicken stock	250 mL
1	can (14 oz/398 mL) artichokes, drained and quartered (about 6 artichoke hearts)	1
2 lbs	skinless, boneless chicken thighs, cut into bite-size pieces	1 kg
¼ cup	freshly squeezed lemon juice	50 mL
2	egg yolks	2
¼ cup	finely chopped dill	50 mL

1. Cut potatoes in half lengthwise, then cut each half into 4 wedges. Pat dry.

2. In a skillet, heat oil over medium-high heat for 30 seconds. Add potatoes, in batches, and cook until nicely browned on all sides, about 7 minutes per batch. Using a slotted spoon, transfer to paper towels to drain. Drain all but 1 tbsp (15 mL) oil from pan.

3. Reduce heat to medium. Add leeks and cook, stirring, until softened, about 5 minutes. Add garlic, Italian seasoning, salt and peppercorns and cook, stirring, for 1 minute. Add wine, bring to a boil and boil for 2 minutes. Stir in stock and artichokes.

4. Arrange chicken evenly over bottom of slow cooker stoneware. Cover with potatoes and vegetable mixture. Cover and cook on Low for 6 hours or on High for 3 hours, until juices run clear when chicken is pierced with a fork.

5. In a bowl, whisk together lemon juice and egg yolks. Gradually whisk in 1 cup (250 mL) of hot liquid from the slow cooker. Return to stoneware and cook on High, stirring until thickened, about 3 minutes. Garnish with dill and serve.

African-Style Chicken in Onion Gravy

If you are desperately seeking a break from the same old thing, try this take on yassa, *a traditional celebratory dish originating in Senegal. It's very simple — chicken braised in a blanket of onions and seasoned stock — but the results are seductive. I like to serve this over steamed brown rice or whole-grain couscous.*

Can Be Halved
see Tips, below

Serves 6

• Medium to large (3½ to 5 quart) slow cooker

2 tsp	finely grated lime zest	10 mL
½ cup	freshly squeezed lime juice	125 mL
6	cloves garlic, minced	6
2 tbsp	soy sauce	25 mL
2 tsp	ground allspice	10 mL
1 tsp	salt	5 mL
1 tsp	cracked black peppercorns	5 mL
3 lbs	skinless bone-in chicken thighs (about 12 thighs)	1.5 kg
2 tbsp	olive oil	25 mL
2	large Spanish or white onions, very thinly sliced on the vertical	2
2	carrots, peeled and diced	2
2 tbsp	minced gingerroot	25 mL
1 cup	chicken stock	250 mL
1 to 2	fresh chile peppers, seeded and minced (see Tips, right)	1 to 2

1. In a large bowl, combine lime zest and juice, garlic, soy sauce, allspice, salt and peppercorns. Pat chicken dry, add to mixture and toss until well coated. Cover and refrigerate for at least 4 hours or overnight.

2. Lift chicken from marinade and transfer to slow cooker stoneware. Set marinade aside.

3. In a skillet, heat oil over medium heat. Add onions and carrots and cook, stirring, until onions just begin to turn golden, about 10 minutes. Add ginger and cook, stirring, for 1 minute. Add reserved marinade and stock and bring to a boil.

4. Transfer to slow cooker stoneware. Cover and cook on Low for 6 hours or on High for 3 hours, until chicken is falling off the bone. Stir in chile pepper and serve.

Tips

If you are halving this recipe, be sure to use a small (2 to 3 quart) slow cooker.

Most fresh chile peppers will work in this recipe, and the quantity you use depends upon their heat quotient and your taste. In this dish, I prefer the flavor of habanero, Scotch bonnet or long red or green chiles. Although jalapeño peppers will provide heat, they have a Tex-Mex flavor that I don't think is appropriate for this dish.

Chicken Cobbler Paprikash

While the flavors in this one-pot meal are classically Hungarian, the cobbler topping is definitely American, making it a fusion version of comfort food. I like to serve this with sliced green beans or sweet peas. It makes a perfectly yummy dinner.

Tips

If you are halving this recipe, be sure to use a small (1½ to 3 quart) slow cooker.

If you're using chicken breasts, reduce the initial cooking time to 3 hours on Low or 1½ hours on High.

If you prefer a topping that is somewhat lower in saturated fat, substitute the one from Traditional Cobbler (see recipe, page 124), which is made with buttermilk and olive oil.

Make Ahead

Complete Step 1. Cover and refrigerate mixture for up to 2 days. When you're ready to cook, complete the recipe.

Serves 6

• Medium to large (3½ to 5 quart) slow cooker

1 tbsp	olive oil	15 mL
3	onions, thinly sliced on the vertical	3
4	cloves garlic, minced	4
1 tsp	caraway seeds	5 mL
1 tsp	dried thyme leaves	5 mL
1 tsp	salt	5 mL
1 tsp	cracked black peppercorns	5 mL
2 tbsp	all-purpose flour	25 mL
1	can (14 oz/398 mL) diced tomatoes with juice	1
1 cup	chicken stock	250 mL
2 lbs	skinless, boneless chicken breasts (see Tips, left) or thighs, cut into 1-inch (2.5 cm) cubes	1 kg
1	red bell pepper, seeded and diced	1
1 tbsp	sweet paprika, preferably Hungarian	15 mL
½ cup	sour cream	125 mL

Topping

1½ cups	all-purpose flour	375 mL
2 tsp	baking powder	10 mL
½ tsp	salt	2 mL
1 tsp	grated lemon zest	5 mL
½ cup	cold butter, cut into 1-inch (2.5 cm) cubes	125 mL
½ cup	sour cream	125 mL

1. In a skillet, heat oil over medium-high heat. Add onions and cook, stirring, just until they begin to turn golden, about 10 minutes. Add garlic, caraway seeds, thyme, salt and peppercorns and cook, stirring for 1 minute. Add flour and cook, stirring, for 1 minute. Add tomatoes with juice and stock and bring to a boil. Cook, stirring, until slightly thickened, about 5 minutes.

2. Arrange chicken evenly over bottom of stoneware and cover with tomato mixture. Cover and cook on Low for 4 hours or on High for 2 hours. Add bell pepper, paprika and sour cream to stoneware and stir well.

3. **Topping:** In a bowl, combine flour, baking powder, salt and lemon zest. Using your fingers or a pastry blender, cut in butter until mixture resembles coarse crumbs. Add sour cream and stir with a fork until a thick batter forms.

4. Using your hands, form batter into 6 biscuit-shaped mounds and place over hot liquid. Cover and cook on High until a tester inserted in the center of a biscuit comes out clean, about 45 minutes.

Variation

Turkey Cobbler Paprikash: Substitute an equal quantity of turkey for the chicken.

Tips

If you are halving this recipe, be sure to use a small (1½ to 3 quart) slow cooker.

I've suggested the addition of tomato paste to enrich the flavor of domestically grown tomatoes. If you are using Italian San Marzano tomatoes, my favorite, they are so rich and flavorful it won't be required.

If you're serving this to guests you may want to reduce the sauce a bit, since it is quite liquidy. After the dish has finished cooking, transfer chicken to a warm deep platter and keep warm. Transfer the sauce to a saucepan and boil over medium heat until desired consistency is reached. Pour over chicken, garnish and serve.

Make Ahead

Complete Step 2. Cover and refrigerate mixture for up to 2 days. When you're ready to cook, complete the recipe.

Chicken Laced with Vinegar

This classic French preparation produces a deliciously tart sauce. Don't be shy of the vinegar — I've actually cut back on the amount compared to traditional recipes, and the quantity of garlic and onion balances the acidity. I like to serve this over mashed potatoes to soak up the lip-smackin' sauce.

Serves 4

• Medium to large (3½ to 5 quart) slow cooker

2 lbs	skinless bone-in chicken thighs (8 thighs)	1 kg
1 tbsp	olive oil	15 mL
2	onions, finely chopped	2
8	cloves garlic, minced	8
1 tsp	dried rosemary leaves	5 mL
1 tsp	salt	5 mL
½ tsp	cracked black peppercorns	2 mL
¼ cup	red wine vinegar	50 mL
1 tbsp	tomato paste (see Tips, left)	15 mL
1	can (14 oz/398 mL) diced tomatoes with juice	1
1 cup	chicken stock	250 mL
	Finely chopped parsley	

1. Arrange chicken evenly over bottom of slow cooker stoneware.

2. In a skillet, heat oil over medium heat. Add onions and cook, stirring, until softened, about 3 minutes. Add garlic, rosemary, salt and peppercorns and cook, stirring, for 1 minute. Add vinegar and cook, stirring, about 1 minute. Add tomato paste, if using, tomatoes with juice and stock and bring to a boil.

3. Transfer to slow cooker stoneware. Cover and cook on Low for 6 hours or on High for 3 hours, until juices run clear when chicken is pierced with a fork. Garnish liberally with parsley.

Tagine of Chicken with Apricots

I love the juxtaposition of hot and sweet flavors in this dish. Apricots and chicken make a surprisingly tasty combination, and the harissa adds a nice hit of heat that is softened by the honey. Bulgur, couscous or rice makes a great accompaniment. For an impressive presentation, arrange the cooked grain in a ring around the edge of a deep platter and fill the center with the chicken mixture. Then garnish with the pine nuts and cilantro.

Can Be Halved
see Tips, below

Serves 6

- Medium to large (3½ to 5 quart) slow cooker

3 lbs	skinless bone-in chicken thighs (about 12 thighs)	1.5 kg
1 tbsp	olive oil	15 mL
2	onions, thinly sliced on the vertical	2
4	cloves garlic, minced	4
1 tbsp	minced gingerroot	15 mL
½ tsp	salt	2 mL
½ tsp	cracked black peppercorns	2 mL
2	bay leaves	2
1	piece (2 inches/5 cm) cinnamon stick	1
24	dried apricots	24
2 cups	chicken stock	500 mL
2 tbsp	harissa (see Tips, right)	25 mL
1 tbsp	liquid honey	15 mL
¼ cup	finely chopped cilantro leaves	50 mL
¼ cup	toasted pine nuts	50 mL

1. Arrange chicken evenly over bottom of stoneware.

2. In a skillet, heat oil over medium heat. Add onions and cook, stirring, until softened, about 3 minutes. Add garlic, ginger, salt, peppercorns, bay leaves and cinnamon stick and cook, stirring, for 1 minute. Stir in apricots and stock.

3. Transfer to slow cooker stoneware. Cover and cook on Low for 5 hours or on High for 2½ hours, until juices run clear when chicken is pierced with a fork. Remove and discard bay leaves.

4. In a small bowl, combine harissa and honey. Mix well. Add to slow cooker and stir well. Cover and cook on High for 10 minutes to blend flavors. Garnish with cilantro and pine nuts and serve.

Tips

If you are halving this recipe, be sure to use a small (2 to 3 quart) slow cooker.

Harissa is a North African condiment made from hot peppers and various seasonings. It is available in specialty food stores. You can easily make your own: In a mini food processor, combine 3 dried red chile peppers (reconstituted in boiling water for 30 minutes), 2 tsp (10 mL) each toasted caraway, coriander and cumin seeds, 2 reconstituted sun-dried tomatoes, 4 cloves garlic, 2 tbsp (25 mL) freshly squeezed lemon juice, 1 tbsp (15 mL) sweet paprika and ½ tsp (2 mL) salt and process until combined. Add 3 tbsp (45 mL) extra virgin olive oil and process until smooth. Store, covered, in the refrigerator for up to 1 month, covering the paste with a bit of olive oil every time you use it. Makes about ⅓ cup (75 mL).

Make Ahead

Complete Step 2. Cover and refrigerate mixture for up to 2 days. When you're ready to cook, complete the recipe.

Can Be Halved
see Tip, below

Tip

If you are halving this recipe, be sure to use a small (2 to 3 quart) slow cooker.

Make Ahead

Complete Step 2. Cover and refrigerate mixture for up to 2 days. When you're ready to cook, complete the recipe.

Miso Mushroom Chicken with Chinese Cabbage

I love the combination of flavors in this luscious stew. Serve it over hot rice, preferably the more nutritious brown variety, for a delicious meal.

Serves 6

- Large (approx. 5 quart) slow cooker

1	package (½ oz/14 g) dried wood ear mushrooms	1
1 cup	hot water	250 mL
1 tbsp	oil	15 mL
2	onions, finely chopped	2
4	stalks celery, diced	4
6	cloves garlic, minced	6
1 tbsp	minced gingerroot	15 mL
1 tsp	cracked black peppercorns	5 mL
½ tsp	salt	2 mL
8 oz	shiitake mushrooms, stems discarded, sliced	250 g
½ cup	mirin	125 mL
¼ cup	soy sauce	50 mL
2 cups	chicken stock	500 mL
2 lbs	skinless bone-in chicken thighs (about 8)	1 kg
½ cup	white miso	125 mL
6 cups	packed shredded napa cabbage	1.5 L

1. In a bowl, combine dried mushrooms and hot water. Let stand for 30 minutes. Drain through a fine sieve, discarding soaking liquid. Pat mushrooms dry with paper towel, chop finely and set aside.

2. In a skillet, heat oil over medium heat. Add onions and celery and cook, stirring, until softened, about 5 minutes. Add garlic, ginger, peppercorns, salt and reserved dried mushrooms and cook, stirring, for 1 minute. Add shiitake mushrooms and toss until coated. Add mirin and bring to a boil. Boil for 1 minute. Stir in soy sauce and stock.

3. Arrange chicken evenly over bottom of stoneware and pour mushroom mixture over. Cover and cook on Low for 6 hours or on High for 3 hours, until chicken is falling off the bone. Stir in miso. Add cabbage, in batches, stirring until each batch is submerged. Cover and cook on High for 15 minutes, until cabbage is wilted and flavors meld.

Can Be Halved
see Tips, below

Simple Soy-Braised Chicken

I've been making variations of this Chinese classic for many years. It's very easy to make and can be tweaked to suit your taste — I particularly like the addition of cayenne or a fresh chile pepper to add a hit of spice. I serve this with stir-fried bok choy and lots of pleasantly glutinous short-grain brown rice.

Tips

If you are halving this recipe, be sure to use a small (1½ to 3 quart) slow cooker.

I recommend making this in a smaller slow cooker because the chicken cooks in a minimum amount of liquid and, depending upon the dimensions, may not be fully submerged in a larger version. If you do make it in a larger cooker, I suggest turning the chicken halfway through the cooking time.

Serves 4

- Medium (approx. 3½ quart) slow cooker (see Tips, left)

1 cup	chicken stock	250 mL
½ cup	soy sauce	125 mL
¼ cup	Shaoxing wine, vodka or dry sherry	50 mL
4	cloves garlic, minced	4
2 tbsp	rice vinegar	25 mL
1 tbsp	packed brown sugar	15 mL
1 tbsp	minced gingerroot	15 mL
1 tsp	grated orange zest	5 mL
½ tsp	cracked black peppercorns	2 mL
1	star anise	1
2 lbs	skinless bone-in chicken thighs (8 thighs)	1 kg
1 tbsp	cornstarch, dissolved in 2 tbsp (25 mL) water	15 mL
¼ tsp	cayenne pepper or one long red chile, seeded and diced, optional	1 mL

1. In a bowl, combine stock, soy sauce, Shaoxing wine, garlic, vinegar, brown sugar, ginger, orange zest, peppercorns and star anise. Stir well.

2. Arrange chicken evenly over bottom of slow cooker stoneware. Cover with sauce. Cover and cook on Low for 6 hours or on High for 3 hours, until chicken is no longer pink.

3. With a slotted spoon, transfer chicken to a serving dish and cover with foil to keep warm. Strain liquid into a saucepan. Whisk in cornstarch mixture and cayenne, if using, and bring to a boil. Reduce heat and simmer, stirring, until thickened, about 3 minutes. Pour over chicken.

Spicy Chicken in Coconut Sauce

The flavor combinations in this dish stray ever so slightly from the beaten track. I love the combination of tomatoes and coconut milk and the hint of Indian curry powder rather than Thai curry paste, which would be a more traditional pairing with the coconut milk. Serve this over steaming rice, preferably whole-grain brown or Thai red rice, for a meal that is destined to become a family favorite.

Entertaining Worthy

Can Be Halved
see Tips, below

Tips

If you are halving this recipe, be sure to use a small (2 to 3 quart) slow cooker.

If you don't have a fresh chile pepper, add ¼ tsp (1 mL) cayenne pepper along with the curry powder.

Serves 6

- Medium to large (3½ to 5 quart) slow cooker

3 lbs	skinless bone-in chicken thighs (12 thighs)	1.5 kg
	Zest and juice of 1 lemon	
1 tbsp	olive oil	15 mL
2	onions, finely chopped	2
4	cloves garlic, minced	4
1 tbsp	minced gingerroot	15 mL
1 tsp	salt	5 mL
1 tsp	cracked black peppercorns	5 mL
1	piece (2 inches/5 cm) cinnamon stick	1
1	can (28 oz/796 mL) diced tomatoes with juice	1
1 cup	coconut milk, divided	250 mL
1 tsp	mild curry powder	5 mL
1	long red chile pepper, seeded and minced (see Tips, right)	1
¼ cup	chopped cilantro	50 mL

1. In a bowl, combine chicken and lemon zest and juice. Cover and set aside for 15 minutes. Drain, reserving liquid, and transfer chicken to slow cooker stoneware.

2. Meanwhile, in a skillet, heat oil over medium heat. Add onions and cook, stirring, until softened, about 3 minutes. Add garlic and ginger and cook, stirring, for 1 minute. Add salt, peppercorns and cinnamon stick and cook, stirring, for 1 minute. Add reserved marinade and bring to a boil. Stir in tomatoes with juice.

3. Transfer to slow cooker stoneware. Cover and cook on Low for 5 hours or on High for 2½ hours, until juices run clear when chicken is pierced with a fork.

4. In a bowl, combine ¼ cup (50 mL) of the coconut milk and curry powder and mix until well blended. Add to slow cooker stoneware along with remaining coconut milk and chile pepper. Cover and cook on High for 15 minutes, until flavors meld and dish is heated through. Garnish with cilantro and serve.

Entertaining Worthy

Can Be Halved
see Tips, below

Island-Style Chicken Curry

In this curry I've tried to capture some of my favorite Caribbean flavors. The allspice and Scotch bonnet pepper provide a definitely Jamaican spin, echoing jerk seasoning, which I love. Serve this in soup plates, ladled over rice, and finish the meal with a tossed salad.

Tips

If you are halving this recipe, be sure to use a small (1½ to 3 quart) slow cooker.

Scotch bonnet and habanero peppers, which figure prominently in Caribbean cuisine, are among the world's hottest chiles, so be cautious when using them. A whole one would make this dish very spicy. I like their unique flavors, but other chiles, such as jalapeños or long red or green chiles, would also work well in this dish.

Serves 4

- Medium to large (3½ to 5 quart) slow cooker

4	cloves garlic, grated or put through a press	4
4	green onions, white part only, minced	4
1 tbsp	minced gingerroot	15 mL
1 tsp	dried thyme leaves	5 mL
1 tsp	ground allspice	5 mL
½ tsp	ground cloves	2 mL
	Finely grated zest and juice of 1 lime	
2 tbsp	soy sauce	25 mL
2 lbs	skinless bone-in chicken thighs (about 8 thighs)	1 kg
1 tbsp	olive oil	15 mL
2	onions, thinly sliced on the vertical	2
2	stalks celery, diced	2
1 tsp	cracked black peppercorns	5 mL
1 tsp	ground turmeric	5 mL
½ tsp	salt	2 mL
2 cups	chicken stock	500 mL
½ to 1	Scotch bonnet or habanero pepper, seeded and diced (see Tips, left)	½ to 1
1 cup	coconut milk	250 mL
	Finely chopped cilantro	

1. In a small bowl, combine garlic, green onions, ginger, thyme, allspice, cloves, lime zest and juice and soy sauce. Using a fork, poke holes in the chicken and rub marinade all over to thoroughly coat. Cover and refrigerate for 6 hours or overnight.

2. Arrange chicken evenly over bottom of slow cooker stoneware, reserving excess marinade.

3. In a skillet, heat oil over medium heat. Add onions and celery and cook, stirring, until softened, about 5 minutes. Add peppercorns, turmeric and salt and cook, stirring, for 1 minute. Add reserved marinade and boil for 1 minute. Add stock and bring to a boil. Transfer to slow cooker stoneware. Cover and cook on Low for 5 hours or on High for 2½ hours, until juices run clear when chicken is pierced with a fork. Stir in chile pepper to taste and coconut milk. Cover and cook on High for 20 minutes, until flavors meld. Garnish with cilantro and serve.

Entertaining Worthy

Can Be Halved
see Tips, below

Fruit-Spiked Chicken Curry

If your taste in curry runs to mild and soothing, this is for you. The addition of apple, banana and currants lends appealingly exotic notes to the broth, and the coconut milk provides a pleasantly creamy finish. Just add plenty of hot rice to soak up the broth.

Tips

If you are halving this recipe, be sure to use a small (1½ to 3 quart) slow cooker.

If you don't have a fresh chile pepper, substitute ¼ tsp (1 mL) cayenne pepper.

Make Ahead

Complete Step 1. Cover and refrigerate mixture for up to 2 days. When you're ready to cook, complete the recipe.

Serves 6

- Medium to large (3½ to 5 quart) slow cooker

1 tbsp	vegetable or coconut oil	15 mL
2	onions, finely chopped	2
2	stalks celery, diced	2
2	carrots, peeled and diced	2
4	cloves garlic, minced	4
1 tsp	salt	5 mL
1 tsp	cracked black peppercorns	5 mL
1 tsp	ground cumin	5 mL
4	whole black cardamom pods, crushed	4
1 tsp	curry powder	5 mL
1	firm apple, peeled and diced	1
1½ cups	chicken stock	375 mL
1½ lbs	skinless boneless chicken thighs, cut into 1-inch (2.5 cm) cubes	750 g
1 cup	coconut milk	250 mL
1	banana, peeled and chopped	1
¼ cup	currants	50 mL
1	long red or green chile pepper, minced (see Tips, left)	1

1. In a skillet, heat oil over medium heat. Add onions, celery and carrots and cook, stirring, until softened, about 7 minutes. Add garlic, salt, peppercorns, cumin, cardamom and curry powder and cook, stirring, for 1 minute. Add apple and toss until coated. Stir in stock.

2. Transfer to slow cooker stoneware. Stir in chicken. Cover and cook on Low for 5 hours or on High for 2½ hours. Add coconut milk, banana, currants and chile pepper. Cover and cook on High for 15 minutes to meld flavors. Remove and discard cardamom pods before serving.

Simple Chicken Curry

If you have a well-stocked spice cupboard, this luscious curry can be put together with ingredients you're likely to have on hand. Serve it with a steaming bowl of rice, a green vegetable and some warm naan to soak up the sauce.

Entertaining Worthy

Can Be Halved
see Tips, below

Serves 4

• Medium to large (3½ to 5 quart) slow cooker

2 lbs	skinless bone-in chicken thighs (8 thighs)	1 kg
1 tbsp	oil or ghee	15 mL
2	onions, finely chopped	2
4	cloves garlic, minced	4
1 tbsp	minced gingerroot	15 mL
2 tsp	garam masala (see Tips, right)	10 mL
2 tsp	cumin seeds, toasted and ground (see Tips, right)	10 mL
1 tsp	fennel seeds, toasted and ground	5 mL
1 tsp	cracked black peppercorns	5 mL
1 tsp	ground turmeric	5 mL
½ tsp	salt	2 mL
1	can (14 oz/398 mL) diced tomatoes with juice	1
1 cup	chicken stock	250 mL
¼ tsp	cayenne pepper (see Tips, right)	1 mL
1 cup	full-fat yogurt	250 mL

1. Arrange chicken evenly over bottom of slow cooker stoneware.

2. In a skillet, heat oil over medium-high heat. Add onions and cook, stirring, until they begin to turn golden, about 5 minutes. Add garlic, ginger, garam masala, cumin, fennel, peppercorns, turmeric and salt and cook, stirring, for 1 minute. Add tomatoes with juice and stock and bring to a boil.

3. Transfer to slow cooker stoneware. Cover and cook on Low for 6 hours or on High for 3 hours, until juices run clear when chicken is pierced with a fork. In a bowl, combine cayenne and yogurt. Stir well. Add to chicken, stir well and cook on Low for 10 minutes to meld flavors.

Tips

If you are halving this recipe, be sure to use a small (1½ to 3 quart) slow cooker.

Garam masala is a spice blend used in Indian cooking that is available in Asian markets or, increasingly, well-stocked supermarkets. It is usually used in the final stages of a dish, but in this recipe I have used it to add hints of coriander, cloves, cinnamon and cardamom to the aromatics.

For the best results, toast and grind the cumin and fennel seeds yourself. Place seeds in a dry skillet over medium heat and cook, stirring, until fragrant, about 3 minutes. Using a mortar and pestle or a spice grinder, pound or grind as finely as you can.

This quantity of cayenne produces a nicely spicy result. If you're a heat seeker, increase the amount, but be cautious, as cayenne is very hot.

Make Ahead

Complete Step 2. Cover and refrigerate mixture for up to 2 days. When you're ready to cook, complete the recipe.

Entertaining Worthy

Can Be Halved
see Tip, below

Tip

If you are halving this recipe, be sure to use a small (1½ to 3 quart) slow cooker.

Make Ahead

Complete Steps 1 and 2. Cover and refrigerate mixture for up to 2 days. When you're ready to cook, complete the recipe.

Peppery Chicken in Coconut-Mushroom Gravy

The flavors in this chicken are vaguely Thai but the shiitake mushrooms add a Chinese twist. There is a good hit of zesty ginger in the sauce and the coconut milk adds a creamy finish. Serve this over hot rice for a simple but satisfying meal.

Serves 4

- Medium to large (3½ to 5 quart) slow cooker

1	package (½ oz/14 g) dried sliced shiitake mushrooms	1
1 cup	hot water	250 L
1 tbsp	vegetable oil	15 mL
1	onion, diced	1
2	carrots, peeled and diced	2
4	cloves garlic, minced	4
2 tbsp	minced gingerroot	25 mL
½ tsp	salt	2 mL
½ tsp	cracked black peppercorns	2 mL
1 cup	chicken stock	250 mL
2 lbs	skinless bone-in chicken thighs (about 8 thighs)	1 kg
2 tbsp	freshly squeezed lime juice	25 mL
¼ tsp	cayenne pepper	1 mL
1 cup	coconut milk	250 mL
1	red bell pepper, seeded and diced	1
½ cup	chopped fresh cilantro leaves	125 mL

1. In a bowl, combine dried mushrooms and hot water. Let stand for 30 minutes. Drain through a fine sieve, reserving soaking liquid. Pat mushrooms dry with paper towel and set aside.

2. In a skillet, heat oil over medium heat. Add onion and carrots and cook, stirring, until carrots are softened, about 7 minutes. Add garlic, ginger, salt, peppercorns and reserved dried mushrooms and cook, stirring, for 1 minute. Add stock and reserved mushroom soaking liquid and bring to a boil.

3. Arrange chicken evenly over bottom of slow cooker stoneware and add vegetable mixture. Cover and cook on Low for 5 hours or on High for 2½ hours, until juices run clear when chicken is pierced with a fork.

4. In a bowl, combine lime juice and cayenne. Stir until cayenne dissolves. Add to slow cooker stoneware along with coconut milk and bell pepper. Stir well. Cover and cook on High for 20 minutes, until pepper is tender and mixture is hot. Garnish with cilantro.

Easy "Paella"

Although this lazy person's adaptation of the classic Spanish dish lacks the complexity of a full-fledged version, it is very easy to make and captures enough of the traditional flavors to satisfy all but sticklers for authenticity. The chorizo provides Spanish resonance, but in a pinch Italian sausage will do.

Can Be Halved
see Tips, below

Serves 4

- Large (approx. 5 quart) slow cooker

2 lbs	skinless bone-in chicken thighs (about 8 thighs)	1 kg
1 tbsp	olive oil	15 mL
4 oz	fresh chorizo or Italian sausage, removed from casings	125 g
1	onion, finely chopped	1
2	stalks celery, diced	2
4	cloves garlic, minced	4
1 tsp	dried oregano leaves	5 mL
1 tsp	salt	5 mL
½ tsp	cracked black peppercorns	2 mL
¼ tsp	saffron threads, crumbled	1 mL
1 cup	long-grain brown rice	250 mL
½ cup	dry white wine (see Tips, right)	125 mL
1	can (14 oz/398 mL) diced tomatoes with juice	1
1½ cups	chicken stock	375 mL
2 tsp	sweet paprika (see Tips, right)	10 mL
1 cup	frozen peas	250 mL
1	red bell pepper, seeded and diced	1
	Finely chopped parsley	
	Hot pepper sauce, optional	

1. Arrange chicken evenly over bottom of slow cooker stoneware.

2. In a skillet, heat oil over medium heat. Add chorizo, onion and celery and cook, stirring, breaking sausage up with a spoon, until vegetables are soft and meat is cooked through, about 6 minutes. Add garlic, oregano, salt, peppercorns and saffron and cook, stirring, for 1 minute. Add rice and toss until evenly coated with mixture. Add wine, bring to a boil and boil for 2 minutes. Add tomatoes with juice and stock and bring to a boil.

3. Transfer to slow cooker stoneware. Place a clean tea towel, folded in half (so you will have 2 layers), over top of stoneware to absorb moisture. Cover and cook on Low for 5 hours or on High for 2½ hours. Sprinkle paprika evenly over top of rice, then stir in peas and bell pepper. Cover and cook on High for 20 minutes, until peas are tender. Garnish liberally with parsley. Pass hot pepper sauce at the table, if using.

Tips

If you are halving this recipe, be sure to use a small (2 to 3 quart) slow cooker.

If you prefer, substitute ½ cup (125 mL) chicken stock mixed with 1 tsp (5 mL) lemon juice for the wine. Add along with the remaining chicken stock.

If you like a bit of heat, substitute 1 tsp (5 mL) of the sweet paprika with an equal quantity of hot paprika, or add a bit of cayenne pepper to taste.

Chili with Black Beans and Grilled Chicken

The addition of grilled chicken adds a flavorful and festive note to this simple chili. I like to use leftover chicken alla diavola, which we often make on the barbecue. It adds pleasant hints of citrus and hot pepper to the mix, but if you're opting for convenience, use a store-bought rotisserie chicken instead. You won't be disappointed.

Tips

For the best results, toast and grind the cumin yourself. Place seeds in a dry skillet over medium heat and cook, stirring, until fragrant, about 3 minutes. Using a mortar and pestle or a spice grinder, pound or grind as finely as you can.

Use a single ground mild chile powder, such as ancho or Anaheim, or a combination thereof.

To make Avocado Topping: Chop 1 whole avocado into ¹/₂-inch (1 cm) cubes and toss with 1 tbsp (15 mL) lime juice, 2 tbsp (25 mL) finely chopped red onion and 2 tbsp (25 mL) finely chopped cilantro. Add salt and pepper to taste.

Make Ahead

Complete Step 1. Cover and refrigerate mixture for up to 2 days. When you're ready to cook, complete the recipe.

Serves 6

• Medium to large (3¹/₂ to 5 quart) slow cooker

1 tbsp	oil	15 mL
2	onions, finely chopped	2
4	stalks celery, diced	4
4	cloves garlic	4
1 tbsp	ground cumin (see Tips, left)	15 mL
2 tsp	dried oregano leaves	10 mL
1 tsp	salt	5 mL
1 tsp	cracked black peppercorns	5 mL
2 tbsp	tomato paste	25 mL
1	can (14 oz/ 398 mL) crushed tomatoes	1
2 cups	chicken stock	500 mL
2 cups	cooked black beans	500 mL
2 tsp	pure chile powder (see Tips, left)	10 mL
¹/₂ tsp	cayenne pepper, optional	2 mL
2 cups	cubed (1 inch/2.5 cm) grilled chicken	500 mL
1	green bell or poblano pepper, seeded and diced	1
1	can (4¹/₂ oz/127 mL) chopped mild green chiles	1
	Avocado Topping (see Tips, left) or shredded Cheddar or Jack cheese or sour cream	
	Finely chopped red or green onion	

1. In a skillet, heat oil over medium heat. Add onions and celery and cook, stirring, until softened, about 5 minutes. Add garlic, cumin, oregano, salt and peppercorns and cook, stirring, for 1 minute. Add tomato paste and tomatoes and bring to a boil.

2. Transfer to slow cooker stoneware. Add stock and beans and stir well. Cover and cook on Low for 6 hours or on High for 3 hours. Stir in chile powder and cayenne, if using. Add chicken, bell pepper and green chiles and stir well. Cover and cook on High for 20 minutes, until bell pepper is tender and chicken is heated through. Serve with topping(s) of your choice.

Can Be
Halved
see Tips, below

African-Style Jambalaya

*This is one of those simple, down-home dishes that has wide appeal.
It's a variation on the theme of Jollof, a one-pot rice dish that is
popular throughout West Africa. I call it jambalaya because, like that
Creole dish, it's a kind of catch-all for whatever the cook has on hand.
The basic ingredients are rice and tomatoes, plus seasonings. Meat,
chicken, fish or seafood can be added to suit the occasion.*

Tips

If you are halving this
recipe, be sure to use a
small (2 to 3 quart) slow
cooker.

For this quantity, soak,
cook and drain 1 cup
(250 mL) dried black-eyed
peas or use 1 can (14 to
19 oz/398 to 540 mL),
drained and rinsed.

To please all palates,
I recommend going easy
on the fresh chiles and
passing hot pepper sauce
a the table. Piri-piri sauce,
a Portuguese condiment
made from the African
pepper of the same name,
is particularly good with
this dish.

Serves 6 to 8

- Medium to large (3½ to 5 quart) slow cooker

2 cups	drained cooked black-eyed peas (see Tips, left)	500 mL
2 tbsp	olive or vegetable oil	25 mL
2	onions, finely chopped	2
4	carrots, peeled and diced	4
6	cloves garlic, minced	6
2 tbsp	minced gingerroot	25 mL
1 tsp	salt	5 mL
1 tsp	cracked black peppercorns	5 mL
1 cup	long-grain brown rice	250 mL
2 cups	chicken stock or water	500 mL
1	can (14 oz/ 398 mL) crushed tomatoes	1
1½ lbs	skinless boneless chicken thighs, cut into ½-inch (1 cm) cubes	750 g
2 cups	sweet green peas, thawed if frozen	500 mL
1 to 2	long red or green chiles, minced (see Tips, left)	1 to 2
2 tsp	curry powder, dissolved in 2 tbsp (25 mL) fresh lemon juice	10 mL

1. In a skillet, heat oil over medium heat. Add onions and carrots and
cook, stirring, until vegetables are softened, about 7 minutes. Add
garlic, ginger, salt and peppercorns and cook, stirring, for 1 minute.
Add rice and toss until well coated with mixture. Add stock and
bring to a boil. Boil for 2 minutes. Stir in tomatoes.

2. Transfer to slow cooker stoneware. Stir in chicken and black-eyed
peas. Place a clean tea towel, folded in half (so you will have 2 layers),
over top of stoneware to absorb moisture. Cover and cook on Low
for 6 hours or on High for 3 hours, until rice is tender. Stir well. Stir
in green peas, chile(s) and curry powder solution. Cover and cook on
High for 15 minutes, until peas are tender and flavors meld.

Horseradish-Spiked Chicken 'n' Noodles

This is a remarkably comforting dish. I love the mild taste of the leek-based sauce, and the chunky bits of chicken are the perfect complement to soft buttered noodles. There's not much you need to add except perhaps a simple green salad, if you're so inclined.

Can Be Halved
see Tips, below

Serves 4 to 6

• Medium to large (3½ to 5 quart) slow cooker

1 tbsp	olive oil	15 mL
2	leeks, cleaned and thinly sliced	2
2	carrots, peeled and diced	2
2	stalks celery, diced	2
2	cloves garlic, minced	2
1 tsp	salt	5 mL
½ tsp	cracked black peppercorns	2 mL
1	bay leaf	1
1 cup	chicken stock	250 mL
2 lbs	skinless boneless chicken thighs, cut into bite-size pieces	1 kg
¼ cup	whipping (35%) cream (see Tips, right)	50 mL
2 tbsp	Dijon mustard	25 mL
1 to 2 tbsp	prepared horseradish (see Tips, right)	15 to 25 mL
8 oz	egg noodles	250 g
1 tbsp	butter	15 mL
	Finely chopped parsley	

1. In a skillet, heat oil over medium heat. Add leeks, carrots and celery and cook, stirring, until softened, about 7 minutes. Add garlic, salt, peppercorns and bay leaf and cook, stirring, for 1 minute. Stir in stock and bring to a boil.

2. Arrange chicken evenly over bottom of slow cooker stoneware. Add sauce and stir well. Cover and cook on Low for 6 hours or on High for 3 hours. Stir in whipping cream, mustard and horseradish. Season to taste with additional salt and freshly ground black pepper, if desired. Remove and discard bay leaf.

3. Meanwhile, cook noodles according to package directions. Drain and toss with butter. To serve, arrange noodles over the bottom of a deep platter or pasta dish. Top with sauce and garnish with parsley.

Tips

If you are halving this recipe, be sure to use a small (1½ to 3 quart) slow cooker.

If you're avoiding cream or dairy in general, you can toss the noodles with extra virgin olive oil in place of the butter and finish the sauce with cornstarch instead of cream. Just dissolve 1 tbsp (15 mL) cornstarch in 2 tbsp (25 mL) water. Stir the mustard and horseradish into the chicken mixture, then add the cornstarch and cook, stirring, until the sauce thickens slightly, about 1 minute.

Vary the quantity of horseradish to suit your taste.

Can Be Halved
see Tips, below

Smoked Turkey Chili

If you're craving the stick-to-the-ribs satisfaction of a zesty chili but feeling the need for something a little different, try this. The black-eyed peas are lighter than traditional red or pinto beans and the smoked turkey adds intriguing depth. If you prefer a creamier finish, increase the quantity of cheese or be sure to add a dollop of sour cream.

Tips

If you are halving this recipe, be sure to use a small (2 to 3 quart) slow cooker.

For this quantity, soak, cook and drain 2 cups (500 mL) dried black-eyed peas or use 2 cans (14 to 19 oz/398 to 540 mL), drained and rinsed.

Use any combination of poblano peppers and red or green bell peppers. If using only sweet peppers, you may want to add an extra jalapeño pepper.

Make Ahead

Complete Step 1. Cover and refrigerate mixture for up to 2 days. When you're ready to cook, complete the recipe.

Serves 8 to 10

- Large (approx. 5 quart) slow cooker

2 tbsp	vegetable or olive oil	25 mL
2	onions, finely chopped	2
4	stalks celery, diced	4
4	cloves garlic, minced	4
2 tsp	ground cumin	10 mL
2 tsp	ground oregano	10 mL
1 tsp	ground allspice	5 mL
1 tsp	cracked black peppercorns	5 mL
1/2 tsp	grated lime zest	2 mL
1	piece (2 inches/5 cm) cinnamon stick	1
1	can (28 oz/796 mL) tomatoes with juice, coarsely chopped	1
1 cup	chicken or turkey stock	250 mL
4 cups	drained cooked black-eyed peas (see Tips, left)	1 L
3	dried ancho, New Mexico or guajillo chiles	3
2 cups	boiling water	500 mL
1 to 2	jalapeño peppers, seeded and diced (see Tips, left)	1 to 2
1/2 cup	coarsely chopped cilantro (leaves and stems)	125 mL
2 tbsp	freshly squeezed lime juice	25 mL
1 tbsp	Mexican chili powder	15 mL
2 lbs	smoked turkey, shredded or cut into cubes	1 kg
2	poblano or green or red bell peppers, seeded and diced	2
1 cup	shredded Monterey Jack or Cheddar cheese	250 mL
	Finely chopped red or green onion, optional	
	Sour cream, optional	

1. In a skillet, heat oil over medium heat. Add onions and celery and cook, stirring, until softened, about 5 minutes. Add garlic, cumin, oregano, allspice, peppercorns, lime zest and cinnamon stick and cook, stirring, for 1 minute. Add tomatoes with juice and stock and bring to a boil.

2. Transfer to slow cooker stoneware. Stir in black-eyed peas. Cover and cook on Low for 6 to 8 hours or on High for 3 to 4 hours, until hot and bubbly.

3. About an hour before recipe has finished cooking, in a heatproof bowl, soak dried chile peppers in boiling water for 30 minutes, weighing down with a cup to ensure they are submerged. Drain, discard stems and chop coarsely. In a blender, combine rehydrated chiles, jalapeño, cilantro, lime juice, chili powder and 1/2 cup (125 mL) liquid from the chili. Purée. Add to stoneware along with smoked turkey and poblano peppers. Cover and cook on High for 20 minutes, until peppers are tender. Stir in cheese and cook on High until melted. Garnish with red onion and/or sour cream, if desired.

Variation

Smoked Chicken Chili: Substitute an equal quantity of smoked chicken for the turkey.

Traditional Cobbler

This is one of those dishes I remember from my childhood — tender chunks of turkey languishing in a creamy sauce punctuated with succulent vegetables, with a pleasant topping to soak it all up. As a contemporary nod I've included tarragon and a splash of white wine, but the spirit of old-fashioned goodness still defines this dish.

Tips

If you are halving this recipe, be sure to use a small (2½ to 3 quart) slow cooker.

If you prefer, substitute an extra ½ cup (125 mL) chicken stock, plus 2 tsp (10 mL) lemon juice, for the white wine.

If using chicken breasts, reduce cooking time to 3 hours on Low or 1½ hours on High. You could also use skinless boneless chicken thighs, which cook for as long as the turkey.

Make sure your slow cooker is turned to High before adding the topping. Otherwise it is likely to be soggy.

Make Ahead

Complete Step 1. Cover and refrigerate mixture for up to 2 days. When you're ready to cook, complete the recipe.

Serves 6

- Large (approx. 5 quart) slow cooker

1 tbsp	olive oil	15 mL
2	leeks, cleaned and finely chopped	2
2	carrots, peeled and diced	2
2	stalks celery, diced	2
2	cloves garlic, minced	2
1 tbsp	dried tarragon leaves	15 mL
1 tsp	each salt and cracked black peppercorns	5 mL
¼ cup	all-purpose flour	50 mL
½ cup	dry white wine (see Tips, left)	125 mL
2 cups	chicken stock	500 mL
8 oz	mushrooms, trimmed and quartered	250 g
4 cups	cubed (½ inch/1 cm) skinless boneless turkey or chicken breast (about 2 lbs/1kg) (see Tips, left)	1 L
2 cups	sweet green peas	500 mL
½ cup	whipping (35%) cream	125 mL

Topping (see Tips, left)

¾ cup	whole wheat flour	175 mL
¾ cup	all-purpose flour	175 mL
½ tsp	salt	2 mL
2 tsp	baking soda	10 mL
¾ cup	buttermilk	175 mL
2 tbsp	olive oil	25 mL

1. In a skillet, heat oil over medium heat. Add leeks, carrots and celery and cook, stirring, until softened, about 5 minutes. Add garlic, tarragon, salt and peppercorns and cook, stirring, for 1 minute. Add flour and cook, stirring, for 1 minute. Add wine and stock and cook, stirring, until mixture comes to a boil and thickens, about 5 minutes.

2. Place mushrooms and turkey in stoneware and add leek mixture. Stir well. Cover and cook on Low for 3½ hours or on High for 1¾ hours. Stir in peas and whipping cream.

3. **Topping:** In a bowl, combine whole wheat and all-purpose flours and salt. Make a well in the middle. In a cup or bowl with a pouring spout, combine baking soda, buttermilk and olive oil. Pour into well and mix until blended. Drop batter by spoonfuls over hot turkey mixture. Cover and cook on High about 45 minutes, until a tester inserted in the center comes out clean.

Tomato-Braised Turkey Breast

If you're tired of the same old thing, try this simple-to-make braised turkey. Serve it with an abundance of fluffy mashed potatoes or, for a change, a mixture of brown and wild rice, both of which work beautifully with the sumptuous sauce. Add some steamed green beans for a perfect special meal.

Tips

If you are halving this recipe, be sure to use a small (2 to 3 quart) slow cooker.

If you prefer, substitute an extra cup (250 mL) of chicken or turkey stock plus 1 tbsp (15 mL) lemon juice for the white wine.

Make Ahead

Complete Step 2. Cover and refrigerate mixture for up to 2 days. When you're ready to cook, complete the recipe.

Serves 4 to 6

- Medium to large (3½ to 5 quart) slow cooker
- Instant-read thermometer

2 tbsp	olive oil	25 mL
1	skin-on turkey breast, 2 to 3 lbs (1 to 1.5 kg)	1
2	onions, thinly sliced on the vertical	2
2	anchovy fillets, minced	2
4	cloves garlic, minced	4
1 tsp	dried oregano leaves	5 mL
1 tsp	cracked black peppercorns	5 mL
½ tsp	salt	2 mL
2 tbsp	all-purpose flour	25 mL
¼ cup	tomato paste	50 mL
1 cup	dry white wine (see Tips, left)	250 mL
2 cups	chicken or turkey stock	500 mL
½ cup	finely chopped parsley	125 mL

1. In a skillet, heat oil over medium-high heat. Add turkey, skin side down, and cook until nicely browned, about 3 minutes. Transfer to slow cooker stoneware, skin side up.

2. Add onions and anchovies to skillet and cook, stirring, until anchovies dissolve and onions begin to turn golden, about 7 minutes. Add garlic, oregano, peppercorns and salt and cook, stirring, for 1 minute. Add flour and cook, stirring, for 1 minute. Stir in tomato paste and wine and cook, stirring and scraping up the brown bits from bottom of the pan, for 2 minutes. Stir in stock and bring to a boil.

3. Transfer to slow cooker stoneware. Cover and cook on Low for 6 hours or on High for 3 hours, until turkey is tender and no longer pink inside or an instant-read thermometer reads 160°F (71°C). To serve, transfer to a deep platter, spoon sauce over turkey and garnish with parsley.

Variation

Tomato-Braised Turkey Legs: Substitute about 3 lbs (1.5 kg) skinless bone-in turkey thighs or legs for the breast. Skip Step 1 and arrange turkey over bottom of slow cooker stoneware. Add oil to skillet and continue with Steps 2 and 3.

Lime-Spiked Turkey Chili with Pinto Beans

Surprisingly light, with a mild hit of hot pepper, this chili is a universal favorite. I like to serve it with buttered whole wheat toast.

Can Be Halved
see Tips, below

Serves 4

- Medium to large (3½ to 5 quart) slow cooker

2 tbsp	olive oil	25 mL
1 lb	ground turkey	500 g
2	onions, finely chopped	2
4	stalks celery, diced	4
4	cloves garlic, minced	4
1 tbsp	ground cumin (see Tips, right)	15 mL
1 tbsp	dried oregano leaves	15 mL
2 tsp	grated lime zest	10 mL
1 tsp	dried thyme leaves	5 mL
1 tsp	ground allspice	5 mL
1 tsp	salt	5 mL
1 tsp	cracked black peppercorns	5 mL
1	piece (2 inches/5 cm) cinnamon stick	1
1	can (5½ oz/156 mL) tomato paste	
2 tsp	brown sugar	10 mL
2 cups	chicken or turkey stock	500 mL
3 cups	cooked pinto beans	750 mL
½ tsp	cayenne pepper, dissolved in 2 tbsp (25 mL) freshly squeezed lime juice	2 mL
1	can (4½ oz/127 mL) minced mild green chiles	1
	Finely chopped cilantro, optional	
	Shredded lettuce, optional	
	Finely chopped red or green onion, optional	
	Shredded Cheddar or Jack cheese, optional	
	Sour cream, optional	

1. In a skillet, heat oil over medium heat. Add turkey, onions and celery and cook until turkey is no longer pink and vegetables are soft, about 7 minutes. Add garlic, cumin, oregano, lime zest, thyme, allspice, salt, peppercorns and cinnamon stick and cook, stirring, for 1 minute. Stir in tomato paste and brown sugar. Add stock and bring to a boil.

2. Transfer to stoneware. Stir in beans. Cover and cook on Low for 6 hours or on High for 3 hours. Stir in cayenne solution and chiles. Cover and cook on High for 10 minutes. Serve garnished with any one or a combination of cilantro, lettuce, onion, cheese or sour cream.

Variation

Lime-Spiked Chicken Chili with Pinto Beans: Substitute an equal quantity of ground chicken for the turkey.

Tips

If you are halving this recipe, be sure to use a small (2 to 3 quart) slow cooker.

For best results, toast and grind the cumin yourself. Place seeds in a dry skillet over medium heat and cook, stirring, until fragrant, about 3 minutes. Using a mortar and pestle or a spice grinder, pound or grind as finely as you can.

Make Ahead

Complete Step 1. Cover and refrigerate mixture for up to 2 days (see Making Ahead, page 17). When you're ready to cook, complete the recipe.

Can Be Halved
see Tips, below

Turkey Meatballs in Tomato Sauce

This should satisfy any yen you might have for an old-fashioned pasta dish. Light and mildly flavored but providing all the satisfaction of its more robust relatives, this is sure to become a family favorite. It's skimpy on sauce, so I recommend serving it over tiny pasta such as orzo, tossed in olive oil or butter. It would even work well with a whole grain such as polenta or a combination of brown and wild rice. Pass Parmesan at the table.

Tips

If you are halving this recipe, be sure to use a small (1½ to 3 quart) slow cooker.

If you prefer, use 1 cup (250 mL) chicken stock or water combined with 2 tsp (10 mL) lemon juice instead of the wine.

I like to use Italian San Marzano tomatoes, which are particularly rich. If you're using domestic tomatoes, add 1 tbsp (15 mL) tomato paste along with the wine.

I like to use parchment when cooking this dish because the recipe doesn't contain much liquid. Creating a tight seal ensures that none evaporates and that the meatballs and sauce are well basted in their own juices.

Make Ahead

Complete Step 3, heating 1 tbsp (15 mL) oil in pan before softening the vegetables. Cover and refrigerate mixture for up to 2 days. When you're ready to cook, complete the recipe.

Serves 6

- Parchment paper
- Large (approx. 5 quart) slow cooker

½ cup	fine bulgur (see Tip, right)	125 mL
½ cup	cold water	125 mL
1 lb	ground turkey	500 g
½ cup	finely chopped red onion	125 mL
2 tsp	dried oregano leaves	10 mL
½ tsp	salt	2 mL
½ tsp	cracked black peppercorns	2 mL
1	egg, beaten	1
2 tbsp	olive oil	25 mL

Tomato Sauce

1	onion, finely chopped	1
2	stalks celery, diced	2
2	carrots, peeled and diced	2
4	cloves garlic, minced	4
2 tsp	dried Italian seasoning	10 mL
1 tsp	salt	5 mL
1 tsp	cracked black peppercorns	5 mL
1 cup	dry white wine or stock (see Tips, left)	250 mL
1	can (28 oz/796 mL) tomatoes with juice, coarsely chopped (see Tips, left)	1

1. In a large bowl, combine bulgur and cold water. Stir well and set aside until liquid is absorbed, about 10 minutes. Add turkey, red onion, oregano, salt, peppercorns and egg. Using your hands, mix until well combined. Form into 12 meatballs, each about 2 inches (5 cm) in diameter.

2. In a skillet, heat oil over medium-high heat. Add meatballs, in batches, and brown well, about 5 minutes per batch. Transfer to slow cooker stoneware. Reduce heat to medium.

3. **Tomato Sauce:** Add onion, celery and carrots to pan and cook, stirring, until carrots are softened, about 7 minutes. Add garlic, Italian seasoning, salt and peppercorns and cook, stirring, for 1 minute. Add wine, bring to a boil and boil for 2 minutes. Stir in tomatoes with juice.

4. Transfer to slow cooker stoneware. Place a large piece of parchment over the mixture, pressing it down to brush the food and extending up the sides of the stoneware so it overlaps the rim. Cover and cook on Low for 6 hours or on High for 3 hours, until mixture is hot and bubbly and juices run clear when meatballs are pierced with a fork.

Variation

Chicken Meatballs in Tomato Sauce: Substitute an equal quantity of ground chicken for the turkey.

Tip

If using coarse bulgur, increase the soaking time to 30 minutes.

Zesty Seafood Chowder

Fish and Seafood

Zesty Seafood Chowder

This robust chowder is a lip-smacking meal-in-a-bowl. I love the hint of smokiness balanced by the heat of the jalapeño.

Can Be Halved
see Tips, below

Tips

If you are halving this recipe, be sure to use a small (2 to 3½ quart) slow cooker.

To clean clams, scrub thoroughly with a wire brush and soak in several changes of cold salted water.

Substitute 2 cans (each 5 oz/142 g) baby clams, drained, for the fresh. Add to slow cooker along with the fish and include 1 cup (250 mL) of water.

Make Ahead

Complete Steps 1 and 2. Cover and refrigerate bacon and vegetable mixture separately for up to 2 days. When you're ready to cook, continue with the recipe.

Serves 6

• Medium to large (3½ to 5 quart) slow cooker

4 oz	smoked bacon, diced	125 g
2	leeks, white part with just a hint of green, thinly sliced	2
2	stalks celery, diced	2
2	cloves garlic, minced	2
1 tsp	Cajun seasoning	5 mL
1 tsp	dried thyme leaves	5 mL
1 tsp	salt	5 mL
½ tsp	cracked black peppercorns	2 mL
2 tbsp	all-purpose flour	25 mL
1 cup	dry white wine (see Tips, page 138)	250 mL
2 cups	fish stock or 1 cup (250 mL) each bottled clam juice and water	500 mL
2	potatoes, peeled and diced	2
3 lbs	small clams, cleaned (see Tips, left)	1.5 kg
1 lb	firm white fish fillets, such as halibut or snapper, cut into 1-inch (2.5 cm) cubes	500 g
1 cup	corn kernels, thawed if frozen	250 mL
1 to 2	jalapeño peppers, seeded and diced	1 to 2
1 cup	whipping (35%) cream	250 mL
	Finely chopped parsley	

1. In a skillet, cook bacon over medium-high heat until crisp. Drain well on paper towel cover and refrigerate until ready to use.

2. Reduce heat to medium. Add leeks and celery to pan and cook, stirring, until softened, about 5 minutes. Add garlic, Cajun seasoning, thyme, salt and peppercorns and cook, stirring, for 1 minute. Add flour and cook, stirring for 1 minute. Add wine, bring to a boil and boil for 2 minutes.

3. Transfer to slow cooker stoneware. Stir in fish stock and potatoes. Cover and cook on Low for 8 hours or on High for 4 hours, until potatoes are tender.

4. Discard any clams that are open. In a large saucepan over medium-high heat, bring 1 cup (250 mL) water to a rapid boil. Add clams, cover and cook, shaking the pot, until all the clams open. Discard any that do not open. Strain cooking liquid through a fine sieve into a bowl. Using a fork, remove clam meat from shells. Add clam cooking liquid and meat to slow cooker, along with fish fillets, reserved bacon, corn, jalapeño and whipping cream. Cover and cook on High for 10 minutes, until fish is cooked through and flavors meld. Ladle soup into bowls and garnish with parsley.

Red Chowder with Fennel

This is a particularly tasty spin on classic Manhattan clam chowder, a little lighter on tomato than the norm and enhanced with the addition of fennel (see Tips, right). It makes a great weeknight dinner served with crusty bread and a simple salad.

Can Be Halved
see Tips, below

Serves 4 as a main course and 6 as a starter

- Medium to large (3½ to 5 quart) slow cooker

4 oz	chunk bacon, diced	125 g
2	onions, diced	2
1	bulb fennel, cored and diced (see Tips, right)	1
2	cloves garlic, minced	2
1 tsp	dried thyme leaves	5 mL
1 tsp	salt	5 mL
½ tsp	cracked black peppercorns	2 mL
2	bay leaves	2
1 cup	dry white wine (see Tips, page 138)	250 mL
1	can (28 oz/796 mL) diced tomatoes with juice	1
2 cups	fish or light vegetable stock	500 mL
1	potato, peeled and shredded	1
3 lbs	small clams, cleaned (see Tips, right)	1.5 kg
½ cup	finely chopped parsley	125 mL

1. In a skillet, cook bacon over medium-high heat until crisp. Drain well on paper towel, cover and refrigerate until ready to use. Drain all but 1 tbsp (15 mL) fat from pan, if necessary.

2. Reduce heat to medium. Add onions and fennel to pan and cook, stirring, until softened, about 5 minutes. Add garlic, thyme, salt, peppercorns and bay leaves and cook, stirring, for 1 minute. Add wine, bring to a boil and boil for 2 minutes. Add tomatoes with juice and return to a boil.

3. Transfer to slow cooker stoneware. Stir in stock and potato. Cover and cook on Low for 8 hours or on High for 4 hours, until potato is tender.

4. Discard any clams that are open. In a large saucepan over medium-high heat, bring 1 cup (250 mL) water to a rapid boil. Add clams, cover and cook, shaking the pot, until all the clams open. Discard any that do not open. Strain cooking liquid through a fine sieve into a bowl. Using a fork, remove clam meat from shells. Add clam cooking liquid and meat to slow cooker, along with reserved bacon. Cover and cook on High for 15 minutes, until heated through. Remove and discard bay leaves. Ladle soup into bowls and garnish with parsley.

Tips

If you are halving this recipe, be sure to use a small (1½ to 3 quart) slow cooker.

The fennel flavor in this chowder is pleasantly light. If you prefer a stronger licorice hit, add ½ tsp (2 mL) crushed fennel seeds along with the peppercorns.

To clean clams, scrub thoroughly with a wire brush and soak in several changes of cold salted water.

Substitute 2 cans (each 5 oz/142 g) baby clams, drained and rinsed, for the fresh clams if desired. Add ½ cup (125 mL) bottled clam juice, mixed with an equal amount of water, along with the tomatoes.

Make Ahead

Complete Steps 1 and 2. Cover and refrigerate bacon and vegetable mixtures separately for up to 2 days. When you're ready to cook, complete the recipe.

South American–Style Shrimp Chowder

Although I've taken more than a few liberties with the concept, this hearty and delicious meal-in-a-bowl was inspired by chupe, *a Peruvian shrimp chowder. I like to serve this with thick chunks of country-style bread and not much else, so I can enjoy as much of the chowder as possible.*

Tips

If you are halving this recipe, be sure to use a small (1½ to 3 quart) slow cooker.

This is fairly substantial chowder, but you could serve small bowls as a prelude to a special meal.

If you are using large shrimp, cut them into thirds after peeling. Smaller shrimp should be halved.

Make Ahead

Complete Steps 1, 2 and 3. Cover and refrigerate shrimp, shrimp stock and vegetable mixtures separately overnight. When you're ready to cook, continue with the recipe.

Serves 6

• Medium to large (3½ to 5 quart) slow cooker

1 lb	peeled deveined shrimp, shells reserved (see Tips, left)	500 g
2 tbsp	freshly squeezed lime juice	25 mL
1 tbsp	Mexican chile powder	15 mL
1 tsp	coarse salt	5 mL
1 tsp	cracked black peppercorns	5 mL
1½ cups	dry white wine	375 mL
1½ cups	water	375 mL
2 tbsp	olive oil, divided	25 mL
2	onions, finely chopped	2
2	stalks celery, diced	2
4	cloves garlic, minced	4
2 tsp	finely grated lime zest	10 mL
½ tsp	salt	2 mL
2 tbsp	tomato paste	25 mL
1	can (14 oz/398 mL) diced tomatoes with juice	1
1	potato, peeled and shredded	1
2	roasted red peppers, diced	2
1	jalapeño pepper, seeded and diced	1
2 cups	corn kernels	500 mL
1 cup	coconut milk	250 mL
	Finely chopped cilantro	

1. In a bowl, combine shrimp, lime juice, chile powder, salt and peppercorns. Stir well. Cover and refrigerate until ready to use.

2. Meanwhile, make shrimp stock. In a saucepan, combine shrimp shells, white wine and water. Bring to a boil, reduce heat and simmer for 15 minutes. Strain, pushing the shells against the sieve to extract as much flavor as possible. Measure 2 cups (500 mL) and set aside. Freeze excess.

3. In a skillet, heat 1 tbsp (15 mL) of the oil over medium heat. Add onions and celery and cook, stirring, until softened, about 5 minutes. Add garlic, lime zest and salt and cook, stirring, for 1 minute. Stir in tomato paste. Add tomatoes with juice and bring to a boil.

4. Transfer to slow cooker stoneware. Add potato and reserved shrimp stock. Cover and cook on Low for 6 hours or on High for 3 hours, until hot and bubbly. Stir in red peppers, jalapeño, corn kernels and coconut milk. Cover and cook on High for 15 minutes, until corn is tender.

5. Meanwhile, in a skillet, heat remaining oil over medium-high heat. Add shrimp, in batches if necessary, and cook, stirring, until they turn pink. Add to stoneware and stir well. Serve chowder garnished with cilantro.

Entertaining
Worthy

Can Be
Halved

see Tips, below

Breton-Style Chowder

There are many versions of this dish, which is known in France as cotriade. Here I've deviated from the norm and added tarragon, which nicely complements the sorrel. This is so tasty I serve it to guests with lots of sliced warm baguette to soak up the exquisite sauce.

Tips

If you are halving this recipe, be sure to use a small (2 to 3½ quart) slow cooker.

Use firm fish such as cod, snapper, halibut or flounder.

Serves 6

• Large (approx. 5 quart) slow cooker

1 tbsp	olive oil	15 mL
2	leeks, white part with just a hint of green, thinly sliced	2
4	cloves garlic, minced	4
1 tsp	salt	5 mL
1 tsp	cracked black peppercorns	5 mL
1 tsp	dried tarragon leaves	5 mL
1	bay leaf	1
2	potatoes, peeled and diced	2
4 cups	fish stock	1 L
4 cups	packed chopped sorrel leaves	1 L
2 lbs	skinless fish fillets, cut into approx. 1-inch (2.5 cm) cubes (see Tips, left)	1 kg
½ cup	whipping (35%) cream or crème fraîche	125 mL
1½ lbs	mussels, cleaned	750 g
½ cup	white wine	125 mL
	Crostini (see Tips, page 150)	

1. In a skillet, heat oil over medium heat. Add leeks and cook, stirring, until softened, about 5 minutes. Add garlic, salt, peppercorns, tarragon and bay leaf and cook, stirring, for 1 minute.

2. Transfer to slow cooker stoneware. Stir in potatoes and fish stock. Cover and cook on Low for 6 hours or on High for 3 hours, until potatoes are tender. Add sorrel and stir well until submerged in liquid. Using an immersion blender, purée. (You can also do this, in batches, in a food processor and return to stoneware.) Stir in fish. Cover and cook on High for 7 minutes, until fish is cooked through. Remove and discard bay leaf. Stir in whipping cream.

3. Meanwhile, in a large saucepan, combine mussels and white wine. Heat over medium-high heat, shaking the pot occasionally, until all the mussels have opened. (Discard any that do not open.) Add to stoneware and adjust seasoning. To serve, place a crostini in each bowl and spoon stew over top.

Deep South Oyster Stew

Make this luscious stew if you're somewhere where oysters are plentiful and inexpensive. Although I don't think oysters from southern climes such as Louisiana have as much pop as those harvested from colder waters, their price makes them appealing for dishes such as this. Add some great bread and crisp cold wine and pass hot pepper sauce at the table.

Entertaining Worthy

Can Be Halved
see Tip, below

Serves 6

- Medium to large (3½ to 5 quart) slow cooker

4 oz	chunk bacon, diced	125 g
2	onions, finely chopped	2
4	stalks celery, diced	4
2	cloves garlic, minced	2
2	bay leaves	2
1 tsp	salt	5 mL
1 tsp	cracked black peppercorns	5 mL
¼ cup	dry sherry	50 mL
4 cups	chicken or vegetable stock	1 L
1	potato, peeled and diced	1
1 tbsp	freshly squeezed lemon juice	15 mL
¼ tsp	cayenne pepper	1 mL
4 cups	finely chopped stemmed spinach	1 L
2 cups	chopped shucked oysters with liquor	500 mL
½ cup	whipping (35%) cream	125 mL
	Hot pepper sauce	

1. In a skillet, cook bacon over medium-high heat until brown and crisp. Using a slotted spoon, transfer to paper towel to drain. Cover and refrigerate until ready to use. Reduce heat to medium.

2. Add onions and celery to pan and cook, stirring, until softened, about 5 minutes. Add garlic, bay leaves, salt and peppercorns and cook, stirring, for 1 minute. Add sherry and bring to a boil. Boil for 1 minute.

3. Transfer to slow cooker stoneware. Stir in stock and potato. Cover and cook on Low for 6 hours or on High for 3 hours. Remove and discard bay leaves.

4. In a small bowl, combine lemon juice and cayenne, stirring until dissolved. Add to stoneware. Add spinach, in batches, stirring until each batch is incorporated. Stir in oysters and whipping cream. Cover and cook on High for 20 minutes, until spinach is cooked and mixture is heated through. Pass hot pepper sauce at the table.

Tip

If you are halving this recipe, be sure to use a small (1½ to 3 quart) slow cooker.

Make Ahead

Complete Steps 1 and 2. Cover and refrigerate bacon and vegetable mixtures separately for up to 2 days. When you're ready to cook, continue with the recipe.

Entertaining Worthy

Can Be Halved
see Tips, below

Spanish-Style Fish Stew

Enlivened by the addition of spicy chorizo sausage and oh-so-good-for-you kale, this dish is easy to make but has the impact of a special occasion dish. It's good on its own, but if you feel the need to kick it up a notch, add the aïoli-brushed crostini.

Serves 6

- Medium to large (3½ to 5 quart) slow cooker

1 tbsp	olive oil	15 mL
1 lb	soft chorizo sausage, removed from casings (see Tips, left)	500 g
2	onions, thinly sliced on the vertical	2
2	stalks celery, diced	2
4	cloves garlic, minced	4
1 tsp	salt	5 mL
1 tsp	cracked black peppercorns	5 mL
2	bay leaves	2
1 cup	dry white wine (see Tips, left)	250 mL
4 cups	fish stock or 2 cups (500 mL) each bottled clam juice and water	1 L
2	potatoes, peeled and shredded	2
1 tsp	smoked paprika	5 mL
4 cups	coarsely chopped kale	1 L
1½ lbs	firm white fish fillets, such as halibut, turbot or haddock, cut into bite-size pieces	750 g
	Aïoli-brushed crostini, optional (see Tips, left)	

1. In a skillet, heat oil over medium heat. Add chorizo, onions and celery and cook, stirring, until meat is cooked, about 7 minutes. Add garlic, salt, peppercorns and bay leaves and cook, stirring, for 1 minute. Add wine, bring to a boil and boil for 2 minutes. Transfer to slow cooker stoneware.

2. Add fish stock and potatoes. Cover and cook on Low for 6 hours or on High for 3 hours, until potatoes are tender. Stir in paprika and kale. Cover and cook on High for 15 minutes. Stir in fish. Cover and cook on High about 7 minutes, until cooked through. Remove and discard bay leaves. Ladle stew into bowls and top with crostini, if using.

Tips

If you are halving this recipe, be sure to use a small (1½ to 3 quart) slow cooker.

Chorizo comes in various degrees of spiciness. I prefer the hot version in this recipe, but use the one that suits your taste.

If you prefer, substitute an extra cup (250 mL) of water plus 1 tbsp (15 mL) lemon juice for the white wine.

To make crostini: Preheat broiler. Brush baguette slices with olive oil on both sides, place on a baking sheet and toast under broiler until lightly browned, turning once. Watch closely. You can use prepared aïoli or make a quick version of your own by combining ¼ cup (50 mL) mayonnaise with 2 tsp (10 mL) finely minced garlic. Brush over crostini just before serving.

Make Ahead

Complete Step 1. Cover mixture, ensuring it cools promptly (see Making Ahead, page 17), and refrigerate for up to 2 days. When you're ready to cook, complete the recipe.

Peppery Fish Stew with Anchovy Crostini

This is a simple fish stew with an in-your-face finish built around olives, a jalapeño pepper and anchovies. It has great flavor and is different enough to charm jaded taste buds.

Serves 6

Entertaining Worthy

Can Be Halved
see Tips, below

- Medium to large (3½ to 5 quart) slow cooker

1 tbsp	olive oil	15 mL
2	onions, finely chopped	2
1	bulb fennel, cored and diced	1
4	cloves garlic, minced	4
2 tsp	dried Italian seasoning	10 mL
1 tsp	salt	5 mL
1 tsp	cracked black peppercorns	5 mL
1 cup	dry white wine (see Tips, right)	250 mL
1	can (28 oz/796 mL) diced tomatoes with juice	1
2 cups	fish stock or 1 cup (250 mL) each bottled clam juice and water	500 mL
1½ lbs	firm white fish fillets, such as halibut, turbot or haddock, cut into bite-size pieces	750 g
½ cup	black olives, pitted and chopped	125 mL
1	jalapeño pepper, seeded and diced	1

Crostini

3 tbsp	extra virgin olive oil, divided	45 mL
2	anchovy fillets, finely minced	2
2 tsp	finely chopped parsley	10 mL
6	slices baguette	6

1. In a skillet, heat oil over medium heat. Add onions and fennel and cook, stirring, until softened, about 5 minutes. Add garlic, Italian seasoning, salt and peppercorns and cook, stirring, for 1 minute. Add wine, bring to a boil and boil for 2 minutes. Add tomatoes with juice and bring to a boil.

2. Transfer to slow cooker stoneware. Add fish stock. Cover and cook on Low for 6 hours or on High for 3 hours. Add fish, olives and jalapeño and stir well. Cover and cook on High about 7 minutes, until fish is cooked through.

3. **Crostini:** Meanwhile, preheat broiler. In a bowl, combine 2 tbsp (25 mL) of the olive oil, anchovies and parsley and mix well. Brush bread on one side with the remaining tbsp (15 mL) of olive oil. Place on baking sheet and toast under broiler until browning around the edges. Turn, brush remaining side with anchovy mixture and toast under broiler until browning around the edges. To serve, ladle stew into soup plates and top with crostini.

Tips

If you are halving this recipe, be sure to use a small (1½ to 3 quart) slow cooker.

If you prefer, substitute an extra cup (250 mL) of water plus 1 tbsp (15 mL) lemon juice for the white wine.

Make Ahead

Complete Step 1. Cover and refrigerate for up to 2 days. When you're ready to cook, complete the recipe.

Down-Home Shrimp

Here's a dish, Cajun-inspired in its ingredients, that packs just a hint of heat and yields a great sense of freshness. Deliciously different, it makes a great one-pot meal served over rice.

Serves 4

Tips

If you are halving this recipe, be sure to use a small (1½ to 3 quart) slow cooker.

Okra, a tropical vegetable, has a great flavor but it becomes unpleasantly sticky when overcooked. Choose young okra pods, 2 to 4 inches (5 to 10 cm) long, that don't feel sticky to the touch. (If sticky they are too ripe.) Gently scrub the pods and cut off the top and tail before slicing.

Make Ahead

Complete Steps 1, 2 and 3. Cover and refrigerate shrimp, shrimp stock and vegetable mixture separately, overnight. When you're ready to cook, continue with the recipe.

- Medium (approx. 3½ quart) slow cooker

1 lb	shrimp, peeled and deveined, shells set aside	500 g
2 tbsp	freshly squeezed lemon juice	25 mL
¼ tsp	cayenne pepper	1 mL
1 cup	dry white wine	250 mL
1 cup	water	250 mL
2 tbsp	olive oil	25 mL
1	onion, finely chopped	1
2	stalks celery, diced	2
1 tsp	salt	5 mL
1 tsp	cracked black peppercorns	5 mL
½ tsp	dried thyme leaves	2 mL
2	bay leaves	2
1	can (14 oz/398 mL) diced tomatoes with juice	1
2 cups	thinly sliced okra (see Tips, left)	500 mL
1 cup	corn kernels	250 mL
1	red or green bell pepper, seeded and diced	1
1 tbsp	butter	15 mL
2	cloves garlic, minced	2

1. In a small bowl, combine shrimp, lemon juice and cayenne. Stir well, cover and refrigerate until ready to use.

2. Meanwhile, make shrimp stock. In a saucepan, combine shrimp shells, white wine and water. Bring to a boil, reduce heat and simmer for 15 minutes. Strain, pushing the shells against the sieve to extract as much flavor as possible. Measure 1 cup (250 mL) and set aside. Freeze excess.

3. In a skillet, heat oil over medium heat. Add onion and celery and cook, stirring, until softened, about 5 minutes. Add salt, peppercorns, thyme and bay leaves and cook, stirring, for 1 minute. Add tomatoes with juice and bring to a boil.

4. Transfer to slow cooker stoneware. Stir in reserved shrimp stock. Cover and cook on Low for 6 hours or on High for 3 hours. Stir in okra, corn and bell pepper. Cover and cook on High for 20 minutes, until okra is tender. Remove and discard bay leaves.

5. When you are ready to serve, melt butter in a small skillet over medium heat. Add garlic and cook, stirring, for 1 minute. Increase heat to medium-high. Using a slotted spoon, immediately add reserved shrimp, in batches, and cook, stirring, until they turn pink. Transfer to slow cooker as completed. Add marinade juices to pan and cook, stirring, for 1 minute. Add to slow cooker, stir well and serve.

**Can Be
Halved**
see Tips, below

Coconut Shrimp Curry

This is one of my favorite Friday night dinners. I serve it over a mound of brown rice along with steamed spinach. A thoroughly chilled bottle of Gewürztraminer makes a perfect finish.

Serves 4

Tips

If you are halving this recipe, be sure to use a small (1½ to 3 quart) slow cooker.

For the best flavor, toast and grind coriander and cumin seeds yourself. Place seeds in a dry skillet over medium heat and cook, stirring, until fragrant, about 3 minutes. Using a mortar and pestle or a spice grinder, pound or grind as finely as you can.

To make shrimp stock: In a saucepan, combine shrimp shells, 1 cup (250 mL) white wine and 1 cup (250 mL) water. Bring to a boil, reduce heat and simmer for 15 minutes. Strain, pushing the shells against the sieve to extract as much flavor as possible. Measure 1 cup (250 mL). Freeze excess.

Make Ahead

Complete Steps 1 and 2. Cover and refrigerate shrimp, stock and vegetable mixtures separately overnight. When you're ready to cook, continue with the recipe.

- Medium (approx. 3½ quart) slow cooker

1 lb	shrimp, peeled and deveined, shells set aside	500 g
2 tbsp	freshly squeezed lemon juice	25 mL
2 tsp	ground coriander (see Tips, left)	10 mL
1 tsp	ground cumin	5 mL
1 tsp	coarse salt	5 mL
½ tsp	ground turmeric	2 mL
¼ tsp	cayenne pepper	1 mL
1 tbsp	olive or coconut oil	15 mL
2	onions, finely chopped	2
2	stalks celery, diced	2
4	cloves garlic, minced	4
2 tbsp	minced gingerroot	25 mL
1 tsp	cracked black peppercorns	5 mL
½ tsp	salt	2 mL
1	can (14 oz/398 mL) crushed tomatoes	1
1 cup	shrimp stock (see Tips, left)	250 mL
1 cup	coconut milk	250 mL
1	green bell pepper, seeded and diced	1
1	long red or green chile pepper, seeded and minced, optional	1
1 tbsp	butter	15 mL

1. In a small bowl, combine shrimp, lemon juice, coriander, cumin, salt, turmeric and cayenne. Stir well, cover and refrigerate. Make shrimp stock (see Tips, left).

2. In a skillet, heat oil over medium heat. Add onions and celery and cook, stirring, until softened, about 5 minutes. Add garlic, ginger, peppercorns and salt and cook, stirring, for 1 minute. Add tomatoes and bring to a boil.

3. Transfer to slow cooker stoneware. Stir in shrimp stock. Cover and cook on Low for 6 hours or on High for 3 hours, until hot and bubbly. Stir in coconut milk, bell pepper and chile pepper, if using. Cover and cook on High for 15 minutes, until pepper is tender.

4. In a large skillet over medium-high heat, melt butter, being careful not to let it brown. Add shrimp and marinade, in batches if necessary, and sauté until shrimp turn pink and seize up, about 3 minutes. Transfer to slow cooker stoneware. Cover and cook on High for 5 minutes, to meld flavors.

Caribbean Pepper Pot

There are two dishes known as pepper pot — one that apparently originated during the American revolutionary war and a Caribbean version. Although both are traditionally based on ingredients the cook has on hand, the results are very different. The original version of Philadelphia pepper pot included tripe and black peppercorns, but in the islands the dish contains a hodgepodge of local ingredients, including incendiary Scotch bonnet peppers and leafy green callaloo. It is often finished with coconut milk, producing a nicely spicy and lusciously creamy stew.

Can Be Halved
see Tips, below

Serves 6

- Large (approx. 5 quart) slow cooker

1 tbsp	olive oil	15 mL
3	onions, thinly sliced on the vertical	3
4	cloves garlic, minced	4
2 tbsp	minced gingerroot	25 mL
1 tsp	salt	5 mL
1 tsp	cracked black peppercorns	5 mL
1 tsp	ground allspice	5 mL
½ tsp	dried thyme leaves	2 mL
2	bay leaves	2
½ cup	short-grain brown rice	125 mL
1	can (14 oz/398 mL) diced tomatoes with juice	1
2 cups	chicken stock	500 mL
4 cups	cubed (1 inch/2.5 cm) butternut squash (about 1)	1 L
1 lb	skinless boneless chicken thighs, cut into 1-inch (2.5 cm) cubes	500 g
4 cups	chopped kale or callaloo (see Tips, right)	1 L
1 lb	cooked, peeled deveined shrimp (see Tips, right)	500 g
1 to 2	diced habanero or Scotch bonnet chile peppers (see Tips, right)	1 to 2
1 cup	coconut milk	250 mL

1. In a skillet, heat oil over medium heat. Add onions and cook, stirring, until softened, about 3 minutes. Add garlic, ginger, salt, peppercorns, allspice, thyme and bay leaves and cook, stirring, for 1 minute. Add rice and toss until well coated with mixture. Stir in tomatoes with juice and stock and bring to a boil. Boil for 1 minute.

2. Transfer to slow cooker stoneware. Stir in squash and chicken. Cover and cook on Low for 6 hours or on High for 3 hours, until chicken is no longer pink. Working in batches, stir in kale. Add shrimp, chile peppers to taste and coconut milk. Cover and cook on High about 20 minutes, until kale is wilted and flavors meld. Remove and discard bay leaves.

Tips

If you are halving this recipe, be sure to use a small (2 to 3½ quart) slow cooker.

Callaloo, also known as pigweed or amaranth leaves, is becoming increasingly available in greengrocers. Also look for it in farmers' markets.

If you are using large shrimp, chop them into bite-size pieces before adding to the stew.

Only use a second habanero pepper if you are a true heat seeker.

Make Ahead

Complete Step 1. Cover and refrigerate for up to 2 days. When you're ready to cook, continue with the recipe.

Can Be Halved
see Tips, below

Spaghetti with Red Clam Sauce

This simple sauce is so easy to make, yet delicious and in its own way quite elegant. The advantage to making it in the slow cooker is that the sauce can simmer away while you do other things. Then when you're ready to eat, you can cook the pasta and prepare the clams.

Tips

If you are halving this recipe, be sure to use a small (2 to 3½ quart) slow cooker.

If you prefer, substitute half a cup (125 mL) water plus 2 tsp (10 mL) lemon juice for the white wine.

Make Ahead

Complete Step 1. Cover and refrigerate for up to 2 days. When you're ready to cook, continue with the recipe.

Serves 6

- Medium to large (3½ to 5 quart) slow cooker

2 tbsp	olive oil	25 mL
2	onions, finely chopped	2
6	cloves garlic, minced	6
1 tsp	salt	5 mL
1 tsp	cracked black peppercorns	5 mL
1 tsp	dried oregano leaves	5 mL
½ cup	dry white wine (see Tips, left)	125 mL
1	can (28 oz/796 mL) tomatoes with juice, coarsely chopped	1
4 lbs	small clams, scrubbed (about 3 dozen)	2 kg
1 to 2	long red or green chile peppers, seeded and diced, optional	1 to 2
1 lb	thin spaghetti	500 g
1 tbsp	butter	15 mL
¼ cup	finely chopped parsley or basil	50 mL

1. In a skillet, heat oil over medium heat. Add onions and cook, stirring, until softened, about 3 minutes. Add garlic, salt, peppercorns and oregano and cook, stirring, for 1 minute. Add wine, bring to a boil and boil for 1 minute. Add tomatoes with juice and return to a boil.

2. Transfer to slow cooker stoneware. Cover and cook on Low for 6 hours or on High for 3 hours.

3. Discard any clams that are open. In a large saucepan over medium-high heat, bring ½ cup (125 mL) water to a rapid boil. Add clams, cover and cook, shaking the pot, until all the clams open, about 5 minutes. Discard any that do not open. Strain cooking liquid through a fine sieve into a bowl. Using a fork, remove clam meat from all but 6 of the shells.

4. Add clam cooking liquid, clam meat, chile peppers to taste, if using, and 6 cooked clams in shells to slow cooker. Cover and cook on High for 10 minutes, until flavors meld.

5. Meanwhile, bring a large pot of salted water to a boil. Add spaghetti and cook according to package instructions. Drain, toss with butter, and place in a large serving dish. Remove clams in shells from slow cooker and set aside. Add clam sauce to spaghetti and toss. Lay cooked clams in shells over top. Garnish with parsley and serve.

Zuppa di Pesce

This is a very simple Italian-style fish stew that is differentiated by an assortment of fish. It doesn't contain any seafood. Its simplicity demands a good-quality broth, which can easily be achieved by simmering fish trimmings with the other ingredients, then removing them before finishing the dish.

Can Be Halved
see Tips, below

Serves 6

- Large (approx. 5 quart) slow cooker

3 tbsp	extra virgin olive oil, divided	45 mL
1 tbsp	freshly squeezed lemon juice	15 mL
1 tsp	fennel seeds, toasted and ground	5 mL
1 tsp	coarse salt, preferably sea salt	5 mL
1 tsp	mild chile powder, such as Aleppo (see Tips, right)	5 mL
2 lbs	assorted skinless fish fillets, cut into chunks (see Tips, right)	1 kg
2	onions, finely chopped	2
4	stalks celery, diced	4
4	cloves garlic, minced	4
2	bay leaves	2
1 tsp	dried oregano leaves	5 mL
1/2 tsp	cracked black peppercorns	2 mL
1 cup	dry white wine (see Tips, right)	250 mL
1	can (28 oz/796 mL) tomatoes with juice, chopped	1
2 lbs	fish trimmings (see Tips, right)	1 kg
6 cups	water	1.5 L
16	Garlic Crostini (see Tips, right)	16
1/2 cup	finely chopped parsley	125 mL

1. In a bowl, combine 2 tbsp (25 mL) of the olive oil, lemon juice, fennel seeds, salt and chile powder. Mix well. Add fish and toss until coated. Cover and refrigerate for 2 hours or overnight, stirring occasionally.

2. In a skillet, heat remaining tbsp (15 mL) of olive oil over medium heat. Add onions and celery and cook, stirring, until softened, about 5 minutes. Add garlic, bay leaves, oregano and peppercorns and cook, stirring, for 1 minute. Add white wine and bring to a boil. Boil for 2 minutes. Stir in tomatoes with juice. Transfer to slow cooker stoneware.

3. In a large square of cheesecloth, tie fish trimmings. Add to stoneware along with water, ensuring trimmings are submerged. Cover and cook on Low for 8 hours or on High for 4 hours. Remove trimmings and discard. Increase heat to High. Add marinated fish and cook about 15 minutes, until fish is tender. Remove and discard bay leaves.

4. To serve, place 2 crostini in each bowl and ladle soup over. Garnish with parsley.

Tips

If you are halving this recipe, be sure to use a small (2 to 3 1/2 quart) slow cooker.

If you don't have Aleppo pepper, substitute 1 tsp (5 mL) sweet paprika mixed with a pinch of cayenne pepper.

Use firm white fish such as halibut, snapper, monkfish or sea bass.

If you prefer, substitute an extra cup (250 mL) of water plus 1 tbsp (15 mL) lemon juice for the white wine.

For best results, when asking for trimmings, be sure to use non-oily fish, which means no salmon.

To make Garlic Crostini: Preheat broiler. In a small bowl, combine 1/4 cup (50 mL) extra virgin olive oil with 2 cloves garlic, peeled and put through a press. Stir well. Brush 16 baguette slices on both sides with infused oil and toast under broiler, turning once.

Make Ahead

Complete Steps 1 and 2. Cover and refrigerate fish and vegetable mixtures separately overnight. When you're ready to cook, complete the recipe.

Entertaining Worthy

Can Be Halved
see Tips, below

Poached Halibut with Dill Hollandaise

This is an elegant dish, perfect for entertaining. I like to serve it with parsleyed potatoes and a green vegetable. Don't be intimidated by the hollandaise. As long as you keep the heat low your eggs won't curdle, and even if they do, the problem is easy to fix (see Step 3).

Tips

If you are halving this recipe, be sure to use a small (2 to 3½ quart) slow cooker.

The cooking time depends upon the configuration of your fish. The thicker it is, the longer it will take. Start checking for doneness after 1 hour. I've made this using a thick chunk of halibut and it took close to 1½ hours.

I use unsalted butter. If you are using butter that is salted, taste before adding salt and adjust the quantity accordingly.

Serves 6 to 8

• Medium to large (3 to 5 quart) slow cooker

Poaching Liquid

1	onion, chopped	1
2	stalks celery, including leaves, chopped	2
4	sprigs parsley	4
8	peppercorns	8
1 tsp	coarse sea or kosher salt	5 mL
2	bay leaves	2
6 cups	water	1.5 L
½ cup	white wine or lemon juice	125 mL
2 lbs	halibut fillet	1 kg

Dill Hollandaise

2	egg yolks	2
1 tbsp	cold water	15 mL
½ cup	butter, cubed	125 mL
1 tbsp	freshly squeezed lemon juice	15 mL
1 tsp	salt (approx.) (see Tips, left)	5 mL
Pinch	cayenne pepper	Pinch
¼ cup	finely chopped dill	50 mL

1. **Poaching Liquid:** In a saucepan, combine onion, celery, parsley, peppercorns, salt, bay leaves, water and wine. Bring to a boil, reduce heat and simmer for 30 minutes. Strain and discard solids.

2. Preheat slow cooker on High for 15 minutes and add hot poaching liquid. Add halibut. Cover and cook on High about 1 hour and 15 minutes, until fish flakes easily when pierced with a knife (see Tips, left). Using a slotted spoon, transfer fish to a warm platter and keep warm. Remove and discard bay leaves.

3. **Dill Hollandaise:** Meanwhile, in a heavy saucepan over low heat (or in the top of a double boiler), whisk egg yolks and water. Add butter, one piece at a time, whisking until each piece melts before adding the next one. (If mixture begins to scramble, remove from heat and whisk in 1 tbsp/15 mL cold water.) When all the butter has been added, continue to whisk until mixture thickens. Whisk in lemon juice, salt and cayenne. Stir in dill. Serve immediately over fish or keep warm over hot water until ready to serve.

Variation

Poached Salmon with Dill Hollandaise: Substitute an equal quantity of salmon fillet for the halibut.

Braised Halibut on a Bed of Creamy Leeks

This luscious dish is perfect for entertaining because it cooks away while your guests are enjoying pre-dinner drinks and nibblies. I serve it over a mound of steaming garlic mashed potatoes accompanied by buttered spinach with a dash of freshly squeezed lemon juice.

Tips

If you are halving this recipe, be sure to use a small (1½ to 3 quart) slow cooker.

If you prefer, substitute an extra ½ cup (125 mL) fish stock plus 2 tsp (10 mL) lemon juice for the white wine.

The cooking time depends upon the configuration of your fish steaks. The thicker they are, the longer it will take. Start checking for doneness after 1 hour. I've made this using a thick chunk of halibut and it took close to 1½ hours.

Make Ahead

Complete Step 1. Cover and refrigerate for up to 2 days. When you're ready to cook, continue with the recipe.

Serves 4

- Parchment paper
- Medium to large (3 to 5 quart) oval slow cooker

¼ cup	butter	50 mL
4	leeks, white part only with just a hint of green, cleaned and thinly sliced (see Tips, page 102)	4
½ tsp	cracked black peppercorns	2 mL
½ tsp	coarse sea salt	2 mL
Pinch	cayenne pepper	Pinch
2	bay leaves	2
½ cup	dry white wine (see Tips, left)	125 mL
½ cup	fish stock	125 mL
2 lbs	halibut steaks or fillet (approx.) (see Tips, left)	1 kg
½ cup	whipping (35%) cream	125 mL
1 tsp	finely grated lemon zest	5 mL
¼ cup	finely chopped dill	50 mL

1. In a skillet over medium heat, melt butter. Add leeks and cook, stirring, until softened, about 8 minutes. Add peppercorns, salt, cayenne and bay leaves and stir well. Add wine and bring to a boil.

2. Transfer to slow cooker stoneware and stir in fish stock. Place halibut on top of leeks and place a piece of parchment paper over the mixture, pressing it down to brush the food and extending up the sides of the stoneware so it overlaps the rim. Cover and cook on High about 1 hour and 15 minutes, until fish flakes easily when pierced with a knife (see Tips, left). Remove and discard bay leaves.

3. To serve, lift out the parchment and discard, being careful not to spill the accumulated liquid into the stoneware. Transfer fish to a warm platter, remove all bones and keep warm. Add whipping cream and lemon zest to leeks and stir well. Taste and adjust seasoning. Pour sauce over halibut and garnish liberally with dill.

Halibut with White Beans and Chorizo

In Portugal and Spain, spicy chorizo is often used to add zest to fish and seafood dishes. Mussels, clams or salt cod are traditional pairings, but halibut, although less conventional, makes a mouth-watering match. The beans provide a starch, so all you need to add is a green salad, and if you're feeling festive, some cold, crisp wine.

Serves 4 to 6

- Medium to large (3½ to 5 quart) slow cooker

1 tbsp	olive oil	15 mL
8 oz	soft chorizo (see Tips, right)	250 g
2	onions, finely chopped	2
4	cloves garlic, minced	4
1 tsp	dried thyme leaves	5 mL
½ tsp	salt	2 mL
½ tsp	cracked black peppercorns	2 mL
¼ cup	dry sherry	50 mL
1	can (28 oz/796 mL) tomatoes with juice, coarsely chopped (see Tips, right)	1
2 cups	cooked cannellini (white kidney) beans	500 mL
1 lb	skinless halibut, cut into 1-inch (2.5 cm) cubes	500 g
2	red peppers, roasted, peeled and cut into strips (see Tips, right)	2

1. In a skillet, heat oil over medium-high heat. Add chorizo and onions and cook, stirring, until sausage is no longer pink and onions are softened, about 3 minutes. Add garlic, thyme, salt and peppercorns and cook, stirring, for 1 minute. Add sherry, bring to a boil and boil for 1 minute. Stir in tomatoes with juice.

2. Transfer to slow cooker stoneware. Add cannellini beans. Cover and cook on Low for 6 to 8 hours or on High for 3 to 4 hours, until hot and bubbly. Add halibut and roasted peppers. Cover and cook on High for 7 minutes, until fish is cooked through.

Can Be Halved
see Tips, below

Tips

If you are halving this recipe, be sure to use a small (1½ to 3 quart) slow cooker.

Chorizo comes in various degrees of spiciness. My butcher makes his extra hot, which makes a zesty version of this dish.

I like to use Italian San Marzano tomatoes, which are particularly rich. If you're using domestic tomatoes, you might want to add 1 tbsp (15 mL) tomato paste subsequent to boiling the sherry.

For this quantity of beans, cook 1 cup (250 mL) dried beans or use 1 can (14 to 19 oz/398 to 540 mL) cannellini beans, drained and rinsed.

You can roast the red peppers yourself, or buy them already roasted and peeled.

Make Ahead

Complete Step 1. Cover mixture, ensuring it cools promptly (see Making Ahead, page 17), and refrigerate for up to 2 days. When you're ready to cook, complete the recipe.

Braised Swordfish

This is a great dish for entertaining because you can assemble it just before your guests arrive and turn the slow cooker on when they come through the door. By the time everyone is enjoying drinks and nibblies, the conversation is flowing and you're thinking about moving to the table, the fish will be cooked. Serve with a big platter of sautéed spinach or rapini alongside. Add a good dessert and await the praise.

Tips

If you are halving this recipe, be sure to use a small (1½ to 3 quart) slow cooker.

If you can't find swordfish that is sustainably caught, that is line or harpooned, substitute another firm white fish such as mahi-mahi, grouper or halibut.

It is hard to be specific about the cooking time as it depends upon the configuration of the steaks (thickness and width). It may take up to 1½ hours.

To make crostini: Preheat broiler. Slice a baguette and brush both sides with olive oil. Toast under broiler, turning once.

Serves 4

- Parchment paper
- Medium to large (3 to 5 quart) oval slow cooker

2	large swordfish steaks (about 2½ lbs/1.25 kg) (see Tips, left)	2
1	sweet onion, such as Vidalia, very thinly sliced on the vertical	1
½ cup	finely chopped parsley	125 mL
1 cup	pitted black olives, preferably kalamata, halved	250 mL
2	cloves garlic, minced	2
1 tsp	mild chili powder such as Aleppo, piment d'Espelette or hot paprika	5 mL
½ tsp	salt	2 mL
½ cup	extra virgin olive oil	125 mL
1½ cups	dry white wine	375 mL
8	crostini (see Tips, left)	8

1. Place swordfish in slow cooker stoneware. Sprinkle with onion, parsley, olives, garlic, chili powder and salt. Pour in olive oil, tipping the stoneware to ensure fish is coated. Pour wine evenly over fish. Place a large piece of parchment paper over the mixture, pressing it down to brush the food and extending up the sides of the stoneware so it overlaps the rim. (This ensures fish is well basted during the cooking process.) Cover and cook until fish flakes easily when pierced with a knife, about 1 hour (see Tips, left).

2. To serve, lift out the parchment and discard, being careful not to spill the accumulated liquid into the stoneware. Lift out fish and cut in half. Place 2 crostini in each soup plate. Place fish on top and spoon braising sauce over.

Mediterranean-Style Mahi-Mahi

I love the in-your-face flavors of the gremolata used to finish this dish. This is another recipe that is great for entertaining because you can time starting the slow cooker so that the fish will be cooked when your guests are ready to eat. I like to serve this with hot buttered orzo and spinach or Swiss chard.

Tips

If you are halving this recipe, be sure to use a small (1½ to 3 quart) slow cooker.

It is difficult to be specific about the timing because of the configuration of the fish, but you should begin checking for doneness after 1 hour. Be aware it may take up to 1½ hours.

Serves 4

• Medium to large (3 to 5 quart) oval slow cooker

2 lbs	mahi-mahi steaks	1 kg
1 tsp	dried oregano leaves	5 mL
1	lemon, thinly sliced	1
1	can (28 oz/796 mL) tomatoes with juice, coarsely chopped	1
½ cup	dry white wine	125 mL
¼ cup	extra virgin olive oil, divided	50 mL
1 tsp	salt	5 mL
	Freshly ground black pepper	

Gremolata

½ cup	finely chopped parsley	125 mL
3 tbsp	capers, drained and minced	45 mL
2	whole anchovies, rinsed and finely chopped	2
	Freshly ground black pepper	

Chopped black olives

1. Place fish in slow cooker stoneware. Sprinkle with oregano and lay lemon slices evenly over top. In a bowl, combine tomatoes with juice, wine, 2 tbsp (25 mL) of the olive oil, salt and pepper to taste. Pour over fish. Cover and cook on High for 1 hour (see Tips, left), until fish flakes easily when pierced with a knife.

2. **Gremolata:** Meanwhile, in a bowl, combine parsley, capers, anchovies, remaining 2 tbsp (25 mL) of the olive oil and pepper to taste. Mix well and set aside in refrigerator until fish is cooked.

3. To serve, transfer fish and tomato sauce to a warm platter. Spoon gremolata evenly over and garnish with olives.

Creamy Coconut Grouper

The sweet potato in this tasty stew lends an appealing hint of sugar that is nicely balanced by the spicy cayenne. If you like heat, add a fresh chile along with the coconut milk. Serve this over plain rice. You won't be disappointed.

Can Be
Halved
see Tip, below

Serves 8

• Medium to large (3½ to 5 quart) slow cooker

1 cup	finely chopped cilantro leaves	250 mL
2 tbsp	freshly squeezed lime juice	25 mL
¼ tsp	cayenne pepper	1 mL
2 lbs	skinless grouper fillets, cut into 1-inch (2.5 cm) cubes	1 kg
1 tbsp	olive or coconut oil	15 mL
2	onions, finely chopped	2
2	stalks celery, diced	2
4	cloves garlic, minced	4
1 tsp	salt	5 mL
1 tsp	cracked black peppercorns	5 mL
1 tsp	dried oregano leaves	5 mL
1	can (28 oz/796 mL) diced tomatoes with juice	1
1	potato, peeled and shredded	1
1	sweet potato, peeled and cubed	1
1 cup	fish or vegetable stock or water	250 mL
1	can (14 oz/400 mL) coconut milk	1
1	long red chile pepper, seeded and minced, optional	1

1. In a bowl, combine cilantro, lime juice, cayenne and grouper. Mix well. Cover and refrigerate until ready to use.

2. In a skillet, heat oil over medium heat. Add onions and celery and cook, stirring, until softened, about 5 minutes. Add garlic, salt, peppercorns and oregano and cook, stirring, for 1 minute. Add tomatoes with juice and bring to a boil.

3. Transfer to slow cooker stoneware. Add potato, sweet potato and fish stock. Cover and cook on Low for 6 hours or on High for 3 hours, until sweet potato is tender. Add grouper mixture, coconut milk and chile, if using. Cover and cook on High about 10 minutes, until fish flakes easily when pierced with a knife and mixture is hot and bubbly.

Tip

If you are halving this recipe, be sure to use a small (2 to 3½ quart) slow cooker.

Make Ahead

Complete Steps 1 and 2. Cover and refrigerate fish and vegetable mixtures separately overnight. When you're ready to cook, continue with the recipe.

Entertaining Worthy

Can Be Halved
see Tips, below

Salmon on a Bed of Lentils with Horseradish Cream

This is a classic French preparation from Alsace. Usually the fish is studded with lardoons, a practice that is too rich for the farmed Atlantic salmon most commonly sold in North America. The horseradish cream, although delicious, is also a bit rich, so I've lightened it with the addition of chives. This is a great dish for entertaining, but because it is quite heavy, I serve smaller portions of fish and round out the meal with big servings of a simple vegetable such as steamed green beans or baby carrots.

Tips

If you are halving this recipe, be sure to use a small (2 to 3½ quart) slow cooker.

Crème fraîche, a thickened cream with a pleasantly nutty taste, is available in specialty stores or well-stocked supermarkets. If you can't find it, substitute ½ cup (125 mL) each sour cream and whipping (35%) cream.

Make Ahead

Complete Step 1. Cover and refrigerate for up to 2 days. When you're ready to cook, continue with recipe.

Serves 6 to 8

- Parchment paper
- Medium to large (3 to 5 quart) oval slow cooker

1 tbsp	olive oil	15 mL
2	onions, finely chopped	2
2	carrots, diced	2
2	stalks celery, diced	2
4	cloves garlic, minced	4
½ tsp	salt	2 mL
½ tsp	cracked black peppercorns	2 mL
2 cups	green or brown lentils (see Tips, page 257)	500 mL
4 cups	vegetable or chicken stock, divided	1 L
1	large salmon fillet (about 1½ lbs/750 g), skin removed	1

Horseradish Cream

1 cup	crème fraîche (see Tips, left)	250 mL
¼ cup	finely chopped chives	50 mL
2 tbsp	prepared horseradish	25 mL

1. In a skillet, heat oil over medium heat. Add onions, carrots and celery and cook, stirring, until carrots are softened, about 7 minutes. Add garlic, salt and peppercorns and cook, stirring, for 1 minute. Add lentils and toss until coated. Add 2 cups (500 mL) of the vegetable stock and bring to a boil.

2. Transfer to slow cooker stoneware. Add remaining vegetable stock. Cover and cook on Low for 5 to 6 hours or on High for 2½ to 3 hours, until lentils are almost tender.

3. Place salmon on top of lentils and place a large piece of parchment paper over the mixture, pressing it down to brush the food and extending up the sides of the stoneware so it overlaps the rim. (This ensures fish is well basted during the cooking process.) Cover and cook on High about 1 hour, until fish flakes easily when pierced with a knife.

4. **Horseradish Cream:** Meanwhile, in a small serving bowl, combine crème fraîche, chives and horseradish. Stir well and refrigerate until ready to serve.

5. To serve, lift out the parchment and discard, being careful not to spill the accumulated liquid into the stoneware. Lift out the salmon and cut into serving-size pieces. Spoon lentils onto plates. Top with fish and garnish with horseradish cream.

Indian-Spiced Salmon in Tomato Sauce with Spinach

If you're fond of salmon but, like me, in a bit of a rut about how to prepare it, here's a dish that will jolt you out of the doldrums. Salmon marinated in gentle spicing is poached with spinach in a light but flavorful tomato sauce. It's so easy to make you can serve it on weekdays, although it's tasty enough to serve to guests. All you really need to add is rice and, if you're feeling in the mood for authenticity, some warm naan.

Tips

If you are halving this recipe, be sure to use a small (1½ to 3 quart) slow cooker.

For the best flavor, toast and grind cumin and coriander seeds yourself. Place seeds in a dry skillet over medium heat and cook, stirring, until fragrant, about 3 minutes. Using a mortar and pestle or a spice grinder, pound or grind as finely as you can.

Make Ahead

Complete Steps 1 and 2. Cover and refrigerate fish and vegetable mixtures separately overnight. When you're ready to cook, continue with the recipe.

Serves 4 to 6

• Medium (approx. 3½ quart) slow cooker

2 tbsp	freshly squeezed lemon juice	25 mL
1 tsp	garam masala	5 mL
¼ tsp	cayenne pepper	1 mL
1½ lbs	salmon fillet, skin removed	750 g
1 tbsp	olive oil or ghee	15 mL
2	onions, finely chopped	2
4	cloves garlic, minced	4
1 tbsp	minced gingerroot	15 mL
1 tbsp	ground cumin (see Tips, left)	15 mL
2 tsp	ground coriander	10 mL
1 tsp	salt	5 mL
1 tsp	cracked black peppercorns	5 mL
½ tsp	ground turmeric	2 mL
1	can (28 oz/796 mL) diced tomatoes with juice	1
4 cups	packed chopped spinach leaves	1 L

1. In a bowl, combine lemon juice, garam masala and cayenne. Stir well. Add salmon and toss until well coated with mixture. Cover and refrigerate until ready to use.

2. In a skillet, heat oil over medium heat. Add onions and cook, stirring, until softened, about 3 minutes. Add garlic, ginger, cumin, coriander, salt, peppercorns and turmeric and cook, stirring, for 1 minute. Add tomatoes with juice and bring to a boil.

3. Transfer to slow cooker stoneware. Cover and cook on Low for 6 hours or on High for 3 hours. Working in batches, stir in spinach. Cover and cook on High for 10 minutes. Add reserved salmon with juices. Cover and cook on High about 7 minutes, until fish flakes easily with a fork.

Basque-Style Tuna

Like many traditional fish dishes, this classic stew, known as marmita, *originated with local fishermen, who prepared it on their boats using some of the day's catch. The classic Basque ingredients — tomatoes, garlic and peppers with a hint of* piment d'Espelette, *a mild red chile pepper from the Basque area of France — are among my favorite combinations.*

Can Be
Halved
see Tips, below

Serves 4 to 6

- Medium to large (3½ to 5 quart) slow cooker

3 tbsp	olive oil, divided	45 mL
1 to 2 tsp	piment d'Espelette or hot paprika (see Tips, right)	5 to 10 mL
1 tsp	sea salt	5 mL
1½ lbs	yellowfin tuna, cut into 1-inch (2 cm) cubes	750 g
2	onions, thinly sliced on the vertical	2
6	cloves garlic, minced	6
1 tsp	cracked black peppercorns	5 mL
½ cup	dry white wine	125 mL
1	can (14 oz/398 mL) diced tomatoes with juice (see Tips, right)	1
2	potatoes, peeled and shredded	2
2 cups	fish stock	500 mL
1	green bell pepper, roasted, peeled and cut into strips	1
4 to 6	Garlic Crostini (see Tips, right)	4 to 6

1. In a bowl, combine 2 tbsp (25 mL) of the olive oil, piment d'Espelette to taste and salt. Mix well. Add fish and toss to coat. Refrigerate until ready to use.

2. In a skillet, heat remaining tbsp (15 mL) of oil over medium heat. Add onions and cook, stirring, until softened, about 3 minutes. Add garlic and peppercorns and cook, stirring, for 1 minute. Add wine, bring to a boil and boil for 1 minute. Add tomatoes with juice and bring to a boil.

3. Transfer to slow cooker stoneware. Add potatoes and fish stock. Cover and cook on Low for 6 hours or on High for 3 hours. Add reserved tuna and roasted pepper. Cover and cook on High for 5 minutes, until tuna is barely cooked through. To serve, place crostini in a bowl and ladle stew over top.

Tips

If you are halving this recipe, be sure to use a small (1½ to 3 quart) slow cooker.

Vary the quantity of Espelette to suit your taste. If you don't have hot paprika or piment d'Espelette, try using an equal quantity of sweet paprika with a pinch or two of cayenne.

I like to use Italian San Marzano tomatoes, which are thick and rich. If you're using domestic tomatoes, you may want to add 1 tbsp (15 mL) tomato paste.

To make Garlic Crostini: In a small bowl, combine ¼ cup (50 mL) extra virgin olive oil with 2 cloves garlic, peeled and put through a press. Stir well. Brush baguette slices on both sides with infused oil and toast under broiler, turning once.

Make Ahead

Complete Steps 1 and 2. Cover and refrigerate fish and vegetable mixtures separately overnight. When you're ready to cook, continue with the recipe.

Short Ribs with
Horseradish Cream

Beef and Veal

Continued on next page.

Short Ribs with Horseradish Cream

This combination of flavors is classic. Serve it for a special Sunday dinner with piping hot mashed potatoes and steamed green beans.

Entertaining Worthy

Can Be Halved
see Tips, below

Serves 6

- Large (approx. 5 quart) slow cooker

4 to 5 lbs	beef short ribs	2 to 2.5 kg
1 tbsp	olive oil	15 mL
3	onions, finely chopped	3
2	carrots, peeled and diced	2
2	stalks celery, diced	2
4	cloves garlic, minced	4
1 tsp	dried thyme leaves	5 mL
1 tsp	salt	5 mL
1 tsp	cracked black peppercorns	5 mL
2	bay leaves	2
2 tbsp	all-purpose flour	25 mL
2 tbsp	tomato paste	25 mL
1 cup	dry red wine	250 mL
2 cups	chicken stock	500 mL
	Salt and freshly ground black pepper	

Horseradish Cream

3 tbsp	prepared horseradish	45 mL
½ cup	sour cream or crème fraîche	125 mL

1. Position broiler rack 6 inches (15 cm) from heat source. Broil ribs on both sides, turning once, for 10 minutes per side. Drain on paper towels. Separate ribs if in strips and place in stoneware.

2. In a large skillet, heat oil over medium heat. Add onions, carrots and celery and cook, stirring, until softened, about 7 minutes. Add garlic, thyme, salt, peppercorns and bay leaves and cook, stirring, for 1 minute. Add flour and cook, stirring, for 1 minute. Stir in tomato paste and wine and cook, stirring, for 2 minutes. Stir in stock and bring to a boil.

3. Transfer vegetable mixture to stoneware. Cover and cook on Low for 8 to 10 hours or on High for 4 to 5 hours, until ribs are falling off the bone. Transfer ribs to a large serving dish and keep warm. Remove and discard bay leaves. Using an immersion blender, purée the sauce and adjust seasoning (see Tips, right). Pour over short ribs.

4. **Horseradish Cream:** Meanwhile, in a small serving bowl, combine horseradish and sour cream. Refrigerate for at least 1 hour to allow flavors to meld. Pass at the table and allow guests to serve themselves.

Tips

If you are halving this recipe, be sure to use a small (2 to 3½ quart) slow cooker.

People differ on how well cooked they like short ribs to be. I prefer mine to be falling off the bone, but if you like a firmer result, or if your slow cooker cooks particularly quickly, reduce the cooking time.

If you don't have an immersion blender, purée the mixture in Step 3 in a food processor.

Make Ahead

Complete Step 2. Cover and refrigerate for up to 2 days. When you're ready to cook, complete the recipe.

Entertaining Worthy

Can Be Halved
see Tips, below

Short Ribs in Rich Mushroom Gravy

This is real stick-to-your-ribs cold-weather cooking — and exceptionally delicious, to boot. Serve over fluffy mashed potatoes, polenta or buttered orzo. It's so good you'll want to invite friends.

Serves 6

Tips

If you are halving this recipe, be sure to use a small (2 to 3½ quart) slow cooker.

People differ on how well cooked they like short ribs to be. I prefer mine to be falling off the bone, but if you like a firmer result, or if your slow cooker cooks particularly quickly, reduce the cooking time.

Make Ahead

Complete Steps 1 and 3. Cover and refrigerate for up to 2 days. When you're ready to cook, complete the recipe.

- Large (approx. 5 quart) slow cooker

1	package (½ oz/14 g) dried porcini mushrooms	1
1 cup	hot water	250 mL
4 lbs	beef short ribs	2 kg
1 tbsp	olive oil	15 mL
2	onions, finely chopped	2
2	carrots, peeled and diced	2
2	stalks celery, diced	2
6	cloves garlic, minced	6
1 tsp	dried thyme leaves	5 mL
1 tsp	salt	5 mL
1 tsp	cracked black peppercorns	5 mL
2	bay leaves	2
1 cup	dry red wine	250 mL
1	can (14 oz/398 mL) tomatoes with juice (see Tips, page 172)	1
8 oz	cremini mushrooms, trimmed and quartered	250 g

1. In a bowl, soak dried mushrooms in hot water for 30 minutes. Strain through a fine sieve, reserving liquid. Chop mushrooms finely and set aside.

2. Meanwhile, position broiler rack 6 inches (15 cm) from heat source. Broil ribs on both sides, turning once, until well browned, about 10 minutes per side. Drain on paper towels. Separate ribs if in strips and place in slow cooker stoneware.

3. In a large skillet, heat oil over medium heat. Add onions, carrots and celery and cook, stirring, until softened, about 7 minutes. Add garlic, thyme, salt, peppercorns, bay leaves and reserved dried mushrooms and cook, stirring, for 1 minute. Add wine, bring to a boil and cook, stirring and scraping up brown bits from bottom of pan, for 2 minutes. Stir in reserved mushroom liquid and tomatoes with juice and bring to a boil.

4. Transfer to stoneware. Stir in cremini mushrooms. Cover and cook on Low for 8 to 10 hours or on High for 4 to 5 hours, until ribs are falling off the bone (see Tips, left). Remove and discard bay leaves.

Chile-Spiced Short Ribs

Here's a short rib recipe that is delectably different yet fairly easy to make. The secret is ancho chile powder and chipotle pepper in adobo sauce, which add incredible depth of flavor with very little effort on the part of the cook. I like to serve this over hot polenta accompanied by steamed runner beans.

Entertaining Worthy

Can Be Halved
see Tips, below

Serves 6

- Large (approx. 5 quart) slow cooker

4 to 5 lbs	beef short ribs	2 to 2.5 kg
1 tbsp	olive oil	15 mL
2	onions, finely chopped	2
2	stalks celery, diced	2
2	carrots, peeled and diced	2
4	cloves garlic, minced	4
1	piece (4 inches/10 cm) cinnamon stick	1
1 tsp	dried thyme leaves	5 mL
1 tsp	cracked black peppercorns	5 mL
1/2 tsp	salt	2 mL
2 tbsp	tomato paste	25 mL
1 cup	dry red wine	250 mL
2 cups	chicken or vegetable stock	500 mL
1 tbsp	ancho chile powder	15 mL
1 to 2	chipotle chiles in adobo sauce, minced (see Tips, right)	1 to 2
	Finely chopped cilantro	

1. Position broiler rack 6 inches (15 cm) from heat source. Broil ribs on both sides, turning once, until well browned, about 10 minutes per side. Drain on paper towels. Separate ribs if in strips and place in slow cooker stoneware.

2. In a skillet, heat oil over medium heat. Add onions, celery and carrots and cook, stirring, until softened, about 7 minutes. Add garlic, cinnamon stick, thyme, peppercorns and salt and cook, stirring, for 1 minute. Stir in tomato paste and wine and bring to a boil. Boil rapidly for 2 minutes.

3. Transfer to slow cooker stoneware. Stir in stock. Cover and cook on Low for 8 to 10 hours or on High for 4 to 5 hours, until ribs are tender and falling off the bone (see Tips, right). Stir in chile powder and chipotle chile with adobo sauce. Cover and cook on High for 30 minutes, until flavors meld. Garnish liberally with cilantro.

Tips

If you are halving this recipe, be sure to use a small (2 to 3½ quart) slow cooker.

Chipotle chiles in abobo sauce lend a great smoky flavor as well as heat to this dish. They are very hot, so unless you are a heat seeker, use only 1 in this recipe. The ancho chile powder is only mildly hot but adds pleasant depth and complexity to the sauce.

People differ on how well cooked they like short ribs to be. I prefer mine to be falling off the bone, but if you like a firmer result, or if your slow cooker cooks particularly quickly, reduce the cooking time.

Make Ahead

Complete Step 2. Cover and refrigerate for up to 2 days. When you're ready to cook, complete the recipe.

Sauerbraten with Gingersnap Gravy

Sauerbraten was one of the first entertaining dishes I learned to make as a young bride. It's pungent and flavorful. For many years I made it with sour cream gravy (see Variation, right), but once I discovered gingersnaps, that became my preferred version. Serve with plenty of fluffy mashed potatoes to soak up the sauce.

Tips

If you are halving this recipe, be sure to use a small (2 to 3½ quart) slow cooker. Reduce cooking time to about 6 hours on Low or 3 hours on High.

You'll need about 3 oz (90 g) gingersnaps to make this quantity of crumbs. Simply purée gingersnaps in a food processor until the desired texture is achieved.

Be aware that these cooking times are general estimates. Not only do cooking times vary substantially among slow cookers (see Cooking Times, page 12), but people have different preferences with regard to how well they like their meat done. If you prefer fork-tender results, start checking after the food has cooked for 6 hours on Low.

Serves 8

- Large (approx. 5 quart) slow cooker

2	onions, thinly sliced on the vertical	2
1	carrot, peeled and diced	1
2	cloves garlic, minced	2
12	whole peppercorns	12
2	bay leaves	2
4	whole cloves	4
1½ cups	red wine vinegar	375 mL
1½ cups	red wine	375 mL
1	beef pot roast (about 4 lbs/2 kg)	1
¼ cup	all-purpose flour	50 mL
1 tbsp	butter	15 mL
1 tbsp	olive oil (approx.)	15 mL
2 tbsp	packed brown sugar	25 mL
1 tbsp	minced gingerroot	15 mL
1 tsp	ground allspice	5 mL
1 tsp	salt	5 mL
1 cup	gingersnap crumbs (see Tips, left)	250 mL
	Finely chopped parsley	

1. In a saucepan, combine onions, carrot, garlic, peppercorns, bay leaves, cloves, vinegar and wine. Bring to a boil over medium heat. Let cool to room temperature.

2. Place meat in a large bowl. Add marinade, cover and refrigerate for 2 to 3 days, turning several times.

3. When you're ready to cook, drain, reserving liquid and solids separately. Pat meat dry. Spread flour on a plate and dredge meat until lightly but evenly coated. Set extra flour aside.

4. In a large skillet over medium-high heat, melt butter and oil. Add roast and brown on all sides, about 10 minutes. Transfer to slow cooker stoneware.

5. Add more oil to pan, if necessary. Add reserved vegetables and cook, stirring, until softened, about 5 minutes. Add brown sugar, ginger, allspice and salt and cook, stirring, for 1 minute. Add reserved flour and cook, stirring, for 1 minute. Add reserved marinade and bring to a boil. Cook, stirring and scraping up brown bits from bottom of pan, until slightly thickened, about 2 minutes.

6. Transfer to slow cooker stoneware. Cover and cook on Low for 8 to 10 hours or on High for 4 to 5 hours, until meat is very tender. Transfer meat to a platter and keep warm. Strain the sauce through a fine sieve and discard vegetables. Transfer sauce to a saucepan and heat over medium heat. Stir in gingersnap crumbs. Taste and adjust seasoning.

7. To serve, slice meat about $1/4$ inch (0.5 cm) thick. Pour a bit of sauce over them and garnish with parsley. Pass remaining gravy in a sauceboat at the table, allowing people to serve themselves.

Variation
Sauerbraten with Sour Cream Gravy: Substitute 1 cup (250 mL) sour cream for the gingersnap crumbs. Be sure not to boil it while on the stove or it will curdle.

Pot Roast in Barolo

Served over polenta, this Italian classic makes a perfect Sunday dinner. Use Barolo to be authentic, but any full-bodied dry red wine will do. I like to finish the meal with a platter of sautéed rapini.

Serves 8 to 10

• Large (approx. 5 quart) slow cooker

2 tbsp	olive oil, divided	25 mL
2 oz	pancetta, diced	60 g
1	boneless rump or chuck roast, about 4 lbs (2 kg)	1
⅓ cup	all-purpose flour (approx.), divided	75 mL
2	onions, finely chopped	2
2	carrots, peeled and diced	2
2	stalks celery, diced	2
4	cloves garlic, minced	4
1 tsp	dried rosemary leaves (see Tips, left)	5 mL
2	bay leaves	2
1	piece (2 inches/5 cm) cinnamon stick	1
1 tsp	each salt and cracked black peppercorns	5 mL
2 tbsp	tomato paste	25 mL
3 cups	dry robust red wine, such as Barolo	750 mL
2 tbsp	butter, softened	25 mL
	Salt and freshly ground black pepper	

Tips

If you are halving this recipe, be sure to use a small (2½ to 3½ quart) slow cooker. Reduce cooking time to 6 to 8 hours on Low or 3 to 4 hours on High.

If you have fresh rosemary on hand, substitute 1 stalk, stem and all, for the dried leaves. Remove and discard stem before serving.

Once roast is in slow cooker, if possible, turn halfway through cooking.

Make Ahead

Complete Steps 1 and 3, using the fat from the pancetta to soften the vegetables. Use the olive oil when you brown the beef, adding more oil if necessary. Cover and refrigerate pancetta and vegetable mixture separately for up to 2 days. When you're ready to cook, complete the recipe.

1. In a skillet, heat 1 tbsp (15 mL) of the oil over medium-high heat. Add pancetta and cook, stirring, until browned, about 3 minutes. Using a slotted spoon, transfer to slow cooker stoneware.

2. Dredge beef in approximately ¼ cup (50 mL) of the flour. Add to pan and brown on all sides, about 8 minutes. Transfer to stoneware.

3. Reduce heat to medium. Add remaining tbsp (15 mL) of oil to pan. Add onions, carrots and celery and cook, stirring, until vegetables are tender, about 7 minutes. Add garlic, rosemary, bay leaves, cinnamon stick, salt and peppercorns and cook, stirring, for 1 minute. Stir in tomato paste. Add wine, bring to a boil, stirring and scraping up brown bits from bottom of pan. Cook, stirring, until slightly reduced and thickened, about 5 minutes.

4. Transfer to slow cooker stoneware. Cover and cook on Low for 8 to 10 hours or on High for 4 to 5 hours, until meat is very tender.

5. Transfer meat to a platter or cutting board, tent with foil and keep warm. Pour sauce into a saucepan. Bring to a boil over medium-high heat and cook until reduced slightly, about 5 minutes. Remove and discard bay leaves. Remove pan from heat. In a small bowl, combine butter and remaining flour. Mix well. Stir into sauce. Return to heat and cook, stirring, until sauce thickens, about 2 minutes. Season to taste with salt and pepper. Slice meat thickly, transfer to a warm platter and smother in sauce.

Mom's Sunday Pot Roast

It doesn't get much more traditional than this. It's the kind of pot roast I grew up with — with a simple but delicious beef gravy served over mounds of mashed potatoes (or if you prefer, cook the potatoes with the roast; see Variation, below). Unlike my mother I've included a bit of red wine to enrich the flavor, but if you prefer, make it with all beef stock and stir in some steak sauce for added flavor.

Serves 6 to 8

- Large (approx. 5 quart) slow cooker

2 tbsp	olive oil, divided	25 mL
1	beef pot roast, about 4 lbs (2 kg), patted dry	1
2	onions, thinly sliced on the vertical	2
2	carrots, peeled and diced	2
2	stalks celery, diced	2
4	cloves garlic, minced	4
1 tsp	each salt and cracked black peppercorns	5 mL
1 tsp	dried thyme leaves	5 mL
¼ cup	all-purpose flour	50 mL
1 tbsp	tomato paste	15 mL
1 cup	dry red wine (see Tips, right)	250 mL
1 cup	beef stock	250 mL
2 tbsp	steak sauce, optional (see Tips, right)	25 mL
¼ cup	finely chopped parsley	50 mL

1. In a skillet, heat 1 tbsp (15 mL) of the oil over medium-high heat. Add roast and brown on all sides, about 10 minutes. Transfer to slow cooker stoneware.

2. Add remaining tbsp (15 mL) of oil to pan. Add onions, carrots and celery and cook, stirring, until vegetables are softened, about 7 minutes. Add garlic, salt, peppercorns and thyme and cook, stirring, for 1 minute. Stir in flour and tomato paste and cook for 1 minute. Add wine, bring to a boil and boil (mixture will be very thick), scraping up brown bits from bottom of pan, for 2 minutes. Add stock and return to a boil.

3. Transfer to slow cooker stoneware. Cover and cook on Low for 8 to 10 hours or on High for 4 to 5 hours, until meat is very tender. Stir in steak sauce, if using. To serve, carve meat thinly and place on a platter. Cover with sauce and garnish with parsley.

Variation

To cook potatoes along with roast, peel and quarter 3 medium potatoes. Place them in a saucepan and cover with cold water. Bring to a boil and boil for 5 minutes. Drain and add to stoneware in Step 3, along with the vegetable mixture.

Tips

If you are halving this recipe, see Tips, page 166.

If you prefer, substitute an additional cup (250 mL) of beef stock for the red wine. Add all at once, bring to a boil and cook, stirring, until the sauce thickens.

To ensure robust flavor in the sauce, I recommend adding the steak sauce if you don't use red wine.

If sauce isn't thick enough for your taste, after roast has finished cooking, transfer it to a deep platter and keep warm. Transfer gravy to a saucepan and bring to a boil over medium-high heat. Reduce heat and simmer for 5 minutes to reduce slightly. Meanwhile, in a small bowl, combine 2 tbsp (25 mL) each softened butter and all-purpose flour. Whisk into sauce and simmer over low heat, stirring, until thickened, about 1 minute. Stir in steak sauce, if using.

Make Ahead

Complete Step 2. Cover and refrigerate for up to 2 days. When you're ready to cook, complete the recipe.

Entertaining
Worthy

Sunday Dinner Braciola

This dish, which is roulade Italian-style, is a traditional Sunday dinner in many Italian-American homes. It is often made with veal and sometimes the filling contains a hard-boiled egg. Pasta such as rigatoni is often an accompaniment, but my own favorite is hot buttered orzo, liberally laced with freshly ground black pepper. Sautéed spinach or rapini makes a perfect pairing, as does some robust red wine.

Tip

When I make this recipe, I have my butcher slice and pound the meat for me. This quantity gives me 3 large, thin slices, each of which I cut in half to make 6 servings.

Make Ahead

Complete Step 5. Cover and refrigerate for up to 2 days. When you're ready to cook, complete the recipe.

Serves 6

- Large (approx. 5 quart) slow cooker

Stuffing

½ cup	water or chicken stock	125 mL
2 cups	cubed (½ inch/1 cm) white country-style bread, crusts removed	500 mL
2	stalks celery, diced	2
2	cloves garlic, minced	2
½ cup	finely chopped parsley	125 mL
¼ cup	freshly grated Parmesan	50 mL
¼ cup	toasted pine nuts	50 mL
4 oz	provolone cheese, diced	125 g
Pinch	salt	Pinch

Braciola

2 lbs	top or bottom round roast (see Tip, left)	1 kg
6	slices prosciutto (about 4 oz/125 g)	6
	Freshly ground black pepper	

Sauce

2 tbsp	olive oil, divided	25 mL
2	onions, finely chopped	2
1	carrot, peeled and diced	1
1	stalk celery, diced	1
2	cloves garlic, minced	2
1 tsp	salt	5 mL
½ tsp	cracked black peppercorns	2 mL
2	bay leaves	2
½ cup	dry white wine	125 mL
1	can (28 oz/796 mL) tomatoes with juice, coarsely chopped (see Tips, page 172)	1

1. **Stuffing:** In a bowl, combine water and bread. Stir well so bread absorbs all the liquid. Squeeze out excess liquid from the bread and discard. Return bread to bowl. Add celery, garlic, parsley, Parmesan, pine nuts, provolone and salt. Mix well and set aside.

2. **Braciola:** Using a sharp knife, cut beef on the horizontal into thin slices (about $1/2$ inch/1 cm thick), then pound with a mallet to about $1/4$ inch (0.5 cm) thick. Cut pieces in half. Cut prosciutto to match. Finely chop trimmings and stir into stuffing.

3. On a work surface, place 1 slice of pounded beef. Lay a slice of prosciutto on top and spread with about $1/4$ cup (50 mL) of the stuffing, leaving a narrow border. Season with pepper to taste. Starting at the narrow end, roll up, then fold over the ends to make a package. Tie around the middle and over the ends with butcher's twine. (If you have gaps, use a small skewer or a second piece of string to close them.) Repeat until all meat and stuffing are used up.

4. In a skillet, heat 1 tbsp (15 mL) of the oil over medium-high heat. Add braciola, in batches, and brown on all sides, about 5 minutes per batch. Transfer to slow cooker stoneware as browned.

5. **Sauce:** Reduce heat to medium. Add remaining tbsp (15 mL) of oil to pan. Add onions, carrot and celery and cook, stirring, until softened. Add garlic, salt, peppercorns and bay leaves and stir well. Add wine, bring to a boil and boil, stirring and scraping up brown bits from bottom of pan, for 2 minutes. Stir in tomatoes with juice and bring to a boil.

6. Transfer to slow cooker stoneware. Cover and cook on Low for 6 to 8 hours or on High for 3 to 4 hours, until beef is tender. Remove and discard bay leaves.

Can Be
Halved
see Tips, below

David's Dream Cholent

Thanks to our friend David Saffir, who passed along his family's treasured cholent recipes. From them I pieced together this version of a Sabbath dish traditionally made by observant Jews. My version is more liquidy than many, but I still serve it with the conventional condiments: horseradish, dill pickles and good mustard.

Serves 10 to 12

- Large (minimum 5 quart) slow cooker

½ cup	dried red kidney beans, soaked and drained	125 mL
½ cup	dried white navy or kidney beans, soaked and drained	125 mL
4 to 5 lbs	double beef brisket, trimmed (see Tips, page 184)	2 to 2.5 kg
2	bone-in English-style short ribs (about 8 oz/250 g)	2
1 tbsp	olive oil	15 mL
2	large potatoes, peeled and cut into ½-inch (1 cm) cubes	2
3	onions, finely chopped	3
4	carrots, peeled and diced	4
6	cloves garlic, minced	6
2 tsp	dried thyme leaves	10 mL
2 tsp	each salt and cracked black peppercorns	10 mL
2 cups	shredded peeled celery root (see Tips, left)	500 mL
½ cup	barley (see Tips, left)	125 mL
4 cups	beef stock, divided	1 L
	Horseradish	
	Dill pickles	
	Dijon or grainy mustard	

1. Pat brisket and short ribs dry. In a large skillet, heat oil over medium-high heat. Add brisket, fat side down, and brown, turning once, about 6 minutes. Transfer to slow cooker stoneware. Add short ribs and cook, turning, until well browned, about 6 minutes. Transfer to stoneware. Add potatoes to skillet, in batches, and cook, stirring, until lightly browned, about 4 minutes. Transfer to stoneware as completed. Drain off all but 2 tbsp (25 mL) of fat.

2. Reduce heat to medium. Add onions and carrots and cook, stirring, until softened, about 7 minutes. Add garlic, thyme, salt and peppercorns and cook, stirring and scraping up brown bits from bottom of pan, for 1 minute. Add celery root and barley and toss to coat. Add beans and 2 cups (500 mL) of the stock and bring to a boil, stirring and scraping up brown bits from pan. Boil for 1 minute.

3. Transfer to stoneware. Add remaining stock and water barely to cover. Cover and cook on Low for 8 to 10 hours or on High for 4 to 5 hours, until meat and beans are very tender. Serve with horseradish, pickles and mustard.

Tips

If you are halving this recipe, be sure to use a small (2½ to 3½ quart) slow cooker.

Celery root is actually a type of celery with crispy white flesh and a pleasing peppery flavor. Since it oxidizes quickly on contact with air, be sure to use it as soon as it is shredded or toss with 1 tbsp (15 mL) lemon juice and water to prevent discoloration. It is usually available in fall and winter. If you can't find it, substitute 6 stalks of diced celery instead. If using celery, soften it in oil along with the carrots and onions.

Use pearled, pot or whole barley in this recipe — whichever you prefer. Whole (also known as hulled) is the most nutritious form of the grain.

Make Ahead

Complete Step 2, adding 1 tbsp (15 mL) oil to pan before softening vegetables. Cover and refrigerate mixture for up to 2 days. When you're ready to cook, complete the recipe.

Corned Beef and Cabbage

Piping hot from the slow cooker, there is nothing quite as succulent as juicy corned beef accompanied by your favorite mustard. Just thinking about it makes my mouth water. Most cooks agree that it is best to cook the vegetables separately to preserve their flavor. I prefer rösti or mashed potatoes, but plain boiled ones tossed in butter and plenty of finely chopped parsley work well, too. Add your favorite veggies, choosing from hot cooked beets, turnips, parsnips and/or carrots.

Can Be
Halved
see Tips, below

Serves 8 to 10

- Large (approx. 5 quart) slow cooker

1	corned beef (about 4 lbs/2 kg)	1
1	small head cabbage, shredded	1
	Apple cider vinegar	
	Butter	
	Salt and freshly ground black pepper	
	Horseradish	
	Mustard	

1. Place beef in slow cooker stoneware. Add water to cover. Cover and cook on Low for 6 to 8 hours or on High for 3 to 4 hours, until the meat can be easily penetrated with a fork. (You don't want it to fall apart, which means it's overcooked.)

2. Fifteen minutes before the meat has finished cooking, bring a large pot of salted water to a boil. Add cabbage, return to a boil and cook until tender to the bite, about 5 minutes. Drain. Toss with vinegar, butter and salt and pepper to taste.

3. To serve, slice the meat and place on a warm platter surrounded by cabbage and the vegetables of your choice. Pass horseradish and/or mustard at the table.

Tips

If you are halving this recipe, be sure to use a small (2 to 3$\frac{1}{2}$ quart) slow cooker. Reduce cooking time to 3 to 4 hours on Low or 1$\frac{1}{2}$ to 2 hours on High.

Be aware that these cooking times are general estimates. Not only do cooking times vary substantially among slow cookers (see Cooking Times, page 12), but people have different preferences with regard to how well they like their meat done. If you prefer fork-tender results, start checking after the food has cooked for 6 hours on Low.

Braised Beef Niçoise

*If you're feeling the need for some robust winter fare, try this hearty
stew. I like to serve it over hot orzo tossed with Parmesan and butter
or extra virgin olive oil, but garlic mashed potatoes or even egg
noodles work well, too.*

Tips

If you are halving this
recipe, be sure to use a
small (2 to 3½ quart)
slow cooker.

To prepare fennel, chop
off top shoots (which
resemble celery) and
discard. If desired, save
feathery green fronds to
use as a garnish. If the
outer sections of fennel
bulb seem old and dry,
peel them with a vegetable
peeler before using.

I like to use Italian San
Marzano tomatoes, which
are very rich. If you're
using domestic tomatoes,
you may want to add
1 tbsp (15 mL) or so of
tomato paste.

I like to use parchment
paper when cooking this
dish because the recipe
doesn't contain a lot of
liquid. The parchment
helps prevent any pieces
of meat not completely
covered by liquid from
oxidizing, in addition
to ensuring that the
vegetables and meat are
well basted in their own
juices.

Make Ahead

Complete Step 2. Cover
and refrigerate for up to
2 days. When you're ready
to cook, complete recipe.

Serves 6 to 8

- Medium to large (3½ to 5 quart) slow cooker
- Parchment paper

2 tbsp	olive oil, divided	25 mL
2 lbs	trimmed stewing beef, cut into 1-inch (2.5 cm) cubes, and patted dry	1 kg
2	onions, finely chopped	2
2	carrots, peeled and diced	2
1	bulb fennel, cored and thinly sliced on the vertical (see Tips, left)	1
4	cloves garlic, minced	4
1 tsp	dried thyme leaves, or 1 sprig fresh thyme, including stem	5 mL
1 tsp	salt	5 mL
1 tsp	cracked black peppercorns	5 mL
2	bay leaves	2
2 tbsp	red wine vinegar	25 mL
1 cup	dry red wine	250 mL
1	can (28 oz/796 mL) tomatoes with juice (see Tips, left)	1
½ cup	pitted black olives, chopped	125 mL
¼ cup	finely chopped parsley	50 mL

1. In a skillet, heat 1 tbsp (15 mL) of oil over medium-high heat. Add beef, in batches, and cook, stirring, until lightly browned on all sides, about 4 minutes per batch. Transfer to slow cooker stoneware as completed.

2. Reduce heat to medium. Add remaining tbsp (15 mL) of oil to pan. Add onions, carrots and fennel and cook, stirring, until softened, about 7 minutes. Add garlic, thyme, salt, peppercorns and bay leaves and cook, stirring, for 1 minute. Add vinegar and wine, bring to a boil and boil, scraping up brown bits from bottom of pan, for 2 minutes. Stir in tomatoes with juice.

3. Transfer to slow cooker stoneware. Place a large piece of parchment paper over the mixture, pressing it down to brush the food and extending up the sides of the stoneware so it overlaps the rim. Cover and cook on Low for 8 hours or on High for 4 hours, until beef is very tender. Lift out and discard parchment, being careful not to spill the accumulated liquid into the stoneware. Remove and discard bay leaves. Garnish with olives, parsley and fennel fronds, if desired (see Tips, left).

Beer-Braised Beef with Collard Greens

There is something very homey and appealing about this dish, which dresses up a classic beer stew with collard greens and a pleasant hit of cayenne. I like to serve this over hot orzo tossed with butter.

Can Be Halved
see Tips, below

Tips

If you are halving this recipe, be sure to use a small (approx. 1½ to 3 quart) slow cooker.

To cut collard greens into a chiffonade, remove any tough veins toward the bottom of the leaves and up the center of the lower portion of the leaf. Stack about 6 in a pile. Roll them up like a cigar, then slice as thinly as you can. Repeat until all the greens are sliced.

Make Ahead

Complete Steps 1 and 3, adding 1 tbsp (15 mL) all-purpose flour where reserved flour is called for. Cover and refrigerate pancetta and onion mixture separately for up to 2 days. When you're ready to cook, continue with the recipe, discarding any excess flour after dredging the beef.

Serves 6

• Large (approx. 5 quart) slow cooker

1 tbsp	olive oil (approx.)	15 mL
4 oz	chunk pancetta or bacon, diced	125 g
2 lbs	stewing beef, cut into 1-inch (2.5 cm) cubes	1 kg
¼ cup	all-purpose flour	50 mL
3	onions, thinly sliced on the vertical	3
2 tbsp	packed brown sugar	25 mL
4	cloves garlic, minced	4
1 tsp	salt	5 mL
1 tsp	cracked black peppercorns	5 mL
4	bay leaves	4
1 tbsp	Dijon mustard	15 mL
2 cups	flat beer	500 mL
1 tbsp	cider vinegar	15 mL
¼ tsp	cayenne pepper	1 mL
4 cups	thinly sliced (chiffonade) stemmed collard greens (about 1 bunch) (see Tips, left)	1 L

1. In a skillet, heat oil over medium-high heat. Add pancetta and cook, stirring, until browned, about 4 minutes. Using a slotted spoon, transfer to slow cooker stoneware.

2. On a plate or in a plastic bag, dredge beef in flour until lightly dusted. Set excess flour aside. Add beef to skillet, in batches, adding more oil as necessary, and cook, stirring, until lightly browned on all sides, about 4 minutes per batch. Transfer to stoneware as completed.

3. Add onions to pan, adding more oil if necessary, and cook, stirring, until they begin to turn golden, about 7 minutes. Add brown sugar and cook for 1 minute. Add garlic, salt, peppercorns and bay leaves and cook, stirring, for 1 minute. Stir in mustard. Add reserved flour and stir well. Add beer and bring to a boil. Cook, stirring and scraping up brown bits from bottom of pan, until slightly thickened, about 2 minutes.

4. Transfer to slow cooker stoneware. Cover and cook on Low for 8 to 10 hours or on High for 4 to 5 hours, until beef is very tender. In a small bowl, combine vinegar and cayenne, stirring until pepper dissolves. Add to stoneware and stir well. Add collard greens, in batches, completely submerging each batch in the liquid before adding another. Cover and cook on High for 30 minutes, until collards are tender. Remove and discard bay leaves.

Beer-Braised Beef with Mushrooms and Caramelized Onions

This flavorful stew is meaty, zesty and delicious. I like to serve it over a mound of steaming garlic mashed potatoes, but hot orzo or noodles work well, too. Carrots or green beans make a perfect accompaniment.

Can Be Halved
see Tips, below

Serves 6

- Medium to large (3½ to 5 quart) slow cooker

4 oz	chunk bacon, diced	125 g
2 lbs	trimmed stewing beef, cut into 1-inch (2.5 cm) cubes, and patted dry	1 kg
¼ cup	all-purpose flour	50 mL
4	onions, thinly sliced on the vertical	4
1 tbsp	packed brown sugar	15 mL
6	cloves garlic, finely chopped	6
2 tbsp	minced gingerroot	25 mL
1 tsp	salt	5 mL
1 tsp	cracked black peppercorns	5 mL
2	bay leaves	2
¼ cup	tomato paste	50 mL
8 oz	mushrooms, trimmed and quartered	250 g
2 cups	flat dark beer	500 mL

1. In a large skillet over medium-high heat, cook bacon until crisp. Using a slotted spoon, transfer to paper towel to drain. Drain off all but 1 tbsp (15 mL) of fat from pan, reserving remainder.

2. On a plate or in a plastic bag, dredge beef in flour until evenly coated. Add beef to skillet, in batches, and cook, stirring, until lightly browned on all sides, about 4 minutes per batch, adding bacon fat as necessary. Transfer to slow cooker stoneware as completed. Discard excess flour.

3. Reduce heat to medium. Add onions and cook, stirring, until softened, about 3 minutes. Add brown sugar and continue to cook and stir until onions caramelize, about 10 minutes. Add garlic, ginger, salt, peppercorns and bay leaves and cook, stirring, for 1 minute. Stir in tomato paste, then mushrooms, tossing until mushrooms are well coated with mixture. Add beer and bring to a boil, stirring and scraping up brown bits from bottom of pan, until slightly thickened, about 2 minutes.

4. Transfer to slow cooker stoneware. Add reserved bacon and stir well. Cover and cook on Low for 8 hours or on High for 4 hours, until beef is very tender. Remove and discard bay leaves.

Tips

If you are halving this recipe, be sure to use a small (approx. 1½ to 3 quart) slow cooker.

Be aware that these cooking times are general estimates. Not only do cooking times vary substantially among slow cookers (see Cooking Times, page 12), but people have different preferences with regard to how well they like their meat done. If you prefer fork-tender results, start checking after the food has cooked for 6 hours on Low.

Make Ahead

Complete Step 3, adding 1 tbsp (15 mL) olive oil to pan before softening vegetables. Cover and refrigerate mixture for up to 2 days. When you're ready to cook, complete the recipe.

Entertaining Worthy

Can Be Halved
see Tips, below

Braised Beef with Crusty Potatoes

This sumptuous combination, which reminds me of an uptown version of shepherd's pie, is home cooking at its best. In fact, it's so good I serve it to guests for an informal Friday night meal. Just add salad and some robust red wine.

Tips

If you are halving this recipe, be sure to use a small (2 to 3½ quart) slow cooker.

If you prefer, substitute 1 cup (250 mL) water for the wine. To ensure your sauce doesn't lack robustness, stir in 1 tbsp (15 mL) steak or Worcestershire sauce just before adding the potatoes.

Use the quantity of horseradish that suits your taste. The smaller amount produces a very mild horseradish flavor.

Make Ahead

Complete Steps 1 through 4. Cover and refrigerate beef stew for up to 2 days. When you're ready to cook, preheat oven to 350°F (180°C). Transfer beef to baking dish, cover with foil and bake until hot and bubbly, about 30 minutes. Remove from oven and continue with Step 5.

Serves 6

- 13- by 9-inch (3 L) baking dish, optional
- Medium to large (3½ to 5 quart) slow cooker

2 lbs	trimmed stewing beef, cut into 1-inch (2.5 cm) cubes, and patted dry	1 kg
¼ cup	all-purpose flour	50 mL
2 tbsp	olive oil (approx.)	25 mL
1 cup	thinly sliced shallots	250 mL
2	stalks celery, diced	2
2	carrots, peeled and diced	2
2	cloves garlic, minced	2
1 tsp	dried thyme leaves	5 mL
1 tsp	salt	5 mL
1 tsp	cracked black peppercorns	5 mL
2	bay leaves	2
8 oz	mushrooms, trimmed and sliced	250 g
1 cup	dry red wine (see Tips, left)	250 mL
1 cup	beef stock	250 mL
3	potatoes, peeled and thinly sliced	3
¾ cup	sour cream or crème fraîche	175 mL
1 to 2 tbsp	prepared horseradish (see Tips, left)	15 to 25 mL
1 tsp	Dijon mustard	5 mL
	Salt and freshly ground black pepper, optional	

1. On a plate or in a plastic bag, dredge beef in flour until lightly dusted. Set any excess flour aside.

2. In a skillet, heat oil over medium-high heat. Add beef, in batches, and cook, stirring, until lightly browned on all sides, adding more oil as necessary, about 4 minutes per batch. Transfer to slow cooker stoneware as completed.

3. Reduce heat to medium. Add shallots, celery and carrots to pan and cook, stirring, until vegetables are softened, about 7 minutes. Add garlic, thyme, salt, peppercorns and bay leaves and cook, stirring, for 1 minute. Add mushrooms and toss until coated. Sprinkle with reserved flour and stir well. Add wine, bring to a boil and cook, stirring and scraping up brown bits from bottom of pan, for 2 minutes. Add stock and bring to a boil.

4. Transfer to slow cooker stoneware. Cover and cook on Low for 8 hours or on High for 4 hours, until beef is very tender. Remove and discard bay leaves.

5. Preheat broiler. Meanwhile, in a large saucepan, cook potatoes until just tender. Drain and return to saucepan. In a small bowl, whisk together sour cream, horseradish and mustard. Add to potatoes and toss until well coated. Season to taste with salt and pepper, if using. Using your fingers, layer potatoes over beef mixture to form a crust (see Tip, right). If there is any additional horseradish mixture, pour it over the top. Place under broiler until potatoes are nicely browned, about 5 minutes. Serve immediately.

Tip

If your slow cooker insert is ovenproof (most are) you can place the potato layer directly over the beef in the stoneware and bake it in the oven. Otherwise, transfer beef to a baking dish before adding the potatoes.

Can Be Halved
see Tips, below

Beef with Beets and Horseradish Cream

While not a traditional combination, beef cooked with beets and topped with horseradish cream makes for a hearty and delicious change. I like to serve this in a tower, with a base of mashed potatoes topped with the beef mixture and finished with a good dollop of horseradish cream.

Tips

If you are halving this recipe, be sure to use a small (2 to 3½ quart) slow cooker.

Be aware that these cooking times are general estimates. Not only do cooking times vary substantially among slow cookers (see Cooking Times, page 12), but people have different preferences with regard to how well they like their meat done. If you prefer fork-tender results, start checking after the food has cooked for 6 hours on Low.

Make Ahead

Complete Step 2, heating 1 tbsp (15 mL) oil in pan before softening vegetables. Cover and refrigerate mixture for up to 2 days. When you're ready to cook, continue with the recipe.

Serves 6

- Cheesecloth
- Medium to large (3½ to 5 quart) slow cooker

1 tbsp	olive oil	15 mL
2 lbs	trimmed stewing beef, cut into 1-inch (2.5 cm) cubes, and patted dry	1 kg
2	onions, finely chopped	2
2	stalks celery, diced	2
4	cloves garlic minced	4
1 tsp	salt	5 mL
½ tsp	cracked black peppercorns	2 mL
1	bay leaf	1
8	whole allspice	8
4	whole cloves	4
1 cup	dry red wine	250 mL
3 cups	beef stock	750 mL
1 tbsp	red wine vinegar	15 mL
1 tbsp	packed brown sugar	15 mL
4	medium beets, peeled and cut into ½-inch (1 cm) cubes	4
½ cup	crème fraîche or sour cream	125 mL
2 tbsp	prepared horseradish	25 mL

1. In a skillet, heat oil over medium-high heat. Add beef, in batches, and cook, stirring, until lightly browned on all sides, about 4 minutes per batch. Transfer to slow cooker stoneware as completed.

2. Reduce heat to medium. Add onions and celery to pan and cook, stirring, until softened, about 5 minutes. Add garlic, salt, peppercorns and bay leaf and cook, stirring, for 1 minute. Tie allspice and cloves in a piece of cheesecloth, creating a spice bag, and add to pan. Add wine, bring to a boil and boil for 2 minutes. Add stock, vinegar and brown sugar and return to a boil.

3. Transfer to slow cooker stoneware. Stir in beets. Cover and cook on Low for 8 hours or on High for 4 hours, until beets and beef are tender. Remove and discard bay leaf, allspice and cloves.

4. In a small bowl, combine crème fraîche and horseradish. Stir well. Serve with beef.

Zesty Braised Beef with New Potatoes

It's hard to believe that this simple combination of ingredients can taste so luscious. I like to serve this with a big platter of roasted carrots. Save leftovers and enjoy in a bowl like a hearty soup.

Serves 6

- Medium to large (3½ to 5 quart) slow cooker

2 tbsp	olive oil, divided	25 mL
2 oz	chunk pancetta, preferably hot pancetta, diced	60 g
2 lbs	trimmed stewing beef, cut into 1-inch (2.5 cm) cubes and patted dry	1 kg
2	onions, finely chopped	2
4	cloves garlic, minced	4
1 tsp	dried thyme leaves	5 mL
1 tsp	salt	5 mL
1 tsp	cracked black peppercorns	5 mL
½ cup	dry white wine (see Tips, page 203)	125 mL
2 cups	chicken stock	500 mL
2 lbs	small new potatoes, scrubbed and thinly sliced (about 30 tiny ones)	1 kg
¼ tsp	cayenne pepper, dissolved in 1 tbsp (15 mL) freshly squeezed lemon juice	1 mL
1 tbsp	all-purpose flour	15 mL
1 tbsp	softened butter	15 mL
	Finely chopped parsley	

1. In a skillet, heat 1 tbsp (15 mL) of the oil over medium-high heat. Add pancetta and cook, stirring, until nicely browned, about 3 minutes. Transfer to slow cooker stoneware.

2. Add beef to skillet, in batches, and cook, stirring, until browned, about 4 minutes per batch. Transfer to stoneware as completed.

3. Reduce heat to medium. Add remaining tbsp (15 mL) of oil to pan. Add onions and cook, stirring, until softened, about 3 minutes. Add garlic, thyme, salt and peppercorns and cook, stirring, for 1 minute. Add wine, bring to a boil and boil, stirring and scraping up brown bits from bottom of pan, for 2 minutes. Add stock and potatoes and bring to a boil. Simmer for 2 minutes.

4. Transfer to stoneware. Cover and cook on Low for 8 hours or on High for 4 hours, until potatoes are tender. Stir in cayenne solution. Cover and cook on High for 10 minutes.

5. Meanwhile, in a small bowl, using a fork, mix flour and butter into a smooth paste. Add to stoneware and stir until sauce thickens slightly, about 1 minute. Transfer to a serving dish and garnish with parsley.

Can Be Halved
see Tips, below

Tips

If you are halving this recipe, be sure to use a small (2 to 3½ quart) slow cooker.

Because it's important to bring the potatoes to a boil in order to ensure they cook in the slow cooker, I do not recommend making part of this dish ahead of time.

Wine-Soaked Beef Bourguignon

I've been enjoying variations of this dish ever since I was a dewy-eyed student wandering through Paris on my first trip to Europe. It's a classic because it's uniquely delicious and, with the help of your slow cooker, it's quite easy to make. You can marinate the meat up to two days ahead of time and, if you prefer, cook the stew overnight. Refrigerating it over the course of a day allows you to spoon off the accumulated fat; it reheats beautifully in the oven (350°F/180°C), covered, in about 30 minutes. Or cook it over the course of a Sunday and enjoy it for a special family meal. I like to serve this with hot orzo tossed in butter, but plain noodles or mashed potatoes work well, too.

Tips

If you are halving this recipe, be sure to use a small (2 to 3½ quart) slow cooker.

While regular white mushrooms work fine in this recipe, I prefer the more robust flavor of cremini.

My family enjoys the flavor of this sauce as is, but some people are particularly sensitive to the alcohol in wine. If that is the case, I recommend boiling off the alcohol before adding the wine to the slow cooker. After you drain the marinade, transfer wine to a saucepan and cook over medium-high heat until it is reduced to about 2 cups (500 mL), about 15 minutes. (You can do this while you're browning the meat and softening the vegetables.) Continue with the recipe, adding 1 cup (250 mL) good beef stock to the skillet along with the reduced wine.

Serves 6

- Cheesecloth
- Large (approx. 5 quart) slow cooker

2	sprigs parsley	2
2	sprigs thyme	2
2	bay leaves	2
5	whole peppercorns	5
5	whole cloves	5
2	cloves garlic, sliced	2
2 lbs	stewing beef, cut into 1-inch (2.5 cm) cubes	1 kg
2	onions, thinly sliced	2
1 tbsp	cognac or plain brandy, optional	15 mL
1	bottle (24 oz/750 mL) dry red wine (see Tips, left)	1
2 oz	chunk bacon, diced	60 g
2	carrots, peeled and diced	2
4	stalks celery, diced	4
12 oz	mushrooms, trimmed and quartered (see Tips, left)	375 g
¼ cup	all-purpose flour	50 mL
1 tbsp	tomato paste	15 mL
1 tsp	salt	5 mL
	Finely chopped parsley	

1. In a square of cheesecloth, tie parsley, thyme, bay leaves, peppercorns, cloves and garlic into a bouquet garni. Place in a large ceramic bowl. Add beef, onions, cognac and wine. Stir to combine, ensuring all or most of the vegetables and meat are submerged in the liquid. (If you are a tad short of liquid, make sure onions are on top.) Cover and refrigerate overnight or for up to 2 days. Drain, reserving onions, meat and liquid separately. Place bouquet garni in slow cooker stoneware. Pat meat dry with paper towel.

2. In a skillet over medium-high heat, cook bacon until browned and crisp, about 3 minutes. Using a slotted spoon, transfer to paper towel to drain. Drain all but 2 tbsp (25 mL) of fat from the pan. (If you don't have enough fat, add olive oil to make up the difference.)

3. Add beef, in batches, and cook, stirring, until lightly browned on all sides, about 4 minutes per batch. Transfer to slow cooker stoneware.

4. Reduce heat to medium. Add drained onions, carrots and celery to pan and cook, stirring, until softened, about 7 minutes. Add mushrooms and toss to coat. Add flour and cook, stirring, for 1 minute. Stir in tomato paste and reserved wine from marinade and cook, stirring, until mixture thickens, about 5 minutes. Stir in salt and transfer to slow cooker stoneware.

5. Cover and cook on Low for 8 hours or on High for 4 to 5 hours, until meat is melt-in-your-mouth tender. Remove and discard bouquet garni. Garnish liberally with parsley before serving.

Tip

Be aware that these cooking times are general estimates. Not only do cooking times vary substantially among slow cookers (see Cooking Times, page 12), but people have different preferences with regard to how well they like their meat done. If you prefer fork-tender results, start checking after the food has cooked for 6 hours on Low.

Entertaining Worthy

Can Be Halved
see Tips, below

Carbonnade Flamande

If you're in the mood for Euro-style eating, try this beer-braised Belgian stew — it's quintessential bistro fare. Serve it over hot buttered noodles with robust red wine or a good beer, depending on your mood.

Serves 6 to 8

- Medium to large (3½ to 5 quart) slow cooker

1 tbsp	olive oil (approx.)	15 mL
4 oz	chunk bacon, diced	125 g
2 lbs	trimmed stewing beef, cut into 1-inch (2.5 cm) cubes, and patted dry	1 kg
½ cup	all-purpose flour	125 mL
3	onions, thinly sliced on the vertical	3
3	carrots, peeled and sliced	3
1 tbsp	packed brown sugar	15 mL
1 tsp	dried thyme leaves	5 mL
1 tsp	salt	5 mL
1 tsp	cracked black peppercorns	5 mL
2	bay leaves	2
4	whole cloves	4
1½ cups	flat brown beer	375 mL
1 cup	beef stock	250 mL

1. In a skillet, heat oil over medium-high heat. Add bacon and brown well. Transfer to slow cooker stoneware.

2. On a plate or in a plastic bag, dredge beef in flour until evenly coated. Set excess flour aside. Add beef to skillet, in batches, and cook, stirring, until lightly browned on all sides, about 4 minutes per batch, adding more oil if necessary. Transfer to slow cooker stoneware as completed.

3. Reduce heat to medium. Add onions and carrots to pan and cook, stirring, until softened, about 7 minutes. Stir in brown sugar. Add thyme, salt, peppercorns, bay leaves and cloves and cook, stirring, for 1 minute. Sprinkle reserved flour over top and cook, stirring, for 1 minute. Add beer and stock, bring to a boil and cook, stirring and scraping up brown bits from bottom of pan, until slightly thickened, about 2 minutes.

4. Transfer to slow cooker stoneware. Stir well. Cover and cook on Low for 8 hours or on High for 4 hours, until beef is very tender. Remove and discard bay leaves.

Tips

If you are halving this recipe, be sure to use a small (approx. 1½ to 3 quart) slow cooker.

Be aware that these cooking times are general estimates. Not only do cooking times vary substantially among slow cookers (see Cooking Times, page 12), but people have different preferences with regard to how well they like their meat done. If you prefer fork-tender results, start checking after the food has cooked for 6 hours on Low.

Make Ahead

Complete Steps 1 and 3, sprinkling mixture with 2 tbsp (25 mL) flour where it calls for reserved flour. Cover and refrigerate bacon and vegetable mixtures separately for up to 2 days. When you're ready to cook, continue with the recipe, discarding the excess flour after dredging the beef.

Onion-Braised Brisket

Impress your friends with this easy-to-make yet absolutely delicious brisket. My next-door neighbor, who was invited in for a tasting, described it as "ambrosial." When it's served alongside steaming garlic mashed potatoes, he's not far wrong.

Entertaining Worthy

Can Be Halved
see Tips, below

Serves 8

- Large (approx. 5 quart) slow cooker

2 tbsp	olive oil, divided	25 mL
4 to 5 lbs	double beef brisket, trimmed (see Tip, page 184)	2 to 2.5 kg
4	onions, thinly sliced on the vertical	4
6	cloves garlic, minced	6
1 tsp	salt	5 mL
1 tsp	cracked black peppercorns	5 mL
1 tsp	dried thyme leaves	5 mL
2 tbsp	red wine vinegar	25 mL
1 tbsp	Dijon mustard	15 mL
1 cup	dry red wine	250 mL
¼ cup	tomato-based chili sauce	50 mL
2 tbsp	tomato paste	25 mL
1 cup	beef stock	250 mL
2 tbsp	cornstarch dissolved in ¼ cup (50 mL) water	25 mL
½ cup	finely chopped parsley	125 mL

1. In a skillet, heat 1 tbsp (15 mL) of the oil over medium-high heat. Add brisket and brown well on both sides, about 6 minutes. Transfer to slow cooker stoneware.

2. Add remaining tbsp (15 mL) of oil to stoneware. Add onions and cook, stirring, until they begin to turn golden, about 5 minutes. Add garlic, salt, peppercorns and thyme and cook, stirring, for 1 minute. Add vinegar, mustard and wine and bring to a boil. Cook, stirring and scraping up brown bits from bottom of pan, for 2 minutes. Stir in chili sauce, tomato paste and stock.

3. Transfer to slow cooker stoneware. Cover and cook on Low for 8 to 10 hours or on High for 4 to 5 hours, until brisket is very tender.

4. Transfer meat to a deep platter, slice and keep warm. Transfer sauce to a saucepan and bring to a boil. Reduce heat and simmer for 5 minutes to slightly reduce. Remove from heat and add cornstarch solution, stirring until sauce thickens. Pour over meat and garnish with parsley.

Tips

If you are halving this recipe, be sure to use a small (2½ to 3½ quart) slow cooker. Reduce cooking time to about 6 hours on Low or 3 hours on High.

Be aware that these cooking times are general estimates. Not only do cooking times vary substantially among slow cookers (see Cooking Times, page 12), but people have different preferences with regard to how well they like their meat done. If you prefer fork-tender results, start checking after the food has cooked for 6 hours on Low.

Make Ahead

Complete Step 2. Cover and refrigerate mixture for up to 2 days. When you're ready to cook, complete the recipe.

Can Be Halved
see Tips, below

Hot 'n' Smoky Brisket Splashed with Whiskey

If you're looking for a beef dish that has strong southwestern flavors but with a difference, this may be it. To maintain the mood, rice and beans is a perfect accompaniment.

Serves 6 to 8

Tips

If you are halving this recipe, be sure to use a small (2½ to 3½ quart) slow cooker. Reduce cooking time to about 6 hours on Low or 3 hours on High.

I like to make this using two chiles, which means it packs a lot of heat, but I have balanced that with sugar to provide sweetness and a hit of citrus in the finish.

If the whole piece of brisket won't fit in your slow cooker, cut it in half and lay the two pieces on top of each other.

For the best flavor, toast and grind the cumin and coriander seeds yourself. Place cumin and coriander seeds in a dry skillet over medium heat and cook, stirring, until fragrant and seeds just begin to brown, about 3 minutes. Using a mortar and pestle or a spice grinder, pound or grind as finely as you can.

Make Ahead

Complete Step 2. Cover and refrigerate mixture for up to 2 days. When you're ready to cook, complete the recipe.

- Large (approx. 5 quart) slow cooker

2 tbsp	olive oil, divided	25 mL
4 to 5 lbs	double beef brisket, trimmed (see Tips, left)	2 to 2.5 kg
2	onions, finely chopped	2
2	stalks celery, diced	2
2	carrots, peeled and diced	2
6	cloves garlic, minced	6
1	piece (2 inches/5 cm) cinnamon stick	1
2	bay leaves	2
2 tsp	finely grated lime zest (1 lime)	10 mL
1 tbsp	each cumin and coriander seeds, toasted and ground (see Tips, left)	15 mL
1½ tsp	salt	7 mL
1 tsp	cracked black peppercorns	5 mL
⅓ cup	whiskey	75 mL
2 tsp	packed brown sugar	10 mL
1½ cups	beef stock	375 mL
1 to 2	chipotle chiles in adobo sauce, minced	1 to 2
2 tbsp	cornstarch, dissolved in 3 tbsp (45 mL) lime juice	25 mL
1 cup	cilantro leaves	250 mL

1. In a skillet, heat 1 tbsp (15 mL) of the oil over medium-high heat. Add brisket and brown well, about 6 minutes. Transfer to stoneware.

2. Reduce heat to medium. Add remaining oil to pan. Add onions, celery and carrots and cook, stirring, until carrots have softened, about 7 minutes. Add garlic, cinnamon, bay leaves, lime zest, cumin and coriander seeds, salt and peppercorns and cook, stirring, for 1 minute. Add whiskey. Bring to a boil and boil, scraping up brown bits from pan, for 1 minute. Stir in brown sugar and stock.

3. Transfer to slow cooker stoneware. Cover and cook on Low for 8 to 10 hours or on High for 4 to 5 hours, until beef is very tender.

4. Transfer brisket to a cutting board and slice. Place in a serving dish or deep platter and keep warm. Transfer sauce to a saucepan. Bring to a boil over medium-high heat and boil rapidly for 5 minutes to reduce slightly. Remove from heat. Remove and discard bay leaves and stir in chipotle chiles. Add cornstarch solution and stir until thickened. Pour over brisket. Garnish with cilantro and serve.

Sherry-Braised Brisket with Saffron

The flavor combination of sherry, sherry vinegar and saffron is Spanish and, perhaps surprisingly, it works very well with brisket. If you have time, make a simple risotto as a side. If not, orzo tossed with extra virgin olive oil and plenty of freshly ground black pepper is also delicious. Invite some friends, open a bottle of good Rioja and add some steamed green beans. Olé!

Entertaining Worthy

Can Be Halved
see Tips, below

Serves 8

- Large (approx. 5 quart) slow cooker

2 tbsp	olive oil, divided	25 mL
4 lbs	double beef brisket, trimmed (see Tips, right)	2 kg
2	onions, finely chopped	2
2	carrots, peeled and diced	2
6	cloves garlic, minced	6
1 tsp	salt	5 mL
¼ tsp	cracked black peppercorns	1 mL
¼ tsp	saffron threads, crumbled	1 mL
2	bay leaves	2
1	piece (2 inches/5 cm) cinnamon stick	1
½ cup	dry sherry	125 mL
2 tbsp	sherry vinegar	25 mL
1 tbsp	packed brown sugar	15 mL
1	can (28 oz/796 mL) diced tomatoes with juice	1
1 cup	chicken stock	250 mL
1	potato, peeled and diced	1
1	green bell pepper, seeded and diced	1
2 tsp	paprika (see Tips, right)	10 mL

1. In a large skillet, heat 1 tbsp (15 mL) of the oil over medium-high heat. Add brisket and brown well on both sides, about 6 minutes. Transfer to slow cooker stoneware.

2. Reduce heat to medium. Add remaining tbsp (15 mL) of oil to pan. Add onions and carrots and cook, stirring, until carrots are softened, about 7 minutes. Add garlic, salt, peppercorns, saffron, bay leaves and cinnamon stick and cook, stirring, for 1 minute. Add sherry, sherry vinegar and brown sugar and bring to a boil. Boil, scraping up brown bits from bottom of pan, for 2 minutes. Stir in tomatoes with juice and stock and return to a boil.

3. Transfer to stoneware. Stir in potato. Cover and cook on Low for 8 to 10 hours or on High for 4 to 5 hours, until beef is very tender. Stir in bell pepper and paprika. Cover and cook on High about 20 minutes, until pepper is tender. Remove and discard bay leaves.

Tips

If you are halving this recipe, be sure to use a small (2½ to 3½ quart) slow cooker. Reduce cooking time to about 6 hours on Low or 3 hours on High.

If the whole piece of brisket won't fit in your slow cooker, cut it in half and lay the two pieces on top of each other.

Substitute hot or smoked paprika for the sweet to produce a different flavor profile.

If desired, after the meat has finished cooking, cover and refrigerate overnight or for up to 2 days. About half an hour before you are ready to serve, skim fat off sauce, slice meat, and place meat and sauce in a Dutch oven. Stir bell pepper and paprika into the sauce. Reheat on stovetop over medium-low heat until hot and bubbly. Serve immediately.

Make Ahead

Complete Step 2. Cover and refrigerate for up to 2 days. When you're ready to cook, complete the recipe.

Can Be Halved
see Tips, below

Braised Brisket with Chile Gravy

Brisket with Mexican overtones is a marriage made in heaven. I love to serve this over a mound of steaming brown rice and beans or in a tortilla. Add some cold lager for a perfect finish.

Serves 8

Tips

If you are halving this recipe, be sure to use a small (2½ to 3½ quart) slow cooker. Reduce cooking time to about 6 hours on Low or 3 hours on High.

Vary the quantity of chiles to suit your level of tolerance for heat. They are all on the mild end of the Scoville scale.

Many people feel that brisket improves in flavor if it is made ahead and reheated. If you prefer to follow this method, complete Steps 1 through 3. Cover and refrigerate overnight or for up to 2 days. Skim off accumulated fat, slice brisket and place in Dutch oven. Spoon off about 1 cup (250 mL) of the liquid and place in a blender. Add cilantro and chiles and purée. Add to Dutch oven along with remaining sauce. Reheat on stovetop over medium-low heat until hot and bubbly. Serve immediately.

Make Ahead

Complete Step 2. Cover and refrigerate for up to 2 days. When you're ready to cook, complete the recipe.

• Large (approx. 5 quart) slow cooker

2 tbsp	olive oil, divided	25 mL
4 to 5 lbs	double beef brisket, trimmed (see Tips, page 187)	2 to 2.5 kg
2	onions, thinly sliced on the vertical	2
4	stalks celery, diced	4
6	cloves garlic, minced	6
1 tbsp	ground cumin (see Tips, page 224)	15 mL
2 tsp	dried oregano leaves	10 mL
1	piece (2 inches/5 cm) cinnamon stick	1
1 tsp	salt	5 mL
1 tsp	cracked black peppercorns	5 mL
1	can (28 oz/796 mL) tomatoes with juice	1
1 cup	chicken stock	250 mL
3 to 4	dried ancho, New Mexico or guajillo chiles (see Tips, left)	3 to 4
2 cups	boiling water	500 mL
1 cup	cilantro, stems and leaves	250 mL
1	jalapeño pepper, seeded and diced, optional	1
1	green bell pepper, diced	1

1. In a large skillet, heat 1 tbsp (15 mL) of the oil over medium-high heat. Add brisket and brown well on both sides, about 6 minutes. Transfer to slow cooker stoneware.

2. Reduce heat to medium. Add remaining tbsp (15 mL) of oil to pan. Add onions and celery and cook, stirring, until softened, about 5 minutes. Add garlic, cumin, oregano, cinnamon stick, salt and peppercorns and cook, stirring, for 1 minute. Add tomatoes with juice and stock. Bring to a boil, stirring and scraping up brown bits from bottom of pan.

3. Transfer to slow cooker stoneware. Cover and cook on Low for 8 to 10 hours or on High for 4 to 5 hours, until beef is very tender.

4. About 1 hour before you are ready to serve, soak chiles in boiling water for 30 minutes, weighing down with a cup to ensure they remain submerged. Drain, discarding soaking liquid and stems. Transfer to a blender and add cilantro, jalapeño, if using, and approximately 1 cup (250 mL) of the brisket cooking liquid. Purée and add to slow cooker along with bell pepper. Cover and cook on High for 20 minutes, until pepper is tender.

Beer-Braised Brisket with Lentils

This is home cookin' at its best. Serve this for Sunday dinner or at an informal Friday night get-together with friends. Just add a green vegetable — steamed green beans and chopped spinach are fabulous accompaniments — and some robust red wine.

Entertaining Worthy

Can Be Halved
see Tips, below

Serves 6 to 8

- Large (approx. 5 quart) slow cooker

2 tbsp	olive oil, divided	25 mL
4 to 5 lbs	double beef brisket, trimmed (see Tips, right)	2 to 2.5 kg
2	onions, finely chopped	2
2	carrots, peeled and diced	2
2	stalks celery, diced	2
4	cloves garlic, minced	4
1 tsp	dried thyme leaves	5 mL
1 tsp	salt	5 mL
1 tsp	cracked black peppercorns	5 mL
2	bay leaves	2
1/4 cup	tomato paste	50 mL
2 tbsp	red wine vinegar	25 mL
2 tbsp	packed brown sugar	25 mL
2 cups	beef stock	500 mL
1 cup	green or brown lentils, rinsed	250 mL
2 cups	flat dark beer, such as Guinness	500 mL

1. In a large skillet, heat 1 tbsp (15 mL) of the oil over medium-high heat. Add brisket and brown well on both sides, about 6 minutes. Transfer to slow cooker stoneware.

2. Reduce heat to medium. Add remaining tbsp (15 mL) of oil to pan. Add onions, carrots and celery and cook, stirring, until carrots have softened, about 7 minutes. Add garlic, thyme, salt, peppercorns and bay leaves and cook, stirring, for 1 minute. Add tomato paste, vinegar and brown sugar and stir well. Add stock and bring to a boil, stirring and scraping up brown bits from bottom of pan.

3. Stir in lentils and beer. Transfer to slow cooker stoneware. Cover and cook on Low for 8 to 10 hours or on High for 4 to 5 hours, until beef is very tender. Remove and discard bay leaves.

Tips

If you are halving this recipe, be sure to use a small (2½ to 3½ quart) slow cooker. Reduce cooking time to about 6 hours on Low or 3 hours on High.

If the whole piece of brisket won't fit in your slow cooker, cut it in half and lay the two pieces on top of each other.

Be aware that these cooking times are general estimates. Not only do cooking times vary substantially among slow cookers (see Cooking Times, page 12), but people have different preferences with regard to how well they like their meat done. If you prefer fork-tender results, start checking after the food has cooked for 6 hours on Low.

Make Ahead

Complete Step 2. Cover and refrigerate mixture for up to 2 days. When you're ready to cook, complete the recipe.

Old-Fashioned Beef Stew with Mushrooms

It doesn't get any better than this family favorite. I serve it with plenty of garlic mashed potatoes to soak up the luscious sauce, imagining I'm 12 years old all over again . . . well, sort of, since my mom never put garlic in the potatoes.

Tips

If you are halving this recipe, be sure to use a small (2 to 3½ quart) slow cooker.

If you prefer, substitute an equal quantity of water or beef stock for the wine.

Be aware that these cooking times are general estimates. Not only do cooking times vary substantially among slow cookers (see Cooking Times, page 12), but people have different preferences with regard to how well they like their meat done. If you prefer fork-tender results, start checking after the food has cooked for 6 hours on Low.

Make Ahead

Complete Step 2. Cover and refrigerate for up to 2 days. When you're ready to cook, complete the recipe.

Serves 6

- Medium to large (3½ to 5 quart) slow cooker

2 lbs	trimmed stewing beef, cut into 1-inch (2.5 cm) cubes, and patted dry	1 kg
¼ cup	all-purpose flour	50 mL
2 tbsp	olive oil (approx.), divided	25 mL
2	onions, finely chopped	2
4	stalks celery, diced	4
2	large carrots, peeled and diced	2
4	cloves garlic, minced	4
1 tsp	dried thyme leaves	5 mL
2	bay leaves	2
1 tsp	salt	5 mL
1 tsp	cracked black peppercorns	5 mL
12 oz	cremini mushrooms, trimmed and sliced	375 g
½ cup	dry red wine (see Tips, left)	125 mL
2 cups	beef stock	500 mL
	Finely chopped parsley	

1. On a plate or in a plastic bag, dredge beef in flour until evenly coated. Set excess flour aside. In a skillet, heat 1 tbsp (15 mL) of the oil over medium-high heat. Add beef, in batches, and cook, stirring, until lightly browned on all sides, about 4 minutes per batch, adding more oil if necessary. Transfer to stoneware as completed.

2. Reduce heat to medium. Add remaining tbsp (15 mL) of oil to pan. Add onions, celery and carrots and cook, stirring, until carrots are softened, about 7 minutes. Add garlic, thyme, bay leaves, salt and peppercorns and cook, stirring, for 1 minute. Add reserved flour and cook, stirring, for 1 minute. Add mushrooms and toss until coated. Add wine, bring to a boil and cook, stirring and scraping up brown bits from pan, for 2 minutes. Stir in stock and bring to a boil.

3. Transfer to slow cooker stoneware. Cover and cook on Low for 8 hours or on High for 4 hours, until beef is very tender. Remove and discard bay leaves. Garnish liberally with parsley.

Can Be Halved
see Tips, below

Smothered Beef Stew

In this recipe I've tried to replicate a beef stew my mother used to make that was smothered in a slightly sweet-and-sour sauce. This is delicious served with a mound of steaming mashed potatoes or even rice. Add a vegetable such as green beans to complete the retro ambiance.

Serves 6

Tips

If you are halving this recipe, be sure to use a small (2 to 3½ quart) slow cooker.

If you're using cayenne, for best results, dissolve it in the Worcestershire sauce before adding to the slow cooker.

Be aware that these cooking times are general estimates. Not only do cooking times vary substantially among slow cookers (see Cooking Times, page 12), but people have different preferences with regard to how well they like their meat done. If you prefer fork-tender results, start checking after the food has cooked for 6 hours on Low.

Make Ahead

Complete Steps 1 and 3. Cover and refrigerate bacon and onion mixtures separately. When you're ready to brown the beef, add 2 tbsp (25 mL) oil to pan. Continue with recipe.

- Medium to large (3½ to 5 quart) slow cooker

4	slices bacon	4
2 lbs	trimmed stewing beef, cut into 1-inch (2.5 cm) cubes, and patted dry	1 kg
¼ cup	all-purpose flour	50 mL
2 tbsp	olive oil	25 mL
2	onions, finely chopped	2
4	cloves garlic, minced	4
1 tbsp	minced gingerroot	15 mL
2	bay leaves	2
2 tbsp	packed brown sugar	25 mL
2 tbsp	red wine vinegar	25 mL
¼ cup	tomato paste	50 mL
2 cups	beef stock	500 mL
1 tbsp	Worcestershire sauce	15 mL
¼ tsp	cayenne pepper, optional (see Tips, left)	1 mL
1	red bell pepper, seeded and diced	1

1. In a skillet over medium-high heat, sauté bacon until crisp. Using a slotted spoon, transfer to paper towel to drain. When cool, crumble. Cover and refrigerate until ready to use. Drain off all but 2 tbsp (25 mL) fat from pan.

2. On a plate or in a plastic bag, dredge beef in flour until evenly coated. Discard excess flour. Add beef to pan, in batches, and cook, stirring, until lightly browned on all sides, about 4 minutes per batch. Transfer to slow cooker stoneware as completed.

3. Reduce heat to medium. Add onions to pan and cook, stirring, until softened, about 3 minutes. Add garlic, ginger and bay leaves and cook, stirring, for 1 minute. Add brown sugar, vinegar, tomato paste and stock. Bring to a boil, scraping up brown bits from the bottom of the pan.

4. Transfer to slow cooker stoneware. Cover and cook on Low for 8 hours or on High for 4 hours, until beef is tender. Add Worcestershire sauce, cayenne, if using, bell pepper and reserved bacon. Cover and cook on High for 15 minutes, until pepper is tender. Remove and discard bay leaves.

Ancho-Spiked Red-Eye Beef with Mushrooms

Red-eye gravy, made with coffee, is an Old West favorite. Here it adds intriguing depth to a beef stew, highlighted by the addition of peppers ranging in intensity from sweet to hot. I like to serve this over a mound of steaming garlic mashed potatoes.

Serves 6

- Medium to large (3½ to 5 quart) slow cooker

2 tbsp	olive oil, divided	25 mL
4 oz	chunk bacon, diced	125 g
2 lbs	trimmed stewing beef, cut into 1-inch (2.5 cm) cubes, and patted dry	1 kg
¼ cup	all-purpose flour	50 mL
2	onions, finely chopped	2
4	stalks celery, diced	4
4	cloves garlic, minced	4
1 tsp	dried thyme leaves	5 mL
1 tsp	salt	5 mL
1 tsp	cracked black peppercorns	5 mL
2	bay leaves	2
2 cups	beef stock	500 mL
½ cup	strong black coffee	125 mL
8 oz	cremini mushrooms, trimmed and quartered	250 g
1 tbsp	ancho chile powder	15 mL
1	red bell pepper, seeded and diced	1
1	jalapeño pepper, seeded and diced	1

1. In a skillet, heat 1 tbsp (15 mL) of the oil over medium-high heat. Add bacon and cook, stirring, until nicely browned, about 4 minutes. Using a slotted spoon, transfer to paper towel to drain. Set aside.

2. On a plate or in a plastic bag, dredge beef in flour until evenly coated. Add to skillet, in batches, and cook, stirring, until lightly browned on all sides, about 4 minutes per batch. Transfer to slow cooker stoneware as completed.

3. Reduce heat to medium. Add remaining tbsp (15 mL) of oil to pan. Add onions and celery and cook, stirring, until softened, about 5 minutes. Add garlic, thyme, salt, peppercorns and bay leaves and cook, stirring, for 1 minute. Add stock and coffee and bring to a boil.

4. Transfer to slow cooker stoneware. Stir in mushrooms. Cover and cook on Low for 8 hours or on High for 4 hours, until beef is very tender. Stir in chile powder, bell pepper, jalapeño and reserved bacon. Cover and cook on High until peppers are tender, about 15 minutes. Remove and discard bay leaves.

Tips

If you are halving this recipe, be sure to use a small (2 to 3½ quart) slow cooker.

Be aware that these cooking times are general estimates. Not only do cooking times vary substantially among slow cookers (see Cooking Times, page 12), but people have different preferences with regard to how well they like their meat done. If you prefer fork-tender results, start checking after the food has cooked for 6 hours on Low.

Make Ahead

Complete Steps 1 and 3. Cover and refrigerate mixture for up to 2 days. When you're ready to cook, complete the recipe.

Beef Tagine with Saffron and Couscous

Although it's very simple to make, the addition of saffron adds a wow factor to this tasty dish. It's perfect for a casual Friday evening with friends. Just add salad and open some robust red wine.

Serves 6

• Medium to large (3½ to 5 quart) slow cooker

2 lbs	trimmed stewing beef, cut into 1-inch (2.5 cm) cubes, and patted dry	1 kg
1 tsp	cracked black peppercorns	5 mL
¼ cup	freshly squeezed lemon juice	50 mL
2 tbsp	olive oil, divided	25 mL
2	onions, finely chopped	2
3	carrots, peeled and diced	3
4	cloves garlic, minced	4
2 tsp	ground cumin (see Tips, left)	10 mL
2 tsp	ground coriander	10 mL
1 tsp	salt	5 mL
½ tsp	ground allspice (see Tips, left)	2 mL
½ tsp	saffron threads, crumbled	2 mL
1	piece (2 inches/5 cm) cinnamon stick	1
1	can (28 oz/796 mL) tomatoes with juice, coarsely chopped	1
2	potatoes, peeled and shredded	2
2 cups	chicken stock	500 mL
1 tsp	ground Aleppo pepper (see Tips, left)	5 mL

Couscous

1½ cups	vegetable or chicken stock or water	375 mL
1 cup	couscous, preferably whole grain	250 mL
	Finely chopped parsley	

1. In a bowl, combine beef, peppercorns and lemon juice. Cover and refrigerate for at least 30 minutes or for up to 2 hours. Drain and pat dry, discarding marinade.

2. In a skillet, heat 1 tbsp (15 mL) of the oil over medium-high heat. Add beef, in batches, and cook, stirring, until lightly browned on all sides, about 4 minutes per batch. Transfer to slow cooker stoneware as completed.

3. Reduce heat to medium. Add remaining tbsp (15 mL) of oil to pan. Add onions and carrots and cook, stirring, until carrots have softened, about 7 minutes. Add garlic, cumin, coriander, salt, allspice, saffron and cinnamon stick and cook, stirring and scraping up brown bits from bottom of pan, for 1 minute. Add tomatoes with juice and bring to a boil.

4. Transfer to slow cooker stoneware. Stir in potatoes and stock. Cover and cook on Low for 8 to 10 hours or on High for 4 to 5 hours, until meat and potatoes are very tender. Stir in Aleppo pepper. Cover and cook for 15 minutes to meld flavors.

5. **Couscous:** Just before adding Aleppo pepper, in a saucepan, bring stock to a boil. Gradually add couscous, stirring well. Remove from heat, cover and let stand for at least 15 minutes. Fluff with a fork before using.

6. To serve, arrange couscous around the edge of a deep platter and ladle beef mixture into the center. Garnish liberally with parsley.

Beef Paprikash

This simple dish, usually made with chicken or veal in Hungary, becomes a robust cold-weather stew when beef is used instead. I like to serve this over buttered broad noodles such as pappardelle, but a bowl of steaming garlic mashed potatoes is delicious, too.

Serves 6

• Medium to large (3½ to 5 quart) slow cooker

2 tbsp	olive oil, divided	25 mL
2 lbs	trimmed stewing beef, cut into 1-inch (2.5 cm) cubes, and patted dry	1 kg
2	onions, finely chopped	2
2	cloves garlic, minced	2
1 tbsp	caraway seeds, crushed	15 mL
1 tsp	dried thyme leaves	5 mL
	Zest of 1 lemon	
½ tsp	salt (see Tips, left)	2 mL
½ tsp	cracked black peppercorns	2 mL
¼ cup	all-purpose flour	50 mL
2 tbsp	tomato paste	25 mL
2 cups	beef stock	500 mL
12 oz	cremini mushrooms, trimmed and quartered (see Tips, left)	375 g
1 tbsp	paprika (see Tips, left)	15 mL
1 tbsp	freshly squeezed lemon juice	15 mL
1	green or red bell pepper, seeded and diced, optional	1
½ cup	sour cream	125 mL
	Finely chopped dill or parsley, optional	

1. In a skillet, heat 1 tbsp (15 mL) of the oil over medium-high heat. Add beef, in batches, and cook, stirring, until lightly browned on all sides, about 4 minutes per batch. Transfer to slow cooker stoneware.

2. Reduce heat to medium. Add remaining tbsp (15 mL) of oil to pan. Add onions and cook, stirring, until softened, about 3 minutes. Add garlic, caraway seeds, thyme, lemon zest, salt and peppercorns and cook, stirring, for 1 minute. Add flour and cook, stirring, for 1 minute. Add tomato paste and stir well. Add stock and cook, stirring and scraping up brown bits from bottom of pan, until mixture thickens, about 5 minutes.

3. Transfer to stoneware. Stir in mushrooms. Cover and cook on Low for 8 hours or on High for 4 hours, until beef is tender.

4. In a small bowl, combine paprika, lemon juice and 1 tbsp (15 mL) water. Add to stoneware along with bell pepper, if using. Cover and cook on High for 20 minutes, until pepper is tender. (If you're not using the pepper just cook for 10 minutes, until flavors meld.) Stir in sour cream. Garnish with dill (see Tips, left).

Tips

If you are halving this recipe, be sure to use a small (2 to 3½ quart) slow cooker.

If your beef stock is very salty, you may want to reduce the quantity of salt.

I like the robust flavor of cremini mushrooms in this stew, but white mushrooms work well, too.

You can vary the kind of paprika to suit your taste. Sweet paprika is traditional, but smoked or hot versions will work well, too.

If you're adding a bell pepper to this dish, I recommend parsley as a garnish. If you're not using a pepper, garnish liberally with dill.

Make Ahead

Complete Step 2. Cover and refrigerate mixture for up to 2 days. When you're ready to cook, complete the recipe.

Italian-Style Goulash

This version of goulash, known as golas, *is from the Friuli region of Italy. Not only does it have great depth of flavor, it also contains its own starch in the form of potatoes, so you don't need to add the traditional noodles. I like to serve this with a big bowl of steamed green beans, crusty bread and a robust red wine.*

Can Be Halved
see Tips, below

Serves 6

- Medium to large (3½ to 5 quart) slow cooker

2 tbsp	olive oil, divided	25 mL
2 lbs	trimmed stewing beef, cut into 1-inch (2.5 cm) cubes, and patted dry	1 kg
2	onions, diced	2
2	stalks celery, diced	2
1	carrot, peeled and diced	1
2	cloves garlic, minced	2
2 tsp	dried oregano leaves	10 mL
1 tsp	dried rosemary leaves or 1 sprig fresh rosemary	5 mL
1 tsp	salt	5 mL
½ tsp	cracked black peppercorns	2 mL
2 tbsp	all-purpose flour	25 mL
¼ cup	tomato paste	50 mL
1 cup	dry red wine	250 mL
2	potatoes, peeled and diced (see Tips, right)	2
2 cups	beef stock	500 mL
1 tbsp	sweet paprika	15 mL
1 tsp	hot paprika (see Tips, right)	5 mL
2 tbsp	water	25 mL

1. In a skillet, heat 1 tbsp (15 mL) of the oil over medium-high heat. Add beef, in batches, and cook, stirring, until lightly browned on all sides, about 4 minutes per batch. Transfer to stoneware as completed.

2. Reduce heat to medium. Add remaining tbsp (15 mL) of oil to pan. Add onions, celery and carrot and cook, stirring, until vegetables are softened, about 7 minutes. Add garlic, oregano, rosemary, salt and peppercorns and cook, stirring, for 1 minute. Stir in flour and cook for 1 minute. Stir in tomato paste and wine. Bring to a boil and cook, stirring and scraping up brown bits from bottom of pan, for 2 minutes.

3. Transfer to slow cooker stoneware. Stir in potatoes and stock. Cover and cook on Low for 8 hours or on High for 4 hours, until meat is very tender and potatoes are cooked through.

4. In a small bowl, dissolve sweet and hot paprika in water. Add to stoneware and stir well. Cover and cook on High for 15 minutes, until flavors meld.

Tips

If you are halving this recipe, see Tips, page 194.

Be sure to dice your potatoes into ½-inch (1 cm) cubes rather than slicing them. Otherwise they are not likely to be cooked at the same time as the meat.

This amount of hot paprika produces a slightly spicy result. Use a bit more or less, depending upon your level of heat tolerance. If you like a hint of smoke, substitute smoked paprika for some or all of the hot paprika.

Be aware that these cooking times are general estimates. Not only do cooking times vary substantially among slow cookers (see Cooking Times, page 12), but people have different preferences with regard to how well they like their meat done. If you prefer fork-tender results, start checking after the food has cooked for 6 hours on Low.

Make Ahead

Complete Step 2. Cover and refrigerate mixture for up to 2 days. When you're ready to cook, complete the recipe.

Entertaining Worthy

Can Be Halved

see Tips, below

Moroccan-Spiced Beef Stew

This delicious mélange is easy to make and so good you'll want to share it with friends. Serve it on a deep platter surrounded by a ring of couscous. If it's available, try barley couscous, a nutritious whole-grain version that is traditional in parts of Morocco — you can find it in specialty stores (my butcher carries it). All you need to add is a simple green vegetable such as steamed beans.

Tips

If you are halving this recipe, be sure to use a small (approx. 1½ to 3 quart) slow cooker.

I prefer this dish to have a strong tomato base, so I used Italian San Marzano tomatoes, which are deep and rich. If you're using domestic tomatoes, add 1 tbsp (15 mL) tomato paste after cooking the spices.

This is about 3 cups (750 mL) of peeled baby carrots.

Harissa is a spice paste indigenous to North Africa that is available in specialty stores. It is useful for adding heat and complexity to soups and stews. If you don't have it, pass your favorite hot pepper sauce at the table.

Make Ahead

Complete Steps 1 and 3. Cover and refrigerate mixtures for up to 2 days. When you're ready to cook, continue with recipe.

Serves 6 to 8

- Medium to large (3½ to 5 quart) slow cooker

1 tbsp	cumin seeds	15 mL
2 tbsp	olive oil, divided	2
2 lbs	stewing beef, cut into 1-inch (2.5 cm) cubes	1 kg
2	onions, thinly sliced on the vertical	2
4	cloves garlic, minced	4
1 tbsp	minced gingerroot	15 mL
1	piece (2 inches/5 cm) cinnamon stick	1
½ tsp	freshly grated nutmeg	2 mL
½ tsp	cracked black peppercorns	2 mL
4	whole cloves	4
1 tbsp	all-purpose flour	15 mL
1	can (14 oz/398 mL) diced tomatoes with juice (see Tips, left)	1
2 cups	beef stock	500 mL
1	bag (12 oz/340 g) peeled baby carrots (see Tips, left)	1
½ cup	finely chopped parsley	125 mL
1 tsp to 1 tbsp	harissa, optional (see Tips, left)	5 to 15 mL

1. In a skillet over medium heat, cook cumin seeds, stirring, until fragrant and seeds just begin to brown, about 3 minutes. Using a mortar and pestle or a spice grinder, pound or grind as finely as you can. Set aside.

2. In same skillet, heat 1 tbsp (15 mL) oil over medium-high heat. Add beef, in batches, and cook, stirring, until lightly browned on all sides, about 4 minutes per batch. Transfer to slow cooker stoneware as completed.

3. Reduce heat to medium. Add remaining tbsp (15 mL) oil to pan. Add onions and cook, stirring, until softened, about 3 minutes. Add garlic, ginger, cinnamon stick, nutmeg, peppercorns, cloves and reserved cumin and cook, stirring, for 1 minute. Add flour and cook, stirring, for 1 minute. Add tomatoes with juice, stock and carrots. Bring to a boil and cook, stirring and scraping up brown bits from bottom of pan, for 2 minutes.

4. Transfer to slow cooker stoneware. Cover and cook on Low for 8 hours or on High for 4 hours, until beef and carrots are tender. Stir in harissa, if using, 1 tsp (5 mL) at a time, tasting after each addition, until desired spiciness is achieved. Cover and cook on High for 10 minutes, until flavors meld.

Persian-Style Beef and Split Pea Stew

If you're looking for something unusual to serve to guests, try this luscious combination of highly seasoned meat and split peas. The substantial hit of saffron coupled with tomato and the unique tang of dried limes is a deliciously exotic flavor. According to Persian food authority Margaret Shaida, this dish is often garnished with fried potatoes, so I have included an oven-baked alternative as an option.

Serves 6 to 8

- Medium to large (3½ to 5 quart) slow cooker

2 tbsp	olive oil, divided	25 mL
2 lbs	trimmed stewing beef, cut into 1-inch (2.5 cm) cubes, and patted dry	1 kg
3	dried limes, pierced with a sharp knife (see Tips, left)	3
2	onions, chopped	2
1 tsp	ground turmeric	5 mL
½ tsp	saffron threads, crumbled	2 mL
½ tsp	salt	2 mL
½ tsp	cracked black peppercorns	2 mL
¼ cup	tomato paste	50 mL
½ cup	yellow split peas, rinsed	125 mL
3 cups	vegetable or chicken stock or water	750 mL
¼ cup	freshly squeezed lemon juice	50 mL
	Oven-Fried Potato Wedges, optional (see Tips, left)	

1. In a skillet, heat 1 tbsp (15 mL) of the oil over medium-high heat. Add beef, in batches, and cook, stirring, until lightly browned on all sides, about 4 minutes per batch. Transfer to slow cooker stoneware as completed. Bury dried limes in meat to keep them submerged.

2. Reduce heat to medium. Add remaining tbsp (15 mL) of oil to pan. Add onions and cook, stirring frequently, until golden, about 10 minutes. Stir in turmeric, saffron, salt and peppercorns and cook for 1 minute. Stir in tomato paste and split peas. Add stock. Bring to a boil and cook, stirring and scraping up brown bits, for 2 minutes.

3. Transfer to slow cooker stoneware. Cover and cook on Low for 8 hours or on High for 4 hours, until beef and peas are tender. Discard dried limes. Stir in lemon juice. Taste and adjust seasoning. To serve, transfer to a deep platter or shallow serving bowl and arrange potato wedges, if using, on top.

Variation

Substitute 2 lbs (1 kg) cubed lamb shoulder for the beef.

Tips

If you are halving this recipe, use 2 limes and be sure to use a small (2 to 3½ quart) slow cooker.

Dried limes are available in Middle Eastern markets or specialty spice shops.

Oven-Fried Potato Wedges: Preheat oven to 400°C (200°F). Thoroughly scrub 4 baking potatoes. Microwave on High for 5 minutes and let stand for 2 minutes. On a cutting board, cut each potato in half, then cut each half into quarters. Brush liberally with olive oil and roast in preheated oven until nicely browned, about 20 minutes.

Make Ahead

Complete Step 2. Cover and refrigerate for up to 2 days. When you're ready to cook, complete the recipe.

Coconut Beef Curry

This aromatic curry is a bit of a hybrid, borrowing from both Indian and Thai cuisines and adding French mustard to complete the mix. While the combination of beef and coconut milk isn't common, it is the basis of masamun curry, an elaborate special occasion dish in Thailand. This much simpler recipe is slightly sweet, with an abundance of ginger and a hint of cardamom. Vary the quantity of chiles to suit your taste. I like to serve this with a mixture of brown basmati rice and Thai red rice and follow the meal with a salad of mesclun greens and avocado tossed in a simple vinaigrette.

Entertaining Worthy

Can Be Halved
see Tips, below

Serves 6 to 8

- Medium (3½ to 4 quart) slow cooker (see Tips, right)

2 tbsp	olive oil, divided	25 mL
2 lbs	trimmed stewing beef, cut into ½-inch (1 cm) cubes, and patted dry	1 kg
2	onions, finely chopped	2
4	cloves garlic, minced	4
2 tbsp	minced gingerroot	25 mL
2 tsp	ground coriander (see Tips, right)	10 mL
1 tsp	ground cumin	5 mL
1 tsp	ground turmeric	5 mL
1 tsp	salt	5 mL
1 tsp	cracked black peppercorns	5 mL
2	black cardamom pods, crushed	2
1	piece (3 inches/7.5 cm) cinnamon stick	1
1 cup	beef, chicken or vegetable stock or water	250 mL
2	long red chiles, seeded and minced	2
1 tsp	Dijon mustard	5 mL
1 cup	coconut milk	250 mL
	Finely chopped cilantro	

1. In a skillet, heat 1 tbsp (15 mL) of the oil over medium-high heat. Add beef, in batches, and cook, stirring, until lightly browned on all sides, about 4 minutes per batch. Transfer to slow cooker stoneware as completed.

2. Add remaining tbsp (15 mL) of the oil to pan. Add onions and cook, stirring, until they being to turn golden, about 5 minutes. Add garlic, ginger, coriander, cumin, turmeric, salt, peppercorns, cardamom and cinnamon stick and cook, stirring, for 1 minute. Add stock and bring to a boil.

3. Transfer to slow cooker stoneware and stir well. Cover and cook on Low for 8 hours or on High for 4 hours, until meat is very tender.

4. In a small bowl, combine chiles, mustard and coconut milk, stirring well to combine. Stir into meat. Cover and cook on High for 30 minutes, until flavors meld. Garnish with cilantro.

Tips

If you are halving this recipe, be sure to use a small (approx. 1½ to 3 quart) slow cooker.

I recommend using a smaller slow cooker to make this dish because it cooks in a small amount of liquid and some of the meat may not be completely covered during the cooking process. If your meat is not completely covered by liquid, stir it once or twice during cooking to ensure the meat doesn't oxidize, or cover with a large piece of parchment paper, pressing it down to brush the food and extending up the sides of the stoneware so it overlaps the rim.

For best results, toast and grind whole coriander and whole cumin seeds yourself. Place in a dry skillet over medium heat and cook, stirring, until fragrant, about 3 minutes. Using a mortar and pestle or a spice grinder, pound or grind as finely as you can.

Make Ahead

Complete Step 2. Cover and refrigerate mixture for up to 2 days. When you're ready to cook, complete the recipe.

Can Be
Halved
see Tips, below

Kentucky Burgoo

Traditionally made with game, burgoo is Kentucky's state dish. Today it is more often a variation on the theme of jambalaya — an anything-goes stew. It is atypical in that it often combines beef and chicken.

Serves 6 to 8

• Large (approx. 5 quart) slow cooker

1 cup	dried lima beans	250 mL
4 oz	chunk bacon, diced	125 g
1 lb	trimmed stewing beef, cut into 1-inch (2.5 cm) cubes, and patted dry	500 g
3	onions, finely chopped	3
2	carrots, peeled and diced	2
2	stalks celery, diced	2
6	cloves garlic, minced	6
1 tsp	each salt and cracked black peppercorns	5 mL
1 tsp	dried thyme leaves (see Tips, left)	5 mL
2	bay leaves	2
1 cup	dry white wine (see Tips, left)	250 mL
6 to 8	skinless bone-in chicken thighs	6 to 8
2 cups	chicken stock	500 mL
1 cup	thinly sliced okra (see Tips, left)	250 mL
1 cup	corn kernels	250 mL
1	red bell pepper, seeded and diced	1
4	reconstituted sun-dried tomatoes, diced	4
1/4 tsp	cayenne pepper, dissolved in 2 tbsp (25 mL) lemon juice (see Tips, left)	1 mL

Tips

If you are halving this recipe, be sure to use a small (2½ to 3½ quart) slow cooker.

If you have some robust stalks of fresh thyme, substitute 2, including stems, for the dried version.

If you prefer, substitute an extra cup (250 mL) of chicken stock plus 1 tbsp (15 mL) lemon juice for the white wine.

If you prefer, substitute a seeded, diced fresh chile pepper for the cayenne.

Okra, a tropical vegetable, has a great flavor but it becomes unpleasantly sticky when overcooked. Choose young okra pods, 2 to 4 inches (5 to 10 cm) long, that don't feel sticky to the touch. (If sticky they are too ripe.) Gently scrub the pods and cut off the top and tail before slicing.

Make Ahead

Complete Steps 1 and 3, adding 1 tbsp (15 mL) oil to pan before softening onions. Cover and refrigerate mixture for up to 2 days. When you're ready to cook, continue with the recipe.

1. In a large saucepan, bring beans to a boil with 4 cups (1 L) water. Boil rapidly for 3 minutes. Turn off element and let stand for 1 hour. Drain and rinse under cold water. Using your fingers, pop beans out of their skins and transfer to a bowl. Cover with cold water and set aside. Discard skins. Drain beans before using.

2. In a skillet over medium-high heat, sauté bacon until crisp. Transfer to stoneware. Add beef to pan, in batches, and cook, stirring, until browned, about 4 minutes per batch. Transfer to stoneware as completed.

3. Reduce heat to medium. Add onions, carrots and celery to pan and cook, stirring, until softened, about 7 minutes. Add garlic, salt, peppercorns, thyme and bay leaves and cook, stirring, for 1 minute. Add reserved beans to pan and toss to coat. Add wine. Bring to a boil and boil, stirring and scraping up brown bits, for 2 minutes.

4. Transfer to stoneware. Add chicken and stir well. Pour in stock and add water to cover. Cover and cook on Low for 8 hours or on High for 4 hours, until beef is tender. Add okra, corn, bell pepper, sun-dried tomatoes and cayenne solution and stir well. Cover and cook on High for 20 minutes, until corn is tender.

Wine-Braised Oxtails with Mushrooms

This hearty dish will more than satisfy the meat lovers in your circle. Cooked on the bone, the beef is particularly succulent and the sauce is deep and rich. Serve this over mashed potatoes or hot orzo accompanied by a green vegetable.

Can Be Halved
see Tips, below

Tips

If you are halving this recipe, be sure to use a small (2 to 3½ quart) slow cooker.

For best results, cook this overnight or a day ahead and chill. Spoon off the fat that rises to the surface and reheat, covered, in a 350°F (180°C) oven until hot and bubbly, about 30 minutes.

I use Italian San Marzano tomatoes, which are particularly rich and flavorful. If you are using domestic tomatoes, you may want to add 1 tbsp (15 mL) tomato paste along with the tomatoes.

Make Ahead

Complete Step 2. Cover and refrigerate for up to 2 days. When you're ready to cook, complete the recipe.

Serves 6 to 8

• Large (approx. 5 quart) slow cooker

4 lbs	oxtails, cut into 2-inch (5 cm) pieces, and patted dry	2 kg
¼ cup	all-purpose flour	50 mL
2 tbsp	olive oil, divided	25 mL
2	onions, finely chopped	2
2	carrots, peeled and diced	2
2	stalks celery, diced	2
4	cloves garlic, minced	4
1 tsp	dried thyme leaves	5 mL
1 tsp	salt	5 mL
2	bay leaves	2
½ tsp	cracked black peppercorns	2 mL
1½ cups	dry red wine	375 mL
1	can (28 oz/796 mL) tomatoes with juice, coarsely chopped (see Tips, left)	1
12 oz	mushrooms, trimmed and quartered	375 g
½ cup	finely chopped parsley	125 mL

1. On a plate or in a plastic bag, dredge oxtails in flour until evenly coated. Discard excess flour.

2. In a skillet, heat 1 tbsp (15 mL) of the oil over medium-high heat. Add oxtails, in batches, and cook, stirring, until lightly browned on all sides, about 4 minutes per batch. Transfer to slow cooker stoneware as completed. Drain off all the fat from the pan.

3. Reduce heat to medium. Add remaining tbsp (15 mL) of oil to pan. Add onions, carrots and celery and cook, stirring, until vegetables are softened, about 7 minutes. Add garlic, thyme, salt, bay leaves and peppercorns and cook, stirring, for 1 minute. Add wine, bring to a boil and boil, stirring and scraping up brown bits from bottom of pan, for 2 minutes. Stir in tomatoes with juice.

4. Transfer to slow cooker stoneware. Add mushrooms and stir well. Cover and cook on Low for 8 to 10 hours or on High for 4 to 5 hours, until meat is falling off the bone (see Tips, page 203). Remove and discard bay leaves. Garnish with parsley.

Roman-Style Oxtails with Celery

This is one of my favorite recipes for oxtails. The sauce is much lighter than most and the abundance of blanched celery adds beautiful flavor. Serve this over polenta for a truly Italian-inspired treat.

Serves 6 to 8

- Large (approx. 5 quart) slow cooker

2 tbsp	olive oil (approx.), divided	25 mL
4 oz	pancetta, diced	125 g
4 lbs	oxtails, cut into 2-inch (5 cm) pieces, and patted dry	2 kg
1	onion, diced	1
2	stalks celery, diced	2
2	cloves garlic, minced	2
1 tsp	salt	5 mL
1 tsp	cracked black peppercorns	5 mL
1 cup	dry white wine (see Tips, right)	250 mL
1/4 cup	tomato paste	50 mL
2 cups	chicken stock	500 mL
6 cups	sliced celery (cut into 1-inch/2.5 cm pieces)	1.5 L
1/2 cup	finely chopped parsley	125 mL

1. In a skillet, heat 1 tbsp (15 mL) of the oil over medium-high heat. Add pancetta and cook, stirring, until nicely browned, about 4 minutes. Transfer to slow cooker stoneware.

2. Add oxtails, in batches, and brown on all sides, about 4 minutes per batch, adding more oil if necessary. Transfer to slow cooker stoneware as completed. Drain off all the fat from pan.

3. Reduce heat to medium. Add remaining tbsp (15 mL) of oil to pan. Add onion, 2 stalks of celery, garlic, salt and peppercorns and cook, stirring, until onions begin to turn golden, about 8 minutes. Add wine, bring to a boil and boil, stirring and scraping up brown bits from bottom on pan, for 2 minutes. Stir in tomato paste and stock.

4. Transfer to slow cooker stoneware. Cover and cook on Low for 8 to 10 hours or on High for 4 to 5 hours, until meat is falling off the bone.

5. When oxtails are almost cooked, bring a large pot of salted water to a boil. Add the sliced celery and return to a boil. Reduce heat and simmer until celery is tender, about 5 minutes. Drain and add to oxtails. Cover and cook on High for 10 minutes, until flavors meld. Garnish with parsley and serve immediately.

Tips

If you are halving this recipe, be sure to use a small (2 to 3 1/2 quart) slow cooker.

If you prefer, substitute an extra cup (250 mL) of chicken stock plus 1 tbsp (15 mL) lemon juice for the white wine.

Be aware that these cooking times are general estimates. Not only do cooking times vary substantially among slow cookers (see Cooking Times, page 12), but people have different preferences with regard to how well they like their meat done. The oxtails should be very tender when cooked within this time frame.

Make Ahead

Complete Steps 1 and 3. Add cooked pancetta to onion mixture. Cover and refrigerate (see Making Ahead, page 17) for up to 2 days. When you're ready to cook, continue with the recipe.

Caribbean Oxtails

I love the textures and flavors in this stick-to-the-ribs one-pot dinner. Add some whole-grain bread and finish with an island-inspired light dessert such as mango sorbet. Yummy!

Serves 6 to 8

Tip

If you are halving this recipe, be sure to use a small (2½ to 3½ quart) slow cooker.

Make Ahead

Complete Step 3. Cover and refrigerate mixture for up to 2 days. When you're ready to cook, complete the recipe.

- Large (approx. 5 quart) slow cooker

1½ cups	dried black-eyed peas, soaked and drained	375 mL
4 lbs	oxtails, cut into 2-inch (5 cm) pieces, and patted dry	2 kg
¼ cup	all-purpose flour	50 mL
2 tbsp	olive oil (approx.), divided	25 mL
2	onions, finely chopped	2
2	carrots, peeled and diced	2
2	stalks celery, diced	2
4	cloves garlic, minced	4
2 tbsp	minced gingerroot	25 mL
1 tsp	grated lime zest	5 mL
1 tsp	dried thyme leaves	5 mL
1 tsp	salt	5 mL
1 tsp	cracked black peppercorns	5 mL
2	bay leaves	2
½ tsp	ground allspice	2 mL
2 tbsp	brandy, optional	25 mL
3 cups	chicken stock	750 mL
1 tbsp	sweet paprika, dissolved in 3 tbsp (45 mL) freshly squeezed lime juice	15 mL
1	Scotch bonnet or habanero chile pepper, seeded and diced	1

1. On a plate or in a plastic bag, dredge oxtails in flour until evenly coated. Discard excess flour.

2. In a skillet, heat 1 tbsp (15 mL) of the oil over medium-high heat. Add oxtails, in batches, and cook, stirring, until lightly browned on all sides, adding more oil if necessary, about 4 minutes per batch. Transfer to slow cooker stoneware as completed. Drain off all fat from pan.

3. Reduce heat to medium. Add remaining tbsp (15 mL) of oil to pan. Add onions, carrots and celery and cook, stirring, until vegetables are softened, about 7 minutes. Add garlic, ginger, lime zest, thyme, salt, peppercorns, bay leaves and allspice and cook, stirring, for 1 minute. Add brandy, if using. Bring to a boil and cook, stirring, for 1 minute. Add stock and cook, stirring and scraping up brown bits from bottom of pan, for 2 minutes.

4. Transfer to stoneware. Add black-eyed peas. Cover and cook on Low for 8 to 10 hours or on High for 4 to 5 hours, until meat is falling off the bone. Stir in paprika solution and chile pepper. Cover and cook on High for 15 minutes.

Steak in Pizzaiola Sauce

In Italy, pizzaiola sauce (so named because it is traditionally used on pizza) is often served with pasta, chicken, fish or seafood. Here it provides a simple but sumptuous topping for a chewy cut of steak, which becomes meltingly tender in the slow cooker. Serve this with plain pasta or risotto and a generous helping of steamed spinach for a very delicious meal.

Can Be Halved
see Tips, below

Serves 6

- Medium (approx. 3½ quart) slow cooker

2 tbsp	olive oil, divided	25 mL
2 to 3 lbs	braising steak, such as round, blade or cross-rib steak	1 to 1.5 kg
4	cloves garlic, minced	4
4	anchovy fillets, chopped (see Tips, right)	4
2 tbsp	chopped parsley	25 mL
1 tbsp	dried oregano leaves, crumbled	15 mL
1 tsp	salt	5 mL
½ tsp	cracked black peppercorns	2 mL
1	can (28 oz/796 mL) tomatoes with juice, coarsely chopped	1
1 tsp	crushed hot red pepper (see Tips, right)	5 mL

1. In a skillet, heat 1 tbsp (15 mL) of the oil over medium-high heat. Add steak, in pieces if necessary, and brown on both sides, about 4 minutes. Transfer to slow cooker stoneware.

2. Reduce heat to medium. Add remaining tbsp (15 mL) of oil to pan. Add garlic, anchovies, parsley, oregano, salt and peppercorns and cook, stirring and scraping up brown bits from the bottom of the pan, until anchovies dissolve. Stir in tomatoes with juice and bring to a boil.

3. Transfer to slow cooker stoneware. Cover and cook on Low for 6 to 8 hours or on High for 3 to 4 hours, until meat is tender. Stir in crushed red pepper and cook on High for 10 minutes, until flavors meld.

Tips

If you are halving this recipe, be sure to use a small (approx. 2 to 3½ quart) slow cooker.

Even if you aren't a fan of anchovies, be sure to use them here. They really enhance the flavor of tomatoes and add depth to the sauce. Their own taste completely disappears in the mix.

Use any variety of hot red pepper to suit your taste, from the usual cayenne to more exotic varieties such as Syrian Aleppo.

Be aware that these cooking times are general estimates. Not only do cooking times vary substantially among slow cookers (see Cooking Times, page 12), but people have different preferences with regard to how well they like their meat done. If you prefer fork-tender results, start checking after the food has cooked for 6 hours on Low.

Make Ahead

Complete Step 2. Cover and refrigerate mixture for up to 2 days. When you're ready to cook, continue with the recipe.

Tea-Braised Beef Stew

This dish was inspired by a recipe of fusion chef Ming Tsai, who uses lapsang souchong tea in a seasoning rub. If you're tired of the same old thing and looking for something a little different, try this technique. The tea adds intriguing smoky notes that are balanced by the sweetness of the parsnips and carrots. Zesty ginger and hot cayenne provide a nice finish. Serve over rice.

Tip

Grind the tea in a mortar with a pestle or using a rolling pin on a cutting board. It gets rid of the fibrous leaves so they're not as intrusive in the sauce.

Make Ahead

Complete Step 3. Cover and refrigerate mixture for up to 2 days. When you're ready to cook, complete the recipe.

Serves 6 to 8

• Medium to large (3½ to 5 quart) slow cooker

Rub

¼ cup	lapsang souchong tea leaves, ground (see Tip, left)	50 mL
1 tbsp	coarse sea or kosher salt	15 mL
2 tsp	Chinese five-spice powder	10 mL
1 tsp	finely grated orange zest	5 mL
2 lbs	stewing beef, cut into 1-inch (2.5 cm) cubes	1 kg
2 tbsp	oil (approx.)	25 mL
2	onions, finely chopped	2
2	carrots, peeled and diced	2
2	parsnips, peeled and diced	2
2	stalks celery, diced	2
4	cloves garlic, minced	4
2 tbsp	minced gingerroot	25 mL
1 tbsp	Demerara or other raw cane sugar	15 mL
1 tsp	cracked black peppercorns	5 mL
1½ cups	dry red wine	375 mL
1½ cups	beef stock	375 mL
1	potato, peeled and shredded	1
1 tbsp	freshly squeezed orange juice	15 mL
¼ tsp	cayenne pepper	1 mL
	Finely chopped cilantro	

1. **Rub:** In a large bowl, combine tea, salt, five-spice powder and orange zest. Mix well. Add beef and toss until well coated. Cover and set aside at room temperature for 15 minutes or refrigerate for up to 2 hours.

2. In a skillet, heat 1 tbsp (15 mL) of the oil over medium-high heat. Pat beef dry. Add to pan, in batches, and cook, stirring, until lightly browned on all sides, about 4 minutes per batch, adding more oil if necessary. Transfer to slow cooker stoneware as completed.

3. Reduce heat to medium. Add remaining tbsp (15 mL) of oil to pan. Add onions, carrots, parsnips and celery and cook, stirring, until softened, about 7 minutes. Add garlic, ginger, sugar and peppercorns and cook, stirring, for 1 minute. Add wine, bring to a boil and boil, stirring and scraping up brown bits from bottom of pan, for 2 minutes. Add stock and return to a boil.

4. Transfer to slow cooker stoneware. Stir in potato. Cover and cook on Low for 8 hours or on High for 4 hours, until beef is very tender. In a bowl, combine orange juice and cayenne. Stir well until cayenne dissolves. Add to stoneware, cover and cook on High for 15 minutes to meld flavors. Garnish with cilantro.

Can Be Halved
see Tips, below

Tips

If you are halving this recipe, be sure to use a small (approx. 1½ to 3 quart) slow cooker.

If you prefer, substitute 1 cup (250 mL) chicken stock plus 1 tbsp (15 mL) lemon juice for the white wine.

Be aware that these cooking times are general estimates. Not only do cooking times vary substantially among slow cookers (see Cooking Times, page 12), but people have different preferences with regard to how well they like their meat done. If you prefer fork-tender results, start checking after the food has cooked for 6 hours on Low.

If you're lucky enough to have anchovy fillets that have been packed in salt (they have the best flavor), soak them in ½ cup (125 mL) milk for 30 minutes before using in this recipe. Rinse thoroughly before chopping.

Make Ahead

Complete Step 2. Cover and refrigerate mixture for up to 2 days. When you're ready to cook, complete the recipe.

Boatmen's Braised Steak

This is a traditional French recipe that originated with the men who ran barges on the Rhône River, a transport route for goods coming inland from the Mediterranean Sea. It is hearty and very warming, and on the boats it was served directly from the pan. It's great with mashed potatoes or new potatoes cooked in their skins, and its enthusiastic flavors cry out for some robust red wine.

Serves 4 to 6

- Medium (approx 3½ quart) slow cooker

2 tbsp	olive oil, divided	25 mL
2 to 3 lbs	braising steak, such as round, blade or cross-rib steak	1 to 1.5 kg
2	onions, thinly sliced on the vertical	2
4	cloves garlic, minced	4
1 tsp	salt	5 mL
1 tsp	cracked black peppercorns	5 mL
1 tsp	dried thyme leaves	5 mL
1	bay leaf	1
1 cup	dry white wine (see Tips, left)	250 mL
2 tbsp	red wine vinegar	25 mL
2 tbsp	all-purpose flour	25 mL
2 tbsp	softened butter	25 mL
1 tbsp	drained capers	15 mL
4	anchovy fillets, finely chopped (see Tips, left)	4
4	gherkins, diced	4

1. In a skillet, heat 1 tbsp (15 mL) of the oil over medium-high heat. Add steak, in pieces if necessary, and brown on both sides, about 4 minutes. Transfer to slow cooker stoneware.

2. Reduce heat to medium. Add remaining tbsp (15 mL) of oil to pan. Add onions and cook, stirring, until softened, about 3 minutes. Add garlic, salt, peppercorns, thyme and bay leaf and cook, stirring and scraping up brown bits from bottom of pan, for 1 minute. Add wine, bring a boil and boil for 2 minutes. Stir in vinegar. Pour over steak.

3. Cover and cook on Low for 6 to 8 hours or on High for 4 to 5 hours, until meat is very tender. Transfer meat to a deep platter and keep warm. Transfer sauce to a saucepan and bring to a boil over medium-high heat. Reduce heat and simmer until slightly reduced, about 5 minutes. Remove and discard bay leaf. Meanwhile, in a bowl, combine flour and butter. Blend well. Stir into sauce and cook, stirring, until slightly thickened, for 1 minute. Stir in capers, anchovies and gherkins. Pour over steak and serve.

Beer-Braised Swiss Steak

Swiss Steak is an American classic. This update enlivens the result with the addition of beer, a hint of paprika and Worcestershire sauce, and the slow cooker saves you the trouble of tenderizing the meat by pounding it with a mallet. Make this the focus of a retro dinner party, served on Fiestaware or Bauer Pottery. Add mounds of mashed potatoes to soak up the rich tomato gravy, plus steamed green beans sprinkled with toasted almonds.

Can Be Halved
see Tips, below

Serves 6 to 8

- Medium (approx. 3½ quart) slow cooker

2 to 3 lbs	braising steak, such as round, blade or cross-rib steak (see Tips, right)	1 to 1.5 kg
¼ cup	all-purpose flour	50 mL
2 tbsp	olive oil, divided	25 mL
2	onions, thinly sliced on the vertical	2
2	stalks celery, diced	2
2	carrots, peeled and diced	2
1 tsp	dried thyme leaves	5 mL
½ tsp	salt	2 mL
½ tsp	cracked black peppercorns	2 mL
1	bay leaf	1
¼ cup	tomato paste	50 mL
1 cup	lager beer	250 mL
1 cup	chicken stock	250 mL
1 tbsp	Worcestershire sauce	15 mL
2 tsp	sweet paprika	10 mL
Pinch	cayenne pepper (see Tips, right)	Pinch
¼ cup	finely chopped parsley	50 mL

1. On a plate, dredge steak in flour until evenly coated. Shake off excess and set aside. In a skillet, heat 1 tbsp (15 mL) of the oil over medium-high heat. Add steak, in pieces if necessary, and brown on both sides, about 4 minutes. Transfer to slow cooker stoneware.

2. Reduce heat to medium. Add remaining tbsp (15 mL) oil to pan. Add onions, celery and carrots and cook, stirring, until vegetables are softened, about 7 minutes. Add thyme, salt, peppercorns, bay leaf and reserved flour and cook, stirring and scraping up brown bits from bottom of pan, for 1 minute. Stir in tomato paste. Add beer and stock and bring to a boil. Cook, stirring, until thickened, about 2 minutes. Transfer to slow cooker stoneware.

3. Cover and cook on Low for 6 to 8 hours or on High for 4 to 5 hours, until meat is very tender. In a small bowl, mix together Worcestershire sauce, paprika and cayenne. Stir into tomato sauce. Cover and cook on High for 10 minutes, until flavors meld. Remove and discard bay leaf. Garnish with parsley.

Tips

If you are halving this recipe, be sure to use a small (approx. 1½ to 3 quart) slow cooker.

While round steak is traditionally used for this dish, an equally successful version can be made with steak that is cut from the blade or cross rib, sometimes identified as "simmering steak." It is available at many supermarkets. If the whole piece won't fit in your slow cooker or skillet, cut it in half.

If you like heat, add as much as ¼ tsp (1 mL) cayenne.

Make Ahead

Complete Step 2. Cover and refrigerate mixture for up to 2 days. When you're ready to cook continue with the recipe.

Can Be Halved
see Tips, below

Steak Smothered in Mushroom Onion Gravy

I don't know why — perhaps there is a Proust moment lurking in the background — but this dish reminds me of growing up. The closest my mother came to this was sautéing sliced white mushrooms in butter as an accompaniment to steak. This is a much more delicious version of that meal — the rich gravy and succulent meat are a real treat.

Tips

If you are halving this recipe, be sure to use a small (2 to 3½ quart) slow cooker.

Be aware that these cooking times are general estimates. Not only do cooking times vary substantially among slow cookers (see Cooking Times, page 12), but people have different preferences with regard to how well they like their meat done. If you prefer fork-tender results, start checking after the food has cooked for 6 hours on Low.

Make Ahead

Complete Step 3. Cover and refrigerate for up to 2 days. When you're ready to cook, continue with the recipe.

Serves 6 to 8

- Medium to large (3½ to 5 quart) slow cooker

1	package (½ oz/14 g) dried porcini mushrooms	1
1 cup	hot water	250 mL
1 tbsp	butter	15 mL
2 tbsp	olive oil, divided	25 mL
2 to 3 lbs	braising steak, such as round, blade or cross-rib steak (see Tips, right)	1 to 1.5 kg
3	onions, thinly sliced on the vertical	3
2	cloves garlic, minced	2
1 tsp	dried thyme leaves	5 mL
½ tsp	salt	2 mL
½ tsp	cracked black peppercorns	2 mL
1	bay leaf	1
1 tbsp	tomato paste	15 mL
2 tbsp	all-purpose flour	25 mL
½ cup	dry sherry	125 mL
8 oz	cremini mushrooms, trimmed and sliced	250 g

1. In a bowl, combine dried mushrooms and hot water. Let stand for 30 minutes, then strain through a fine sieve, reserving liquid. Pat mushrooms dry with paper towel and chop finely. Set liquid and mushrooms aside.

2. In a skillet, melt butter with 1 tbsp (15 mL) of the oil over medium-high heat. Add steak and brown, in pieces if necessary, on both sides, about 4 minutes. Transfer to slow cooker stoneware.

3. Reduce heat to medium. Add remaining tbsp (15 mL) of oil to pan. Add onions and cook, stirring, until they begin to turn golden, about 7 minutes. Add garlic, thyme, salt, peppercorns, bay leaf and reserved dried mushrooms and cook, stirring and scraping up brown bits from bottom of pan, for 1 minute. Stir in tomato paste. Sprinkle flour over mixture and cook, tossing, for 1 minute. Add sherry and cook, stirring, for 1 minute. Stir in reserved mushroom liquid and 1 cup (250 mL) water. Bring to a boil and cook, stirring, until slightly thickened, about 3 minutes.

4. Transfer to slow cooker. Stir in cremini mushrooms. Cover and cook on Low for 6 to 8 hours or on High for 3 to 4 hours, until meat is very tender. Remove and discard bay leaf.

Variation

Steak Smothered in Creamy Mushroom Onion Gravy: Stir in $1/4$ cup (50 mL) whipping (35%) cream after recipe has finished cooking.

Tip

While round steak is traditionally used for this dish, an equally successful version can be made with steak that is cut from the blade or cross rib, sometimes identified as "simmering steak." It is available at many supermarkets. If the whole piece won't fit in your slow cooker or skillet, cut it in half.

Indian-Spiced Beef with Eggplant

Because it uses ground beef, this dish is very easy to make, yet the results seem exotic. The eggplant adds luscious texture and the mild Indian spicing produces intriguing flavor. I serve this over brown rice and add a simple green salad to complete the meal.

Can Be Halved
see Tip, below

Tip

If you are halving this recipe, be sure to use a small (2 to 3½ quart) slow cooker.

Make Ahead

Complete Steps 1, 2 and 3. Cover mixture, ensuring it cools promptly (see Making Ahead, page 17), and refrigerate for up to 2 days. When you're ready to cook, complete the recipe.

Serves 6

• Medium to large (3½ to 5 quart) slow cooker

1	large eggplant (about 1½ lbs/750 g), peeled and cut into 2-inch (5 cm) cubes	1
2 tsp	kosher salt	10 mL
3 tbsp	olive oil (approx.)	45 mL
2 lbs	lean ground beef	1 kg
2	onions, finely chopped	2
4	cloves garlic, minced	4
1 tbsp	minced gingerroot	15 mL
2 tsp	ground cumin	10 mL
1 tsp	ground coriander	5 mL
1 tsp	salt	5 mL
1 tsp	cracked black peppercorns	5 mL
1	can (28 oz/796 mL) diced tomatoes with juice	1
½ cup	beef stock	125 mL
1 cup	full-fat plain yogurt	250 mL
1 tbsp	garam masala	15 mL
1	green bell pepper, seeded and diced	1
1	long red chile pepper, seeded and minced	1

1. In a colander over a sink, combine eggplant and salt. Toss and let stand for 30 minutes. Rinse thoroughly under cold running water. Lay a clean tea towel on a work surface. Working in batches over the sink and using your hands, squeeze liquid out of the eggplant. Transfer to the tea towel. When batches are complete, roll the towel up and press down to remove remaining liquid.

2. In a nonstick skillet, heat 1 tbsp (15 mL) of the oil over medium-high heat. Add sweated eggplant, in batches, and cook until browned, adding more oil as necessary. Transfer to slow cooker stoneware.

3. Add remaining oil to pan. Add beef and onions and cook, stirring, until meat is no longer pink, about 7 minutes. Add garlic, ginger, cumin, coriander, salt and peppercorns and cook, stirring, for 1 minute. Add tomatoes with juice and stock and bring to a boil.

4. Transfer to slow cooker stoneware. Cover and cook on Low for 6 to 8 hours or on High for 3 to 4 hours, until hot and bubbly.

5. In a small bowl, combine yogurt and garam masala. Add to stoneware along with bell pepper and chile pepper. Stir well, cover and cook on High until pepper is tender, about 15 minutes.

Meatball Goulash

I love the flavors in this sauce — paprika, sweet peppers and tomatoes, with just a hint of caraway seed. Served over hot buttered noodles, this dish is positively ambrosial.

Serves 6 to 8

- Medium to large (3½ to 5 quart) slow cooker

½ cup	fine bulgur (see Tips, right)	125 mL
½ cup	cold water	175 mL
1	onion, quartered	1
2	cloves garlic, chopped	2
½ cup	parsley leaves	125 mL
1 tsp	salt	5 mL
	Freshly ground black pepper	
1 lb	each lean ground beef and ground pork	500 g
1	egg, beaten	1
2 tbsp	olive oil, divided	25 mL
2	onions, finely chopped	2
4	cloves garlic, minced	4
1 tsp	caraway seeds	5 mL
½ tsp	each salt and cracked black peppercorns	2 mL
1	can (28 oz/796 mL) tomatoes with juice, coarsely chopped	1
1 cup	beef stock	250 mL
2	red bell peppers, seeded and diced	2
1 tbsp	paprika (sweet or hot), dissolved in 2 tbsp (25 mL) lemon juice	15 mL
½ cup	finely chopped dill	125 mL
	Sour cream, optional	

1. In a bowl, combine bulgur and water. Stir well and set aside until liquid is absorbed, about 10 minutes.

2. In a food processor, combine onion, garlic, parsley, salt and pepper to taste. Process until onion is finely chopped. Add beef, pork, egg and bulgur, in batches, and pulse to combine. Shape mixture into 12 equal balls.

3. In a skillet, heat 1 tbsp (15 mL) of the oil over medium-high heat. Add meatballs, in batches, and brown well, about 5 minutes per batch. Transfer to slow cooker stoneware.

4. Reduce heat to medium. Add remaining tbsp (15 mL) of oil to pan. Add onions and cook, stirring, until softened, about 3 minutes. Add garlic, caraway, salt and peppercorns and cook, stirring, for 1 minute. Add tomatoes with juice and stock and bring to a boil.

5. Pour over meatballs. Cover and cook on Low for 6 to 8 hours or on High for 3 to 4 hours. Stir in bell peppers and paprika solution. Cover and cook on High for 30 minutes, until peppers are tender and flavors meld. Garnish with dill and a dollop of sour cream, if using.

Can Be Halved
see Tips, below

Tips

If you are halving this recipe, be sure to use a small (2 to 3½ quart) slow cooker.

If using coarse bulgur, increase the soaking time to 30 minutes.

Make Ahead

Complete Step 4. Cover and refrigerate for up to 2 days. When you're ready to cook, complete the recipe.

Tip

Be aware that the cooking times are general estimates. Cooking times vary substantially among slow cookers (see Cooking Times, page 12) and lasagna seems particularly sensitive to overcooking in the slow cooker. Begin checking this recipe after the food has cooked for 5 hours on Low or 2½ hours on High.

Make Ahead

Complete Step 1. Cover mixture, ensuring it cools promptly (see Making Ahead, page 17), and refrigerate for up to 2 days. When you're ready to cook, complete the recipe.

Classic Lasagna

I don't think any book about comfort food could omit lasagna, a wonderfully soothing combination of soft noodles and warm cheese blended with a robust tomato sauce.

Serves 6 to 8

- Lightly greased stoneware
- Large (approx. 5 quart) oval slow cooker

2 tbsp	olive oil	25 mL
1 lb	lean ground beef	500 mL
8 oz	Italian sausage, removed from casings	250 g
2	onions, finely chopped	2
2	stalks celery, diced	2
1	carrot, peeled and diced	1
4	cloves garlic, minced	4
1 tbsp	dried Italian seasoning	15 mL
1 tsp	salt	5 mL
1 tsp	cracked black peppercorns	5 mL
1 cup	dry red wine	250 mL
1	can (28 oz/796 mL) tomatoes with juice, coarsely chopped (see Tips, page 202)	1
2 cups	ricotta cheese	500 mL
1	egg yolk	1
½ tsp	freshly grated nutmeg	2 mL
12	oven-ready lasagna noodles	12
2 cups	shredded mozzarella	500 mL
½ cup	finely grated Parmesan	125 mL

1. In a large skillet, heat oil over medium-high heat. Add ground beef, sausage, onions, celery and carrot and cook, stirring, until meat is no longer pink, about 10 minutes. Add garlic, Italian seasoning, salt and peppercorns and cook, stirring, for 1 minute. Add wine, bring to a boil and boil, stirring and scraping up brown bits on bottom of pan, for 2 minutes. Add tomatoes with juice and bring to a boil. Reduce heat and simmer for 5 minutes to meld flavors. Remove from heat and set aside.

2. In a bowl, combine ricotta, egg yolk and nutmeg. Using your hands, mix well and set aside.

3. Spread one-quarter of meat sauce over bottom of prepared stoneware. Cover with 4 noodles, breaking to fit where necessary. Spread with a thin layer of meat sauce, half the ricotta mixture and one-third each of the Parmesan and mozzarella. Repeat. Arrange final layer of noodles over cheeses. Pour remaining sauce over top and sprinkle with remaining mozzarella and Parmesan.

4. Place a clean tea towel, folded in half (so you will have 2 layers), over top of stoneware to absorb moisture. Cover and cook on Low for 5 to 6 hours or on High for 2½ to 3 hours, until hot and bubbly.

Tip

Bolognese sauce should be thick. Placing the tea towels over the top of the slow cooker absorbs generated moisture that would dilute the sauce.

Make Ahead

Complete Step 2. Cover mixture, ensuring it cools promptly (see Making Ahead, page 17), and refrigerate for up to 2 days. When you're ready to cook, complete the recipe.

Best-Ever Bolognese Sauce

This version of the classic Italian meat sauce, which is known for its heartiness, combines beef, pork and pancetta with traditional vegetables and robust porcini mushrooms. Traditionally the sauce develops flavor from long, slow simmering, making it perfect for the slow cooker. I like to serve this over spaghetti, but other long noodles such as fettuccine work well, too.

Serves 6

- Medium to large (3½ to 5 quart) slow cooker

1	package (½ oz/14 g) dried porcini mushrooms	1
1 cup	hot water	250 mL
1 tbsp	olive oil (approx.)	15 mL
2 oz	chunk pancetta, diced	60 g
1 lb	lean ground beef	500 g
8 oz	ground pork	250 g
2	onions, diced	2
2	stalks celery, diced	2
2	carrots, peeled and diced	2
4	cloves garlic, minced	4
1 tbsp	dried Italian seasoning	15 mL
2	bay leaves	2
1 tsp	salt	5 mL
½ tsp	cracked black peppercorns	2 mL
½ tsp	ground cinnamon	2 mL
1 cup	dry red wine	250 mL
1	can (28 oz/796 mL) tomatoes with juice, coarsely chopped (see Tips, page 202)	1
¼ cup	tomato paste	50 mL
1 lb	dried pasta, preferably whole grain, cooked and drained	500 g
	Freshly grated Parmesan	

1. In a bowl, combine dried mushrooms and hot water. Let stand for 30 minutes. Drain through a fine sieve, reserving liquid. Pat mushrooms dry with paper towel and chop finely. Set liquid and mushrooms aside.

2. Meanwhile, in a large skillet, heat oil over medium-high heat. Add pancetta and cook, stirring, until browned, about 3 minutes. Using a slotted spoon, transfer to slow cooker stoneware. Add more oil to pan if necessary. (You should have about 1 tbsp/15 mL.) Add beef, pork, onions, celery and carrots and cook, stirring, until carrots have softened and meat is no longer pink, about 7 minutes. Add garlic, Italian seasoning, bay leaves, salt, peppercorns, cinnamon and reserved dried mushrooms and cook, stirring, for 1 minute. Add wine, bring to a boil and boil, stirring and scraping up brown bits from bottom of pan, for 2 minutes. Add reserved mushroom liquid.

3. Transfer to slow cooker stoneware. Add tomatoes with juice and stir well. Stir in tomato paste. Place 2 clean tea towels, each folded in half (so you will have 4 layers), over top of stoneware to absorb moisture. Cover and cook on Low for 6 to 8 hours or on High for 3 to 4 hours. Serve over hot pasta, liberally garnished with Parmesan.

Can Be
Halved
see Tips, below

Catalonian Meatballs

This is an adaptation of a dish from the French part of Catalonia, boules de picolat, *that appears in Anne Willan's book* The Country Cooking of France. *These meatballs are traditionally cooked in an earthenware dish known as a* cassola, *but the slow cooker makes a wonderful substitute. In Spain a smaller and slightly different version is often served as tapas. Serve these over rice, or as hot sandwiches on crusty bread such as ciabatta.*

Tips

If you are halving this recipe, be sure to use a small (approx. 1½ to 3 quart) slow cooker.

If you prefer, substitute ½ cup (125 mL) fine fresh bread crumbs for the bulgur and water.

If using coarse bulgur, increase the soaking time to 30 minutes.

Make Ahead

Complete Step 4, heating 1 tbsp (15 mL) olive oil before adding onions to pan. Cover and refrigerate mixture for up to 2 days. When you're ready to cook, complete the recipe.

Serves 6

• Medium to large (3½ to 5 quart) slow cooker

¼ cup	fine bulgur (see Tips, left)	50 mL
¼ cup	cold water	50 mL
1 lb	lean ground beef	500 g
8 oz	ground pork	250 g
4	cloves garlic, minced	4
1	egg, beaten	1
1 tsp	salt	5 mL
	Freshly ground black pepper	
¼ cup	all-purpose or whole wheat flour	50 mL
1 tbsp	olive oil	15 mL
2 oz	chunk bacon, diced	60 g

Sauce Rousse

2	onions, finely chopped	2
½ tsp	cracked black peppercorns	2 mL
1	piece (2 inches/5 cm) cinnamon stick	1
2 cups	beef, chicken or vegetable stock	500 mL
1 tbsp	tomato paste	15 mL
½ cup	sliced pimento-stuffed olives	125 mL
⅛ tsp	cayenne pepper	0.5 mL
¼ cup	finely chopped parsley	50 mL

1. In a bowl, combine bulgur and water. Stir well and set aside until liquid is absorbed, about 10 minutes.

2. In a large bowl, combine beef, pork, garlic, egg, salt, pepper to taste, and soaked bulgur. Mix well. Shape into 12 equal balls. Spread flour on a plate and dredge meatballs in it until well coated. Set excess flour aside.

3. In a skillet, heat oil over medium-high heat. Add bacon and cook, stirring, until lightly browned, about 5 minutes. Using a slotted spoon, transfer to slow cooker stoneware. Working in batches, add meatballs to pan and cook until lightly browned on all sides, about 6 minutes per batch. Transfer to slow cooker stoneware as completed.

4. **Sauce Rousse:** Add onions to pan and cook, stirring, until softened, about 3 minutes. Add peppercorns and cinnamon stick and cook, stirring, for 1 minute. Sprinkle reserved flour over mixture and cook, stirring, for 1 minute. Stir in stock and tomato paste and bring to a boil.

5. Pour over meatballs. Cover and cook on Low for 6 to 8 hours or on High for 3 to 4 hours, until hot and bubbly and meatballs are cooked through. Add olives and cayenne to stoneware and stir well. Cover and cook on High for 20 minutes, until olives are heated through and flavors meld. Garnish with parsley.

Can Be Halved
see Tips, below

Cheese-Stuffed Meatballs in Tomato Sauce

Served with whole-grain pasta, these tasty meatballs in tomato sauce make a delicious and nutritious meal. Kids love the molten cheese centers, which lend a dimension of discovery to a great family meal.

Tips

If you are halving this recipe, be sure to use a small (approx. 1½ to 3 quart) slow cooker.

I like the taste of Asiago cheese in these meatballs, but other good melting cheeses, such as mozzarella, provolone or fontina, would also work well.

Make Ahead

Complete Step 3. Cover and refrigerate sauce for up to 2 days. When you're ready to cook, complete the recipe.

Serves 6 to 8

- Medium to large (3½ to 5 quart) slow cooker

Meatballs

1 lb	lean ground beef	500 g
8 oz	ground pork	250 g
¾ cup	fine dry bread crumbs	175 mL
¼ cup	freshly grated Parmesan	50 mL
¼ cup	finely chopped parsley	50 mL
½ tsp	salt	2 mL
	Freshly ground black pepper	
1	egg, beaten	1
3 oz	Asiago cheese, cut into 12 equal cubes (see Tips, left)	90 g
¼ cup	all-purpose or whole wheat flour	50 mL
2 tbsp	olive oil (approx.), divided	25 mL
1	onion, finely chopped	1
2	stalks celery, diced	2
2	carrots, peeled and diced	2
4	cloves garlic, minced	4
1 tsp	dried thyme leaves	5 mL
½ tsp	dried rosemary leaves	2 mL
½ tsp	salt	2 mL
½ tsp	cracked black peppercorns	2 mL
1	can (28 oz/796 mL) tomatoes with juice, coarsely chopped	1
¼ cup	tomato paste	50 mL

1. In a bowl, combine beef, pork, bread crumbs, Parmesan, parsley, salt and pepper to taste. Mix well. Add egg and, using your hands, mix until well combined. Shape mixture into 12 equal balls. Stuff a cube of cheese into the center of each meatball and roll to enclose the cheese. Spread flour evenly over a plate and roll meatballs in it until evenly coated.

2. In a skillet, heat 1 tbsp (15 mL) of the oil over medium-high heat. Add meatballs, in batches, and cook, turning, until lightly browned on all sides, about 6 minutes per batch, adding more oil if necessary. Transfer to slow cooker stoneware.

3. Reduce heat to medium. Add remaining tbsp (15 mL) of oil to pan. Add onion, celery and carrots and cook, stirring, until carrots are softened, about 7 minutes. Add garlic, thyme, rosemary, salt and peppercorns and cook, stirring, for 1 minute. Add tomatoes with juice and tomato paste and cook, stirring, until mixture comes to a boil.

4. Transfer to slow cooker stoneware. Cover and cook on Low for 6 to 8 hours or on High for 3 to 4 hours, until sauce is hot and bubbly and meatballs are cooked through.

Can Be
Halved
see Tips, below

Mexican Meatballs

*These simple meatballs are revved up with the addition of zesty
chipotle chiles. I find that two chiles provide a nice level of punch.
If you're a heat seeker, use three; if you are heat-averse, stick with
one. These are great served over Mexican-Style Beans and Grains
(see page 323) but they also work well with plain rice, beans or hot
tortillas, preferably made from corn.*

Tips

If you are halving this
recipe, be sure to use a
small (2 to 3½ quart)
slow cooker.

I like to use bulgur in
meatballs because it is
a nutritious whole grain.
If you prefer, substitute
½ cup (125 mL) fine
dry bread crumbs for
this quantity of bulgur
and water.

If using coarse bulgur,
increase the soaking time
to 30 minutes.

Use the flour of your
choice. I prefer whole
wheat, but all-purpose,
barley or even oatmeal
flour would work well, too.

Make Ahead

Complete Step 4. Cover
and refrigerate mixture for
up to 2 days. When you're
ready to cook, complete
the recipe.

Serves 6

- Medium to large (3½ to 5 quart) slow cooker

Meatballs

⅓ cup	fine bulgur (see Tips, left)	75 mL
½ cup	cold water	125 mL
1 lb	lean ground beef	500 g
1 lb	ground pork	500 g
1	onion, finely chopped	1
2 tsp	dried oregano leaves	10 mL
1 tsp	ground cumin	5 mL
½ tsp	salt	2 mL
	Freshly ground black pepper	
1	egg, beaten	1
¼ cup	flour (see Tips, left)	50 mL
2 tbsp	olive oil, divided	25 mL
¼ cup	minced onion	50 mL
4	stalks celery, diced	4
4	cloves garlic, minced	4
1 tsp	dried oregano leaves	5 mL
½ tsp	salt	2 mL
½ tsp	cracked black peppercorns	2 mL
¼ cup	tomato paste	50 mL
1	can (28 oz/796 mL) tomatoes with juice, coarsely chopped	1
½ cup	chicken, beef or vegetable stock	125 mL
1 to 2	chipotle chile in abobo sauce, minced	1 to 2
	Finely chopped cilantro	

1. In a bowl, combine bulgur and water. Stir well and set aside until
   liquid is absorbed, about 10 minutes.

2. In a bowl, combine beef, pork, onion, oregano, cumin, soaked bulgur
   and salt and pepper to taste. Mix well. Add egg and using your
   hands, mix until well combined. Shape mixture into 12 equal balls.
   Spread flour evenly over a plate and roll meatballs in it until evenly
   coated. Discard excess flour.

3. In a skillet, heat 1 tbsp (15 mL) of the oil over medium-high heat. Add meatballs, in batches, and cook, turning, until lightly browned on all sides, about 3 minutes per batch. Transfer to slow cooker stoneware.

4. Reduce heat to medium. Add remaining tbsp (15 mL) of oil to pan. Add minced onion and celery and cook, stirring and scraping up brown bits from bottom of pan, until softened, about 5 minutes. Add garlic, oregano, salt and peppercorns and cook, stirring, for 1 minute. Stir in tomato paste. Add tomatoes with juice and stock and cook, stirring, until mixture comes to a boil.

5. Transfer to slow cooker stoneware. Cover and cook on Low for 6 to 8 hours or on High for 3 to 4 hours, until hot and bubbly and meatballs are cooked through. Stir in chipotle chile. Cover and cook on High for 15 minutes, until flavors blend. Garnish with cilantro.

Can Be Halved
see Tips, below

Sloppy Joes

This American classic is a great dish for those evenings when everyone is coming and going at different times. Just leave the fixin's for salad. People can toast themselves a bun, scoop up a serving of this delicious mélange and enjoy a satisfying and nutritious meal.

Tips

If you are halving this recipe, be sure to use a small (approx. 1½ to 3 quart) slow cooker.

For best results, toast and grind whole cumin seeds yourself. To toast cumin seeds, place in a dry skillet over medium heat and cook, stirring, until fragrant, about 3 minutes. Using a mortar and pestle or a spice grinder, pound or grind as finely as you can.

Make Ahead

Complete Steps 1 and 2. Cover and refrigerate meat and vegetable mixtures separately for up to 2 days. When you're ready to cook, complete the recipe.

Serves 4

• Small to medium (2 to 4 quart) slow cooker

2 tbsp	olive oil, divided	25 mL
1 lb	lean ground beef	500 g
2	onions, finely chopped	2
2	stalks celery, diced	2
2	cloves garlic, minced	2
2 tsp	ground cumin (see Tips, left)	10 mL
2 tsp	dried oregano leaves	10 mL
1 tsp	salt	5 mL
½ tsp	cracked black peppercorns	2 mL
1	can (14 oz/398 mL) diced tomatoes with juice	1
1 tbsp	tomato paste	15 mL
1 tbsp	balsamic vinegar	15 mL
1 tbsp	packed brown sugar	15 mL
1 tbsp	Dijon mustard	15 mL
1	green bell pepper, seeded and diced	1
1	jalapeño pepper, seeded and diced	1
	Toasted buns	

1. In a skillet, heat 1 tbsp (15 mL) of the oil over medium-high heat. Add beef and cook, stirring, until meat is no longer pink, about 5 minutes. Transfer to slow cooker stoneware.

2. Reduce heat to medium. Add remaining tbsp (15 mL) of oil to pan. Add onions and celery and cook, stirring and scraping up brown bits from bottom of pan, until softened, about 5 minutes. Add garlic, cumin, oregano, salt and peppercorns and cook, stirring, for 1 minute. Stir in tomatoes with juice, tomato paste, vinegar, brown sugar and mustard and bring to a boil.

3. Transfer to slow cooker stoneware. Cover and cook on Low for 6 hours or on High for 3 hours, until hot and bubbly. Stir in bell and jalapeño peppers. Cover and cook on High for 20 minutes, until peppers are tender. Ladle over hot toasted buns and serve immediately.

Vegetarian Alternative

Substitute 2 cups (500 mL) cooked brown or green lentils, drained and rinsed, for the ground beef. Add along with the mustard.

Easy Chili con Carne

Simple and classic. Chili made with ground beef is among the easiest to prepare and has a homestyle flavor that I love. Make extra because you'll enjoy the leftovers. I like to serve this with buttered whole-grain toast.

Serves 6 to 8

Can Be Halved
see Tips, below

- Medium to large (3½ to 5 quart) slow cooker

2 tbsp	olive oil	25 mL
1½ lbs	lean ground beef	750 g
2	onions, finely chopped	2
4	stalks celery, diced	4
4	cloves garlic, minced	4
2 tbsp	ground cumin (see Tips, right)	25 mL
1 tbsp	dried oregano leaves	15 mL
1 tsp	salt	5 mL
1 tsp	cracked black peppercorns	5 mL
1 tsp	caraway seeds	5 mL
1 tbsp	packed brown sugar	15 mL
1	can (28 oz/796 mL) crushed tomatoes	1
3 cups	cooked red kidney beans, drained (see Tips, right)	750 mL
2 tbsp	Mexican chili powder	25 mL
1 tbsp	apple cider vinegar	15 mL
1 tbsp	water	15 mL
1	green bell pepper, seeded and diced	1

1. In a large skillet, heat oil over medium-high heat. Add beef, onions and celery and cook, stirring, until beef is no longer pink, about 7 minutes. Add garlic, cumin, oregano, salt, peppercorns and caraway seeds and cook, stirring, for 1 minute. Add brown sugar and tomatoes and bring to a boil.

2. Transfer to slow cooker stoneware. Add kidney beans and stir well. Cover and cook on Low for 6 to 8 hours or on High for 3 to 4 hours, until hot and bubbly.

3. In a small bowl, combine chili powder, vinegar and water. Mix until blended. Add to stoneware and stir well. Add bell pepper and stir well. Cover and cook on High about 20 minutes, until pepper is tender.

Tips

If you are halving this recipe, be sure to use a small (approx. 1½ to 3 quart) slow cooker.

To maximize flavor, instead of using ground cumin, toast and grind whole cumin seeds yourself. Place seeds in a dry skillet over medium heat, stirring until fragrant, about 3 minutes. Using a mortar and pestle or a spice grinder, pound or grind as finely as you can.

For this quantity, use canned beans and rinse them well, or soak and cook 1½ cups (375 mL) dried beans.

Make Ahead

Complete Step 1. Cover mixture, ensuring it cools promptly (see Making Ahead, page 17), and refrigerate for up to 2 days. When you're ready to cook, complete the recipe.

Spice-Laced Shepherd's Pie with Potato Parsnip Topping

Although it diverges from the traditional, this version of shepherd's pie — with mild Indian spicing and parsnips in the topping — is truly delicious. It makes a great weeknight meal. Steamed green beans or a tossed salad is all you need to add. If you prefer a crispy topping, after the dish has finished cooking, remove the lid and place the stoneware under a preheated broiler until the top browns.

Tip

For the best flavor, toast and grind the cumin and coriander seeds yourself. Place seeds in a dry skillet over medium heat and cook, stirring, until fragrant and seeds just begin to brown, about 3 minutes. Using a mortar and pestle or a spice grinder, pound or grind as finely as you can.

Make Ahead

This dish can be partially prepared the night before it is cooked. Make Topping, cover and refrigerate. Complete Steps 2 and 3, chilling cooked meat and onion mixtures separately. Refrigerate overnight. The next morning, continue cooking as directed in Step 4.

Serves 4

- Medium to large (3½ to 5 quart) oval slow cooker

Topping

2	potatoes (each about 6 oz/175 g), peeled and quartered	2
4	parsnips (each about 3 oz/90 g), peeled and cut into 2-inch (5 cm) chunks	4
¼ cup	cream or milk	50 mL
1 tbsp	butter	15 mL
1 tsp	curry powder	5 mL
	Salt and freshly ground pepper	

Filling

2 tbsp	olive oil, divided	25 mL
1 lb	lean ground beef	500 g
2	onions, finely chopped	2
2	stalks celery, diced	2
4	cloves garlic, minced	4
1 tbsp	minced gingerroot	15 mL
1 tsp	ground cumin (see Tip, left)	5 mL
1 tsp	ground coriander	5 mL
1 tsp	salt	5 mL
½ tsp	cracked black peppercorns	2 mL
3 tbsp	tomato paste	45 mL
2 tbsp	all-purpose flour	25 mL
1 cup	beef stock	250 mL

1. **Topping:** In a large pot of boiling water, cook potatoes and parsnips until tender. Drain and mash or put through a ricer. Add cream, butter, curry powder and salt and pepper to taste. Cover and refrigerate until ready to use.

2. **Filling:** Meanwhile, in a skillet, heat 1 tbsp (15 mL) of the oil over medium-high heat. Add beef and cook, breaking up with the back of a spoon, until meat is no longer pink, about 5 minutes. Using a slotted spoon, transfer to slow cooker stoneware. Drain off liquid.

3. Reduce heat to medium. Add remaining tbsp (15 mL) of oil to pan. Add onions and celery and cook, stirring, until softened, about 5 minutes. Add garlic, ginger, cumin, coriander, salt and peppercorns and cook, stirring, for 1 minute. Stir in tomato paste. Sprinkle flour over mixture and cook, stirring, for 1 minute. Stir in stock and bring to a boil. Cook, stirring, until slightly thickened, about 2 minutes.

4. Transfer to slow cooker stoneware. Stir well. Cover and cook on Low for 6 hours or on High for 3 hours. Spread topping evenly over meat mixture. Cover and cook on High for 1 hour, until mixture is hot and bubbly.

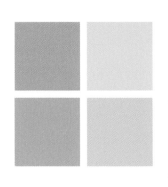

Shepherd's Pie with Horseradish-Spiked Topping

This is an almost traditional approach to shepherd's pie, but the pleasant hint of horseradish knocks it up a notch. If you like a crispy topping, after the dish has finished cooking, remove the lid and place the stoneware under a preheated broiler until the top browns.

Serves 4

- Medium to large (3½ to 5 quart) oval slow cooker

Topping

4	large potatoes (each about 8 oz/250 g), peeled and quartered	4
¼ cup	cream or milk	50 mL
2 tbsp	prepared horseradish	25 mL
1 tbsp	butter	15 mL
	Salt and freshly ground pepper	

Filling

2 tbsp	olive oil, divided	25 mL
1 lb	lean ground beef	500 g
2	onions, thinly sliced on the vertical	2
2	carrots, peeled and diced	2
2	parsnips, peeled and diced	2
4	cloves garlic, minced	4
1 tsp	dried thyme leaves	5 mL
1 tsp	salt	5 mL
1 tsp	cracked black peppercorns	5 mL
¼ cup	tomato paste	50 mL
¼ cup	all-purpose flour	50 mL
2 cups	beef stock	500 mL

1. **Topping:** In a large pot of boiling water, cook potatoes until tender. Drain and mash or put through a ricer. Add cream, horseradish, butter and salt and pepper to taste. Cover and refrigerate until ready to use.

2. **Filling:** Meanwhile, in a skillet, heat 1 tbsp (15 mL) of the oil over medium-high heat. Add beef and cook, breaking up with the back of a spoon, until meat is no longer pink, about 5 minutes. Using a slotted spoon, transfer to slow cooker stoneware. Drain off liquid.

Tip

After refrigeration, the potatoes will solidify. Simply remove them from the container, place on a cutting board and cut into thin slices. Lay the slices as evenly as you can over top of the ground meat mixture. They will soften as they heat in the hot liquid.

Make Ahead

This dish can be partially prepared the night before it is cooked. Make Topping, cover and refrigerate. Complete Steps 2 and 3, chilling cooked meat and onion mixtures separately. Refrigerate overnight. The next morning, continue cooking as directed in Step 4.

3. Reduce heat to medium. Add remaining tbsp (15 mL) of oil to pan. Add onions, carrots and parsnips and cook, stirring, until softened, about 7 minutes. Add garlic, thyme, salt and peppercorns and cook, stirring, for 1 minute. Stir in tomato paste. Sprinkle flour over mixture and cook, stirring, for 1 minute. Stir in stock and bring to a boil. Cook, stirring, until slightly thickened, about 2 minutes.

4. Transfer to slow cooker stoneware. Stir well. Cover and cook on Low for 6 hours or on High for 3 hours. Spread reserved topping evenly over meat mixture (see Tip, left). Cover and cook on High for 1 hour, until mixture is hot and bubbly.

Almost Classic Moussaka

This is my husband's favorite moussaka — I think he likes it so much because it includes potatoes. Lightly browned in the oven and mixed in with eggplant, they create a heavenly combination. If you're more of a traditionalist, omit the potatoes and increase the quantity of eggplant (see Variation, right). Either way, this is a great dish for a casual evening with friends.

Tips

If you are halving this recipe, be sure to use a small (2½ to 3½ quart) slow cooker.

If you prefer, substitute an equal quantity of beef stock for the wine.

This is the quantity in 1 large can (12 oz/370 mL) evaporated milk.

Make Ahead

Complete Step 2. Cover mixture, ensuring it cools promptly (see Making Ahead, page 17), and refrigerate for up to 2 days. When you're ready to cook, complete the recipe.

Serves 8

- 2 rimmed baking sheets
- Lightly greased slow cooker stoneware
- Large (minimum 5 quart) oval slow cooker

2	medium eggplants (each about 12 oz/375 g), peeled and sliced into ½-inch (1 cm) thick slices	2
1 tbsp	kosher or sea salt	15 mL
2	large potatoes, peeled and sliced into ¼-inch (0.5 cm) slices	2
¼ cup	olive oil, divided	50 mL
1½ lbs	lean ground beef or lamb	750 g
2	onions, finely chopped	2
4	cloves garlic, minced	4
2 tsp	dried oregano leaves	10 mL
1 tsp	ground cinnamon	5 mL
1 tsp	salt	5 mL
1 tsp	cracked black peppercorns	5 mL
½ cup	dry red wine (see Tips, left)	125 mL
1	can (28 oz/796 mL) tomatoes with juice, coarsely chopped	1

Topping

¼ cup	butter	50 mL
¼ cup	all-purpose flour	50 mL
1½ cups	warm evaporated milk (see Tips, left)	375 mL
1½ cups	warm water	375 mL
½ tsp	salt	2 mL
½ tsp	freshly grated nutmeg	2 mL
3	egg yolks	3
¼ cup	finely grated Parmesan	50 mL

1. Sprinkle eggplant with salt and let stand in a colander for 30 minutes to 1 hour. Rinse thoroughly under cold running water and pat dry. Meanwhile, preheat oven to 425°F (220°C). Brush eggplant and potato slices on both sides with about 2 tbsp (25 mL) of the olive oil. Spread evenly on baking sheets and bake in preheated oven until soft and golden, turning once, about 20 minutes. Remove from oven and set aside.

2. In a skillet, heat remaining 2 tbsp (25 mL) olive oil over medium-high heat. Add beef and onions and cook, stirring, until meat is lightly browned and no trace of pink remains, about 8 minutes. Add garlic, oregano, cinnamon, salt and peppercorns and cook, stirring, for 1 minute. Add wine, bring to a boil and boil for 2 minutes. Add tomatoes with juice and return to a boil. Remove from heat and set aside.

3. **Topping:** In a saucepan over medium-high heat, melt butter. Add flour, whisking until smooth and mixture begins to turn golden, about 2 minutes. Reduce heat and gradually add milk and water, whisking constantly. Stir in salt and nutmeg. Cook, stirring frequently, until mixture thickens, about 10 minutes. Remove from heat. In a small bowl, beat egg yolks. Gradually beat in 1 cup (250 mL) of the hot sauce, whisking constantly. Return to saucepan and stir well.

4. In prepared stoneware, place half the eggplant and potatoes, overlapping as necessary. Spread with half of the meat mixture. Repeat. Spread with topping and sprinkle with Parmesan. Place 2 clean tea towels, each folded in half (so you will have 4 layers), over top of stoneware to absorb moisture. Cover and cook on High for 3 hours, until mixture is bubbly and slightly brown around the edges. If desired, place under a preheated broiler to brown top.

Variation

Classic Moussaka: Substitute an additional medium eggplant for the potatoes.

Braised Veal with Pearl Onions and Sweet Peas

Here veal is braised in white wine and chicken stock to produce a richly satisfying yet surprisingly light stew. I serve this with a simple risotto — one made with just onions and chicken stock and seasoned liberally with black pepper — for a delicious meal.

Tips

If you are halving this recipe, be sure to use a small (approx. 1½ to 3 quart) slow cooker.

To peel pearl onions, cut an "x" in the root end and drop them into a pot of rapidly boiling water for about 30 seconds. Drain in a colander and run under cold running water. The skins should lift off quite easily with a little prodding from you and a sharp paring knife.

Make Ahead

Complete Step 3. Cover and refrigerate for up to 2 days. When you're ready to cook, complete the recipe.

Serves 6

- Medium to large (3½ to 5 quart) slow cooker

2 tbsp	olive oil (approx.), divided	25 mL
2 oz	pancetta, diced	60 g
2 lbs	trimmed stewing veal, cut into 1-inch (2.5 cm) cubes	1 kg
¼ cup	all-purpose flour	50 mL
2	carrots, peeled and diced	2
2	stalks celery, diced	2
2	cloves garlic, minced	2
1 tsp	dried thyme leaves	5 mL
1 tsp	salt	5 mL
½ tsp	cracked black peppercorns	2 mL
2	bay leaves	2
1 cup	dry white wine	250 mL
2 cups	chicken or veal stock	500 mL
24	pearl onions, peeled (see Tips, left)	24
2 cups	sweet green peas, thawed if frozen	500 mL
	Freshly ground black pepper	
	Whipping (35%) cream, optional	

1. In a skillet, heat 1 tbsp (15 mL) of the oil over medium-high heat. Add pancetta and cook, stirring, until browned, about 3 minutes. Using a slotted spoon, transfer to stoneware. Set pan aside.

2. On a plate or in a plastic bag, dredge veal in flour until evenly coated. Return pan to element over medium-high heat. Add veal, in batches, and brown on all sides, transferring to stoneware as completed and adding more oil if necessary.

3. Reduce heat to medium. Add remaining tbsp (15 mL) of oil to pan. Add carrots and celery and cook, stirring, until softened, about 7 minutes. Add garlic, thyme, salt, peppercorns and bay leaves and cook, stirring, for 1 minute. Add wine, bring to a boil and boil for 2 minutes, stirring and scraping up brown bits from the bottom of the pan. Add stock. Return to a boil.

4. Transfer to stoneware. Stir in onions. Cover and cook on Low for 8 hours or on High for 4 hours, until veal is very tender. Add peas and cook on High about 10 minutes, until tender. Season to taste with pepper. If desired, add a drizzle of cream. Serve immediately.

Entertaining Worthy

Can Be Halved
see Tips, below

Braised Veal in Creamy Sorrel Sauce

Sorrel, which looks and tastes like sour spinach, is often used in French cooking to balance rich foods such as cream. Here it complements a veal breast braised with leeks and tarragon and finished with eggs and cream. Save this for a special occasion in late spring when there is still a nip in the air but the first harvest of sorrel has reached farmers' markets. It's wonderful with new potatoes simply boiled in their skins.

Serves 6 to 8

- Medium to large (3½ to 5 quart) slow cooker
- Instant-read meat thermometer

2 tbsp	butter	25 mL
1	boneless veal breast (2 to 3 lbs/1 to 1.5 kg) (see Tips, left)	1
2	leeks, white part only with just a hint of green, thinly sliced	2
1 tbsp	dried tarragon leaves	15 mL
1 tsp	salt	5 mL
1 tsp	cracked black peppercorns	5 mL
1 cup	dry white wine (see Tips, left)	500 mL
1 cup	veal or chicken stock	250 mL
4 cups	packed chopped sorrel leaves	1 L
1 tsp	Dijon mustard	5 mL
1 cup	whipping (35%) cream or crème fraîche	250 mL
1	egg, beaten	1

1. In a skillet over medium-high heat, melt butter. Immediately add veal (you don't want the butter to burn), fat side down, and cook until lightly browned, about 4 minutes. Repeat (the other side will not brown as nicely). Transfer to slow cooker stoneware.

2. Reduce heat to medium. Add leeks to pan and cook, stirring, until softened, about 5 minutes. Add tarragon, salt and peppercorns and cook, stirring, for 1 minute. Add wine, bring to a boil and boil, scraping up brown bits on bottom of pan, for 2 minutes. Stir in stock.

3. Pour over veal. Cover and cook on Low for 6 hours or on High for 3 hours, until an instant-read meat thermometer registers 140°F (60°C). Remove meat from slow cooker and keep warm.

4. Working in batches, stir sorrel into slow cooker. Add mustard and cream and stir well. Cover and cook on High for 10 minutes, until sorrel is wilted. Using an immersion blender, purée. (You can also do this in a food processor, in batches, and return to stoneware.)

5. In a small bowl, beat egg. Gradually beat in 1 cup (250 mL) of the hot sorrel sauce, whisking constantly. Add egg mixture to stoneware and cook on High for 1 minute, stirring constantly. Pour over veal.

Tips

If you are halving this recipe, be sure to use a small (approx. 1½ to 3 quart) slow cooker.

Veal breast comes from the same part of the cow as brisket and shanks. It is usually sold rolled but my butcher provides it flat, like a brisket, which I prefer. If you have a rolled version, by all means use it here. It will take about 10 minutes to brown because you'll need to turn it more.

If you're using a flat piece of meat and it won't fit in your slow cooker, cut it in half and overlap the two pieces.

If you prefer, substitute an extra cup (250 mL) of veal or chicken stock plus 1 tbsp (15 mL) lemon juice for the white wine.

Make Ahead

Complete Step 2, adding 1 tbsp (15 mL) olive oil to pan before softening vegetables. Cover and refrigerate for up to 2 days. When you're ready to cook, complete the recipe.

Rigatoni with Veal Shank Ragù

Served over fat pasta such as rigatoni or bucatelli (a kind of elongated macaroni), this thick, luscious ragù is the perfect dish for a winter weekend in the country or après-ski. With a fire in the fireplace, a tossed salad and some robust red wine, what could be better?

Serves 6

- Medium to large (3½ to 5 quart) slow cooker

1	package (½ oz/14 g) dried porcini mushrooms, rehydrated and finely chopped (see Tips, right)	1
2	veal shanks, each about ¾ lb (375 g)	2
¼ cup	all-purpose flour	50 mL
2 tbsp	olive oil, divided	25 mL
1 tbsp	butter	15 mL
2	onions, finely chopped	2
2	carrots, peeled and diced	2
2	stalks celery, diced	2
4	cloves garlic, minced	4
1 tsp	dried thyme leaves	5 mL
1 tsp	salt	5 mL
½ tsp	cracked black peppercorns	2 mL
1 cup	dry white wine (see Tips, right)	250 mL
1	can (14 oz/398 mL) tomatoes with juice, coarsely chopped	1
1 lb	thick pasta, such as rigatoni, cooked and drained	500 g
	Freshly grated Parmesan	

1. On a plate, dredge veal in flour until lightly coated, shaking off excess. Set excess flour aside.

2. In a skillet, heat 1 tbsp (15 mL) of the oil and butter over medium heat. Add veal and cook until lightly browned on both sides, about 4 minutes. Transfer to slow cooker stoneware.

3. Add remaining tbsp (15 mL) of oil to pan. Add onions, carrots and celery and cook, stirring, until softened, about 7 minutes. Add garlic, thyme, salt, peppercorns and reserved porcini and cook, stirring, for 1 minute. Add reserved flour and cook, stirring, for 1 minute. Add wine, bring to a boil and boil, stirring and scraping up brown bits from bottom of pan, for 2 minutes. Add tomatoes with juice and reserved mushroom liquid and bring to a boil.

4. Transfer to stoneware. Cover and cook on Low for 12 hours or on High for 6 hours, until veal is tender. Transfer veal to a cutting board and chop into bite-size pieces. Return to slow cooker. Using a coffee spoon, scoop marrow from the bones and stir into stew. Taste and adjust seasoning. Serve over hot pasta and pass the Parmesan.

Tips

If you are halving this recipe, be sure to use a small (approx. 1½ to 3 quart) slow cooker.

Combine porcini mushrooms and 1 cup (250 mL) hot water in a bowl. Let stand for 30 minutes. Drain through a fine sieve, reserving liquid. Pat mushrooms dry with a paper towel and chop finely.

If you prefer, substitute 1 cup (250 mL) chicken stock mixed with 2 tsp (10 mL) lemon juice for the wine.

Make Ahead

Complete Step 3. Cover and refrigerate for up to 2 days. When you're ready to cook, complete the recipe.

Hot Sausage Sandwiches

Pork and Lamb

Hot Sausage Sandwiches

These Italian-inspired sandwiches make a great weeknight meal that's a big hit with both kids and adults. If you like your sandwiches spicy, garnish them with roasted banana peppers. All this needs is a tossed salad to complete the meal.

Tip

If you are halving this recipe, be sure to use a small (approx. 1½ to 3 quart) slow cooker.

Make Ahead

Complete Step 1. Cover mixture, ensuring it cools promptly (see Making Ahead, page 17), and refrigerate for up to 2 days. When you're ready to cook, complete the recipe.

Serves 4

- Medium to large (3½ to 5 quart) slow cooker
- Rimmed baking sheet

1 tbsp	olive oil	15 mL
1 lb	Italian sausage, casings removed	500 g
1	onion, finely chopped	1
2	stalks celery, diced	2
1	carrot, peeled and diced	1
2 tsp	dried oregano leaves	10 mL
½ tsp	salt	2 mL
½ tsp	cracked black peppercorns	2 mL
1	piece (2 inches/5 cm) cinnamon stick	1
½ cup	dry white wine, optional	125 mL
1	can (28 oz/796 mL) diced tomatoes, drained	1
1	French baguette, cut into 4 pieces and split horizontally	1
1 cup	shredded mozzarella	250 mL
	Roasted banana peppers, optional	

1. In a skillet, heat oil over medium-high heat. Add sausage, onion, celery and carrot and cook, stirring, until sausage is no longer pink, about 7 minutes. Add oregano, salt, peppercorns and cinnamon stick and cook, stirring, for 1 minute. Add wine, if using, bring to a boil and boil, scraping up brown bits from bottom of pan, for 2 minutes. Stir in tomatoes.

2. Transfer to slow cooker stoneware. Cover and cook on Low for 6 to 8 hours or on High for 3 to 4 hours.

3. When ready to serve, preheat broiler. Place top halves of baguette on baking sheet and sprinkle liberally with mozzarella. Place under broiler until cheese melts and begins to brown. To serve, place 1 bottom half of baguette on each plate. Spoon sausage mixture over, garnish with hot peppers, if using, and top with grilled cheese half.

Spicy Sausage with Beans

This recipe is very versatile. Not only can you vary the kind of sausage to suit whatever is available, the dish itself can be used in a variety of ways. It makes a great main course accompanied by salad or a terrific addition to a buffet, and can even function as a side if your main course is a light one.

Can Be Halved
see Tips, below

Serves 4 to 6

- Medium to large (3½ to 5 quart) slow cooker

2 cups	cooked white beans, drained and rinsed (see Tips, right)	500 mL
1 tbsp	olive oil	15 mL
1 lb	soft spicy sausage, removed from casings (see Tips, right)	500 g
1	onion, chopped	1
4	stalks celery, diced	4
2	cloves garlic, minced	2
1 tsp	salt	5 mL
½ tsp	cracked black peppercorns	2 mL
1	can (28 oz/796 mL) tomatoes with juice, coarsely chopped	1
1 tsp	smoked paprika, optional (see Tips, page 256)	5 mL

1. In a skillet, heat oil over medium-high heat. Add sausage, onion and celery and cook, stirring, until sausage is no longer pink, about 5 minutes. Add garlic, salt and peppercorns and cook, stirring and scraping up brown bits from bottom of pan, for 1 minute. Stir in tomatoes with juice.

2. Transfer to slow cooker stoneware. Stir in beans. Cover and cook on Low for 6 to 8 hours or on High for 3 to 4 hours. If using, dissolve smoked paprika in 1 tbsp (15 mL) water and stir in. Cook on High for 15 minutes to meld flavors.

Tips

If you are halving this recipe, be sure to use a small (approx. 1½ to 3 quart) slow cooker.

Any kind of white bean, such as navy, great Northern or cannellini, works well in this recipe. You can use canned beans or cook dried beans yourself (see Basic Beans, page 341).

If you're looking for a bit of "wow" factor, make this recipe using merguez sausage, a North African specialty made with lamb and seasoned with harissa. The flavor is fantastic. It is also great made with chorizo, or even Italian sausage from the supermarket. The choice is yours.

Make Ahead

Complete Step 1. Cover mixture, ensuring it cools promptly (see Making Ahead, page 17), and refrigerate for up to 2 days. When you're ready to cook, complete the recipe.

Can Be Halved
see Tips, below

Sausage-Spiked Chickpeas with Yogurt

It's hard to believe that a dish so simple to make can taste so delicious. This is the perfect combination of ingredients — they seem to work synergistically, each enhancing the others. The slightly sour tang of the yogurt makes a particularly nice finish.

Tips

If you are halving this recipe, be sure to use a small (approx. 1½ to 3 quart) slow cooker.

If you're looking for some "wow" factor, make this recipe using merguez sausage, a North African specialty made with lamb and seasoned with harissa. The flavor is fantastic. It is also great made with chorizo, or even Italian sausage from the supermarket. The choice is yours.

Make Ahead

Complete Step 1. Cover mixture, ensuring it cools promptly (see Making Ahead, page 17), and refrigerate for up to 2 days. When you're ready to cook, complete the recipe.

Serves 4

- Medium to large (3½ to 5 quart) slow cooker

1 tbsp	olive oil	15 mL
1 lb	spicy sausage, removed from casings (see Tips, left)	500 g
2	onions, finely chopped	2
1 tbsp	ground cumin	15 mL
2 tbsp	tomato paste	25 mL
1	can (28 oz/796 mL) tomatoes with juice	1
1 cup	chicken stock or water	250 mL
1	potato, peeled and shredded	1
3 cups	cooked chickpeas	750 mL
½ cup	plain yogurt	125 mL
¼ cup	finely chopped parsley leaves	50 mL

1. In a skillet, heat oil over medium-high heat. Add sausage and onions and cook, stirring and breaking up with a spoon, until sausage is cooked through, about 7 minutes. Add cumin and cook, stirring, for 1 minute. Stir in tomato paste. Add tomatoes with juice and stock and bring to a boil, scraping up brown bits from bottom of pan.

2. Transfer to slow cooker stoneware. Stir in potato and chickpeas. Cover and cook on Low for 6 to 8 hours or on High for 3 to 4 hours, until hot and bubbly. To serve, ladle into bowls, top with yogurt and garnish with parsley.

Kale-Spiked Sausages and Beans

Here's a very simple yet delicious dish that is a perfect weeknight meal. Chorizo makes the flavors authentically Spanish or Portuguese, but I've also used my Greek butcher's homemade leek sausage, with splendid results.

Can Be Halved
see Tips, below

Serves 4

- Large (approx. 5 quart) slow cooker

1 tbsp	olive oil	15 mL
2	onions, finely chopped	2
2	stalks celery, diced	2
1 lb	fresh pork sausage, such as chorizo or Italian, removed from casings	500 g
2	cloves garlic, minced	2
½ tsp	salt	2 mL
½ tsp	cracked black peppercorns	2 mL
4 cups	cooked white beans, such as cannellini (see Tips, right)	1 L
1 cup	chicken broth	250 mL
4 cups	packed chopped kale (about 1 bunch)	1 L
2 tbsp	red wine vinegar	25 mL

1. In a large skillet, heat oil over medium-high heat. Add onions, celery and sausage and cook, stirring, until sausage is no longer pink, about 7 minutes. Add garlic, salt and peppercorns and cook, stirring, for 1 minute. Stir in beans and chicken broth and bring to a boil, scraping up brown bits from bottom of pan.

2. Transfer to slow cooker stoneware. Cover and cook on Low for 6 hours or on High for 3 hours, until hot and bubbly. Add kale, in batches, stirring to submerge before adding the next batch. Cover and cook on High about 15 minutes, until kale is tender. Stir in vinegar and serve.

Tips

If you are halving this recipe, be sure to use a small (2 to 3½ quart) slow cooker.

Cook 2 cups (500 mL) dried beans yourself (see Basic Beans, page 341) or use 2 cans (each 14 to 19 oz/398 to 540 mL) beans, thoroughly rinsed and drained.

Make Ahead

Complete Step 1. Cover mixture, ensuring it cools promptly (see Making Ahead, page 17), and refrigerate for up to 2 days. When you're ready to cook, complete the recipe.

Entertaining Worthy

Can Be Halved
see Tips, below

Tex-Mex Pork Stew

I love the combination of flavors in this delicious stew, which is a perfect dish for a casual evening with friends. I like to serve it over polenta, adding a big tossed salad to complete the meal, but a simple green vegetable and warm tortillas will also do the trick.

Serves 6

- Medium to large (3½ to 8 quart) slow cooker

1 tbsp	cumin seeds	15 mL
1 tbsp	coriander seeds	15 mL
1 tbsp	fennel seeds	15 mL
2 lbs	trimmed pork shoulder or blade (butt), cut into 1-inch (2.5 cm) cubes, and patted dry	1 kg
2 tbsp	olive oil, divided	25 mL
2	onions, finely chopped	2
2	carrots, peeled and diced	2
2	stalks celery, diced	2
4	cloves garlic, minced	4
2 tsp	dried oregano leaves	10 mL
2 tsp	dried thyme leaves	10 mL
1 tsp	salt	5 mL
1 tsp	finely grated lemon zest	5 mL
½ tsp	cracked black peppercorns	2 mL
1 cup	dry white wine (see Tips, left)	250 mL
2 cups	chicken stock	500 mL
2	dried mild New Mexico, ancho or guajillo chiles	2
2 cups	boiling water	500 mL
½ cup	packed cilantro leaves	125 mL
¼ cup	freshly squeezed lemon juice	50 mL
1 to 2	jalapeño pepper(s), seeded and coarsely chopped (see Tips, left)	1 to 2

1. In a dry skillet over medium heat, toast cumin, coriander and fennel seeds until fragrant, about 3 minutes. Using a mortar and pestle or a spice grinder, pound or grind as finely as you can. Toss with pork. Cover and refrigerate overnight.

2. In a large skillet, heat 1 tbsp (15 mL) of the oil over medium-high heat. Add pork, in batches, and cook, stirring, until lightly browned, about 4 minutes per batch. Transfer to slow cooker stoneware as completed.

Tips

If you are halving this recipe, be sure to use a small (approx. 1½ to 3 quart) slow cooker.

If you prefer, instead of wine, substitute 1 cup (250 mL) chicken stock plus 1 tbsp (15 mL) lemon juice.

One jalapeño pepper produces a mildly spiced stew. If you're a heat seeker, use two. If you like a bit of smoke and more spice, substitute an equal quantity of chipotle peppers in adobo sauce.

Make Ahead

Complete Steps 1, 3 and 4. Cover and refrigerate pork, vegetable and chile mixtures separately for up to 2 days. (The chile mixture will lose some of its vibrancy. For best results, complete Step 4 while the stew is cooking.) When you're ready to cook, brown the pork and complete the recipe. Or, if you prefer, add the unbrowned pork to the stoneware along with the vegetable mixture, being aware that the result will not be as flavorful as that produced using browned meat.

3. Reduce heat to medium. Add remaining tbsp (15 mL) of the oil to pan. Add onions, carrots and celery and cook, stirring, until carrots have softened, about 7 minutes. Add garlic, oregano, thyme, salt, lemon zest and peppercorns and cook, stirring, for 1 minute. Add wine, bring to a boil and boil for 2 minutes, scraping up brown bits from bottom of pan. Transfer to slow cooker stoneware. Add chicken stock and stir well.

4. About 1 hour before the stew has finished cooking, in a heatproof bowl, soak dried chiles in boiling water for 30 minutes, weighing down with a cup to ensure they remain submerged. Drain, discarding soaking liquid and stems, and chop coarsely. Transfer to a blender. Add cilantro, lemon juice and jalapeño. Purée, scraping down the sides of the blender if necessary.

5. Add chile mixture to stoneware. Cover and cook on High for 30 minutes, until hot and bubbly and flavors meld.

Can Be Halved
see Tips, below

Bacon-Studded Lentils with Smoked Sausage

This dish is reminiscent of French country cooking. Adding the cherry tomatoes at the end gives great flavor and texture to a classically simple dish. Serve this with a tossed green salad for a delicious meal.

Serves 6 to 8

Tips

If you are halving this recipe, be sure to use a small (approx. 1½ to 3 quart) slow cooker.

For best results, use Puy lentils, a French green lentil with robust flavor that holds its shape during cooking. Red lentils, which are very soft and dissolve during cooking, would not work well in this recipe.

Make Ahead

Complete Step 2. Cover and refrigerate mixture for up to 2 days. When you're ready to cook, complete the recipe.

• Medium to large (3½ to 5 quart) slow cooker

4	slices bacon	4
2	onions, finely chopped	2
2	stalks celery, diced	2
2	carrots, peeled and diced	2
4	cloves garlic, minced	4
1 tsp	ground turmeric	5 mL
1 tsp	salt	5 mL
½ tsp	cracked black peppercorns	2 mL
2 cups	green or brown lentils (see Tips, left)	500 mL
2 tbsp	red wine vinegar	25 mL
1 tbsp	Dijon mustard	15 mL
1	can (14 oz/398 mL) diced tomatoes with juice	1
3 cups	chicken or vegetable stock	750 mL
8 oz	smoked sausage, such as kielbasa, sliced	250 g
1 cup	cherry tomatoes, halved	250 mL

1. In a skillet over medium-high heat, sauté bacon until crisp. Using a slotted spoon, transfer to a paper towel to drain. When cool, crumble and refrigerate. Drain off all but 2 tbsp (25 mL) fat from pan or add enough olive oil to make the required quantity.

2. Reduce heat to medium. Add onions, celery and carrots and cook, stirring, until softened, about 7 minutes. Add garlic, turmeric, salt and peppercorns and cook, stirring, for 1 minute. Add lentils and toss until coated. Add vinegar, Dijon mustard and canned tomatoes with juice and cook, stirring and scraping up brown bits from bottom of pan, until mixture is hot and bubbly.

3. Transfer to slow cooker stoneware. Stir in stock. Cover and cook on Low for 8 hours or on High for 4 hours, until lentils are tender. Stir in smoked sausage, cherry tomatoes and reserved bacon. Cover and cook on High for 15 minutes, until heated through.

Choucroute Ragoût

If you like sauerkraut — and I do — this is superb winter fare. If you have access to smoked pork chops, substitute an equal quantity for the sausage. I like to serve this with country-style bread and a pot of good Dijon mustard. Little dollops of mustard on the frankfurters add a lovely touch.

Can Be Halved
see Tips, below

Serves 6

- Medium to large (3½ to 5 quart) slow cooker

4 cups	sauerkraut, soaked, drained and rinsed (see Tips, right)	1 L
4 oz	chunk bacon, diced	125 g
2	onions, finely chopped	2
2	carrots, peeled and diced	2
1 tsp	cracked black peppercorns	5 mL
1 tsp	caraway seeds	5 mL
1	bay leaf	1
1 cup	dry white wine (see Tips, page 242)	250 mL
2	potatoes, peeled and shredded	2
2 cups	chicken stock	500 mL
2	frankfurters, sliced	2
8 oz	smoked pork sausage, such as kielbasa, cubed	250 g

1. In a skillet, cook bacon over medium-high heat until browned. Using a slotted spoon, transfer to paper towels to drain. Set aside. Drain all but 2 tbsp (25 mL) fat from pan, if necessary.

2. Add onions and carrots to pan and cook, stirring, until softened, about 7 minutes. Add peppercorns, caraway seeds and bay leaf and cook, stirring, for 1 minute. Add wine, bring to a boil and boil for 2 minutes, scraping up brown bits from bottom of pan.

3. Transfer to slow cooker stoneware. Add drained sauerkraut, potatoes, chicken stock and reserved bacon. Cover and cook on Low for 6 hours or on High for 3 hours. Add frankfurters and smoked sausage. Cover and cook on High for 15 minutes, until frankfurters are heated through.

Tips

If you are halving this recipe, be sure to use a small (approx. 1½ to 3 quart) slow cooker.

The quality of your sauerkraut makes a big difference to the results you'll achieve with this dish. If I don't have any of my own homemade sauerkraut on hand, I buy it at a farmers' market or from a local Alsatian chef. Supermarket sauerkraut is usually highly acidic, which I believe is why so many people dislike the product — they have never tasted the real thing. For best results, before using, soak the sauerkraut in a large bowl of water for about an hour and rinse in several changes of water to reduce the bitter vinegar taste.

Make Ahead

Complete Steps 1 and 2, refrigerating cooked bacon and vegetable mixtures separately for up to 2 days. When you're ready to cook, complete the recipe.

Can Be Halved
see Tips, below

Tips

If you are halving this recipe, be sure to use a small (approx. 1½ to 3 quart) slow cooker.

To rehydrate ancho chiles for this recipe, about 1 hour before recipe has finished cooking, in a heatproof bowl, soak dried ancho peppers in boiling water for 30 minutes, weighing down with a cup to ensure they are submerged. Drain, reserving ½ cup (125 mL) of the soaking liquid. Discard stems and chop chiles coarsely.

Make Ahead

Complete Steps 2 and 4. Cover and refrigerate vegetable and chile mixtures separately for up to 2 days. (The chile mixture will lose some of its vibrancy if held this long. For best results, complete Step 4 while the chili is cooking.) When you're ready to cook, brown the pork and continue with the recipe. Or, if you prefer, add the unbrowned pork to the stoneware along with the vegetable mixture, being aware that the result will not be as flavorful as that produced using browned meat.

Red Chili with Anchos

This robust chili is a meal in itself. I like to serve it with warm whole-grain rolls and an abundance of garnishes to lighten it up.

Serves 8

- Large (minimum 5 quart) slow cooker

2 tbsp	olive oil, divided	25 mL
2 lbs	trimmed pork shoulder or blade (butt), cut into 1-inch (2.5 cm) cubes, and patted dry (see Tips, page 248)	1 kg
2	onions, finely chopped	2
4	stalks celery, diced	4
4	cloves garlic, minced	4
1 tbsp	dried oregano leaves	15 mL
1 tbsp	ground cumin (see Tips, page 248)	15 mL
1 tsp	salt	5 mL
1 tsp	cracked black peppercorns	5 mL
1	piece (2 inches/5 cm) cinnamon stick	1
1 tbsp	cider vinegar	15 mL
1	can (28 oz/796 mL) crushed tomatoes	1
3 cups	cooked pinto beans (see Tips, page 292)	750 mL
2	dried ancho chiles, rehydrated (see Tips, left)	2
2	jalapeño peppers, seeded and chopped	2
½ cup	celery leaves or parsley	125 mL
	Sour cream or shredded Cheddar or Jack cheese	
	Shredded lettuce	
	Finely chopped red or green onion	

1. In a skillet, heat 1 tbsp (15 mL) of the oil over medium-high heat. Add pork, in batches, and cook, stirring, until browned, about 4 minutes per batch. Transfer to stoneware as completed.

2. Reduce heat to medium. Add remaining tbsp (15 mL) of oil to the pan. Add onions and celery and cook, stirring, until softened, about 5 minutes. Add garlic, oregano, cumin, salt, peppercorns and cinnamon stick and cook, stirring, for 1 minute. Add vinegar and boil until evaporated, about 10 seconds. Add tomatoes and bring to a boil scraping up brown bits from bottom of pan.

3. Transfer to stoneware. Add beans and stir well. Cover and cook on Low for 8 hours or on High for 4 hours, until meat is tender.

4. In a blender, combine rehydrated chiles, jalapeños, celery leaves and reserved soaking liquid (see Tips, left). Purée.

5. Add chile mixture to stoneware and stir well. Cover and cook on High for 30 minutes, until hot and bubbly and flavors meld. Pass sour cream, shredded lettuce and chopped onion at the table and let people help themselves.

Chipotle Pork Tacos

Liberally garnished, these yummy tacos are a meal in themselves. They make a great weeknight dinner, and they're a perfect solution for those nights when everyone is coming and going at different times. Just shred the pork, keep it warm in the sauce and leave the accompaniments within easy reach.

Can Be Halved
see Tips, below

Serves 6

- Medium to large (3½ to 5 quart) slow cooker

2 tbsp	olive oil, divided	25 mL
2 lbs	trimmed boneless pork shoulder or blade (butt), patted dry	1 kg
2	onions, thinly sliced on the vertical	2
2	stalks celery, diced	2
4	cloves garlic, minced	4
1 tbsp	ground cumin (see Tips, page 248)	15 mL
1 tbsp	dried oregano leaves	15 mL
1 tsp	salt	5 mL
1 tsp	cracked black peppercorns	5 mL
1	piece (2 inches/5 cm) cinnamon stick	1
2	bay leaves	2
1	can (28 oz/796 mL) tomatoes with juice, coarsely chopped	1
1 to 2	chipotle pepper(s) in adobo sauce, minced (see Tips, right)	1 to 2
	Warm soft tortillas	
	Diced avocado tossed in fresh lime juice	
	Shredded lettuce	
	Crumbled soft fresh cheese, such as goat cheese or Mexican queso fresco	
	Finely chopped green or red onion	

1. In a skillet, heat 1 tbsp (15 mL) of the oil over medium-high heat. Add pork and brown well, about 3 minutes per side. Transfer to slow cooker stoneware.

2. Add remaining tbsp (15 mL) of oil to pan. Add onions and celery and cook, stirring, until softened, about 5 minutes. Add garlic, cumin, oregano, salt, peppercorns, cinnamon stick and bay leaves and cook, stirring, for 1 minute. Add tomatoes with juice and bring to a boil, scraping up brown bits from bottom of pan.

3. Transfer to slow cooker stoneware. Cover and cook on Low for 8 hours or on High for 4 hours, until pork is very tender. Add chipotle pepper(s), stir well, cover and cook on High for 10 minutes.

4. Transfer pork to a cutting board and, using 2 forks, shred. To serve, spoon pork onto tortillas and spoon sauce to taste over it (see Tips, right). Garnish with avocado, lettuce, cheese and onion and roll up. Serve immediately.

Tips

If you are halving this recipe, be sure to use a small (approx. 1½ to 3 quart) slow cooker.

In my opinion, this recipe makes slightly too much sauce for the pork, so I spoon it over the shredded pork in a quantity that suits my taste. I refrigerate the excess. When I'm ready for lunch, I heat it to the boiling point and add lots of shredded Cheddar or Jack cheese. It's great over toast.

Chipotle peppers pack quite a wallop, so only add the second one if you're a real heat seeker.

Make Ahead

Complete Step 2. Cover and refrigerate mixture for up to 2 days. When you're ready to cook, brown the pork and continue with the recipe. Or, if you prefer, add the unbrowned pork to the stoneware along with the vegetable mixture, being aware that the result will not be as flavorful as that produced using browned meat.

Entertaining
Worthy

Can Be
Halved
see Tips, below

Ancho-Embraced Pork with Tomatillos

I love the flavors in this simple but sumptuous stew. Serve it over polenta or plain white rice, with plenty of tortillas to soak up the sauce. Make more than you think you'll need — requests for seconds are the norm.

Tips

If you are halving this recipe, be sure to use a small (2½ to 3½ quart) slow cooker.

Many butchers sell cut-up pork stewing meat, which is fine to use in this recipe.

To maximize flavor, instead of buying ground cumin, buy cumin seeds and toast and grind them yourself. Place seeds in a dry skillet over medium heat, stirring, until fragrant, about 3 minutes. Using a mortar and pestle or a spice grinder, pound or grind as finely as you can.

Although ancho chiles are among the mildest chile peppers, 3 chiles produces a zesty dish. If you're heat averse, reduce the quantity to 2.

If you like the taste of cilantro, chop some stems and substitute them for an equal quantity of the leaves called for.

Make Ahead

Complete Step 2. Cover and refrigerate for up to 2 days. When you're ready to cook, complete the recipe.

Serves 6

• Medium to large (3½ to 8 quart) slow cooker

2 tbsp	olive oil, divided	25 mL
2 lbs	trimmed pork shoulder or blade (butt), cut into 1-inch (2.5 cm) cubes, and patted dry (see Tips, left)	1 kg
2	onions, thinly sliced on the vertical	2
2	stalks celery, diced	2
2	carrots, peeled and diced	2
4	cloves garlic, minced	4
2 tsp	ground cumin (see Tips, left)	10 mL
2 tsp	dried oregano leaves, preferably Mexican, crumbled	10 mL
2	bay leaves	2
1 tsp	salt	5 mL
½ tsp	cracked black peppercorns	2 mL
2 tbsp	cider or white vinegar	25 mL
1	can (28 oz/796 mL) tomatillos, drained and coarsely chopped	1
2 cups	chicken stock	500 mL
2 to 3	dried ancho chiles (see Tips, left)	2 to 3
2 cups	boiling water	500 mL
½ cup	packed cilantro leaves (see Tips, left)	125 mL

1. In a skillet, heat 1 tbsp (15 mL) of the oil over medium-high heat. Add pork, in batches, and brown on all sides, about 4 minutes per batch. Transfer to slow cooker stoneware as completed.

2. Reduce heat to medium. Add remaining tbsp (15 mL) of oil to pan. Add onions, celery and carrots and cook, stirring, until vegetables are softened, about 7 minutes. Add garlic, cumin, oregano, bay leaves, salt and peppercorns and cook, stirring, for 1 minute. Add vinegar and cook, stirring, for 1 minute, scraping up brown bits from bottom of pan. Add tomatillos and stir well.

3. Transfer to slow cooker stoneware. Add chicken stock and stir well. Cover and cook on Low for 8 hours or on High for 4 hours, until pork is very tender.

4. About 1 hour before recipe has finished cooking, in a heatproof bowl, soak dried chiles in boiling water for 30 minutes, weighing down with a cup to ensure they remain submerged. Drain, discarding soaking liquid and stems, and chop coarsely. Transfer to a blender along with cilantro. Scoop out 1/2 cup (125 mL) of the cooking broth from the pork and add to blender. Purée. Stir puréed mixture into stoneware. Cover and cook on High for 30 minutes, until flavors meld.

Farmhouse Pork Stew

This Italian-inspired stew is rustic and flavorful. On a cold winter's day there is nothing better than a steaming serving accompanied by polenta and a bottle of good Chianti.

Serves 6

- Medium to large (3½ to 8 quart) slow cooker

2 tbsp	olive oil, divided	25 mL
2 oz	pancetta, diced	60 g
2 lbs	trimmed pork shoulder or blade (butt), cut into 1-inch (2.5 cm) cubes, and patted dry (see Tips, left)	1 kg
2	onions, finely chopped	2
2	carrots, peeled and diced	2
2	stalks celery, diced	2
6	cloves garlic, minced	6
1 tsp	salt	5 mL
½ tsp	cracked black peppercorns	2 mL
3 to 4	sprigs rosemary with stems, or 1 tbsp (15 mL) dried rosemary	3 to 4
1 cup	dry white wine (see Tips, left)	250 mL
1	can (28 oz/796 mL) tomatoes with juice, coarsely chopped	1
2 tbsp	freshly squeezed lemon juice	25 mL
1 tbsp	sweet paprika	15 mL
¼ tsp	cayenne pepper	1 mL

1. In a skillet, heat 1 tbsp (15 mL) of the oil over medium-high heat. Add pancetta and cook, stirring, until crisp. Using a slotted spoon, transfer to slow cooker stoneware. Add pork, in batches, and cook, stirring, until browned, about 4 minutes per batch. Transfer to slow cooker stoneware.

2. Reduce heat to medium. Add remaining tbsp (15 mL) of oil to pan. Add onions, carrots and celery and cook, stirring, until vegetables are softened, about 7 minutes. Add garlic, salt, peppercorns and rosemary and toss until coated. Add wine, bring to a boil and cook, stirring for 2 minutes, scraping up brown bits from bottom of pan. Stir in tomatoes with juice.

3. Transfer to slow cooker stoneware. Cover and cook on Low for 8 hours or on High for 4 hours, until meat is very tender.

4. In a small bowl, combine lemon juice, paprika and cayenne, stirring until spices dissolve. Add to slow cooker and stir well. Cover and cook on High for 10 minutes, until flavors meld.

Tips

If you are halving this recipe, be sure to use a small (2½ to 3½ quart) slow cooker.

Many butchers sell cut-up pork stewing meat, which is fine to use in this recipe.

If you prefer, substitute 1 cup (250 mL) chicken stock plus 1 tbsp (15 mL) lemon juice for the wine.

Make Ahead

Complete Step 2. Cover and refrigerate for up to 2 days. When you're ready to cook, complete the recipe.

Home-Style Pork and Beans

There is nothing fancy about this dish — it's real down-home cooking that is simply delicious. Serve it with thick slices of hearty bread, a big salad and cold beer or robust red wine. This is a great recipe for a tailgate or Super Bowl party.

Serves 6

- Medium to large (3½ to 6 quart) slow cooker

2 cups	dried white beans such as great Northern or navy, soaked, drained and rinsed (see Tips, right)	500 mL
½ cup	pure maple syrup	125 mL
½ cup	grainy mustard	125 mL
½ cup	ketchup	125 mL
½ cup	tomato paste	125 mL
1 tsp	salt	5 mL
1 tsp	cracked black peppercorns	5 mL
8 oz	chunk pork belly or bacon (see Tips, right)	250 g
3	onions, finely chopped	3
4	cloves garlic, minced	4

1. In a saucepan, combine rinsed beans with 6 cups (1.5 L) fresh cold water (see Tips, right). Bring to a boil over medium heat. Reduce heat and simmer until beans are just tender to the bite but not fully cooked, about 30 minutes. Scoop out 1½ cups (375 mL) of the cooking liquid and set aside. Drain beans and set aside, discarding remaining liquid.

2. In a large measuring cup, combine maple syrup, mustard, ketchup, tomato paste, salt, peppercorns and ½ cup (125 mL) of the bean cooking liquid. Stir well and set aside.

3. In slow cooker stoneware, place half the pork. Add half the onions and garlic, sprinkling evenly over bottom of stoneware. Add half of the beans and remaining pork. Repeat with remaining onion, garlic and beans. Pour tomato mixture evenly over top.

4. Cover and cook on Low for 8 hours or on High for 4 hours, adding more bean cooking liquid, if necessary to keep beans moist, until beans are tender and mixture is hot and bubbly.

Tips

If you are halving this recipe, be sure to use a small (approx. 1½ to 3 quart) slow cooker.

If you prefer, cook the beans in your slow cooker (see Basic Beans, page 341) and skip Step 2, reserving 1½ cups (375 mL) of the cooking liquid.

If you are using pork belly, cut it into two equal pieces. If bacon, slice it thinly.

Make Ahead

Complete Step 1, retaining enough cooking liquid to cover the cooked beans. Cover and refrigerate for up to 2 days. When you're ready to cook, drain the beans, reserving 1½ cups (375 mL) of the cooking liquid, and continue with the recipe.

Pork Belly with Flageolets

This is, quite simply, pork and beans for gourmands. Made with luscious pork belly, which melts into the mélange and falls apart after cooking, and flageolets, the Rolls-Royce of dried beans, it is the ne plus ultra *of rustic cooking. Just add a tossed green salad, lots of crusty bread and, perhaps, an appropriate bottle of wine.*

Tips

If you are halving this recipe, be sure to use a small (approx. 1½ to 3 quart) slow cooker.

To soak the flageolets, combine them in a saucepan with 6 cups (1.5 L) cold water. Bring to a boil over medium heat and boil rapidly for 3 minutes. Turn off element and let stand for 1 hour. Or soak overnight in cold water. Drain and rinse thoroughly under cold running water.

Make Ahead

Complete Step 2. Cover and refrigerate mixture for up to 2 days. When you're ready to cook, complete the recipe.

Serves 6

- Medium to large (3½ to 5 quart) slow cooker

2 cups	dried flageolets, soaked and drained (see Tips, left)	500 mL
1 lb	boneless pork belly	500 g
1 tbsp	olive oil	15 mL
2	onions, finely chopped	2
2	carrots, peeled and diced	2
2	stalks celery, diced	2
4	cloves garlic, minced	4
1 tsp	dried thyme leaves	5 mL
1 tsp	dried rosemary leaves	5 mL
1 tsp	salt	5 mL
½ tsp	cracked black peppercorns	2 mL
1 cup	dry white wine	250 mL
¼ cup	tomato paste	50 mL
2 cups	chicken stock	500 mL

1. Place pork belly in slow cooker stoneware.

2. In a skillet, heat oil over medium heat. Add onions, carrots and celery and cook, stirring, until softened, about 7 minutes. Add garlic, thyme, rosemary, salt and peppercorns and cook, stirring, for 1 minute. Add flageolets and toss until well coated with mixture. Add wine and tomato paste, bring to a boil and boil for 2 minutes. Stir in chicken stock.

3. Transfer to slow cooker stoneware. Cover and cook on Low for 8 hours or on High for 4 hours, until beans are very tender.

Wine-Spiked Pork and Beans

Serve this dish whenever you need a supplementary main course or a substantial additional side. It's perfect for a potluck or as part of a buffet. Delicious but rich, in small portions it also makes a nutritious dinner accompanied by salad and some whole-grain bread.

Can Be Halved
see Tips, below

Serves 8 to 10

- Medium to large (3½ to 5 quart) slow cooker

1½ cups	dried white beans (navy or haricot) soaked, drained and rinsed (see Basic Beans, page 341)	375 mL
2 tbsp	olive oil	25 mL
2	onions, finely chopped	2
2	carrots, peeled and diced	2
2	stalks celery, diced	2
4	cloves garlic, minced	4
2 tsp	dried thyme leaves	10 mL
1 tsp	salt	5 mL
1 tsp	cracked black peppercorns	5 mL
¼ cup	tomato paste	50 mL
1½ cups	dry red wine	375 mL
3 cups	water or chicken stock	750 mL
8 oz	pork belly, including fat, chopped	250 g

1. In a skillet, heat oil over medium heat. Add onions, carrots and celery and cook, stirring, until vegetables are softened, about 7 minutes. Add garlic, thyme, salt and peppercorns and cook, stirring, for 1 minute. Stir in tomato paste and wine, bring to a boil and boil for 2 minutes.

2. Transfer to slow cooker stoneware. Add drained beans, water and pork and stir well. Cover and cook on Low for 8 to 10 hours or on High for 4 to 5 hours, until beans are tender.

Tips

If you are halving this recipe, be sure to use a small (approx. 1½ to 3 quart) slow cooker.

Slow cookers tend to cook at different rates and, in my experience, some slow cookers simply do not produce tender beans even after 8 hours of cooking on Low. If this is your experience, you have two options. Bring the beans to a boil on top of the stove with the water or stock called for in the recipe and simmer them for at least 10 minutes before adding to the stoneware. Cooking them on High should also do the trick.

Make Ahead

Complete Step 1. Cover and refrigerate mixture for up to 2 days. When you're ready to cook, complete the recipe.

Beer-Braised Chili

If you're tired of beef-based chilies with red beans, try this equally delicious but lighter version. It makes a great potluck dish or the centerpiece for a casual evening with friends. For a special occasion, serve with hot cornbread.

Serves 8

Tips

If you are halving this recipe, be sure to use a small (2½ to 3½ quart) slow cooker.

For this quantity of beans, use 2 cans (14 to 19 oz/398 to 540 mL) drained and rinsed black-eyed peas, or soak and cook 2 cups (500 mL) dried beans yourself (see Basic Beans, page 341).

Many butchers sell cut-up pork stewing meat, which is fine to use in this recipe.

For best results, toast and grind the cumin and coriander seeds yourself. Place seeds in a dry skillet over medium heat, stirring until fragrant, about 3 minutes. Using a mortar and pestle or a spice grinder, pound or grind as finely as you can.

Make Ahead

Complete Step 2. Cover and refrigerate mixture for up to 2 days. When you're ready to cook, complete the recipe.

- Large (minimum 5 quart) slow cooker

4 cups	cooked black-eyed peas (see Tips, left)	1 L
2 tbsp	olive oil, divided	25 mL
4 oz	chunk bacon, diced	125 g
2 lbs	trimmed pork shoulder or blade (butt), cut into 1-inch (2.5 cm) cubes, and patted dry (see Tips, left)	1 kg
2	onions, finely chopped	2
4	stalks celery, diced	4
4	cloves garlic, minced	4
2 tsp	ground cumin (see Tips, left)	10 mL
2 tsp	ground coriander	10 mL
2 tsp	dried oregano leaves, crumbled	10 mL
1 tsp	salt	5 mL
1 tsp	cracked black peppercorns	5 mL
1	piece (2 inches/5 cm) cinnamon stick	1
1 cup	flat beer	250 mL
1	can (14 oz/398 mL) crushed tomatoes	1
1	each red and green bell peppers, seeded and diced	1
1 to 2	chipotle peppers in adobo sauce, minced	1 to 2
	Sour cream	
	Finely chopped red onion	
	Shredded Monterey Jack cheese	

1. In a skillet, heat 1 tbsp (15 mL) of the oil over medium-high heat. Add bacon and cook, stirring, until browned and crisp, about 4 minutes. Using a slotted spoon, transfer to slow cooker stoneware. Add pork, in batches, and cook, stirring, until browned, about 4 minutes per batch. Transfer to stoneware as completed.

2. Reduce heat to medium. Add remaining tbsp (15 mL) of oil to pan. Add onions and celery and cook, stirring, until softened, about 5 minutes. Add garlic, cumin, coriander, oregano, salt, peppercorns and cinnamon and cook, stirring, for 1 minute. Add beer, bring to a boil and boil for 1 minute, scraping up brown bits. Stir in tomatoes.

3. Transfer to stoneware. Stir in peas. Cover and cook on Low for 6 hours or on High for 3 hours. Stir in bell peppers and chipotles. Cover and cook on High about 20 minutes, until peppers are tender. Garnish with any combination of sour cream, onion and/or cheese.

Barbecue Pork on a Bun

In my books, this succulent pork tastes every bit as authentic as slow-cooked Southern barbecue, even though the smokiness is Spanish in origin. The mystery ingredient is smoked paprika. Use either the hot or sweet version to suit your taste. This is great fare for a tailgating party. To complete the Deep South theme, serve this with ice-cold beer and coleslaw.

Tips

If you are halving this recipe, be sure to use a small (approx. 1½ to 3 quart) slow cooker.

Because the pork will not be submerged in the sauce, I recommend turning it at least once during the cooking process and spooning the pan juices over top.

Use hot smoked paprika if you like heat and sweet paprika if you're heat averse. Either way, you'll love the flavor.

Serves 6

• Medium (approx. 4 quart) slow cooker

1 tbsp	Demerara or other raw cane sugar	15 mL
1 tbsp	cracked black peppercorns	15 mL
4	cloves garlic, minced	4
½ tsp	salt	2 mL
2 lbs	trimmed boneless pork shoulder or blade (butt) roast, patted dry (see Tips, page 259)	1 kg

Barbecue Sauce

1 cup	tomato-based chili sauce	250 mL
⅓ cup	apple cider vinegar	75 mL
⅓ cup	Demerara or other raw cane sugar	75 mL
½ tsp	salt	2 mL
2 tsp	smoked paprika (see Tips, left)	10 mL
	Kaiser or onion buns, halved and warmed	

1. In a small bowl, combine sugar, peppercorns, garlic and salt. Rub all over pork. Place in a bowl and cover or in a large resealable plastic bag and refrigerate overnight.

2. **Barbecue Sauce:** In a bowl, combine chili sauce, vinegar, sugar and salt.

3. Place pork in slow cooker stoneware and cover with sauce. Cover and cook on Low for 10 to 12 hours or on High for 5 to 6 hours, until pork is falling apart. Stir in smoked paprika. Cover and cook on High for 20 minutes, until flavors meld.

4. Transfer pork to a cutting board and shred, using two forks. Return to sauce and keep warm. When ready to serve, spoon shredded pork and sauce over warm buns.

Country-Style Salted Pork with Lentils

Entertaining Worthy

Can Be Halved
see Tips, below

This is my variation of a classic French country dish — dry-brined pork simmered with lentils and aromatics. It makes a sumptuous winter meal. Steamed baby turnips along with sliced green beans are the perfect accompaniment.

Serves 6 to 8

- Medium (approx. 4 quart) slow cooker

1 tbsp	fennel seeds, toasted and ground	15 mL
1 tbsp	puréed garlic	15 mL
2 tsp	coarse salt	10 mL
1 tsp	cracked black peppercorns	5 mL
2 lbs	trimmed boneless pork shoulder or blade (butt), patted dry	1 kg
2 tbsp	olive oil, divided	25 mL
2	onions, finely chopped	2
2	stalks celery, diced	2
2	carrots, peeled and diced	2
4	cloves garlic, minced	4
2	whole cloves	2
2	bay leaves	2
1½ cups	green or brown lentils (see Tips, right)	375 mL
1 cup	dry white wine (see Tips, right)	250 mL
4 cups	chicken stock	1 L

1. In a small bowl, combine fennel seeds, garlic, salt and peppercorns. Mix well. Pat meat dry and rub all over with mixture. Cover and refrigerate overnight. Set any juices aside.

2. In a skillet, heat 1 tbsp (15 mL) of the oil over medium-high heat. Add pork and brown, about 4 minutes per side. Transfer to slow cooker stoneware.

3. Reduce heat to medium. Add remaining tbsp (15 mL) of oil to pan. Add onions, celery and carrots and cook, stirring, until vegetables are softened, about 7 minutes. Add garlic, cloves and bay leaves and cook, stirring, for 1 minute. Add lentils and toss until coated. Stir in any reserved meat juices. Add wine, bring to a boil and boil for 2 minutes, scraping up brown bits from bottom of pan. Transfer to slow cooker stoneware. Pour in chicken stock.

4. Cover and cook on Low for 8 hours or on High for 4 hours, until pork is very tender.

Tips

If you are halving this recipe, be sure to use a small (2½ to 3½ quart) slow cooker.

For best results, use Puy lentils, a French green lentil with robust flavor that holds its shape during cooking. Red lentils, which are very soft and dissolve during cooking, would not work well in this recipe.

If you prefer, substitute 1 cup (250 mL) chicken stock plus 1 tbsp (15 mL) lemon juice for the wine.

Make Ahead

Complete Steps 1 and 3, refrigerating meat and vegetable mixtures separately for up to 2 days. When you're ready to cook, brown the pork and continue with the recipe. Or, if you prefer, add the unbrowned pork to the stoneware along with the vegetable mixture, being aware that the result will not be as flavorful as that produced using browned meat.

Entertaining Worthy

Can Be Halved
see Tips, below

Braised Canadian Bacon with Sauerkraut

Also known as peameal bacon in its country of origin, Canadian bacon is made by curing (and sometimes smoking) a loin of pork, which is then rolled in cornmeal. If you're a fan of sauerkraut, which I am, this is a delicious stick-to-the-ribs cold-weather dish. Although it makes a large quantity, it reheats well.

Tips

If you are halving this recipe, be sure to use a small (approx. $1\frac{1}{2}$ to 3 quart) slow cooker.

The quality of your sauerkraut makes a big difference to the results you'll achieve with this dish. If I don't have any of my own homemade sauerkraut on hand, I buy it at a farmers' market or from a local Alsatian chef. Supermarket sauerkraut is usually highly acidic, which I believe explains why so many people dislike the product. For best results, rinse sauerkraut thoroughly in several changes of water to reduce the bitter taste.

Make Ahead

Complete Step 2. Cover and refrigerate mixture for up to 2 days. When you're ready to cook, complete the recipe. Or, if you prefer, add the unbrowned bacon to the stoneware before adding the vegetable mixture, being aware that the result will not be as flavorful as that produced using browned meat.

Serves 8

- Parchment paper
- Medium to large (4 to 8 quart) oval slow cooker

4 cups	sauerkraut, soaked, drained and rinsed (see Tips, left)	1 L
2 tbsp	olive oil	25 mL
1	piece Canadian bacon (about 3 lbs/1.5 kg)	1
1	onion, finely chopped	1
2	carrots, peeled and diced	2
1 tsp	caraway seeds	5 mL
1 tsp	cracked black peppercorns	5 mL
1	bay leaf	1
1 cup	dry white wine (see Tips, page 257)	250 mL
1 cup	chicken stock	250 mL

1. In a skillet, heat 1 tbsp (15 mL) of the oil over medium-high heat. Add bacon and brown on all sides, about 8 minutes. Transfer to slow cooker stoneware.

2. Reduce heat to medium. Add remaining tbsp (15 mL) of oil to pan. Add onion and carrots and cook, stirring, until softened, about 7 minutes. Add caraway seeds, peppercorns and bay leaf and cook, stirring, for 1 minute. Add wine, bring to a boil and boil for 2 minutes, scraping up brown bits from bottom of pan. Add chicken stock.

3. Stir in sauerkraut. Transfer to slow cooker stoneware. Place a large piece of parchment paper over the mixture, pressing it down to brush the food and extending up the sides of the stoneware so it overlaps the rim. (This ensures the mixture will baste in its own flavorful juices during the cooking process.) Cover and cook on Low for 5 hours or on High for $2\frac{1}{2}$ hours, until hot and bubbly. Lift out parchment and discard, being careful not to spill the accumulated liquid into the sauce. To serve, slice or shred bacon and top with sauerkraut mixture.

Savory Braised Pork

This pork is very easy to make but it's disproportionately delicious because marinating it overnight imbues the meat with deep flavor. Add some garlic mashed potatoes and a green vegetable for a terrific Sunday dinner.

Serves 6 to 8

• Medium (3 to 4 quart) slow cooker

2 tsp	coriander seeds	10 mL
2 tsp	cumin seeds	10 mL
1 tsp	cracked black peppercorns	5 mL
6	cloves garlic, puréed	6
1 tsp	coarse salt	5 mL
2 tbsp	olive oil, divided	25 mL
3 lbs	pork shoulder or blade (butt) roast (see Tips, right)	1.5 kg
2	onions, finely chopped	2
2	stalks celery, diced	2
2	carrots, peeled and diced	2
2	bay leaves	2
½ cup	water or chicken stock	125 mL

1. In a skillet over medium heat, toast coriander and cumin seeds until fragrant, about 3 minutes. Transfer to a mortar or a spice grinder. Add peppercorns and coarsely pound or grind. Transfer to a bowl and combine with garlic, salt and 1 tbsp (15 mL) of the oil. Make slits all over meat and fill with spice paste. Rub remainder all over meat. Cover and refrigerate overnight or for up to 24 hours, turning several times, if possible.

2. In a skillet, heat remaining tbsp (15 mL) of oil over medium-high heat. Add pork and brown on all sides, about 10 minutes. Transfer to slow cooker stoneware.

3. Reduce heat to medium. Add onions, celery and carrots and cook, stirring, until softened, about 7 minutes. Stir in bay leaves and water and bring to a boil, scraping up brown bits from bottom of pan.

4. Pour over pork. Cover and cook on Low for 8 hours or on High for 4 hours, until pork is very tender. Transfer meat to a deep platter and keep warm. Transfer sauce to a saucepan and skim off fat. Bring to a boil over medium-high heat and cook until reduced by one-quarter, about 7 minutes. Taste and adjust seasoning. Spoon over pork and serve.

Tips

You can use a bone-in or boneless roast for this recipe, ranging in weight from about 3 to 4 lbs (1.5 to 2 kg). I do, however, suggest you use one from which the skin has been removed, to reduce the quantity of fat.

Pork shoulder can be very fatty. If your pork shoulder isn't trimmed of fat when you purchase it, I recommend removing the string and trimming off as much fat as possible before using.

Make Ahead

Complete Steps 1 and 3. Cover and refrigerate mixtures overnight. When you're ready to cook, brown the pork and continue with the recipe. Or, if you prefer, add the unbrowned marinated pork to the stoneware, then cover with the vegetable mixture, being aware that the result will not be as flavorful as that produced using browned meat.

Cheater's Cassoulet

While it is still a fair bit of work to make this version of the classic French dish, it is not nearly as onerous as the traditional approach, which first roasts the pork and braises the lamb, then combines them with the beans and sausage to simmer. Cassoulet has a real mystique, perhaps because it usually takes several days to make, but it is actually a country dish — rich, delicious and substantial.

Tips

If you are halving this recipe, be sure to use a small (approx. 3 quart) slow cooker.

Be sure to use sausage that is seasoned with "traditional spices." Those containing chile pepper, such as chorizo, will disrupt the flavors of the dish.

Many butchers sell cut-up pork stewing meat, which is fine to use in this recipe.

If you prefer, substitute 1½ cups (375 mL) chicken stock plus 2 tbsp (25 mL) lemon juice for the white wine.

Make Ahead

Complete Step 2. Cover and refrigerate mixture for up to 2 days. When you're ready to cook, complete the recipe.

Serves 12

- Large (minimum 6 quart) slow cooker

4 cups	cooked white beans, such as navy or great Northern, drained and rinsed (see Basic Beans, page 341)	1 L
2 tbsp	olive oil, divided	25 mL
1 lb	pork sausage, removed from casings (see Tips, left)	500 g
2 lbs	trimmed boneless pork shoulder or blade (butt), cut into 1-inch (2.5 cm) cubes, and patted dry (see Tips, left)	1 kg
1 lb	trimmed lamb shoulder, cut into 1-inch (2.5 cm) cubes, and patted dry	500 g
4	onions, chopped	4
6	cloves garlic, minced	6
2 tsp	dried thyme leaves	10
2	bay leaves	2
1 tsp	salt	5 mL
1 tsp	cracked black peppercorns	5 mL
1	can (5½ oz/156 mL) tomato paste	1
1½ cups	dry white wine (see Tips, left)	375 mL
3 cups	chicken stock	750 mL
8 oz	pork belly, thinly sliced	250 g

Topping

2 cups	bread crumbs	500 mL
½ cup	finely chopped parsley	125 mL
2	cloves garlic, minced	2
	Freshly ground black pepper	
¼ cup	melted butter	50 mL

1. In a skillet, heat 1 tbsp (15 mL) of the oil over medium-high heat. Add sausage and cook, stirring, until no hint of pink remains, about 5 minutes. Transfer to slow cooker stoneware. Add pork shoulder, in batches, and cook, stirring, until browned, about 4 minutes per batch. Transfer to slow cooker stoneware. Add lamb, in batches, and cook, stirring, until browned, about 4 minutes per batch. Transfer to stoneware.

2. Reduce heat to medium. Add remaining tbsp (15 mL) of oil to pan. Add onions and cook, stirring, until softened, about 5 minutes. Add garlic, thyme, bay leaves, salt and peppercorns and cook, stirring, for 1 minute. Stir in tomato paste. Add wine, bring to a boil and boil for 2 minutes, scraping up brown bits from bottom of pan.

3. Transfer to slow cooker stoneware. Add chicken stock, pork belly and cooked beans. Stir well. Cover and cook on Low for 8 to 10 hours or on High for 4 to 5 hours, until hot and bubbly.

4. **Topping:** Preheat oven to 350°F (180°C). In a bowl, combine bread crumbs, parsley, garlic and pepper to taste. Mix well. Spread evenly over bean mixture. Drizzle with butter. Bake in preheated oven until top has formed a crust, about 30 minutes.

Variation

If you are serving this to guests, you can easily bump it up a notch if you have access to prepared duck confit (many butchers are selling it these days). Just cut it into bite-size pieces and add to the cooked cassoulet before adding the topping. Don't use more than 8 oz (250 g).

Can Be
Halved
see Tips, below

Tomato-Braised Pork with Winter Vegetables

Here's a simple combination of ingredients that is surprisingly lush — partly due to the wonderful sweetness of the parsnips. Serve this over a mound of steaming mashed potatoes to complete the root vegetables theme.

Tips

If you are halving this recipe, be sure to use a small (2 to 3½ quart) slow cooker.

If you are using chicken stock rather than wine, add 2 tsp (10 mL) fresh lemon juice along with the stock. The sauce, which has a lovely sweetness from the parsnips, benefits from the hint of acidity.

Make Ahead

Complete Step 2. Cover and refrigerate mixture for up to 2 days. When you're ready to cook, brown the pork and complete the recipe. Or, if you prefer, add the unbrowned pork to the stoneware along with the vegetable mixture, being aware that the result will not be as flavorful as that produced using browned meat.

Serves 6

• Large (approx. 5 quart) slow cooker

2 tbsp	olive oil, divided	25 mL
2 lbs	trimmed boneless pork shoulder or blade (butt), patted dry	1 kg
3	onions, thinly sliced on the vertical	3
3	carrots, peeled and diced	3
3	parsnips, peeled and diced	3
6	cloves garlic, minced	6
1 tsp	dried thyme leaves	5 mL
1 tsp	salt	5 mL
1 tsp	cracked black peppercorns	5 mL
1 cup	dry white wine or chicken stock (see Tips, left)	250 mL
1	can (28 oz/796 mL) tomatoes with juice, coarsely chopped	1

1. In a large skillet, heat 1 tbsp (15 mL) of the oil over medium-high heat. Add pork and brown on all sides, about 10 minutes. Transfer to slow cooker stoneware.

2. Reduce heat to medium. Add remaining tbsp (15 mL) of oil to pan. Add onions, carrots and parsnips and cook, stirring, until softened, about 7 minutes. Add garlic, thyme, salt and peppercorns and cook, stirring, for 1 minute. Add wine, bring to a boil and boil for 2 minutes, scraping up brown bits from bottom of pan. Add tomatoes with juice and return to a boil.

3. Transfer to slow cooker stoneware. Cover and cook on Low for 8 hours or on High for 4 hours, until meat is very tender.

Simply Braised Pork with Jerk Spicing

Many years ago I took a trip to Jamaica with a friend who had grown up there. We traveled around that beautiful island eating, among other delights, succulent jerk pork cooked over oil-drum barbecues and sold on the side of the road. Since then, the flavors of Jamaican jerk spicing are among my favorites.

Can Be Halved
see Tips, below

Serves 6

- Rimmed baking sheet
- Medium (approx. 4 quart) slow cooker
- Parchment paper

1 tbsp	olive oil	15 mL
1 tbsp	minced gingerroot	15 mL
4	green onions, white part with a bit of green, minced	4
4	cloves garlic, puréed (see Tips, page 266)	4
2 tsp	coarse salt, crushed	10 mL
2 tsp	ground cumin	10 mL
1 tsp	ground coriander	5 mL
1 tsp	cracked black peppercorns	5 mL
1 tsp	ground allspice (see Tips, right)	5 mL
1/2 tsp	ground cinnamon	2 mL
3 lbs	pork shoulder or blade (butt) roast, patted dry (see Tips, right)	1.5 kg
1 tsp	finely grated lime zest	5 mL
1/4 cup	freshly squeezed lime juice	50 mL
2 tbsp	soy sauce	25 mL
1 to 2	habanero or Scotch bonnet peppers, minced	1 to 2

1. In a small bowl, combine olive oil, ginger, green onions, garlic, salt, cumin, coriander, peppercorns, allspice and cinnamon. Rub all over meat. Cover and refrigerate overnight or for up to 24 hours, turning several times, if possible.

2. When you're ready to cook, preheat broiler. Transfer pork to rimmed baking sheet and broil, turning, until skin and sides brown evenly, about 15 minutes. Transfer to slow cooker stoneware.

3. In a bowl, combine lime zest and juice and soy sauce. Pour over pork. Place a large sheet of parchment paper over the pork, pressing it down to brush the meat and extending up the sides of the stoneware so it overlaps the rim. Cover and cook on Low for 6 to 8 hours or on High for 3 to 4 hours, until pork is very tender. Lift off the parchment and discard, being careful not to spill the accumulated liquid, which will dilute the sauce. To serve, tear the pork into chunks (it will pretty well fall apart). Add hot peppers to the pan juices and spoon over pork.

Tips

If you are halving this recipe, be sure to use a small (approx. 1 1/2 to 3 quart) slow cooker. Reduce cooking time to about 4 hours on Low.

For the best flavor, toast and grind cumin and coriander seeds and allspice berries yourself. Simply stir in a dry skillet over medium heat until fragrant, about 3 minutes. Using a mortar and pestle or a spice grinder, pound or grind as finely as you can.

Pork shoulder can be very fatty. If your pork shoulder isn't trimmed of fat when you purchase it, I recommend removing the string and trimming off as much fat as possible before using.

Be aware that these cooking times are general estimates. Not only do cooking times vary substantially among slow cookers (see Cooking Times, page 12), but people have different preferences with regard to how well they like their meat done. If you prefer fork-tender results, start checking after the food has cooked for 6 hours on Low.

Pork in Mushroom Tomato Gravy

Here's an absolutely luscious way to serve pork — wallowing in a rich tomato gravy flavored with robust porcini mushrooms. Add the cayenne if you like a bit of heat. I serve this over polenta, but it would be great with chunky pasta such as rigatoni or even over a mound of steaming mashed potatoes.

Can Be Halved
see Tips, below

Tips

If you are halving this recipe, be sure to use a small (2 to 3½ quart) slow cooker. Reduce cooking time to about 4 hours on Low.

To rehydrate mushrooms, place in a bowl with 1 cup (250 mL) hot water. Let stand for 30 minutes. Drain through a fine sieve, reserving liquid. Pat mushrooms dry with a paper towel and chop finely.

If you prefer, substitute 1 cup (250 mL) chicken stock plus 1 tbsp (15 mL) lemon juice for the wine.

Make Ahead

Complete Step 2. Cover and refrigerate mixture for up to 2 days. When you're ready to cook, complete the recipe.

Serves 6

- Large (approx. 5 quart) slow cooker

1	package (½ oz/14g) dried porcini mushrooms, rehydrated and chopped (see Tips, left)	1
2 tbsp	olive oil, divided	25 mL
4 oz	chunk pancetta, diced	125 g
3 lbs	trimmed pork shoulder or blade (butt) roast, patted dry (see Tips, page 259)	1.5 kg
2	onions, finely chopped	2
2	carrots, peeled and diced	2
4	cloves garlic, minced	4
2 tsp	dried oregano leaves	10 mL
1 tsp	dried thyme leaves	5 mL
1 tsp	salt	5 mL
1 tsp	cracked black peppercorns	5 mL
2	bay leaves	2
1 cup	dry white wine (see Tips, left)	250 mL
1	can (28 oz/796 mL) tomatoes with juice, coarsely chopped (see Tips, page 202)	1
¼ to ½ tsp	cayenne pepper, dissolved in 1 tbsp (15 mL) lemon juice, optional	1 to 2 mL

1. In a large skillet, heat oil over medium-high heat. Add pancetta and cook, stirring, until browned, about 4 minutes. Using a slotted spoon, transfer to slow cooker stoneware. Add pork and brown on all sides, about 10 minutes. Drain off fat from pan.

2. Reduce heat to medium. Add remaining tbsp (15 mL) of oil to pan. Add onions and carrots and cook, stirring, until carrots are softened, about 7 minutes. Add reserved mushrooms, garlic, oregano, thyme, salt, peppercorns and bay leaves and cook, stirring, for 1 minute. Add wine, bring to a boil and boil for 2 minutes. Add tomatoes with juice and reserved mushroom soaking liquid (see Tips, left) and return to a boil, breaking tomatoes up with the back of a spoon and scraping up brown bits from bottom of pan.

3. Transfer to slow cooker stoneware. Cover and cook on Low for 6 to 8 hours or on High for 3 to 4 hours, until pork is very tender. Stir in cayenne solution, if using. Cover and cook for on High for 10 minutes.

Ribs 'n' Rigatoni

This hearty meat ragù, served with thick pasta, is almost a meal in itself — just add salad and some robust red wine. Other thick tubular pastas such as ziti, bucatini or even stubby ditali work well, too.

Serves 6

Can Be Halved
see Tips, below

- Large (approx. 5 quart) slow cooker

1 tbsp	olive oil	15 mL
3 lbs	country-style pork spareribs, cut into individual ribs, and patted dry (see Tips, right)	1.5 kg
8 oz	mild Italian sausage, removed from casings	250 g
2	onions, finely chopped	2
2	carrots, peeled and diced	2
2	stalks celery, diced	2
4	cloves garlic, minced	4
1 tsp	salt	5 mL
½ tsp	cracked black peppercorns	2 mL
6	whole cloves	6
2	sprigs fresh rosemary or 1 tbsp (15 mL) dried rosemary leaves	2
½ tsp	freshly grated nutmeg	2 mL
¼ cup	tomato paste	50 mL
1 cup	dry white wine (see Tips, right)	250 mL
1 cup	chicken stock	250 mL
½ cup	finely chopped parsley	125 mL
¼ cup	whipping (35%) cream	50 mL
1 lb	rigatoni or other thick tubular pasta, cooked and drained	500 g
	Freshly grated Parmesan	

1. In a skillet, heat oil over medium-high heat. Add ribs, in batches, and brown on both sides, about 4 minutes per batch. Transfer to slow cooker stoneware. Add sausage and cook, breaking up with a spoon, until lightly browned and no hint of pink remains. Drain all but 1 tbsp (15 mL) fat from pan.

2. Reduce heat to medium. Add onions, carrots and celery to pan and cook, stirring, until softened, about 7 minutes. Add garlic, salt, peppercorns, cloves, rosemary and nutmeg and cook, stirring, for 1 minute. Stir in tomato paste. Add wine, bring to a boil and cook, stirring, for 2 minutes, scraping up brown bits from bottom of pan. Stir in chicken stock.

3. Transfer to slow cooker stoneware. Cover and cook on Low for 5 hours or on High for 2½ hours, until ribs are very tender.

4. Discard rosemary, if using sprigs, and whole cloves. Stir in parsley and cream. Cover and cook for 5 minutes to meld flavors. Place cooked pasta in a serving bowl and spoon ribs and sauce over all. Pass the Parmesan in a small bowl.

Tips

If you are halving this recipe, be sure to use a small (2 to 3½ quart) slow cooker.

Calling for country-style ribs in a recipe may confuse consumers because, in my experience, they vary dramatically in presentation. Most recently, my butcher has been providing a long piece of meat with small bones at either end, which cooks in a chunk. Sometimes they are sold in small chunks on a piece of bone. Don't worry about how they look. All will cook beautifully in the slow cooker, so long as you don't overcook them and dry them out.

If you prefer, omit the wine and substitute an extra cup (250 mL) chicken stock plus 1 tbsp (15 mL) lemon juice.

Make Ahead

Complete Step 2, adding 1 tbsp (15 mL) olive oil to the pan before softening the vegetables. Cover and refrigerate for up to 2 days. When you're ready to cook, complete the recipe.

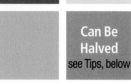

Entertaining Worthy

Can Be Halved
see Tips, below

Chinese-Style Braised Pork

This recipe is so easy to make you can dish it up as a weekday meal, but it's also delicious enough to serve to guests, with the appropriate sides. I like to accompany it with a mélange of whole-grain rice (you can buy wonderful prepared mixes at many supermarkets now) and a platter of stir-fried bok choy. If you're offering wine, a cold Gewürztraminer is a perfect fit.

Tips

If you are halving this recipe, be sure to use a small (approx. 1½ to 3 quart) slow cooker.

To purée garlic, use a fine, sharp-toothed grater, such as those made by Microplane.

If the whole piece of pork won't fit in your slow cooker, cut it in half and lay the two pieces on top of each other.

Pork shoulder can be very fatty. If your pork shoulder isn't trimmed of fat when you purchase it, I recommend removing the string and trimming off as much fat as possible before using. Broiling will render some of the fat.

I prefer to make this with dry sherry rather than traditional Chinese Shaoxing rice wine as, in my experience, the North American offerings of this product are extremely salty and combine with the soy sauce to produce a result that tastes overwhelmingly of salt.

Serves 6

- Rimmed baking sheet
- Medium (3 to 4 quart) slow cooker

6	cloves garlic, puréed (see Tips, left)	6
1 tbsp	finely minced gingerroot	15 mL
1 tsp	cracked black peppercorns	5 mL
1 tsp	dry mustard	5 mL
½ tsp	salt	2 mL
3 lbs	pork shoulder or blade (butt) roast (see Tips, left)	1.5 kg
½ cup	soy sauce, preferably reduced-sodium	125 mL
¼ cup	dry sherry (see Tips, left)	50 mL
2 tbsp	packed brown sugar	25 mL
3	star anise	3
¼ cup	chopped green onions	50 mL

1. In a small bowl, combine garlic, ginger, peppercorns, mustard and salt. Rub all over meat. Cover and refrigerate overnight or for up to 24 hours, turning several times, if possible.

2. When you're ready to cook, preheat broiler. Transfer pork to rimmed baking sheet and broil, turning, until skin and sides brown evenly, about 15 minutes. Transfer to slow cooker stoneware.

3. In a bowl, combine soy sauce, sherry, brown sugar and star anise. Pour over pork. Cover and cook on Low for 8 hours or on High for 4 hours, until pork falls apart. To serve, cut pork into chunks, spoon pan juices over and garnish with green onions.

Entertaining Worthy

Can Be Halved
see Tips, below

Rustic Italian Ribs

Here's a very simple but delicious ribs-and-pasta combo. The sauce is quite soupy but has excellent flavor. I serve this with a green vegetable such as broccoli and follow the meal with a green salad.

Serves 6

- Large (approx. 5 quart) slow cooker

2 tbsp	olive oil (approx.)	25 mL
3 lbs	country-style pork spareribs, cut into individual ribs, if possible (see Tips, left), and patted dry	1.5 kg
2	onions, thinly sliced on the vertical	2
4	stalks celery, diced	4
4	cloves garlic, minced	4
3	anchovy fillets, minced	3
1 tbsp	dried rosemary or 2 to 3 fresh sprigs (including stem)	15 mL
1 tsp	salt	5 mL
1 tsp	cracked black peppercorns	5 mL
1 cup	dry white wine	250 mL
1	can (28 oz/796 mL) tomatoes with juice	1
1 lb	tubular pasta, such as penne or tubetti	500 g
	Butter	
	Freshly ground black pepper	

1. In a skillet, heat oil over medium-high heat. Add ribs, in batches, and brown on both sides, about 4 minutes per batch. Transfer to slow cooker stoneware. Drain off all but 2 tbsp (25 mL) fat from pan (see Tips, left).

2. Reduce heat to medium. Add onions and celery and cook, stirring, until softened, about 5 minutes. Add garlic and anchovies and cook, stirring, for 1 minute. Add rosemary, salt and peppercorns and cook, stirring, for 1 minute. Add wine, bring to a boil and boil for 2 minutes, scraping up brown bits from bottom of pan. Add tomatoes with juice and return to a boil, breaking up with a spoon.

3. Transfer to slow cooker stoneware. Cover and cook on Low for 5 hours or on High for 2½ hours, until ribs are very tender.

4. Cook pasta according to package directions. Drain, transfer to a serving bowl and toss with butter and pepper to taste. Spoon ribs and sauce over pasta and serve.

Tips

If you are halving this recipe, be sure to use a small (2 to 3½ quart) slow cooker.

Calling for country-style ribs in a recipe may confuse consumers because, in my experience, they vary dramatically in presentation. Most recently, my butcher has been providing a long piece of meat with small bones at either end, which cooks in a chunk. Sometimes they are sold in small chunks on a piece of bone. Don't worry about how they look. All will cook beautifully in the slow cooker, so long as you don't overcook them and dry them out.

The quantity of fat left in the pan after browning the ribs can vary dramatically. If you don't have 2 tbsp (25 mL) left over, add olive oil to make up the difference.

Make Ahead

Complete Step 2, adding 1 tbsp (15 mL) olive oil to the pan before softening the vegetables. Cover and refrigerate for up to 2 days. When you're ready to cook, complete the recipe.

Smothered Country-Style Ribs

These are the kind of ribs my mother used to make when I was growing up. They have real down-home flavor. I like to serve them over steamed rice with coleslaw on the side. Yum!

Serves 6

Can Be Halved
see Tips, below

- Large (approx. 5 quart) slow cooker

1 tbsp	olive oil	15 mL
3 lbs	country-style pork spareribs, cut into individual ribs, if possible, and patted dry (see Tips, page 268)	1.5 kg
2	onions, finely chopped	2
4	cloves garlic, minced	4
1 tsp	salt	5 mL
1 tsp	cracked black peppercorns	5 mL
1 tsp	dry mustard	5 mL
1 cup	tomato-based chili sauce	250 mL
1/4 cup	Demerara or other raw cane sugar	50 mL
1/4 cup	apple cider vinegar	50 mL

1. In a skillet, heat oil over medium-high heat. Add ribs, in batches, and brown on both sides, about 4 minutes per batch. Transfer to slow cooker stoneware.

2. Add onions to pan and cook, stirring, until softened, about 3 minutes. Add garlic, salt, peppercorns and mustard and cook, stirring, for 1 minute. Add chili sauce, sugar and vinegar. Bring to a boil, stirring and scraping up brown bits from bottom of pan.

3. Pour over ribs. Cover and cook on Low for 5 hours or on High for 2 1/2 hours, until ribs are tender (see Tips, right).

Tips

If you are halving this recipe, be sure to use a small (2 to 3 1/2 quart) slow cooker.

How long you cook your ribs is a matter of personal taste. Some people prefer them a bit firm, in which case cooking for less time makes sense. While I like them falling off the bone, I have also found that if there isn't enough fat in the meat they tend to dry out, so the timing is a bit of a balancing act. Once you know how quickly your slow cooker cooks and assess that against your personal preference, you'll be able to find the timing that really works for you.

Make Ahead

Complete Step 2, adding 1 tbsp (15 mL) olive oil to the pan before softening the vegetables. Cover and refrigerate for up to 2 days. When you're ready to cook, complete the recipe.

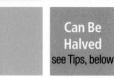
Braised Ribs with Sauerkraut

Here's a dish that will warm the cockles of your heart on a blustery day. There's not much you'll need to add — perhaps some plain boiled potatoes tossed with butter and parsley.

Tips

If you are halving this recipe, be sure to use a small (2 to 3½ quart) slow cooker.

Calling for country-style ribs in a recipe can confuse consumers, because, in my experience, they vary dramatically in presentation. Most recently, my butcher has been providing a long piece of meat with small bones at either end, which cooks in a chunk. Sometimes they are sold in small chunks on a piece of bone. Don't worry about how they look. All will cook beautifully in the slow cooker, so long as you don't overcook them and dry them out.

Because this dish cooks in a minimum of liquid, adding the parchment helps to ensure that none evaporates and that the food bastes in its own succulent juices.

Make Ahead

Complete Step 2, adding 1 tbsp (15 mL) olive oil to the pan before softening the vegetables. Cover and refrigerate for up to 2 days. When you're ready to cook, complete the recipe.

Serves 6

- Large (approx. 5 quart) slow cooker
- Parchment paper

4 cups	sauerkraut, soaked, drained and rinsed	1 L
1 tbsp	olive oil	15 mL
2 oz	chunk bacon, diced	60 g
3 lbs	country-style pork spareribs, cut into individual ribs, if possible, and patted dry (see Tips, left)	1.5 kg
2	onions, finely chopped	2
2	carrots, peeled and diced	2
4	cloves garlic, minced	4
1 tsp	caraway seeds	5 mL
1 tsp	salt	5 mL
1 tsp	cracked black peppercorns	5 mL
1	bay leaf	1
1 cup	dry white wine (see Tips, page 265)	250 mL
1 cup	chicken stock	250 mL

1. In a skillet, heat oil over medium-high heat. Add bacon and cook, stirring, until browned, about 4 minutes. Place on a paper towel to drain and set aside. Add ribs, in batches, and cook, stirring, until browned, about 4 minutes per batch. Transfer to slow cooker stoneware. Drain off all but 1 tbsp (15 mL) fat from pan.

2. Reduce heat to medium. Add onions and carrots to pan and cook, stirring, until carrots are softened, about 7 minutes. Add garlic, caraway seeds, salt, peppercorns and bay leaf and cook, stirring, for 1 minute. Add wine, bring to a boil and boil for 2 minutes, scraping up brown bits from bottom of pan. Stir in chicken stock.

3. Transfer to slow cooker stoneware. Add sauerkraut and reserved bacon and stir gently. Place a large piece of parchment paper over the mixture, pressing it down to brush the food and extending up the sides of the stoneware so it overlaps the rim. Cover and cook on Low for 5 hours or on High for 2½ hours, until pork is tender. Lift off parchment and discard, being careful not to spill the accumulated liquid, which will dilute the sauce. Discard bay leaf.

Barley-Studded Irish Stew

The proper ingredients for a good Irish stew are much debated in Ireland. Many argue for only meat, potatoes and onions, plus cooking liquid. Although barley is not the norm, it does turn up in some traditional recipes, and I really like the added texture it provides.

Entertaining Worthy

Can Be Halved
see Tip, below

Serves 6

- Large (approx. 5 quart) slow cooker

2 tbsp	olive oil (approx.)	25 mL
2 lbs	trimmed stewing lamb, cut into 1-inch (2.5 cm) cubes, and patted dry	1 kg
2	onions, finely chopped	2
2	carrots, peeled and diced	2
1 tsp	dried thyme leaves	5 mL
1 tsp	salt	5 mL
1 tsp	cracked black peppercorns	5 mL
¼ cup	barley	50 mL
¼ cup	tomato paste	50 mL
2 cups	chicken stock	500 mL
2	potatoes, peeled and diced	2
1½ cups	green peas, thawed if frozen	375 mL
1 tbsp	Worcestershire sauce	15 mL

1. In a skillet, heat 1 tbsp (15 mL) of the oil over medium heat. Add lamb, in batches, and cook, stirring, until browned, about 4 minutes per batch, adding more oil if necessary. Transfer to slow cooker stoneware as completed.

2. Add remaining tbsp (15 mL) of oil to pan. Add onions and carrots and cook, stirring, until softened, about 7 minutes. Add thyme, salt and peppercorns and cook, stirring, for 1 minute. Add barley and toss to coat. Stir in tomato paste and stock and bring to a boil, scraping up brown bits from the bottom of the pan.

3. Transfer to slow cooker stoneware. Stir in potatoes. Cover and cook on Low for 8 hours or on High for 5 hours, until lamb is tender. Stir in peas and Worcestershire sauce. Cover and cook on High about 20 minutes, until peas are tender.

Tip

If you are halving this recipe, be sure to use a small (2 to 3½ quart) slow cooker.

Make Ahead

Complete Step 2. Cover and refrigerate for up to 2 days. When you're ready to cook, complete the recipe.

Lamb with Flageolet Gratin

This ambrosial concoction of highly seasoned lamb, fennel and flageolets (small dried beans that traditionally accompany lamb in France) is a superb dish for entertaining. For an elegant presentation, I like to transfer the mixture to individual gratin dishes, which I place under the broiler, but if your slow cooker stoneware is ovenproof you can do it directly in the stoneware and serve from that.

Tips

If you are halving this recipe, be sure to use a small (2 to 3½ quart) slow cooker.

Use a fine-tooth grater to purée the garlic.

To toast fennel seeds: Place seeds in a dry skillet over medium heat, stirring until fragrant, about 3 minutes. Using a mortar and pestle or a clean spice grinder, pound or grind as finely as you can.

Flageolets are available in well-stocked supermarkets or specialty stores. Although they usually do not need to be soaked before using, I find they cook better in the slow cooker if they receive a quick soak as directed.

Aleppo pepper is a mild chile pepper from Syria. It is available in specialty stores or supermarkets with a well-stocked spice section. If you want a bit of heat and don't have it, substitute ¼ tsp (1 mL) cayenne pepper.

Serves 6 to 8

• Large (approx. 5 quart) slow cooker

Marinade

2 tbsp	olive oil	25 mL
1 tbsp	puréed garlic (3 to 4 cloves) (see Tips, left)	15 mL
1 tsp	dried thyme leaves	5 mL
1 tsp	dried rosemary leaves	5 mL
1 tsp	fennel seeds, toasted and ground (see Tips, left)	5 mL
1 tsp	cracked black peppercorns	5 mL
2 lbs	trimmed stewing lamb, cut into 1-inch (2.5 cm) cubes, and patted dry	1 kg
1½ cups	dried flageolets (see Tips, left)	375 mL
2 cups	chicken stock	500 mL
2 cups	water	500 mL
2 tbsp	olive oil, divided	25 mL
2	onions, thinly sliced on the vertical	2
1	bulb fennel, cored and diced	1
4	cloves garlic, minced	4
1 tsp	dried thyme leaves or 1 sprig fresh thyme	5 mL
1 tsp	dried rosemary or 1 sprig fresh rosemary	5 mL
2	bay leaves	2
1 tsp	salt	5 mL

Topping

2 cups	dry bread crumbs	500 mL
½ cup	finely chopped parsley	125 mL
1 tsp	Aleppo pepper, optional (see Tips, left)	5 mL
¼ tsp	salt	1 mL
¼ cup	melted butter	50 mL

1. **Marinade:** In a bowl, combine olive oil, garlic, thyme, rosemary, fennel and peppercorns. Mix well. Add lamb and toss until well coated. Cover and refrigerate overnight or up to 2 days.

2. In a saucepan, combine flageolets, stock and water. Bring to a boil and boil rapidly for 2 minutes. Set aside for 20 minutes.

3. In a skillet, heat 1 tbsp (15 mL) of the oil over medium-high heat. Add lamb, in batches, and cook, stirring, until browned, about 4 minutes per batch, transferring to slow cooker stoneware as completed.

4. Reduce heat to medium. Add remaining tbsp (15 mL) oil to pan. Add onions and fennel and cook, stirring, until softened, about 5 minutes. Add garlic, thyme, rosemary, bay leaves and salt and cook, stirring, for 1 minute, scraping up brown bits from bottom of pan.

5. Transfer to slow cooker stoneware. Add flageolets with liquid. Stir well. Cover and cook on Low for 8 hours or on High for 4 hours, until flageolets are tender.

6. **Topping:** Preheat broiler. After lamb has cooked, ladle it into individual heatproof tureens. (If your stoneware is ovenproof, you may prefer to leave it in that.) In a bowl, combine bread crumbs, parsley, Aleppo pepper, if using, and salt and mix well. Sprinkle over lamb mixture and drizzle with butter. Place under broiler until topping is lightly browned and mixture is bubbly, about 3 minutes.

Make Ahead
Complete Steps 1 and 4, adding 1 cup (250 mL) of the chicken stock called for in Step 2 to the onion mixture after sautéing the garlic, etc. Cover and refrigerate for up to 2 days. When you're ready to cook, complete the recipe.

Lamb Tagine with Dates

If you're in the mood for something a little different, try this. The dates add sumptuous fruity notes that are slightly unexpected when combined with rosemary and a hint of tomato. Serve this over whole-grain couscous for a special treat.

Serves 6 to 8

- Large (approx. 5 quart) slow cooker

2	onions, quartered	2
4	cloves garlic, minced	4
1 tbsp	finely chopped fresh rosemary leaves or 2 tsp (10 mL) dried rosemary leaves	15 mL
½ tsp	salt	2 mL
½ tsp	cracked black peppercorns	2 mL
1	piece (2 inches/5 cm) cinnamon stick	1
2 lbs	trimmed stewing lamb, cut into 1-inch (2.5 cm) cubes	1 kg
2 tbsp	tomato paste	25 mL
2 cups	chicken stock	500 mL
2	sweet potatoes, peeled and cut into 1-inch (2.5 cm) cubes	2
¾ cup	chopped pitted dates (about 4 oz/125 g)	175 mL
	Finely chopped cilantro	

1. In a food processor, pulse onions until a grated consistency is achieved. (You can also do this on a box grater, if you prefer.) Transfer to a bowl. Add garlic, rosemary, salt, peppercorns and cinnamon stick and stir well. Add lamb and toss until well coated with mixture. Cover and refrigerate for at least 6 hours or overnight.

2. In slow cooker stoneware, combine tomato paste and chicken stock. Mix well. Add sweet potatoes and lamb mixture. Stir well. Cover and cook on Low for 8 hours or on High for 4 hours, until lamb is very tender. Stir in dates. Cover and cook on High for 15 minutes, until heated through. Garnish with cilantro.

Tip

If you are halving this recipe, be sure to use a small (2 to 3½ quart) slow cooker.

Make Ahead

Complete Step 1. Cover and refrigerate for up to 2 days. When you're ready to cook, complete the recipe.

Spicy Chinese Lamb with Mushrooms

Although there are lots of deep flavors in this hearty stew, it is not heavy because the quantity of vegetables acts as a balance. I like to serve this with a steaming bowl of mixed whole-grain rice — wild, brown and perhaps some robust red, such as Wehani.

Serves 4 to 6

- Large (approx. 5 quart) slow cooker

2 tbsp	soy sauce (see Tip, right)	25 mL
2 tbsp	Demerara or other raw cane sugar, divided	25 mL
1 tbsp	finely grated orange zest	15 mL
1½ lbs	lamb shoulder, cut into 1-inch (2.5 cm) cubes	750 g
2 tbsp	olive oil, divided	25 mL
2	onions, finely chopped	2
2	carrots, peeled and diced	2
6	cloves garlic, minced	6
1 tbsp	minced gingerroot	15 mL
½ tsp	cracked black peppercorns	2 mL
2 tbsp	balsamic vinegar	25 mL
½ cup	freshly squeezed orange juice	125 mL
2 cups	chicken stock	500 mL
2	Japanese eggplants, skin-on, sliced	2
8 oz	sliced cremini mushrooms	250 g
1 to 2	long red chiles, minced	1 to 2
2 tbsp	cornstarch	25 mL

1. In a bowl, combine soy sauce, 1 tbsp (15 mL) of the sugar and orange zest. Mix well. Add lamb and toss until well coated with mixture. Cover and refrigerate overnight.

2. In a skillet, heat 1 tbsp (15 mL) of the oil over medium-high heat. Add lamb, in batches, and cook, stirring, until browned, about 4 minutes per batch. Transfer to slow cooker stoneware as completed.

3. Add remaining tbsp (15 mL) of oil to pan. Add onions and carrots and cook, stirring, until softened, about 7 minutes. Add garlic, ginger and peppercorns and cook, stirring, for 1 minute. Stir in remaining sugar, vinegar and orange juice. Add chicken stock and bring to a boil, scraping up brown bits from bottom of pan.

4. Transfer to slow cooker stoneware. Add eggplant and mushrooms and stir well. Cover and cook on Low for 8 hours or on High for 4 hours, until lamb is tender. Stir in chile. Cover and cook on High for 15 minutes to meld flavors. When you're ready to serve, scoop out about ⅓ cup (75 mL) of liquid from the stoneware and, in a small bowl, whisk into cornstarch. Return to stoneware and cook, stirring, until sauce is thickened, about 1 minute.

Tip

Regular soy sauce works fine in this recipe, but if you have dark or mushroom soy sauce on hand, use 1 tbsp (15 mL) of it and an equal quantity of the regular kind for deeper flavor.

Make Ahead

Complete Step 3. Cover and refrigerate mixture for up to 2 days. When you're ready to cook, complete the recipe.

Entertaining Worthy

Can Be Halved
see Tips, below

Lamb Shanks Braised in Tomato Sauce with Lemon Gremolata

Braised in a light tomato sauce and finished with lemon gremolata, these lamb shanks have Mediterranean overtones, which is why I like to serve them with buttered orzo or polenta. That said, a bed of mashed potatoes is pretty good, too.

Tips

If you are halving this recipe, see Tip, page 254.

Whether you cook the lamb shanks whole, halved or have them cut into pieces is a matter of preference. However, if the shanks are left whole, you will be able to serve only four people — each will receive one large shank.

This recipe generates a lot of liquid, which I think works well if you're serving it over orzo or polenta. If you prefer a thicker sauce, remove the shanks with a slotted spoon, cover and keep warm. Transfer sauce to a saucepan, bring to a boil and simmer for 10 minutes to reduce slightly. Meanwhile, combine 1 tbsp (15 mL) each softened butter and all-purpose flour until blended. Remove sauce from the heat and whisk flour mixture in for 1 minute, until slightly thickened.

Make Ahead

Complete Step 2. Cover and refrigerate for up to 2 days. When you're ready to cook, complete recipe.

Serves 4 to 8

- Large (approx. 5 quart) slow cooker

2 tbsp	olive oil, divided	25 mL
4	large lamb shanks (about 4 lbs/2 kg) (see Tips, left)	4
3	onions, finely chopped	3
2	stalks celery, diced	2
2	carrots, peeled and diced	2
6	cloves garlic, minced	6
1 tsp	dried thyme leaves or several whole sprigs, stems and all	5 mL
1 tsp	each salt and cracked black peppercorns	5 mL
1 cup	dry white wine (see Tips, page 257)	250 mL
1 cup	chicken stock	250 mL
1	can (28 oz/796 mL) tomatoes with juice, coarsely chopped (see Tips, page 202)	1

Lemon Gremolata

2	cloves garlic, minced	2
1 cup	finely chopped parsley	250 mL
	Grated zest of 1 lemon	
1 tbsp	extra virgin olive oil	15 mL

1. In a large skillet, heat 1 tbsp (15 mL) oil over medium-high heat. Add lamb, in batches, and brown on all sides, about 8 minutes per batch. Transfer to stoneware as completed. Drain off fat from pan.

2. Reduce heat to medium. Add remaining tbsp (15 mL) of oil to pan. Add onions, celery and carrots and cook, stirring, until vegetables are softened, about 7 minutes. Add garlic, thyme, salt and peppercorns and cook, stirring, for 1 minute. Add wine, bring to a boil and boil for 2 minutes, scraping up brown bits from bottom of pan. Stir in chicken stock and tomatoes with juice.

3. Transfer to slow cooker stoneware. Cover and cook on Low for 10 to 12 hours or on High for 5 to 6 hours, until meat is falling off the bone.

4. **Lemon Gremolata:** About half an hour before serving, in a small serving bowl, combine garlic, parsley, lemon zest and olive oil. Pass around the table, allowing guests to individually garnish their meat.

Suneeta's Lamb in Almond Sauce

This is an adaptation of a recipe that appears in Suneeta Vaswani's The Complete Book of Indian Cooking. *Suneeta calls it sensuous, an apt description. Serve this over plain rice, with perhaps a side of puréed spinach.*

Tip

If you are halving this recipe, be sure to use a small (approx. 1½ to 3 quart) slow cooker.

Make Ahead

Complete Steps 1, 2, 3 and 4. Cover and refrigerate lamb and onion mixtures separately overnight. When you're ready to cook, complete the recipe.

Serves 6

- Medium to large (4 to 6 quart) slow cooker

1 tsp	saffron threads	5 mL
1 cup	plain full-fat yogurt	250 mL
1 tbsp	ground cumin (see Tip, right)	15 mL
1 tsp	salt or to taste	5 mL
½ tsp	cracked black peppercorns	2 mL
2 lbs	trimmed stewing lamb, cut into 1-inch (2.5 cm) cubes	1 kg
¾ cup	blanched almonds	175 mL
¾ cup	very hot water	175 mL
2 tbsp	olive or coconut oil	25 mL
1	piece (2 inches/5 cm) cinnamon stick	1
12	green cardamom pods, crushed	12
6	whole cloves	6
3	onions, finely chopped	3
6	cloves garlic, minced	6
2 tbsp	minced gingerroot	25 mL
1 tsp	cayenne pepper	5 mL
1 cup	coconut milk, divided	250 mL
2 tbsp	sliced or slivered almonds, toasted	25 mL

1. In a small bowl, soak saffron threads in 2 tbsp (25 mL) very hot water for 10 minutes.

2. In a large bowl, combine yogurt, cumin, salt and peppercorns. Add saffron with soaking liquid and stir well. Stir in lamb until well coated with mixture. Cover and set aside at room temperature for 30 minutes or refrigerate for up to 24 hours.

3. In a bowl, combine blanched almonds and very hot water. Set aside for 10 minutes. Transfer mixture to a blender and purée. Set aside.

4. In a saucepan, heat oil over medium-high heat. Add cinnamon stick, cardamom pods and cloves and sauté for 30 seconds. Add onions and cook, stirring, until golden, about 8 minutes. Add garlic and ginger and cook, stirring, for 1 minute. Stir in almond purée.

5. Transfer to slow cooker stoneware. Add meat with marinade and stir well. Place a large piece of parchment paper over the mixture, pressing it down to brush the food and extending up the sides of the stoneware so it overlaps the rim. Cover and cook on Low for 6 to 8 hours or on High for 3 to 4 hours, until meat is tender. Lift out parchment and discard, being careful not to spill the accumulated liquid into the sauce.

6. In a small bowl, blend cayenne with 2 tbsp (25 mL) of the coconut milk until smooth. Stir into lamb. Add remainder of coconut milk and stir well. Cover and cook on High for 15 minutes to meld flavors. Garnish with toasted almonds before serving.

Tip

To maximize flavor, toast and grind cumin seeds yourself. Place seeds in a dry skillet over medium heat and cook, stirring, until fragrant, about 3 minutes. Using a mortar and pestle or a clean spice grinder, pound or grind as finely as you can.

Spicy Lamb with Chickpeas

Here's a dish with robust flavor that will delight even your most discriminating guests. Serve over whole-grain couscous or, for a New World spin, hot quinoa, and open a good Rioja for a perfect accompaniment.

Tips

If you are halving this recipe, be sure to use a small (2 to 3½ quart) slow cooker.

For the best flavor, toast and grind the cumin and coriander yourself, rather than buying the ground versions. Place seeds in a dry skillet over medium heat, stirring until fragrant, about 3 minutes. Using a mortar and pestle or a spice grinder, pound or grind as finely as you can.

You can cook your own chickpeas (see Basic Beans, page 341) or use canned chickpeas, thoroughly rinsed and drained.

Aleppo pepper is a mild Syrian chile pepper. It is increasingly available in specialty shops or well-stocked supermarkets. If you don't have it, substitute another mild chile powder such as ancho or New Mexico, or add another ¼ tsp (1 mL) cayenne.

Make Ahead

Complete Steps 1 and 3. Cover and refrigerate overnight. When you're ready to cook, complete the recipe.

Serves 6

- Medium to large (4 to 6 quart) slow cooker

1 tbsp	ground cumin (see Tips, left)	15 mL
2 tsp	ground coriander	10 mL
1 tsp	ground turmeric	5 mL
1 tsp	salt	5 mL
1 tsp	cracked black peppercorns	5 mL
1 tsp	finely grated lime zest	5 mL
2 tbsp	freshly squeezed lime juice	25 mL
2 lbs	trimmed stewing lamb, cut into 1-inch (2.5 cm) cubes	1 kg
2 tbsp	olive oil, divided	25 mL
2	onions, finely chopped	2
2	carrots, diced	2
2	parsnips, peeled and diced	2
4	cloves garlic, minced	4
2 tbsp	minced gingerroot	25 mL
4	black cardamom pods, crushed	4
1	piece (2 inches/5 cm) cinnamon stick	1
6	whole cloves	6
½ tsp	salt	2 mL
½ tsp	cracked black peppercorns	2 mL
1	can (28 oz/796 mL) tomatoes with juice, coarsely chopped	1
1 cup	chicken or vegetable stock	250 mL
3 cups	cooked chickpeas, mashed (see Tips, left)	750 mL
1 tsp	Aleppo pepper (see Tips, left)	5 mL
¼ tsp	cayenne pepper	1 mL

1. In a bowl, combine cumin, coriander, turmeric, salt, peppercorns and lime zest and juice. Stir well. Add lamb and toss to coat. Cover and set aside in refrigerator for 4 hours or overnight.

2. Pat lamb dry. In a skillet, heat 1 tbsp (15 mL) of the oil over medium heat. Add lamb, in batches, and cook, stirring, until lightly browned, about 4 minutes per batch. Transfer to slow cooker as completed.

3. Add remaining tbsp (15 mL) oil to pan. Add onions, carrots and parsnips and cook, stirring and scraping up brown bits from the bottom of the pan, until carrots are softened, about 7 minutes. Add garlic, ginger, cardamom, cinnamon stick, cloves, salt and peppercorns and cook, stirring, for 1 minute. Add tomatoes with juice and chicken stock and bring to a boil, scraping up brown bits from bottom of pan.

4. Transfer to slow cooker stoneware. Stir in chickpeas. Cover and cook on Low for 8 hours or on High for 4 to 5 hours, until meat is very tender. Stir in Aleppo and cayenne. Cover and cook on High for 10 minutes to meld flavors.

Quince-Laced Lamb Shanks with Yellow Split Peas

This is a version of a traditional Middle Eastern dish. Fragrant quince, which is very fibrous in its raw state, cooks up beautifully in the slow cooker and pairs with the hint of pomegranate to add luscious fruitiness. Serve this over couscous, preferably a whole wheat version possibly made from spelt or Kamut.

Serves 4 to 8

- Large (approx. 5 quart) slow cooker

2 tsp	cumin seeds	10 mL
2 tsp	coriander seeds	10 mL
2 tbsp	olive oil, divided	25 mL
4	large lamb shanks, halved (about 4 lbs/2 kg) (see Tips, left)	4
2	onions, finely chopped	2
4	cloves garlic, minced	4
2 tbsp	minced gingerroot	15 mL
1/2 tsp	salt (see Tips, left)	2 mL
1/2 tsp	cracked black peppercorns	2 mL
3	quinces (about 1 1/2 lbs/750 g), peeled, cored and sliced (see Tips, left)	3
1/4 cup	yellow split peas	50 mL
2 cups	chicken stock	500 mL
2 tbsp	pomegranate molasses	25 mL

1. In a large dry skillet over medium heat, toast cumin and coriander seeds, stirring constantly, until fragrant, about 3 minutes. Using a mortar and pestle or a spice grinder, pound or grind as finely as you can. Set aside.

2. Return skillet to element and heat 1 tbsp (15 mL) oil. Add lamb, in batches, and brown on all sides, about 4 minutes per batch. Transfer to slow cooker stoneware. Drain off fat from pan.

3. Reduce heat to medium. Add remaining tbsp (15 mL) of oil to pan. Add onions and cook, stirring, until softened, about 3 minutes. Add garlic, ginger, salt, peppercorns and reserved cumin and coriander and cook, stirring, for 1 minute. Add quinces and toss to coat. Add split peas and toss to coat. Stir in chicken stock and pomegranate molasses and bring to a boil, scraping up brown bits from bottom of pan.

4. Transfer to slow cooker stoneware. Cover and cook on Low for 10 to 12 hours or on High for 5 to 6 hours, until meat is falling off the bone.

Tips

If you are halving this recipe, be sure to use a small (2 to 3 1/2 quart) slow cooker.

Whether you cook the lamb shanks whole, halved or have them cut into pieces is a matter of preference. However, if the shanks are left whole, you will be able to serve only four people — each will receive one large shank.

The quantity of salt will vary depending upon how salty your stock is.

Depending upon where you live, quinces are in season usually from late fall through to early January. If you can't find them, substitute 4 Granny Smith apples, peeled, cored and thinly sliced, and add them to the stew 2 hours before it is finished, if you're cooking on Low, or 1 hour, if you're cooking on High.

Make Ahead

Complete Step 3. Cover and refrigerate mixture for up to 2 days. When you're ready to cook, complete the recipe.

Chile-Spiked Lamb Shanks

I love the flavors in this dish — a sweet-and-sour combination with a bit of heat. The sauce is great with polenta.

Serves 4 to 8

Entertaining Worthy

Can Be Halved
see Tips, below

- Large (approx. 5 quart) slow cooker

2 tbsp	olive oil, divided	25 mL
4	large lamb shanks (about 4 lbs/2 kg), patted dry (see Tips, right)	4
2	onions, finely chopped	2
2	carrots, peeled and diced	2
2	stalks celery, diced	2
6	cloves garlic, minced	6
1 tsp	dried thyme leaves	5 mL
1 tsp	salt	5 mL
1 tsp	cracked black peppercorns	5 mL
1	cup dry red wine	250 mL
¼ cup	packed brown sugar	50 mL
¼ cup	red wine vinegar	50 mL
2 cups	chicken stock	500 mL
2 to 4	jalapeño peppers, seeded and diced	2 to 4
	Finely chopped parsley, optional	

1. In a large skillet, heat 1 tbsp (15 mL) oil over medium-high heat. Add lamb, in batches, and brown on all sides, about 8 minutes per batch. Transfer to slow cooker stoneware as completed. Drain off fat from pan.

2. Reduce heat to medium. Add remaining tbsp (15 mL) of oil to pan. Add onions, carrots and celery to pan and cook, stirring, until carrots are soft, about 7 minutes. Add garlic, thyme, salt and peppercorns and cook, stirring, for 1 minute. Add wine, bring to a boil and boil for 2 minutes, scraping up brown bits from bottom of pan. Add brown sugar and vinegar and stir well.

3. Transfer to slow cooker stoneware. Stir in chicken stock. Cover and cook on Low for 10 to 12 hours or on High for 5 to 6 hours, until meat is falling off the bone. Stir in jalapeños and cook on High for 15 minutes, until flavors meld. Garnish with parsley, if using.

Tips

If you are halving this recipe, be sure to use a small (2 to 3½ quart) slow cooker.

Whether you cook the lamb shanks whole, halved or have them cut into pieces is a matter of preference. However, if the shanks are left whole, you will be able to serve only four people — each will receive one large shank.

For a more sophisticated version, after the dish has finished cooking, transfer the lamb to a deep platter and keep warm. Transfer the sauce to a saucepan and cook over medium heat until reduced by a third, about 10 minutes. Purée using an immersion blender. Pour over shanks and garnish liberally with parsley, if using.

Make Ahead

Complete Step 2. Cover and refrigerate mixture for up to 2 days. When you're ready to cook, complete the recipe.

Lentil Vegetable Stew

Meatless Mains

Vegan Friendly

Can Be Halved
see Tips, below

Lentil Vegetable Stew

Served over rice or a whole grain such as quinoa or couscous, this one-pot meal makes a delicious dinner. It also works as a course for a multi-dish Indian meal.

Serves 6

- Large (approx. 5 quart) slow cooker

1 tbsp	coriander seeds	15 mL
1 tbsp	cumin seeds	15 mL
1 tsp	fennel seeds	5 mL
2 tbsp	olive or coconut oil or ghee (approx.)	25 mL
1	medium eggplant (about 1¼ lbs/625 g), peeled, cut into 1-inch (2.5 cm) cubes, and sweated (see Tips, left)	1
2	onions, finely chopped	2
4	cloves garlic, minced	4
2 tbsp	minced gingerroot	25 mL
1 tsp	ground turmeric	5 mL
1 tsp	cracked black peppercorns	5 mL
6	green cardamom pods	6
4	whole cloves	4
1	piece (2 inches/5 cm) cinnamon stick	1
2 cups	brown or green lentils	500 mL
1	can (28 oz/796 mL) diced tomatoes with juice	1
2 cups	vegetable stock	500 mL
2 cups	corn kernels, thawed if frozen	500 mL
½ tsp	cayenne pepper	2 mL
½ cup	finely chopped cilantro	125 mL

1. In a large dry skillet over medium heat, toast coriander, cumin and fennel seeds, stirring, until fragrant, about 3 minutes. Using a mortar and pestle or a spice grinder, pound or grind as finely as you can.

2. In same skillet, heat 1 tbsp (15 mL) of the oil over medium heat. Add eggplant, in batches, and cook, stirring, until it begins to brown, adding more oil as necessary. Transfer to stoneware as completed.

3. Add remaining tbsp (15 mL) of oil to the pan. Add onions and cook, stirring, until softened, about 3 minutes. Add garlic, ginger, turmeric, peppercorns, cardamom, cloves, cinnamon stick and reserved coriander, cumin and fennel and cook, stirring, for 1 minute. Add lentils and toss until coated. Add tomatoes and bring to a boil.

4. Transfer to stoneware. Stir in vegetable stock. Cover and cook on Low for 8 hours or on High for 4 hours, until lentils are tender. Stir in corn and cayenne. Cover and cook on High for 20 minutes, until corn is tender and flavors meld. Garnish with cilantro.

Tips

If you are halving this recipe, be sure to use a small (2 to 3½ quart) slow cooker.

To sweat eggplant, sprinkle with salt and set aside in a colander for 1 to 2 hours. (If time is short, blanch pieces in heavily salted water.) In either case, rinse thoroughly in fresh cold water and, using your hands, squeeze out the excess moisture. Pat dry with paper towels.

Make Ahead

Complete Steps 1, 2 and 3. Cover and refrigerate mixture for up to 2 days. When you're ready to cook, complete the recipe.

Gingery Red Lentils with Spinach and Coconut

I love this recipe! The red lentils and shredded potato melt into the sauce, creating a luscious texture, and the flavors are so appealing, even non-vegetarians will lap it up. It makes a great main course served over rice or another whole grain, or a beautiful substitute for dal as part of an Indian meal.

Serves 6

- Medium to large (3½ to 5 quart) slow cooker

1 tbsp	olive or coconut oil or ghee (see Tips, right)	25 mL
2	onions, finely chopped	2
2	stalks celery, diced	2
2	carrots, peeled and diced	2
4	cloves garlic, minced	4
2 tbsp	minced gingerroot	25 mL
2 tsp	ground cumin	10 mL
2 tsp	ground turmeric	10 mL
1 tsp	salt	5 mL
½ tsp	cracked black peppercorns	2 mL
1 cup	red lentils, rinsed	250 mL
3 cups	vegetable broth	750 mL
1	potato, peeled and shredded	1
1 cup	coconut milk, divided	250 mL
¼ tsp	cayenne pepper	1 mL
1 lb	fresh spinach leaves, stems removed and coarsely chopped (see Tip, right)	500 g

1. In a skillet, heat oil over medium heat. Add onions, celery and carrots and cook, stirring, until carrots are softened, about 7 minutes. Add garlic, ginger, cumin, turmeric, salt and peppercorns and cook, stirring, for 1 minute. Add lentils and toss to coat. Add vegetable broth and bring to a boil.

2. Transfer to slow cooker stoneware. Stir in potato. Cover and cook on Low for 8 hours or on High for 4 hours, until lentils are tender and slightly puréed.

3. In a small bowl, combine 1 tbsp (15 mL) of the coconut milk and cayenne. Stir until blended. Add to stoneware along with remaining coconut milk and spinach. Cover and cook on High for 20 minutes, until spinach is wilted and flavors meld. Serve immediately.

Tips

If you are halving this recipe, be sure to use a small (2 to 3½ quart) slow cooker.

Because this is an Asian-inspired recipe, I like to use coconut oil or ghee, an Indian version of clarified butter, to soften the vegetables.

If you prefer, substitute 1 package (10 oz/300 g) frozen spinach, thawed and squeezed dry, for the fresh.

Make Ahead

Complete Step 1. When you're ready to cook, complete the recipe.

Saffron-Spiked Squash Tagine with Couscous

Punctuated with sweet green peas and seasoned with just a hint of bitter saffron, this tagine is not only delicious but very pretty. Served over whole wheat couscous, which is far more nutritious than the kind made from refined wheat flour, it is a complete protein that makes an impressive presentation.

Tips

I like to use parchment when cooking this dish because the recipe doesn't contain much liquid. Creating a tight seal ensures that the ingredients baste in their own juices, intensifying the flavors.

For this quantity of chickpeas use 1 cup (250 mL) dried chickpeas, soaked, cooked and drained (see Basic Beans, page 341), or 1 can (14 to 19 oz/398 to 540 mL) chickpeas, drained and rinsed.

Harissa is a North African chili paste that is often added to couscous to give it some bite. If you don't have it, pass your favorite hot pepper sauce at the table to satisfy any heat seekers in the group.

Make Ahead

Complete Step 1. Cover and refrigerate mixture for up to 2 days. When you're ready to cook, complete the recipe.

Serves 6 to 8

- Large (approx. 5 quart) slow cooker
- Parchment paper

1 tbsp	olive oil	15 mL
2	onions, finely chopped	2
2	carrots, peeled and diced	2
2	stalks celery, diced	2
4	cloves garlic, minced	4
2 tbsp	minced gingerroot	25 mL
1 tsp	salt	5 mL
1 tsp	cracked black peppercorns	5 mL
½ tsp	ground turmeric	2 mL
¼ tsp	saffron threads, crumbled	1 mL
1	piece (2 inches/ 5cm) cinnamon stick	1
1	can (14 oz/398 mL) tomatoes with juice	1
4 cups	cubed (1 inch/2.5 cm) peeled pumpkin or winter squash	1 L
2 cups	cooked chickpeas, drained and rinsed (see Tips, left)	500 mL
1 cup	sweet green peas, thawed if frozen	250 mL
2 cups	water or vegetable stock	500 mL
1 tsp	harissa, optional (see Tips, left)	5 mL
1½ cups	whole wheat, spelt, Kamut or barley couscous	375 mL
½ cup	toasted slivered almonds	125 mL

1. In a skillet, heat oil over medium heat. Add onions, carrots and celery and cook, stirring, until vegetables are softened, about 7 minutes. Add garlic, ginger, salt, peppercorns, turmeric, saffron and cinnamon stick and cook, stirring, for 1 minute. Stir in tomatoes with juice and bring to a boil.

2. Arrange squash evenly over bottom of stoneware. Place chickpeas on top and cover with tomato mixture. Place a large piece of parchment over the mixture, pressing it down to brush the food and extending up the sides of the stoneware so it overlaps the rim. Cover and cook on Low for 6 hours or on High for 3 hours. Lift off the parchment and discard, being careful not to spill the accumulated liquid, which will dilute the sauce. Stir in green peas. Cover and cook on High for 5 minutes, until tender.

3. About 20 minutes before you're ready to serve, bring water to a boil. Stir in harissa, if using. Add couscous in a steady stream, stirring constantly. Remove from heat. Cover and let stand until liquid is absorbed, about 15 minutes. Fluff with a fork.

4. To serve, spread couscous over a deep platter. Arrange tagine evenly over top, leaving a border around the edges. Garnish with toasted almonds.

Entertaining Worthy

Vegan Friendly

Can Be Halved
see Tip, right

Chickpea and Potato Curry with Cauliflower

This colorful mélange, which is vaguely Indian in origin, makes a very tasty and nutritious main course. Serve it over rice or couscous, preferably whole grain, to provide a complete protein.

Serves 6 to 8

- Medium to large (3½ to 5 quart) slow cooker

1 tbsp	olive or coconut oil or ghee	15 mL
2	onions, finely chopped	2
2	carrots, peeled and diced	2
2	stalks celery, diced	2
4	cloves garlic, minced	4
2 tbsp	minced gingerroot	25 mL
1 tbsp	ground turmeric	15 mL
1 tbsp	ground cumin (see Tips, page 292)	15 mL
2 tsp	ground coriander	10 mL
1 tsp	salt	5 mL
½ tsp	cracked black peppercorns	2 mL
2 tbsp	tomato paste	25 mL
3 cups	vegetable stock (see Tips, left)	750 mL
2	potatoes, peeled and shredded	2
2 cups	cooked chickpeas (see Tips, left)	500 mL
¼ tsp	cayenne pepper	1 mL
4 cups	cooked cauliflower florets (about 1 small head) (see Tips, left)	1 L

1. In a skillet, heat oil over medium heat. Add onions, carrots and celery and cook, stirring, until carrots are softened, about 7 minutes. Add garlic, ginger, turmeric, cumin, coriander, salt and peppercorns and cook, stirring, for 1 minute. Add tomato paste and vegetable stock and stir well.

2. Transfer to slow cooker stoneware. Add potatoes and chickpeas. Cover and cook on Low for 6 hours or on High for 3 hours, until vegetables are tender. Stir in cayenne and cauliflower. Cover and cook on High for 15 minutes to meld flavors.

Tips

If you're using prepared vegetable stock, be aware that some brands are extremely strong, resembling vegetable juice more than stock. If this is the case, dilute your stock with up to 1½ cups (375 mL) water to suit your taste. Otherwise, the stock will overpower the recipe.

For this quantity of chickpeas, cook 1 cup (250 mL) soaked, dried chickpeas (see Basic Beans, page 341), or use 1 can (14 to 19 oz/ 398 to 540 mL), drained and rinsed.

For added flavor, roast the cauliflower rather than blanching it. *To roast cauliflower:* In a baking dish, toss the uncooked florets in 2 tbsp (25 mL) olive oil and season with salt and freshly ground black pepper. Place in a preheated (350°F/180°C) oven, cover with foil and roast until tender, stirring once, about 30 minutes.

Make Ahead

Complete Step 1. Cover and refrigerate mixture for up to 2 days. When you're ready to cook, complete the recipe.

Tomato-Mushroom Sauce with Lentils

Although this robust sauce is very tasty over hot pasta tossed with extra virgin olive oil or butter, for a more nutritious option serve it over polenta made with stone-ground cornmeal, or cooked whole grains such as barley or wheat berries.

Entertaining Worthy

Vegan Friendly

Can Be Halved
see Tip, below

Serves 6 to 8

- Medium to large (3½ to 5 quart) slow cooker

1	package (½ oz/14 g) dried porcini mushrooms	1
1 cup	hot water	250 mL
2 tbsp	olive oil	25 mL
2	onions, finely chopped	2
2	stalks celery, diced	2
1	carrot, peeled and diced	1
4	cloves garlic, minced	4
2 tsp	dried Italian seasoning	10 mL
1 tsp	salt	5 mL
1 tsp	cracked black peppercorns	5 mL
1 cup	green or brown lentils, rinsed	250 mL
1 cup	vegetable stock	250 mL
1	can (28 oz/796 mL) tomatoes with juice, coarsely chopped	1
8 oz	cremini mushrooms, trimmed and sliced	250 g
	Finely chopped parsley	

1. In a bowl, combine dried mushrooms with hot water. Let stand for 30 minutes. Strain through a fine sieve, reserving liquid. Pat mushrooms dry and chop finely. Set mushrooms and liquid aside, separately.

2. In a skillet, heat oil over medium heat. Add onions, celery and carrot and cook, stirring, until vegetables are softened, about 7 minutes. Add garlic, Italian seasoning, salt, peppercorns and reserved porcini mushrooms and cook, stirring, for 1 minute. Add lentils and toss well. Add vegetable stock, reserved mushroom liquid and tomatoes with juice and bring to a boil.

3. Transfer to slow cooker stoneware. Add cremini mushrooms and stir well. Cover and cook on Low for 6 hours or on High for 3 hours, until lentils are tender and mixture is hot and bubbly. Garnish with parsley.

Tip

If you are halving this recipe, be sure to use a small (2 to 3½ quart) slow cooker.

Make Ahead

Complete Steps 1 and 2. Cover and refrigerate mixture for up to 2 days. When you're ready to cook, complete the recipe.

Vegan Friendly

Can Be Halved
see Tips, below

Pinto Bean Chili with Corn and Kale

Here's a chili that's very easy to make yet loaded with flavor and nutrition. There is so much goodness here you don't need to add a great deal — perhaps some wholesome brown rice to complete the protein.

Tips

If you're halving this recipe, be sure to use a small (2 to 3½ quart) slow cooker.

To maximize flavor, instead of using ground cumin, toast and grind cumin seeds yourself. Place seeds in a dry skillet over medium heat and cook, stirring, until fragrant, about 3 minutes. Using a mortar and pestle or a clean spice grinder, pound or grind as finely as you can.

Use 1 can (14 to 19 oz/ 398 to 540 mL) pinto beans, drained and rinsed, or 1 cup (250 mL) dried pinto beans, soaked, cooked and drained (see Basic Beans, page 341).

Make Ahead

Complete Steps 1 and 3. Cover and refrigerate vegetable and chile mixtures separately for up to 2 days. (The chile mixture will lose some of its vibrancy. For best results, complete Step 3 while the recipe is cooking.) When you're ready to cook, complete the recipe.

Serves 6

- Large (approx. 5 quart) slow cooker

1 tbsp	olive oil	15 mL
2	onions, finely chopped	2
4	stalks celery, diced	4
4	cloves garlic, minced	4
2 tsp	ground cumin (see Tips, left)	10 mL
1 tsp	dried oregano leaves, crumbled	5 mL
1 tsp	salt	5 mL
½ tsp	cracked black peppercorns	2 mL
1	can (28 oz/796 mL) diced tomatoes with juice	1
2 cups	cooked pinto beans (see Tips, left), drained and rinsed	500 mL
2	dried ancho, New Mexico or guajillo chile peppers	2
1	jalapeño pepper, optional	1
2 cups	corn kernels	500 mL
6 cups	packed chopped kale	1.5 L
	Sour cream or shredded Cheddar or Jack cheese, optional	

1. In a skillet, heat oil over medium heat. Add onions and celery and cook, stirring, until softened, about 5 minutes. Add garlic, cumin, oregano, salt and peppercorns and cook, stirring, for 1 minute. Add tomatoes with juice and bring to a boil.

2. Transfer to slow cooker stoneware. Stir in beans. Cover and cook on Low for 6 hours or on High for 3 hours, until mixture is hot and bubbly.

3. About 1 hour before the chili has finished cooking, in a heatproof bowl, soak dried chile peppers in boiling water for 30 minutes, weighing down with a cup to ensure they remain submerged. Drain and set soaking water aside. Discard stems and chop coarsely. Transfer to a blender. Add jalapeño, if using, and ½ cup (125 mL) of the chile soaking liquid (discard remainder). Purée.

4. Add chile mixture to stoneware and stir well. Stir in corn. Add kale, in batches, stirring after each addition to submerge leaves in liquid. Cover and cook on High for 20 minutes, until corn and kale are tender. Ladle into bowls and garnish with sour cream, if using.

Chile-Spiked Hominy Ragoût with Collard Greens

I suppose you could call this a fusion dish — traditional Mexican ingredients, such as hominy, red beans and chiles, combined with collard greens, which I traditionally associate with the American South. Whatever you call it, it sure tastes good, and in my books that's what matters most.

Serves 6 to 8

- Large (approx. 5 quart) slow cooker

1 tbsp	olive oil	15 mL
2	onions, finely chopped	2
4	stalks celery, diced	4
4	cloves garlic, minced	4
2 tsp	ground cumin (see Tips, right)	10 mL
2 tsp	dried oregano leaves, crumbled	10 mL
1	can (28 oz/796 mL) crushed tomatoes	1
2 cups	vegetable stock	500 mL
2	cans (each 15 oz/425 g) hominy, drained and rinsed	2
2 cups	cooked red kidney beans (see Tips, right)	500 mL
2	dried ancho chile peppers	2
2 cups	boiling water	500 mL
4 cups	thinly sliced (chiffonade) stemmed collard greens or kale (about 1 bunch)	1 L

1. In a skillet, heat oil over medium heat. Add onions and celery and cook, stirring, until softened, about 5 minutes. Add garlic, cumin and oregano and cook, stirring, for 1 minute. Add tomatoes and bring to a boil.

2. Transfer to slow cooker stoneware. Stir in vegetable stock, hominy and beans. Cover and cook on Low for 6 hours or on High for 3 hours, until hot and bubbly.

3. About 1 hour before the recipe has finished cooking, in a heatproof bowl, soak dried chiles in boiling water for 30 minutes, weighing down with a cup to ensure they remain submerged. Drain, discarding soaking liquid and stems, and chop coarsely. Transfer to a blender. Add 1 cup (250 mL) of cooking liquid from the ragoût. Purée. Add to stoneware and stir well. Add collard greens, in batches, completely submerging each batch in the liquid before adding another. Cover and cook on High for 30 minutes, until collards are tender.

Tips

If you're halving this recipe, be sure to use a small (2 to 3½ quart) slow cooker.

To maximize flavor, toast and grind cumin seeds yourself. Place seeds in a dry skillet over medium heat and cook, stirring, until fragrant, about 3 minutes. Using a mortar and pestle or a clean spice grinder, pound or grind as finely as you can.

Use 1 can (14 to 19 oz/ 398 to 540 mL) red kidney beans, drained and rinsed, or 1 cup (250 mL) dried red kidney beans, soaked, cooked and drained (see Basic Beans, page 341).

Make Ahead

Complete Steps 1 and 3, substituting 1 cup (250 mL) of the vegetable stock for the cooking liquid when puréeing the chiles. Cover and refrigerate vegetable and chile mixtures separately for up to 2 days. (The chile mixture will lose some of its vibrancy. For best results, complete Step 3 while the recipe is cooking.) When you're ready to cook, complete the recipe.

Mushroom "Cassoulet"

Served with salad and crusty whole-grain bread, this makes a tasty and substantial meal. If you want to impress your guests, add the toasted bread crumbs — a great way to use up day-old bread.

Tips

If you are halving this recipe, be sure to use a small (2 to 3½ quart) slow cooker.

For added depth of flavor, add a sprig of fresh thyme or rosemary along with the garlic. Use the whole stem. The leaves will fall off during cooking and the stem can be discarded before serving.

To make bread crumbs: For 2 cups (500 mL) bread crumbs, use about 3 slices from a large loaf, each about 1 inch (2.5 cm) thick. Cut each slice into quarters and process in a food processor fitted with a metal blade, until the crumbs are the size of split peas, about 40 seconds. Season to taste with salt and freshly ground pepper and pulse to combine.

Make Ahead

Complete Steps 1 and 2. Cover and refrigerate mixture for up to 2 days. When you're ready to cook, complete the recipe.

Serves 6

- Medium (approx. 4 quart) slow cooker

1	package (½ oz/14 g) dried porcini mushrooms	1
1 cup	hot water	250 mL
1 tbsp	olive oil	15 mL
2	onions, finely chopped	2
2	carrots, peeled and diced	2
2	parsnips, peeled and diced	2
2	stalks celery, diced	2
6	cloves garlic, minced	6
1 tbsp	herbes de Provence	15 mL
2	bay leaves	2
1 tsp	salt	5 mL
1 tsp	cracked black peppercorns	5 mL
1	can (28 oz/796 mL) crushed tomatoes	1
1 lb	cremini mushrooms, trimmed and quartered	500 g
3 cups	cooked white beans, such as navy or cannellini	750 mL
½ cup	finely chopped parsley	125 mL

Garlic Toasted Bread Crumbs, optional

3 tbsp	butter or olive oil	45 mL
1 tbsp	minced garlic	15 mL
2 cups	fresh bread crumbs (see Tips, left)	500 mL

1. In a bowl, combine dried mushrooms with hot water. Let stand for 30 minutes. Strain through a fine sieve, reserving liquid. Pat mushrooms dry and chop finely. Set mushrooms and soaking liquid aside, separately.

2. In a skillet, heat oil over medium heat. Add onions, carrots, parsnips and celery and cook, stirring, until vegetables are softened, about 7 minutes. Add garlic, herbes de Provence, bay leaves, salt, peppercorns and reserved dried mushrooms and cook, stirring, for 1 minute. Stir in crushed tomatoes and reserved mushroom soaking liquid and bring to a boil.

3. Transfer to slow cooker stoneware. Add cremini mushrooms and beans and stir well. Cover and cook on Low for 6 hours or on High for 3 hours, until hot and bubbly. Garnish with parsley.

4. **Garlic Toasted Bread Crumbs, optional:** In a skillet over medium-high heat, melt butter. Add garlic and stir well. Add bread crumbs and cook, stirring, until evenly browned, about 5 minutes. Sprinkle over cassoulet.

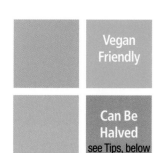

Vegan Friendly

Can Be Halved
see Tips, below

Smoky Butternut Hominy Chili

Adding chipotle peppers to this chili gives it an enticing flavor. Add the smoked paprika only if you really like the flavor of smoke. This is a meal in itself — the combination of hominy (a whole grain) and beans provides a complete protein. You might want to add a green salad and some whole-grain bread to complete the meal.

Tips

If you're halving this recipe, be sure to use a small (2 to 3½ quart) slow cooker.

For best results, toast and grind the cumin yourself. Place seeds in a dry skillet over medium heat and cook, stirring, until fragrant, about 3 minutes. Using a mortar and pestle or a clean spice grinder, pound or grind as finely as you can.

Chipotle chiles are pretty powerful, so unless you're a heat seeker, err on the side of caution and use only one. Include a bit of the adobo sauce, which adds flavor in addition to heat.

Make Ahead

Complete Step 1. Cover and refrigerate mixture for up to 2 days. When you're ready to cook, complete the recipe.

Serves 6 to 8

• Large (approx. 5 quart) slow cooker

1 tbsp	oil	15 mL
2	onions, finely chopped	2
4	stalks celery, diced	4
2	carrots, peeled and diced	2
6	cloves garlic, minced	6
1 tbsp	ground cumin (see Tips, left)	15 mL
1 tbsp	dried oregano leaves, crumbled	15 mL
1 tsp	ground allspice	5 mL
1 tsp	salt	5 mL
½ tsp	cracked black peppercorns	2 mL
1	piece (2 inches/5 cm) cinnamon stick	1
1	can (28 oz/796 mL) tomatoes with juice, coarsely chopped	1
3 cups	cubed (1 inch/2.5 cm) peeled butternut squash	750 mL
2 cups	cooked black beans	500 mL
1	can (15 oz/425 g) hominy, drained	1
1 to 2	chipotle chiles in adobo sauce, minced (see Tips, left)	1 to 2
	Smoked paprika, optional	

1. In a skillet, heat oil over medium heat. Add onions, celery and carrots and cook, stirring, until softened, about 7 minutes. Add garlic, cumin, oregano, allspice, salt, peppercorns and cinnamon stick and cook, stirring, for 1 minute. Stir in tomatoes with juice and bring to a boil, breaking up with a spoon. Remove from heat.

2. In slow cooker stoneware, combine squash, beans and hominy. Add tomato mixture and stir well. Cover and cook on Low for 6 hours or on High for 3 hours, until squash is tender. Stir in chile(s) and smoked paprika to taste, if using. Cover and cook on High for 10 minutes to meld flavors.

Mushroom Chili

Here's a vegetarian chili that is particularly rich and lush, thanks to the addition of robust cremini mushrooms. Serve this with whole-grain bread and a tossed green salad for a delicious meal.

Vegan Friendly

Can Be Halved
see Tips, below

Serves 6

- Large (approx. 5 quart) slow cooker

2 cups	cooked red kidney beans (see Tips, right)	500 mL
1 tbsp	olive oil	15 mL
2	onions, finely chopped	2
4	stalks celery, diced	4
4	cloves garlic, minced	4
1 tbsp	dried oregano leaves	15 mL
1 tbsp	ground cumin (see Tips, right)	15 mL
2 tsp	ground coriander seeds	10 mL
1 tsp	salt	5 mL
1 tsp	cracked black peppercorns	5 mL
1	can (14 oz/398 mL) crushed tomatoes	1
1 lb	cremini mushrooms, trimmed and quartered	500 g
1 cup	vegetable stock or water	250 mL
1	jalapeño pepper, seeded and diced	1
1 tsp	ancho or Mexican chile powder	15 mL
	Chopped red or green onion, optional	
	Avocado Topping (see Tips, right), optional	
	Sour cream, optional	
	Shredded Cheddar or Monterey Jack cheese, optional	

1. In a skillet, heat oil over medium heat. Add onions and celery and cook, stirring, until softened, about 3 minutes. Add garlic, oregano, cumin, coriander, salt and peppercorns and cook, stirring, for 1 minute. Stir in crushed tomatoes and bring to a boil.

2. Transfer to slow cooker stoneware. Add mushrooms, vegetable stock and kidney beans. Cover and cook on Low for 6 hours or on High for 3 hours, until hot and bubbly. Stir in jalapeño and ancho chile powder. Cover and cook on High for 10 minutes to blend flavors. Serve garnished with any combination of red onion, Avocado Topping, sour cream, and/or shredded cheese.

Tips

If you're halving this recipe, be sure to use a small (approx. 2 quart) slow cooker.

Use 1 can (14 to 19 oz/ 398 to 540 mL) red kidney beans, drained and rinsed, or soak and cook 1 cup (250 mL) dried beans yourself (see Basic Beans, page 341).

To maximize flavor, toast and grind the cumin yourself. Place seeds in a dry skillet over medium heat and cook, stirring, until fragrant, about 3 minutes. Using a mortar and pestle or a clean spice grinder, pound or grind as finely as you can.

To make Avocado Topping: Chop 1 whole avocado into ½-inch (1 cm) cubes and toss with 1 tbsp (15 mL) lime juice, 2 tbsp (25 mL) finely chopped red onion and 2 tbsp (25 mL) finely chopped cilantro. Add salt and pepper to taste.

Make Ahead

Complete Step 1. Cover and refrigerate mixture for up to 2 days. When you're ready to cook, complete the recipe.

Vegan Friendly

Can Be Halved
see Tips, below

Black Bean Chili with Hominy and Sweet Corn

This is a particularly thick and luscious chili, rich with the goodness of corn. It doesn't need much more than a simple green salad and perhaps some whole-grain bread to complete the meal.

Serves 6 to 8

- Large (approx. 5 quart) slow cooker

1 tbsp	olive oil	15 mL
2	onions, finely chopped	2
4	stalks celery, diced	4
2	carrots, peeled and diced	2
4	cloves garlic, minced	4
1 tbsp	ground cumin (see Tips, left)	15 mL
2 tsp	dried oregano leaves	10 mL
1 tsp	salt	5 mL
1 tsp	cracked black peppercorns	5 mL
1	can (28 oz/796 mL) crushed tomatoes	1
3 cups	cooked black beans (see Tips, left)	750 mL
1	can (14 oz/398 mL) hominy, drained	1
1 to 2 tbsp	ancho or New Mexico chili powder	15 to 25 mL
1 cup	corn kernels	250 mL
1 to 2	jalapeño peppers, seeded and diced	1 to 2

1. In a skillet, heat oil over medium heat. Add onions, celery and carrots and cook, stirring, until softened, about 7 minutes. Add garlic, cumin, oregano, salt and peppercorns and cook, stirring, for 1 minute. Stir in tomatoes and bring to a boil.

2. Transfer to slow cooker stoneware. Add beans and hominy and stir well. Cover and cook on Low for 6 hours or on High for 3 hours, until hot and bubbly. Add ancho chile powder and stir well. Stir in corn and jalapeno to taste. Cover and cook on High for 20 minutes, until corn is tender.

Tips

If you are halving this recipe, be sure to use a small (approx. 1½ to 2 quart) slow cooker.

For best results, toast and grind the cumin yourself. Place seeds in a dry skillet over medium heat and cook, stirring, until fragrant, about 3 minutes. Using a mortar and pestle or a clean spice grinder, pound or grind as finely as you can.

For this quantity of black beans, use 2 cans (14 to 19 oz/398 to 540 mL), drained and rinsed, and set excess aside for another use, or cook 1½ cups (375 mL) dried black beans (see Basic Beans, page 341).

Make Ahead

Complete Step 1. Cover and refrigerate mixture for up to 2 days. When you're ready to cook, complete the recipe.

Lentil Shepherd's Pie with Sweet Potato Topping

It's not often that a vegetarian dish can be described as "stick-to-your-ribs," but this one qualifies. Traditionalists may miss the meat and white potatoes, but others will appreciate the nutritional benefits provided by lentils and sweet potatoes.

Vegetarian Friendly

Can Be Halved
see Tips, below

Serves 6 to 8

- Medium to large (3½ to 5 quart) slow cooker

1 tbsp	olive oil	15 mL
2	onions, finely chopped	2
2	stalks celery, diced	2
2	carrots, peeled and diced	2
2	cloves garlic, minced	2
1 tsp	salt	5 mL
1 tsp	dried thyme leaves	5 mL
½ tsp	cracked black peppercorns	2 mL
1½ cups	green or brown lentils, rinsed	375 mL
1	can (28 oz/796 mL) diced tomatoes with juice	1
2 cups	vegetable stock (see Tips, right)	500 mL

Topping

4 cups	mashed cooked sweet potatoes (about 3 medium-large)	1 L
2 tbsp	butter	25 mL
1 cup	dry bread crumbs	250 mL
½ cup	shredded Cheddar cheese, optional	125 mL

1. In a large skillet, heat oil over medium heat. Add onions, celery and carrots and cook, stirring, until carrots have softened, about 7 minutes. Add garlic, salt, thyme and peppercorns and cook, stirring, for 1 minute. Add lentils and toss until coated. Add tomatoes with juice and bring to a boil.

2. Transfer to slow cooker stoneware. Stir in vegetable stock.

3. **Topping:** In a bowl, combine mashed sweet potatoes and butter. Stir in bread crumbs and cheese, if using. Spread evenly over lentils. (The best way to do this is to add the mixture in dollops, then spread with the back of a spoon. You can submerge it a bit in the liquid, which will ease spreading.) Cover and cook on Low for 6 hours or on High for 3 hours, until lentils are tender and mixture is hot and bubbly.

Vegan Alternative

Substitute olive oil for the butter and vegan Cheddar cheese for the regular version.

Tips

If you are halving this recipe, be sure to use a small (approx. 1½ to 2 quart) slow cooker.

If you're using prepared vegetable stock, be aware than some brands are extremely strong, resembling vegetable juice more than stock. If this is the case, dilute your stock with up to 1½ cups (375 mL) water to suit your taste. Otherwise, the stock will overpower the recipe.

Make Ahead

Complete Step 1. Cover and refrigerate mixture for up to 2 days. When you're ready to cook, complete the recipe.

Spicy Peanut Stew with Tofu and Coconut

Serve this over hot rice for a delightfully different meal that will please everyone. The lush stew contains a wide range of vegetables along with the tofu, and the slightly sweet coconut finish enhances its pleasantly mild curry flavor.

Tips

If you are halving this recipe, be sure to use a small (approx. 1½ to 2 quart) slow cooker.

Because the flavors in this dish are fundamentally Asian, I like to use coconut oil when softening the vegetables. Many people believe it has unique health benefits — certainly its mild coconut flavor complements the recipe.

Make Ahead

Complete Step 1. Cover and refrigerate mixture for up to 2 days. When you're ready to cook, complete the recipe.

• Medium to large (3½ to 5 quart) slow cooker

1 tbsp	olive or coconut oil (see Tips, left)	15 mL
2	onions, finely chopped	2
2	carrots, peeled and diced	2
2	stalks celery, diced	2
4	cloves garlic, minced	4
1 tbsp	minced gingerroot	15 mL
1 tsp	salt	5 mL
½ tsp	cracked black peppercorns	2 mL
1	can (28 oz/796 mL) diced tomatoes with juice	1
2 cups	cubed (1 inch/2.5 cm) sweet potatoes	500 mL
1 lb	extra-firm tofu, cut into 1-inch (2.5 cm) cubes	500 g
2 cups	vegetable stock	500 mL
3 tbsp	smooth natural peanut butter	45 mL
2 tbsp	freshly squeezed lime juice	25 mL
2 tbsp	soy sauce	25 mL
1 tsp	Thai red curry paste	5 mL
½ cup	coconut milk	125 mL
1	red bell pepper, diced	1
¼ cup	chopped roasted peanuts	50 mL
¼ cup	finely chopped cilantro	50 mL

1. In a skillet, heat oil over medium heat. Add onions, carrots and celery and cook, stirring, until carrots are softened, about 7 minutes. Add garlic, ginger, salt and peppercorns and cook, stirring, for 1 minute. Add tomatoes with juice and bring to a boil.

2. Transfer to slow cooker stoneware. Add sweet potatoes, tofu and vegetable stock and stir well. Cover and cook on Low for 5 hours or on High for 2½ hours, until hot and bubbly.

3. In a bowl, combine peanut butter, lime juice, soy sauce and red curry paste. Mix well. Add to slow cooker stoneware and stir well. Add coconut milk and red pepper and stir well. Cover and cook on High for 20 minutes, until pepper is tender and mixture is hot. Garnish with peanuts and cilantro.

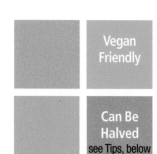

Vegan Friendly

Can Be Halved
see Tips, below

Butterbeans with Artichokes and Rice

This recipe is loaded with ingredients I find terrifically soothing — rice, artichokes and butterbeans (also known as lima beans) — and which combine beautifully. I particularly love this dish topped with a runny poached egg.

Tips

If you are halving this recipe, be sure to use a small (approx. 1½ to 2 quart) slow cooker.

For the best flavor, toast and grind cumin seeds yourself. Place seeds in a dry skillet over medium heat and stir until fragrant, about 3 minutes. Using a mortar and pestle or a clean spice grinder, pound or grind as finely as you can.

Make Ahead

Complete Steps 1 and 2. Cover and refrigerate mixture for up to 2 days. When you're ready to cook, complete the recipe.

Serves 4 to 6

- Medium (approx. 3½ quart) slow cooker

1 cup	dried lima beans	250 mL
3 cups	cold water	750 mL
1 tbsp	olive oil	15 mL
2	onions, thinly sliced on the vertical	2
4	cloves garlic, minced	4
1 tbsp	ground cumin (see Tips, left)	15 mL
1 tsp	finely grated lemon zest	5 mL
1 tsp	salt	5 mL
½ tsp	cracked black peppercorns	2 mL
1 cup	short-grain brown rice, rinsed	250 mL
3 cups	vegetable or chicken stock	750 mL
1	can (14 oz/398 mL) artichoke hearts, drained and quartered	1
1 tbsp	freshly squeezed lemon juice	15 mL
1 tsp	hot paprika	5 mL
	Freshly grated Parmesan, optional	
	Poached eggs, optional	

1. In a large saucepan, bring lima beans and cold water to a boil. Boil rapidly for 3 minutes. Turn off heat, cover and set aside for 1 hour. Drain in a colander, rinse thoroughly under cold running water and pop beans out of their skins. Discard skins. If you're not using the beans immediately, submerge them in cold water.

2. In a skillet, heat oil over medium heat. Add onions and cook, stirring, until softened, about 3 minutes. Add garlic, cumin, lemon zest, salt and peppercorns and cook, stirring, for 1 minute. Add rice and toss until well coated with mixture. Stir in reserved beans. Add stock and bring to a boil. Boil rapidly for 2 minutes.

3. Transfer to slow cooker stoneware. Stir in artichokes. Place a clean tea towel, folded in half (so you will have 2 layers), over top of stoneware to absorb moisture. Cover and cook on Low for 6 hours or on High for 3 hours.

4. In a small bowl, combine lemon juice and paprika. Stir into cooked rice. To serve, spoon onto plates and sprinkle with Parmesan, if using. If desired, top each serving with a freshly poached egg.

Yellow and Green Pea Coconut Dal

This dish is almost too pretty to eat — but not quite. It's a yummy combination of healthful ingredients that makes a great main course served over rice, a splendid dish for a multi-course Indian meal, or an eye-catching component of a party buffet.

Entertaining Worthy

Vegan Friendly

Can Be Halved
see Tips, below

Serves 8

- Large (approx. 5 quart) slow cooker

1 cup	yellow split peas (see Tips, right)	250 mL
1 tbsp	olive or coconut oil	15 mL
2	onions, finely chopped	2
2	carrots, peeled and diced	2
2	stalks celery, diced	2
6	cloves garlic, minced	6
2 tbsp	minced gingerroot	25 mL
1 tbsp	ground cumin (see Tips, right)	15 mL
2 tsp	ground coriander	10 mL
1 tsp	salt	5 mL
1 tsp	cracked black peppercorns	5 mL
1	can (14 oz/398 mL) diced tomatoes with juice	1
2	potatoes, peeled and shredded	2
2 cups	vegetable stock	500 mL
2 cups	sweet green peas, thawed if frozen	500 mL
1 cup	coconut milk	250 mL
1 to 2	long red or green chile(s), seeded and minced (see Tips, right)	1 to 2

1. In a large saucepan, combine 4 cups (1 L) water and split peas. Bring to a boil. Reduce heat to low and simmer until peas are almost tender, about 25 minutes. Drain and set aside.

2. In a skillet, heat oil over medium heat. Add onions, carrots and celery and cook, stirring, until softened, about 7 minutes. Add garlic, ginger, cumin, coriander, salt and peppercorns and cook, stirring, for 1 minute. Stir in tomatoes with juice and split peas and bring to a boil.

3. Transfer to slow cooker stoneware. Add potatoes and vegetable stock. Cover and cook on Low for 6 hours or on High for 3 hours, until hot and bubbly. Add green peas, coconut milk and chile(s). Cover and cook on High for 20 minutes, until peas are tender and flavors meld.

Tips

If you're halving this recipe, be sure to use a small (2 to 3½ quart) slow cooker.

I like to give the split peas a bit of a precooking to ensure they are almost dissolved in the sauce when the dish is finished. If you prefer a firmer texture, simply bring them to a boil, boil for 3 minutes and let them sit while you prepare the remainder of the ingredients. Drain before adding to the recipe.

For the best flavor, toast and grind the cumin and coriander seeds yourself. Place seeds in a dry skillet over medium heat and stir until fragrant, about 3 minutes. Using a mortar and pestle or a clean spice grinder, pound or grind as finely as you can.

Vary the quantity of chiles to suit your taste. One produces a mild result and two are quite spicy.

Make Ahead

Complete Steps 1 and 2. Cover and refrigerate mixture for up to 2 days. When you're ready to cook, complete the recipe.

| Entertaining Worthy | Vegan Friendly |
| Can Be Halved see Tips, below | |

Tofu Enchiladas

Why do we like enchiladas? There is something very soothing about filled tortillas baked in a sauce.

Tips

If you're halving this recipe, be sure to use a small (2 to 3½ quart) oval slow cooker.

Use the kind of flour you prefer — all-purpose, whole wheat or, if you are gluten adverse, sorghum or buckwheat.

For best flavor, toast and grind the cumin yourself. Place seeds in a dry skillet over medium heat, stirring until fragrant, about 3 minutes. Using a mortar and pestle or a clean spice grinder, pound or grind as finely as you can.

For best results, use corn tortillas — they have much more flavor than those made from wheat.

Make Ahead

Complete Step 3. Cover and refrigerate mixture for up to 2 days. When you're ready to cook, complete the recipe.

Serves 6 to 8

- Large (approx. 5 quart) slow cooker

Filling

2 tbsp	flour (see Tips, left)	25 mL
2 tsp	Mexican chili powder	10 mL
1 lb	extra-firm tofu, cut into ½-inch (1 cm) cubes	500 g
2 tbsp	olive oil (approx.), divided	25 mL
2	onions, finely chopped	2
4	stalks celery, diced	4
2	cloves garlic, minced	2
2 tsp	ground cumin (see Tips, left)	10 mL
2 tsp	ground oregano leaves	10 mL
1 tsp	salt	5 mL
1 tsp	cracked black peppercorns	5 mL
1	can (28 oz/796 mL) tomatoes with juice, chopped	1
8	soft tortillas (see Tips, left)	8
1 cup	chopped green onion	250 mL
2 cups	shredded Monterey Jack cheese or vegan alternative, divided	500 mL
	Pickled jalapeño peppers	
	Sour cream or vegan alternative	
	Cilantro	

1. On a plate, combine flour and chili powder. Add tofu, in batches, and coat well.

2. In a skillet, heat 1 tbsp (15 mL) of the oil over medium-high heat. Add dredged tofu, in batches, and cook, turning once, until golden, about 4 minutes, adding more oil if necessary. Remove with a slotted spoon and drain on paper towel.

3. Reduce heat to medium. Add remaining oil to pan. Add onions and celery and cook, stirring, until softened, about 5 minutes. Add garlic, cumin, oregano, salt and peppercorns and cook, stirring, for 1 minute. Add tomatoes with juice and bring to a boil. Set aside.

4. Lay 1 tortilla on a work surface. Arrange tofu in the center, sprinkle with approximately 1 tbsp (15 mL) green onion and 2 tbsp (25 mL) shredded cheese. Fold ends over and roll up. Repeat with remaining tortillas. (When you're finished you should have about ½ cup/125 mL green onion and 1 cup/250 mL of cheese left over.)

5. Lay filled tortillas, seam side down, in stoneware. Cover with tomato sauce and sprinkle with remaining cheese and onions. Cover and cook on Low for 6 hours or on High for 3 hours, until hot and bubbly. Garnish with jalapeños, sour cream and cilantro.

Raghavan's Braised Potatoes and Eggplant

This recipe appears in a marvelous book, 660 Curries, *written by my friend Raghavan Iyer. It's very easy to make — simple yet delicious, with a pitch-perfect combination of ingredients. I've adapted it a bit for the slow cooker, and I believe it maintains all the virtues of the original. Serve over hot rice with naan for a complete meal.*

Serves 6

- Medium to large (3½ to 5 quart) slow cooker

10	small purple Indian (or 1 large Italian) eggplants (about 1¼ lbs/625 g total)	10
2 to 4	fresh green Thai, cayenne or long chiles	2 to 4
2 tbsp	olive oil or ghee	25 mL
2 tsp	whole cumin seeds	10 mL
½ tsp	ground turmeric	2 mL
1½ lbs	russet or Yukon gold potatoes, peeled and finely diced (see Tips, right)	750 g
½ cup	water	125 mL
1	can (14 oz/398 mL) diced tomatoes with juice	1
2 tsp	coarse salt (kosher or sea)	10 mL
1 tbsp	whole cumin seeds, toasted and ground	15 mL
2 tbsp	finely chopped cilantro	25 mL

1. Remove stems from eggplants and cut into 2- by 1-inch (5 by 2.5 cm) pieces. Remove stems from chile peppers. Cut crosswise into ¼-inch (0.5 cm) slices (do not remove the seeds).

2. In a large skillet, heat oil over medium-high heat. Add 2 tsp (10 mL) whole cumin seeds and cook until they sizzle, about 10 seconds. Stir in turmeric. Add potatoes and cook, tossing, for 3 minutes. Add eggplant and toss until coated. Transfer to slow cooker stoneware.

3. Add water, tomatoes with juice and salt to pan and bring to a boil, scraping up brown bits on the bottom. Pour over eggplant mixture. Place a large piece of parchment paper over the mixture, pressing down to brush the food and extending up the sides of the stoneware so it overlaps the rim. Cover and cook on Low for 6 hours or on high for 3 hours. Lift out parchment and discard, being careful not to spill the accumulated liquid into the sauce. Sprinkle with sliced chiles and 1 tbsp (15 mL) ground toasted cumin seeds. Cover and cook about 10 minutes, until flavors meld. Garnish with cilantro.

Tips

If you are halving this recipe, be sure to use a small (2 to 3½ quart) slow cooker.

Potatoes cook particularly slowly in the slow cooker, so I recommend cutting them into a fine dice to ensure they will not be *al dente* when the rest of the dish has finished cooking. Because they oxidize quickly on contact with air, after they are diced, submerge them in a bowl of cold water to prevent browning.

I like to use parchment when cooking this dish because it doesn't contain much liquid. Creating a tight seal ensures that none evaporates and that the vegetables are well basted in their own juices.

Entertaining Worthy

Vegan Friendly

Can Be Halved
see Tips, below

Ratatouille with Roasted Peppers

Ratatouille is probably the first vegetarian dish I learned to appreciate. I have very fond memories of making it from freshly picked produce at a friend's farmhouse, faithfully following Julia Child's recipe. I have maintained respect for her dictum that the individual elements should be cooked separately, then assembled to briefly meld. However, using the slow cooker permits a few shortcuts. I enjoy ratatouille as a main course, but it also makes a great side and is equally delicious hot or cold.

Tips

If you are halving this recipe, be sure to use a small (2 to 3½ quart) slow cooker.

Whether you peel the eggplant and zucchini is a matter of taste.

Green bell peppers provide a nice color contrast in this dish, but if you're opting for convenience, by all means use prepared roasted red peppers instead.

Make Ahead

Complete Steps 1 through 5. Cover and refrigerate tomato mixture, eggplant and zucchini separately for up to 2 days. When you're ready to cook, complete the recipe.

Serves 6

- Medium to large (3½ to 5 quart) slow cooker

1	eggplant (about 1 lb/500 g), cut into 2-inch (5 cm) cubes (see Tips, left)	1
2 tsp	salt, divided	10 mL
2	medium zucchini (each about 12 oz/375 g)	2
¼ cup	olive oil (approx.)	50 mL
2	onions, finely chopped	2
4	cloves garlic, minced	4
1 tsp	cracked black peppercorns	5 mL
½ tsp	dried thyme leaves	2 mL
1	can (28 oz/796 mL) tomatoes with juice, coarsely chopped	1
2	green bell peppers, roasted, peeled, seeded and cut into strips (see Tips, left)	2

1. Sprinkle eggplant with ½ tsp (2 mL) of the salt and set aside in a bowl for 30 minutes. Rinse thoroughly in fresh cold water and, using your hands, squeeze out excess moisture. Pat dry with paper towels.

2. Cut zucchini in half lengthwise and slice into 1-inch (2.5 cm) pieces. In a separate bowl, toss with ½ tsp (2 mL) of the salt. Set aside for 30 minutes. Rinse thoroughly in fresh cold water and pat dry with paper towels.

3. In a skillet, heat 1 tbsp (15 mL) of the oil over medium heat. Add eggplant, in batches, and cook, stirring, until nicely browned, about 4 minutes per batch, adding more oil as necessary. Transfer to slow cooker stoneware as completed.

4. In same skillet, heat remaining oil. Add zucchini, in batches, and cook, stirring, until softened and nicely browned, about 6 minutes per batch. Transfer to a bowl, cover and refrigerate.

5. Add more oil to pan if necessary. Add onions and cook, stirring, until softened, about 3 minutes. Add garlic and cook, stirring, for 1 minute. Add 1 tsp (5 mL) of salt, peppercorns and thyme and cook, stirring, for 1 minute. Add tomatoes with juice and bring to a boil.

6. Transfer to slow cooker stoneware. Cover and cook on Low for 6 hours or on High for 3 hours, until eggplant is very tender. Stir in reserved zucchini and roasted peppers. Cover and cook on High for 15 minutes to meld flavors.

Variation

Ratatouille Gratin: You can easily turn this into an elegant buffet dish. After ratatouille has finished cooking, transfer to a 13- by 9-inch (3 L) baking dish. In a bowl, combine 1 cup (250 mL) dry bread crumbs with $\frac{1}{4}$ cup (50 mL) each melted butter and finely chopped parsley or basil. Sprinkle over ratatouille and place under preheated broiler until topping is lightly browned and mixture is bubbling. (Or refrigerate it for up to 2 days before completing this step — just make sure to reheat the ratatouille before adding the topping.)

Entertaining
Worthy

Vegetarian
Friendly

Artichoke and Onion Strata

This is a great dish for brunch because you can assemble it the night before, then put it in the slow cooker in the morning to be ready as your guests arrive. However, it tastes so good I like to have it for dinner, too. Served with a green salad, it makes a lovely meal.

Tips

Use white or light whole wheat bread in this recipe. Heavier bread such as multigrain will overwhelm the flavors.

I recommend soaking the mixture in a large mixing bowl because the bread condenses as it absorbs the liquid. It will subsequently fit into the baking dish.

Make Ahead

Complete Steps 1 and 2. Cover and refrigerate as per Step 2 for up to 2 days. When you're ready to cook, complete the recipe.

Serves 6

- Lightly greased 8-cup (2 L) soufflé dish
- Large (minimum 5 quart) oval slow cooker

1 tbsp	olive oil	15 mL
1	large Spanish onion, thinly sliced on the vertical	1
4	cloves garlic, minced	4
1 tbsp	dried Italian seasoning	15 mL
½ tsp	salt	2 mL
½ tsp	cracked black peppercorns	2 mL
1	can (14 oz/398 mL) artichokes, drained and quartered	1
1½ cups	shredded Cheddar cheese	375 mL
3	slices bread (about 1 inch/2.5 cm thick), cubed (see Tips, left)	3
4	eggs	4
1	can (12 oz or 370 mL) evaporated milk	1
2 tbsp	grated Parmesan	25 mL

1. In a skillet, heat oil over medium heat. Add onion and cook, stirring, until softened, about 3 minutes. Add garlic, Italian seasoning, salt and peppercorns and cook, stirring, for 1 minute. Add artichokes and toss to coat. Remove from heat and stir in cheese. Transfer to a large mixing bowl. Add bread and toss well.

2. In a bowl, beat eggs and evaporated milk. Pour mixture over bread and stir well. Cover with plastic wrap and, using your hands, push the bread down so it is submerged in the liquid. Refrigerate overnight, pushing the bread down into the liquid once or twice, if possible.

3. Transfer to prepared dish. Cover with foil and tie tightly with a string. Place dish in slow cooker stoneware and add boiling water to come 1 inch (2.5 cm) up the sides. Cover and cook on High for 3 hours, until strata is puffed.

4. Meanwhile, preheat broiler. Remove foil and sprinkle Parmesan evenly over top of strata. Place under broiler until melted and nicely browned. Serve immediately.

Savory Bread-and-Butter Pudding

Served hot from the slow cooker, this dish is so yummy I always have seconds. It's a fabulous combination of soothing foods such as cheese, eggs, milk and bread. Make it with olive bread for some Mediterranean flair. Add a simple green salad and enjoy a great lunch, brunch or dinner.

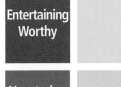

Entertaining Worthy

Vegetarian Friendly

Serves 6

- Lightly greased 8-cup (2 L) baking or soufflé dish
- Large (minimum 5 quart) oval slow cooker

3	thick slices bread (about 1 inch/2.5 cm thick) (see Tips, right)	3
¼ cup	softened butter (approx.)	50 mL
2 cups	baby spinach	500 mL
1½ cups	shredded old Cheddar cheese	375 mL
1 cup	chopped green onions	250 mL
4	eggs	4
2	egg yolks	2
1 cup	evaporated milk	250 mL
2 tsp	Dijon mustard	10 mL
1 tsp	salt	5 mL
1 tsp	cracked black peppercorns	5 mL
1	can (28 oz/796 mL) diced tomatoes with juice	1
¼ cup	grated Parmesan	50 mL

1. Butter the bread on both sides and cut into 1-inch (2.5 cm) cubes. Place in a large mixing bowl (see Tips, page 308). Add spinach, cheese and green onions and toss well.

2. In a separate bowl, whisk together eggs, egg yolks, evaporated milk, mustard, salt and peppercorns, until blended. Whisk in tomatoes with juice. Pour over bread mixture, stirring until well covered. Cover with plastic wrap and, using your hands, push the bread down so it is submerged in the liquid. Refrigerate overnight, pushing the bread down into the liquid once or twice, if possible.

3. Transfer to prepared dish. Cover with foil and tie tightly with a string. Place dish in slow cooker stoneware and add boiling water to come 1 inch (2.5 cm) up the sides. Cover and cook on High for 3 to 4 hours, until pudding is puffed.

4. Meanwhile, preheat broiler. Remove foil and sprinkle Parmesan evenly over top of pudding. Place under broiler until melted and nicely browned.

Tips

Use white or light whole wheat bread in this recipe. Olive bread is also a good choice. Do not use a heavy whole wheat or multigrain bread because it would overwhelm the other flavors.

Don't worry about the large quantity — this reheats in the microwave very well. Also, at least one friend of mine thoroughly enjoys it served cold.

Make Ahead

Complete Steps 1 and 2. Cover and refrigerate as per Step 2 for up to 2 days. When you're ready to cook, complete the recipe.

Indian-Spiced Tofu in Tomato Sauce with Spinach

Here's a delightfully different dinner that even non-vegans will love. It's a complete meal — there's nothing you need to add.

Tips

If you are halving this recipe, be sure to use a small (approx. 1½ to 2 quart) slow cooker.

If you prefer, substitute 1 tsp (5 mL) hot or smoked hot paprika for the paprika and cayenne.

To maximize flavor, toast and grind the cumin and coriander seeds yourself. Place seeds in a dry skillet over medium heat and cook, stirring, until fragrant, about 3 minutes. Using a mortar and pestle or a clean spice grinder, pound or grind as finely as you can.

Make Ahead

Complete Steps 1 and 2. Cover and refrigerate tofu and tomato mixture separately for up to 2 days. When you're ready to cook, complete the recipe.

Serves 6

• Medium to large (3½ to 5 quart) slow cooker

2 tbsp	whole wheat or all-purpose flour	25 mL
2 tsp	paprika (see Tips, left)	10 mL
¼ tsp	cayenne pepper	1 mL
1 lb	extra-firm tofu, cut into 1-inch (2.5 cm) squares	500 g
2 tbsp	olive oil (approx.), divided	25 mL
2	onions, finely chopped	2
2	stalks celery, diced	2
4	cloves garlic, minced	4
1 tbsp	minced gingerroot	15 mL
1 tbsp	ground cumin (see Tips, left)	15 mL
2 tsp	ground coriander	10 mL
1 tsp	ground turmeric	5 mL
1 tsp	salt	5 mL
1 tsp	cracked black peppercorns	5 mL
1	can (28 oz/796 mL) diced tomatoes with juice	1
1 cup	vegetable stock	250 mL
4 cups	packed chopped spinach leaves	1 L

1. On a plate or in a plastic bag, combine flour, paprika and cayenne. Mix well. Add tofu and toss until well coated with mixture. In a skillet, heat 1 tbsp (15 mL) of the oil over medium-high heat. Add tofu, in batches, and brown, turning once, about 4 minutes per batch, adding more oil if necessary. Transfer to a paper towel to drain, then cover and refrigerate until ready to use.

2. Add remaining tbsp (15 mL) of oil to pan. Add onions and celery and cook, stirring, until onions just begin to turn golden, about 5 minutes. Add garlic, ginger, cumin, coriander, turmeric, salt and peppercorns and cook, stirring, for 1 minute. Add tomatoes with juice and vegetable stock and bring to a boil.

3. Transfer to slow cooker stoneware. Cover and cook on Low for 6 hours or on High for 3 hours, until hot and bubbly.

4. Add spinach, stirring well until it is submerged in the liquid, then add reserved tofu. Cover and cook on High for 15 minutes, until spinach is wilted and tofu is heated through.

Mushroom Crisp

If you're looking for something a little different, this is it. Rich and dense, with dark, flavorful mushrooms and an almond-speckled topping, this is almost like a nut loaf. Serve smallish portions, accompanied by a lighter dish such as a simple salad of tossed greens.

Serves 6 to 8

- Medium (approx. 3 quart) oval slow cooker

1	package (½ oz/14 g) dried wild mushrooms, such as porcini	1
1 cup	hot water	250 mL
1 tbsp	olive oil	15 mL
2	onions, finely chopped	2
2	stalks celery, diced	2
2	carrots, peeled and diced	2
4	cloves garlic, minced	4
1 tsp	dried thyme leaves	5 mL
1 tsp	cracked black peppercorns	5 mL
½ tsp	salt	2 mL
2 tbsp	whole wheat or all-purpose flour	25 mL
2 tbsp	balsamic vinegar	25 mL
1 lb	cremini mushrooms, sliced	500 g

Topping

½ cup	rolled oats	125 mL
½ cup	whole wheat or all-purpose flour	125 mL
½ cup	toasted chopped almonds	125 mL
¼ cup	softened butter	50 mL
2 tbsp	finely chopped parsley	25 mL

1. In a bowl, combine dried mushrooms and hot water. Let stand for 30 minutes. Strain through a fine sieve, reserving liquid. Chop mushrooms finely and set aside.

2. In a skillet, heat oil over medium heat. Add onions, celery and carrots and cook, stirring, until softened, about 7 minutes. Add garlic, thyme, peppercorns, salt and reserved dried mushrooms and cook, stirring, for 1 minute. Add flour and cook, stirring, for 1 minute. Add 1 cup (250 mL) water, vinegar and reserved mushroom liquid and bring to a boil. Cook, stirring, until slightly thickened, about 2 minutes.

3. Transfer to slow cooker stoneware. Stir in cremini mushrooms.

4. **Topping:** In a bowl, combine rolled oats, flour, almonds, butter and parsley. Using two forks or your fingers, combine until crumbly. Sprinkle evenly over mushroom mixture. Place 2 clean tea towels, each folded in half (so you will have 4 layers), over top of stoneware. Cover and cook on High for 3 to 4 hours, until hot and bubbly. Remove lid and towel and let stand for 5 minutes before serving.

Tip

If you're halving this recipe, be sure to use a small (approx. 1½ to 2 quart) slow cooker.

Make Ahead

Complete Steps 1 and 2. Cover and refrigerate mixture for up to 2 days. When you're ready to cook, complete the recipe.

Fennel Braised with Tomatoes

Grains and Sides

Entertaining Worthy

Vegan Friendly

Can Be Halved
see Tips, below

Fennel Braised with Tomatoes

Here's a perfectly luscious side dish that makes a great companion for grilled or roasted fish and meats or a splendid topping for hot whole grains such as wheat berries, barley or brown rice. The gratin variation, which adds a fancy finish and nice texture, is particularly attractive on a buffet table.

Tips

If you are halving this recipe, be sure to use a small (approx. 1½ to 2 quart) slow cooker.

If the outer sections of your fennel bulb seem old and dry, peel them with a vegetable peeler before using. *To prepare fennel:* Chop off the top shoots (which resemble celery) and discard. If desired, save the feathery green fronds to use as a garnish.

I like to use parchment when cooking this dish because it doesn't contain much liquid. Creating a tight seal ensures that none evaporates and that the vegetables are well basted in their own juices.

Serves 6

- Medium (approx. 3½ quart) slow cooker
- Parchment paper

2 tbsp	olive oil	25 mL
1	onion, thinly sliced on the vertical	1
3	bulbs fennel, cored and thinly sliced on the vertical (see Tips, left)	3
4	cloves garlic, minced	4
½ tsp	salt	2 mL
½ tsp	cracked black peppercorns	2 mL
1	can (14 oz/398 mL) diced tomatoes with juice	1
	Fennel fronds, optional	

1. In a large skillet, heat oil over medium heat. Add onion and fennel and cook, tossing, until fennel begins to brown, about 5 minutes. Add garlic, salt and peppercorns and cook, stirring, for 1 minute. Add tomatoes with juice and bring to a boil.

2. Transfer to slow cooker stoneware. Place a large piece of parchment over the mixture, pressing it down to brush the food and extending up the sides of the stoneware so it overlaps the rim.

3. Cover and cook on Low for 6 hours or on High for 3 hours, until fennel is tender. Lift out parchment and discard, being careful not to spill the accumulated liquid into the sauce. Garnish with fennel fronds, if using.

Variation

Fennel and Tomato Gratin: After the fennel has finished cooking, preheat broiler. Scoop out about ¼ cup (50 mL) of the cooking liquid and set aside. In a bowl, combine ½ cup (125 mL) each dry bread crumbs and finely grated Parmesan and ¼ tsp (1 mL) finely grated lemon zest. Sprinkle evenly over fennel and drizzle with reserved cooking liquid. Place under broiler until cheese melts and top is browned. Garnish with fennel fronds, if desired.

Parmesan-Spiked Wheat Berries

I like to serve this for a change when I'm tired of potatoes or rice but have a hankering for a comforting carb. It's a great accompaniment for a grilled veal chop, roast chicken or a platter of roasted vegetables. This makes a large quantity but you can easily cut the recipe in half.

Serves 8

- Lightly greased slow cooker stoneware
- Small to medium (2 to 3½ quart) slow cooker

1 tbsp	olive oil	15 mL
1	onion, finely chopped	1
2	cloves garlic, minced	2
½ tsp	salt	2 mL
½ tsp	cracked black peppercorns	2 mL
1 cup	wheat, spelt or Kamut berries	250 mL
½ cup	dry white wine (see Tips, right)	125 mL
2 cups	vegetable or chicken stock	500 mL
½ cup	freshly grated Parmesan or vegan alternative	125 mL
¼ cup	finely chopped parsley	50 mL
	Freshly ground black pepper	

1. In a skillet, heat oil over medium heat. Add onion and cook, stirring, until softened, about 3 minutes. Add garlic, salt and peppercorns and cook, stirring, for 1 minute. Add wheat berries and toss to coat. Add wine, bring to a boil and boil for 2 minutes. Add vegetable stock and bring to a boil.

2. Transfer to slow cooker stoneware and stir well. Cover and cook on Low for 6 to 8 hours or on High for 3 to 4 hours, until wheat berries are tender. Stir well. Stir in Parmesan and parsley and season to taste with pepper.

Vegan Friendly

Can Be Halved
see Tips, below

Tips

If you are halving this recipe, be sure to use a small (approx. 1½ to 2 quart) slow cooker.

If you prefer, substitute ½ cup (125 mL) vegetable or chicken stock plus 1 tsp (5 mL) lemon juice for the white wine.

Make Ahead

Complete Step 1. Cover and refrigerate for up to 2 days. When you're ready to cook, continue with the recipe.

Polenta with Mushrooms

This is a great dish to serve with robust meat dishes such as Pot Roast in Barolo (see recipe, page 166) or to round out the protein in a meatless meal. I recommend using the far more nutritious stone-ground cornmeal rather than the refined version, which has lost its bran and germ layers and in the process most of its B vitamins, fiber, iron and healthful phytochemicals.

Tips

If you are halving this recipe, I recommend cooking directly in a small (approx. 1½ quart) slow cooker, lightly greased.

You can cook the polenta directly in the slow cooker stoneware or in a 6-cup (1.5 L) baking dish, lightly greased. If you are cooking directly in the stoneware, I recommend using a small (maximum 3½ quart) slow cooker, lightly greased. If you are using a baking dish, you will need a large (minimum 5 quart) oval slow cooker.

Serves 6

• Small to large (2 to 8 quart) slow cooker (see Tips, left)

4 cups	vegetable or chicken stock or water	1 L
1 tsp	salt	5 mL
1¼ cups	cornmeal, preferably stone-ground	300 mL
1	package (½ oz/14 g) dried porcini mushrooms	1
1 cup	hot water	250 mL
2 tbsp	butter	25 mL
2	cloves garlic, minced	2
8 oz	mushrooms, trimmed and sliced	250 g
½ cup	whipping (35%) cream	125 mL
½ cup	grated Parmesan	125 mL
	Salt and freshly ground black pepper	

1. In a saucepan over medium heat, bring stock and salt to a boil. Add cornmeal in a thin stream, stirring constantly.

2. **Direct method:** Transfer mixture to prepared stoneware (see Tips, left). Cover and cook on Low for 1½ hours.

   Baking dish method: Transfer mixture to prepared baking dish (see Tips, left). Cover tightly with foil. Place dish in slow cooker stoneware and pour in enough boiling water to come 1 inch (2.5 cm) up the sides of the dish. Cover and cook on Low for 1½ hours.

3. Meanwhile, in a small bowl, combine dried mushrooms with hot water. Set aside until softened, about 25 minutes. Strain through a fine sieve, discarding liquid. Pat mushrooms dry and chop finely.

4. In a skillet over medium heat, melt butter. Add garlic, sliced mushrooms and reconstituted dried mushrooms and cook, stirring, until mushrooms release their liquid, about 7 minutes. Add cream and Parmesan. Bring to a boil and cook, stirring, until flavors meld, about 2 minutes. Remove from heat. Season to taste with salt and pepper. To serve, stir into cooked polenta.

Vegan Alternative

Substitute olive oil for the butter, soy creamer for the cream and vegan Parmesan for the regular version.

Cheesy Grits

I just love good grits — by good I mean those that are stone-ground, preferably from an heirloom variety of corn. Seasoned with cheese and chile (see Variation, below), they are so delicious I can make a meal out of grits alone.

Serves 4

- 4-cup (1 L) baking dish, lightly greased
- Large (approx. 5 quart) oval slow cooker

1 tbsp	olive oil	15 mL
1	onion, finely chopped	1
4	cloves garlic, minced	4
½ tsp	cracked black peppercorns	2 mL
2 cups	vegetable or chicken stock	500 mL
½ cup	stone-ground grits (see Tip, right)	125 mL
1½ cups	shredded old Cheddar cheese or vegan alternative, divided	375 mL

1. In a large skillet, heat oil over medium heat. Add onion and cook, stirring, until softened, about 3 minutes. Add garlic and peppercorns and cook, stirring, for 1 minute. Add vegetable stock and bring to a boil. Gradually add grits, stirring constantly, until smooth and blended. Continue cooking and stirring until grits are slightly thickened, about 4 minutes. Stir in 1 cup (250 mL) of the cheese. Transfer to prepared baking dish. Cover tightly with foil and secure with a string.

2. Place in slow cooker stoneware and pour in enough boiling water to come 1 inch (2.5 cm) up the sides of the dish. Cover and cook on Low for 8 hours or on High for 4 hours. Stir well and let stand uncovered for 2 to 3 minutes to absorb any liquid.

3. Meanwhile, preheat broiler. Sprinkle remaining cheese over top of grits and place under broiler until melted and lightly browned.

Variation

Chile-Spiked Cheesy Grits: If you like a little heat, finely mince 1 chipotle chile in adobo sauce. Stir in along with the peppercorns.

Tip

Stone-ground grits are dried corn that has been crushed between millstones and ground the old-fashioned way, with the power of water. They are one of the whole-grain forms of field corn and although they can be difficult to find, they are worth the extra effort, not only for their flavor but also for their nutritional profile. Stone-ground grits contain a good range of minerals such as magnesium, potassium and selenium and are particularly high in antioxidants. For best flavor and nutrition, look for coarse texture and dark flecks of germ and bran scattered throughout. Because the germ is loaded with healthful unsaturated oils, grits are very perishable, so buy from a source with high turnover. Store grits in an airtight container, in the refrigerator for up to 2 months or in the freezer for up to 6 months.

Tips

If you are halving this recipe, be sure to use a small (approx. 1½ to 2 quart) slow cooker.

Use the variety of barley you prefer — pearled, pot or whole. Whole (also known as hulled) barley is the most nutritious form of the grain.

If you prefer, substitute an extra cup (250 mL) vegetable stock plus 1 tbsp (15 mL) lemon juice for the white wine.

If you prefer a creamier risotto, stir in 2 tbsp (25 mL) cream along with the butter.

Make Ahead

Complete Step 1. Cover and refrigerate mixture for up to 2 days. When you're ready to cook, complete the recipe.

Three-Grain Risotto with Artichokes

This recipe was inspired by one that appears in American Brasserie, *by Chicago chefs Rick Tramonto and Gale Grand. It makes a robust and nutritious side dish. Loaded with whole-grain goodness, it is delicious with salmon, roast turkey and chicken, or a big plate of your favorite salad. I particularly like it with broccoli slaw. It also makes a great addition to a buffet.*

Serves 6

- Lightly greased stoneware
- Small (2 to 3½ quart) slow cooker

1 tbsp	olive oil	15 mL
1	onion, diced	1
2	stalks celery, diced	2
2	cloves garlic, minced	2
1 tsp	dried Italian seasoning	5 mL
½ tsp	salt	2 mL
½ tsp	cracked black peppercorns	2 mL
½ cup	barley (see Tips, left)	125 mL
½ cup	wild rice	125 mL
½ cup	short-grain brown rice	125 mL
1 cup	dry white wine (see Tips, left)	250 mL
2½ cups	vegetable or chicken stock	625 mL
1	can (14 oz/398 mL) artichoke hearts, drained and quartered	1
¼ cup	finely chopped parsley	50 mL
2 tbsp	butter	25 mL
2 tbsp	finely grated Parmesan	25 mL

1. In a skillet, heat oil over medium heat. Add onion and celery and cook, stirring, until softened, about 5 minutes. Add garlic, Italian seasoning, salt and peppercorns and cook, stirring, for 1 minute. Add barley, wild rice and brown rice and toss until well coated. Add wine, bring to a boil and boil for 2 minutes. Add stock and return to a boil.

2. Transfer to prepared stoneware. Stir in artichokes. Place a clean tea towel, folded in half (so you will have 2 layers), over top of slow cooker stoneware to absorb moisture. Cover and cook on Low for 7 to 8 hours or on High for $3\frac{1}{2}$ to 4 hours, until rice is tender and liquid has been absorbed. Sir in parsley, butter and Parmesan and serve. Pass additional Parmesan at the table.

Vegan Alternative
Substitute olive oil for the butter and vegan Parmesan for the regular version.

Barley Risotto with Tomatoes

This stick-to-your-ribs side makes a great accompaniment to grilled chicken or meat or a plate of roasted vegetables. With the addition of rice and salad, it can do double duty as a main course.

Serves 8

Tips

If you are halving this recipe, be sure to use a small (approx. 1½ to 2 quart) slow cooker.

If you prefer, substitute ½ cup (125 mL) chicken or vegetable stock plus 1 tsp (5 mL) lemon juice for the white wine.

Make Ahead

Complete Step 1. Cover and refrigerate mixture for up to 2 days. (If you are using pancetta, ensure it cools promptly; see Making Ahead, page 17.) When you're ready to cook, complete the recipe.

• Small (2 to 3½ quart) slow cooker

1 tbsp	olive oil	15 mL
4 oz	pancetta, diced, optional	125 g
1	onion, finely chopped	1
2	cloves garlic, minced	2
1 tsp	dried thyme leaves	5 mL
1 tsp	salt	5 mL
½ tsp	cracked black peppercorns	2 mL
1 cup	barley, rinsed	250 mL
½ cup	dry white wine (see Tips, left)	125 mL
2 cups	chicken or vegetable stock	500 mL
1	can (28 oz/796 mL) diced tomatoes with juice	1

1. In a skillet, heat oil over medium-high heat. Add pancetta, if using, and onion and cook, stirring, until onion begins to turn golden, about 5 minutes. Add garlic, thyme, salt and peppercorns and cook, stirring, for 1 minute. Add barley and toss until well coated with mixture. Add wine, bring to a boil and boil for 1 minute. Add stock and bring to a boil for 2 minutes.

2. Transfer to slow cooker stoneware. Stir in tomatoes with juice. Cover and cook on Low for 8 hours or on High for 4 hours, until barley is very tender.

Brown and Wild Rice with Bay Leaves

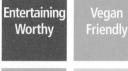

This recipe was inspired by one developed by the late film producer and cook Ismail Merchant, which used plain long-grain brown rice. I have found that a combination of wild and brown rice produces excellent results in the slow cooker and makes a great pairing with grilled salmon or braised vegetables.

Serves 4 to 6

- Small (2 to 3½ quart) slow cooker

2 tbsp	butter or olive oil	25 mL
4	bay leaves	4
½ tsp	cracked black peppercorns	2 mL
2½ cups	vegetable or chicken stock	625 mL
1 cup	long-grain brown and wild rice mixture (see Tip, right)	250 mL

1. In a saucepan over low heat, melt butter. Add bay leaves and peppercorns and cook, stirring, for 1 minute. Add stock and bring to a boil. Stir in rice. Return to a boil and boil for 1 minute. Transfer to slow cooker stoneware.

2. Place a clean tea towel, folded in half (so you will have 2 layers), over top of stoneware to absorb moisture. Cover and cook on Low for 8 hours or on High for 4 hours, until rice is tender and liquid is absorbed. Remove and discard bay leaves.

Tip

You can buy prepackaged combinations of brown and wild rice or make your own, using equal portions of each. I have also made this using ¼ cup (50 mL) each long-grain and wild rice and ½ cup (125 mL) French red rice from the Camargue, with excellent results.

Vegan Friendly

Plantain-Spiked Frijoles with Rice

I've adapted this recipe from Marian Maria Baez Kijac's excellent book The South American Table. *This is a Colombian approach to rice and beans and according to her, it is eaten as a main course with a green salad. If desired, you can add diced cooked bacon after the dish has finished cooking. I like to serve this as an accompaniment to a zesty stew.*

Tips

I've specified red kidney beans for convenience. If you prefer, use another type of red bean. Bala or frijol boludo are Colombian beans, available in Latin American markets.

For this quantity of beans use 2 cans (14 to 19 oz/ 398 to 540 mL), drained and rinsed, or soak and cook 1 cup (250 mL) dried beans yourself (see Basic Beans, page 341).

Serves 4 to 6

- Small to medium (2 to 3½ quart) slow cooker

2 cups	rinsed, drained cooked red kidney beans (see Tips, left)	500 mL
1	onion, chopped	1
1	carrot, peeled and chopped	1
1	potato, peeled and chopped	1
2	cloves garlic, minced	2
1½ cups	vegetable stock or water	375 mL
1	unripe plantain, peeled and cut into cubes	1
	Salt and freshly ground black pepper	
1 cup	cooked brown or white rice	250 mL

1. In a food processor, process onion, carrot, potato, garlic and vegetable stock until smooth.

2. In slow cooker stoneware, combine puréed vegetables, beans, plantain and salt and pepper to taste. Cover and cook on Low for 8 hours or on High for 4 hours, until hot and bubbly. Stir in rice.

Mexican-Style Beans and Grains

This recipe was inspired by a dish traditionally made in Oaxaca and documented by Diana Kennedy, the doyenne of Mexican cooking. It makes a great accompaniment to zesty stews such as Mexican Meatballs (see recipe, page 222) and is an excellent way to use up various bits of grains you may have in the pantry. Add the topping if you are serving it alongside a dish that doesn't have much sauce.

Entertaining Worthy

Vegetarian Friendly

Can Be Halved
see Tips, below

Serves 6

- Small (2 to 3½ quart) slow cooker

3 cups	vegetable stock	750 mL
1 cup	rinsed, drained cooked red or black beans	250 mL
1 tbsp	olive oil	15 mL
1	onion, finely chopped	1
4	cloves garlic, minced	4
1	bay leaf	1
½ tsp	cracked black peppercorns	2 mL
1 cup	long-cooking whole grains (see Tips, right)	250 mL

Topping, optional

½ cup	crème fraîche	125 mL
⅓ cup	crumbled soft goat cheese	75 mL

1. In a blender, combine vegetable stock and beans. Purée and set aside.

2. In a skillet, heat oil over medium heat. Add onion and cook, stirring, until softened, about 3 minutes. Add garlic, bay leaf and peppercorns and cook, stirring, for 1 minute. Add grains and cook, stirring, until coated. Add bean mixture and bring to a boil. Boil rapidly for 2 minutes.

3. Transfer to slow cooker stoneware. Place a clean tea towel, folded in half (so you will have 2 layers), over top of stoneware to absorb moisture. Cover and cook on Low for 8 hours or on High for 4 hours, until grains are tender. Stir well. Remove and discard bay leaf.

4. **Topping, optional:** Transfer mixture to a serving dish and drizzle with crème fraîche. Sprinkle cheese over top.

Tips

If you are halving this recipe, be sure to use a small (approx. 1½ to 2 quart) slow cooker.

This recipe works well with any long-cooking grain, such as wheat berries, barley, brown or wild rice, or any combination thereof.

Make Ahead

Complete Steps 1 and 2. Cover and refrigerate for up to 2 days. When you're ready to cook, complete the recipe.

Entertaining Worthy

Vegan Friendly

Can Be Halved
see Tip, below

Orange-Spiked Carrots Braised in Vermouth

I love the combination of flavors in this dish, which makes a great accompaniment to just about anything. Served glazed (see Variation, below), it is perfect for a special occasion meal.

Tip

If you are halving this recipe, be sure to use a small (approx. 1½ to 2 quart) slow cooker.

Serves 6 to 8

- Medium (approx. 4 quart) slow cooker

12	carrots, peeled and sliced	12
2 tbsp	melted butter or olive oil	25 mL
2 tsp	finely grated orange zest	10 mL
½ tsp	salt	2 mL
½ tsp	cracked black peppercorns	2 mL
½ tsp	granulated sugar	2 mL
½ cup	dry vermouth	125 mL
2 tbsp	freshly squeezed orange juice	25 mL

1. In slow cooker stoneware, combine carrots, butter and orange zest. Stir well. Place a clean tea towel, folded in half (so you have 2 layers), over top of stoneware to absorb moisture. Cover and cook on High for 1 hour. Add salt, peppercorns, sugar, vermouth and orange juice. Cover and cook on Low for 4 hours or on High for 2 hours, until carrots are tender.

Variation

I particularly enjoy these carrots in a slightly bumped-up version. After they are cooked, transfer the contents of the slow cooker, including liquid, to a gratin dish. Sprinkle with granulated sugar and, if desired, a bit a cinnamon, to taste. (I've also used vanilla sugar, which produced excellent results.) Place under a preheated broiler until the sugar glazes. One advantage to this is convenience — you can keep the carrots on Warm in the slow cooker and finish them off (adding the sugar and placing them under the broiler) when the timing suits you.

Simple Braised Leeks

Leeks have a mild onion flavor that is both delicate and rich. They are a wonderful accompaniment to grilled fish and meats or roast chicken. If you're a vegetarian, with a topping of bread crumbs and cheese (see Variation, below) they can be a main course all on their own.

Serves 4 to 6

- Small to medium (2 to 4 quart) slow cooker

6 to 8	leeks, white part only with just a hint of green, cleaned and sliced into quarters on the vertical (see Tips, left)	6 to 8
3 tbsp	melted butter or olive oil	45 mL
1 cup	vegetable or chicken stock	250 mL
	Salt and freshly ground black pepper	
1/4 cup	finely chopped parsley	50 mL

Tips

If you are halving this recipe, be sure to use a small (approx. 1$\frac{1}{2}$ to 2 quart) slow cooker.

Leeks can be gritty and need to be thoroughly cleaned before cooking. Peel off the tough outer layer(s) and cut off the root. Slice leeks according to recipe instructions and submerge in a basin of lukewarm water, swishing them around to remove all traces of dirt. Transfer to a colander and rinse under cold water.

1. Pat leeks dry and place in slow cooker stoneware. Add butter and toss until well coated. Place a clean tea towel, folded in half (so you will have 2 layers), over top of stoneware to absorb moisture. Cover and cook on High for 1 hour. Stir well. Remove tea towel and add stock.

2. Cover and cook on Low for 5 to 6 hours or on High for 2$\frac{1}{2}$ to 3 hours, until leeks are very tender. Season to taste with salt and pepper. Garnish with parsley and serve.

Variation

Leeks Gratin: After the leeks have finished cooking, drain off the liquid and set aside. Do not garnish with parsley. Transfer leeks to an ovenproof serving dish and keep warm. Place the liquid in a saucepan, bring to a boil, and cook until reduced by at least half. (You'll want about $\frac{1}{2}$ cup/125 mL of liquid.)

Meanwhile, preheat broiler. In a bowl, combine $\frac{1}{2}$ cup (125 mL) dry bread crumbs, $\frac{1}{4}$ cup (50 mL) finely grated Parmesan and 2 tbsp (25 mL) finely chopped parsley. Pour reduced cooking liquid over leeks and sprinkle bread crumb mixture evenly over top. Place under broiler until cheese is melted and top is browned.

Bourbon-Braised Onions

This is a Southern treatment for onions that I adapted from a recipe in James Beard's classic American Cookery. *It is quite wonderful. The onions are sweet, soft and sauce-like — a perfect accompaniment for roast meats or vegetables.*

Entertaining Worthy

Vegetarian Friendly

Can Be Halved
see Tip, below

Serves 6

- Small to medium (2 to 3½ quart) slow cooker

2 tbsp	butter	25 mL
2 tbsp	olive oil	25 mL
6	onions, thinly sliced on the vertical	6
1 tsp	salt	5 mL
½ tsp	cracked black peppercorns	2 mL
¼ cup	bourbon	50 mL
¼ cup	vegetable or chicken stock or water	50 mL

1. In a large skillet over medium-high heat, melt butter with oil. Add onions and cook, stirring, until onions begin to turn golden, about 5 minutes. Add salt, peppercorns and bourbon and cook, stirring, until bourbon almost evaporates, about 3 minutes. Add stock and stir well.

2. Transfer to slow cooker stoneware. Cover and cook on Low for 6 hours or on High for 3 hours.

Vegan Alternative

Substitute an equal quantity of olive oil for the butter.

Tip

If you are halving this recipe, be sure to use a small (approx. 1½ to 2 quart) slow cooker.

Make Ahead

Complete Step 1. Cover and refrigerate for up to 2 days. When you're ready to cook, complete the recipe.

Tip

If you are halving this recipe, be sure to use a small (approx. 1½ to 2 quart) slow cooker.

Braised Belgian Endive

Endive's bitter flavor can be an acquired taste, but once you "get it," this intriguing vegetable can be mildly addictive. Usually eaten raw, often in salads like its relative radicchio, endive also sparkles when cooked. It lends itself to long, slow braising and is particularly delectable served as a gratin. This dish makes a great accompaniment to grilled meat, roast chicken or whole grains.

Serves 6

- Small to medium (2 to 3½ quart) slow cooker
- Parchment paper

6	medium Belgian endives	6
3 tbsp	butter or olive oil (approx.)	45 mL
½ cup	vegetable or chicken stock	125 mL
1 tbsp	freshly squeezed lemon juice	15 mL
½ tsp	salt	2 mL
½ tsp	cracked black peppercorns	2 mL

1. Trim off the stem ends of endives and, using a sharp paring knife, dig out the hard cores and discard. Then halve lengthwise.

2. In a large skillet over medium heat, melt butter. Add endive, cut side down, in batches if necessary, and cook, stirring, until nicely browned, about 4 minutes per batch, adding more butter if necessary. Transfer to slow cooker stoneware as completed. Add stock, lemon juice, salt and peppercorns to pan and bring to a boil, scraping up brown bits from bottom of pan. Pour over endive. Place a large piece of parchment over the mixture, pressing it down to brush the food and extending up the sides of the stoneware so it overlaps the rim.

3. Cover and cook on Low for 6 hours or on High for 3 hours, until endive is tender. Lift out parchment and discard, being careful not to spill the accumulated liquid into the sauce.

Variation

Belgian Endive Gratin: After the endive has finished cooking, transfer to a lightly greased gratin dish. In a small bowl, combine 1 cup (250 mL) each shredded Gruyère cheese and dry bread crumbs and ½ tsp (2 mL) finely grated lemon zest. Sprinkle evenly over endive. Place under broiler until cheese has melted and mixture is browned.

Cumin-Spiced Potatoes

This classic Indian way of preparing potatoes makes a perfect accompaniment for grilled or roasted meat or a platter of roasted vegetables. If you have access to new potatoes, they work very well, too (see Tips, right).

Serves 4 to 6

- Small (2 to 3½ quart) slow cooker
- Parchment paper

3	large potatoes (each about 8 oz/250 g)	3
3 tbsp	olive oil	45 mL
2 tsp	cumin seeds, toasted and ground	10 mL
½ tsp	ground turmeric	2 mL
1 tsp	salt	5 mL
½ tsp	cracked black peppercorns	2 mL
1 cup	vegetable stock or water	250 mL
¼ cup	plain full-fat yogurt or vegan sour cream	50 mL
¼ tsp	cayenne pepper	1 mL
	Finely chopped cilantro, optional	

1. Peel potatoes and cut in half lengthwise, then cut each half into 4 wedges. Pat dry.

2. In a skillet, heat oil over medium-high heat. Add cumin seeds and cook, stirring, until they sizzle, about 10 seconds. Stir in turmeric. Add potatoes, in batches, and cook until they are lightly browned on all sides, about 7 minutes per batch. Using a slotted spoon, transfer to slow cooker stoneware. Drain all but 1 tbsp (15 mL) oil from pan.

3. Add salt and peppercorns to pan and cook, stirring, for 1 minute. Add vegetable stock and bring to a boil, scraping up brown bits from the bottom of the pan. Transfer to slow cooker stoneware. Place a large piece of parchment paper over the potatoes, pressing it down to brush the food and extending up the sides of the stoneware so it overlaps the rim.

4. Cover and cook on Low for 6 hours or on High for 3 hours, until potatoes are tender. Lift out the parchment and discard, being careful not to spill the accumulated liquid into the stoneware. Stir in yogurt and cayenne. Garnish with cilantro, if using.

Tips

If you are halving this recipe, be sure to use a small (approx. 1½ to 2 quart) slow cooker.

If using new potatoes, scrub well and cut into halves but do not peel. Brown on the cut side only.

Entertaining
Worthy

Vegetarian
Friendly

Braised Potatoes with Mushrooms and Leeks

This is a rich and delicious side meant for a special occasion dinner or perhaps even a buffet. A small serving makes a wonderful accompaniment to traditional roast beef or leg of lamb and would also add sparkle to a luscious platter of roasted vegetables. It's a great dish for entertaining because you can make it in the slow cooker, keep it warm, and finish it off in the oven when you're ready to serve.

Tips

Crumbling dried mushrooms saves you the trouble of chopping them. Just remove them from the package and break them up, using your fingers.

This is also delicious made with new potatoes. Depending upon their size, you'll need about 30. Simply scrub and quarter them and follow the recipe.

Serves 8

- Small to medium (2 to 4 quart) slow cooker
- Ovenproof serving dish

2 tbsp	melted butter	25 mL
2	leeks, white part with just a hint of green, cleaned and sliced (see Tips, page 326)	2
2	cloves garlic, minced	2
½ tsp	cracked black peppercorns	2 mL
1	package (½ oz/14 g) dried wild mushrooms, crumbled (see Tips, left)	1
2 cups	hot vegetable or chicken stock	500 mL
4	large potatoes, scrubbed and thinly sliced (see Tips, left)	4
1 tsp	salt	5 mL
2 tsp	fresh thyme leaves	10 mL
	Freshly grated nutmeg	
⅓ cup	whipping (35%) cream	75 mL

1. In slow cooker stoneware, combine butter, leeks, garlic and peppercorns. Stir well. Place a clean tea towel, folded in half (so you have 2 layers), over top of stoneware to absorb moisture. Cover and cook on High, stirring occasionally, for 1 hour.

2. Meanwhile, in a bowl, combine mushrooms and hot stock. Set aside until mushrooms have softened and rehydrated. Strain through a fine sieve or paper coffee filter, setting mushrooms and liquid aside.

3. When leeks have softened, add potatoes, rehydrated mushrooms and soaking liquid and salt to stoneware. Stir well. Add water barely to cover. Cover and cook on Low for 6 hours or on High or 3 hours, until potatoes are tender.

4. When you're almost ready to serve, preheat oven to 400°F (200°C). Transfer mixture to an ovenproof serving dish. Sprinkle with thyme and nutmeg to taste. Pour cream over top and bake until mixture is bubbly and top is lightly browned, about 15 minutes.

Vegan Alternative

Substitute olive oil for the butter and soy creamer for the whipping cream.

Sweet Potato Pudding

This dish makes a wonderful accompaniment to poultry, which is why it is traditionally served with roast turkey. It's slightly sweet, so if you're feeling the urge, enjoy leftovers with a little cream for dessert or an afternoon snack.

Make Ahead

Complete Step 1. Cover and refrigerate for up to 2 days. When you're ready to cook, continue with the recipe.

Serves 6

- Greased baking dish
- Large (approx. 5 quart) slow cooker

4	medium sweet potatoes, cooked and peeled (2 lbs/1 kg)	4
2 tbsp	butter	25 mL
2 tbsp	Demerara or other raw cane sugar	25 mL
½ tsp	salt	2 mL
½ tsp	freshly ground black pepper	2 mL
½ tsp	freshly grated nutmeg	2 mL
2	eggs	2

Topping

½ cup	chopped pecans	125 mL
½ cup	dry bread crumbs	125 mL
2 tbsp	Demerara or other raw cane sugar	25 mL
1 tsp	ground cinnamon	5 mL
2 tbsp	melted butter	25 mL

1. In a food processor, combine sweet potatoes, butter, sugar, salt, pepper and nutmeg. Pulse until blended. Add eggs and process until smooth. Transfer to prepared dish. Cover with foil and secure with a string.

2. Place in slow cooker stoneware and pour in enough hot water to come 1 inch (2.5 cm) up the sides of the bowl. Cover and cook on High for 3 to 3½ hours, until pudding is set.

3. **Topping:** In a bowl, combine pecans, bread crumbs, brown sugar and cinnamon. Mix well. Add butter and mix to blend. When pudding has finished cooking, preheat broiler. Remove foil and sprinkle topping evenly over pudding. Place under broiler until browned.

Creamy Celery

This is a great way to use up the tougher outer stalks of celery. It is beautifully creamy and makes a splendid complement to roast meat or grilled fish.

Serves 4

- Small to medium (2 to 3½ quart) slow cooker

1 tbsp	butter	15 mL
2	shallots, finely chopped	2
12	stalks celery, peeled and cut into 2-inch (5 cm) lengths	12
½ cup	vegetable or chicken stock or water	125 mL
2	egg yolks	2
¼ cup	whipping (35%) cream	50 mL
	Salt and freshly ground black pepper	
	Finely chopped parsley	

1. In a skillet over medium heat, melt butter. Add shallots and cook, stirring, until softened, about 3 minutes. Add celery and toss until coated. Add stock and bring to a boil.

2. Transfer to slow cooker stoneware. Cover and cook on Low for 6 to 7 hours or on High for 3 to 4 hours, until celery is tender.

3. In a bowl, beat egg yolks and cream with salt and pepper to taste. Add to celery in stoneware and cook on High, stirring, about 3 minutes, until thickened. Garnish liberally with parsley.

Tip

If you are halving this recipe, be sure to use a small (approx. 1½ to 2 quart) slow cooker.

Braised Butternut Squash

One advantage to making squash in the slow cooker is that you can get it ready and forget about it until it's cooked, which is a big help if you're preparing a multi-course meal. Another is that you can cook in a minimum amount of liquid, conserving precious nutrients and flavor.

Tips

If you are halving this recipe, be sure to use a small (approx. 1½ to 2 quart) slow cooker.

I like to use parchment when cooking this dish because the recipe doesn't contain much liquid. Creating a tight seal ensures that the ingredients baste in their own juices, intensifying the flavors.

If you prefer, substitute another winter squash, such as acorn, calabaza or pumpkin.

Serves 6

- Medium (3½ quart) slow cooker
- Parchment paper (see Tips, left)

8 cups	cubed (1 inch/2.5 cm) butternut squash (about 1 large) (see Tips, left)	2 L
1 tbsp	butter	15 mL
1	onion, finely chopped	1
2	cloves garlic, minced	2
½ tsp	salt	2 mL
½ tsp	cracked black peppercorns	2 mL
½ cup	water or vegetable stock	125 mL
2 tbsp	whipping (35%) cream	25 mL
1 tbsp	fresh thyme leaves or finely snipped chives	15 mL

1. Place squash in slow cooker stoneware.

2. In a skillet over medium heat, melt butter. Add onion and cook, stirring, until it begins to turn golden, about 5 minutes. Add garlic, salt and peppercorns and cook, stirring, for 1 minute. Add water and bring to a boil, scraping up brown bits from the bottom of the pan.

3. Transfer to slow cooker stoneware. Stir well. Place a large piece of parchment paper over the squash, pressing it down to brush the food and extending up the sides of the stoneware so it overlaps the rim. Cover and cook on Low for 6 hours or on High for 3 hours, until squash is very tender. Remove and discard parchment, being careful not to spill accumulated liquid onto squash. Using a wooden spoon, mash squash until desired consistency is achieved. Stir in cream and thyme. Serve hot.

Vegan Alternative

Substitute olive oil for the butter and soy creamer for the whipping cream.

Braised Red Cabbage

This is one of my favorite winter vegetables — in my opinion, the best possible accompaniment to a pork roast. It is also delicious on its own with buttered rye bread or a serving of whole grains such as barley, wheat berries or a combination of brown and wild rice.

Entertaining Worthy

Vegan Friendly

Can Be Halved
see Tip, below

Serves 6 to 8

- Medium to large (3½ to 5 quart) slow cooker

2 tbsp	butter or olive oil	25 mL
2	onions, thinly sliced	2
2	apples, peeled, cored and chopped	2
1 tsp	salt	5 mL
½ tsp	cracked black peppercorns	2 mL
4	whole cloves	4
1	piece (2 inches/5 cm) cinnamon stick	1
1	small red cabbage, shredded	1
3 tbsp	balsamic vinegar	45 mL
2 tbsp	packed brown sugar	25 mL
2 tbsp	water	25 mL

1. In a large skillet over medium heat, melt butter. Add onions and cook, stirring, until softened, about 3 minutes. Add apples, salt, peppercorns, cloves and cinnamon stick and cook, stirring, for 1 minute. Add cabbage, in batches, stirring until it begins to wilt before adding more. Stir in vinegar, brown sugar and water.

2. Transfer to slow cooker stoneware. Cover and cook on High, stirring once or twice, for 3 hours, until cabbage is tender.

Tip

If you are halving this recipe, be sure to use a small (approx. 1½ to 3½ quart) slow cooker.

Down-Home Tomatoes with Okra

This is a great side dish. A particularly mouthwatering combination of flavors, it makes a perfect accompaniment to grilled meat, fish or seafood. Leftovers make a delicious filling for an omelet.

Tips

If you are halving this recipe, be sure to use a small (approx. 1½ to 2 quart) slow cooker.

Okra, a tropical vegetable, has a great flavor but becomes unpleasantly sticky when overcooked. Choose young okra pods 2 to 4 inches (5 to 10 cm) long that don't feel sticky to the touch (if sticky, they are too ripe). Gently scrub the pods and cut off the top and tail. Okra can also be found in the freezer section of the grocery store. Thaw before adding to the slow cooker.

Serves 6

- Medium (approx. 3½ quart) slow cooker

1 tbsp	olive oil	15 mL
4 oz	chunk bacon, diced, optional	125 g
1	onion, finely chopped	1
2	cloves garlic, minced	2
1 tsp	salt	5 mL
1 tsp	cracked black peppercorns	5 mL
1	can (28 oz/796 mL) tomatoes with juice	1
1	green bell pepper, seeded and diced	1
2 cups	sliced (½ inch/1 cm) okra, about 12 oz (375 g) (see Tips, left)	500 mL

1. In a skillet, heat oil over medium-high heat. Add bacon, if using, and cook, stirring, until nicely browned, about 4 minutes. Using a slotted spoon, transfer to slow cooker stoneware. Add onion and cook, stirring, until softened, about 3 minutes. Add garlic, salt and peppercorns and cook, stirring, for 1 minute. Add tomatoes with juice and bring to a boil. Transfer to slow cooker stoneware.

2. Cover and cook on Low for 6 hours or on High for 3 hours, until hot and bubbly. Add bell pepper and okra. Cover and cook on High for about 30 minutes, until okra is tender.

Hoppin' John with Collard Greens

Can Be Halved
see Tips, below

In the American South, where it is served over rice with a liberal dash of local hot sauce, this is a traditional New Year's dish. At my house it often appears as a side to roast pork, but it also makes a main course on its own, accompanied by a bowl of mixed whole-grain rice.

Tips

If you are halving this recipe, be sure to use a small (approx. 1½ to 2 quart) slow cooker.

I've served this over a combination of brown, black and red varieties of rice, and it's particularly delicious.

Serves 8

• Medium (approx. 4 quart) slow cooker

2 cups	soaked black-eyed peas, drained and rinsed	500 mL
2 oz	chunk bacon, diced	60 g
2	large onions, finely chopped	2
4	stalks celery, finely chopped	4
4	cloves garlic, minced	4
1 tsp	dried thyme leaves	5 mL
1 tsp	salt	5 mL
½ tsp	cracked black peppercorns	2 mL
2	bay leaves	2
4 cups	vegetable or chicken stock	1 L
½ tsp	cayenne pepper, optional	2 mL
8 cups	collard greens, stems removed, chopped	2 L
1 tbsp	apple cider vinegar	15 mL
	Butter or butter substitute	
	Salt and freshly ground black pepper	

1. In a skillet over medium-high heat, cook bacon until browned and crisp, about 3 minutes. Drain on paper towel and set aside. Drain all but 2 tbsp (25 mL) of fat from the pan. (If you don't have enough fat, add olive oil to make up the difference.) Reduce heat to medium.

2. Add onions and celery to pan and cook, stirring, until celery is softened, about 5 minutes. Add garlic, thyme, salt, peppercorns and bay leaves and cook, stirring, for 1 minute. Transfer to slow cooker stoneware. Add peas, vegetable stock and reserved bacon.

3. Cover and cook on Low for 8 hours or on High for 4 hours, until peas are tender. Stir in cayenne, if using. Remove and discard bay leaves.

4. In a vegetable steamer, steam greens until tender, about 10 minutes. Toss with cider vinegar and butter or butter substitute. Season with salt and pepper to taste. Add to pea mixture and stir to combine. Serve immediately.

Vegan and Vegetarian Alternatives

For vegans, omit bacon and use 2 tbsp (25 mL) olive oil to soften the vegetables. For vegetarians, you may use 4 slices of meatless bacon strips, chopped.

Butterbeans Braised with Celery

This is an adaptation of a recipe developed by Greek cooking expert Diane Kochilas. It's a traditional way of cooking gigantes, the large dried lima beans that feature in a variety of Greek dishes. You can buy them at stores specializing in Greek provisions or substitute slightly smaller lima beans instead. This makes a wonderful side for grilled or roasted fish, meat or vegetables and is a great dish for a buffet. Stirring the beans a few times before serving encourages a lusciously creamy texture.

Vegan Friendly

Can Be Halved
see Tips, below

Serves 6

- Medium (approx. 3½ quart) slow cooker

1 cup	dried butterbeans, lima beans or gigantes, soaked, drained and popped out of their skins (see Tips, right)	250 mL
2 tbsp	olive oil	25 mL
1	whole bunch celery, with leaves, diced	1
4	cloves garlic, minced	4
1 tsp	salt	5 mL
½ tsp	cracked black peppercorns	2 mL
1	bay leaf	1
¼ cup	tomato paste	50 mL
1½ cups	water	375 mL
1 cup	finely chopped parsley leaves	250 mL
¼ cup	freshly squeezed lemon juice	50 mL
	Extra virgin olive oil	

1. In a large pot of water, cook soaked beans until tender to the bite (you do not want them to be fully cooked), about 20 minutes. Drain and transfer to slow cooker stoneware.

2. In a skillet, heat oil over medium heat. Add celery and garlic and cook, stirring, until celery is softened, about 5 minutes. Add salt, peppercorns and bay leaf and cook, stirring, for 1 minute. Stir in tomato paste. Add water and bring to a boil.

3. Transfer to slow cooker stoneware. Stir well. Cover and cook on Low for 6 hours or on High for 3 hours, until beans are meltingly tender. Stir in parsley. Cover and cook on High for 15 minutes. Stir in lemon juice and adjust seasoning, adding more lemon juice if desired. Stir well. Remove and discard bay leaf. Drizzle with olive oil and serve warm.

Tips

If you are halving this recipe, be sure to use a small (approx. 1½ to 2 quart) slow cooker.

To soak the beans for this recipe, bring them to a boil in 4 cups (1 L) water over medium heat. Boil rapidly for 3 minutes. Cover, turn off element and let stand for 1 hour. Drain in a colander placed over a sink and rinse thoroughly under cold running water. Using your hands, pop the beans out of their skins. Discard skins and cook beans as per Step 1.

Make Ahead

Complete Steps 1 and 2. Cover and refrigerate for up to 2 days. When you're ready to cook, complete the recipe.

Can Be Halved
see Tips, below

Butterbeans with Bacon

A slightly different twist on Boston baked beans, this makes a great accompaniment to hearty meat dishes such as ribs or a smoked brisket. Removed from their skins, the lima beans become quite soft, dissolving in the sauce to produce a deliciously creamy result.

Serves 8

Tips

If you are halving this recipe, be sure to use a small (approx. 1½ to 3½ quart) slow cooker.

To soak the beans for this recipe, bring them to a boil in 6 cups (1.5 L) water over medium heat. Boil rapidly for 3 minutes. Cover, turn off element and let stand for 1 hour. Drain in a colander placed over a sink and rinse thoroughly under cold running water. Using your hands, pop the beans out of their skins. Discard skins and cook beans as per Step 1.

• Medium to large (3½ to 5 quart) slow cooker

2 cups	large lima beans, soaked, cooked and drained (see Tips, left)	500 mL
8 oz	bacon, preferably smoked, diced	500 g
1	onion, minced	1
2	cloves garlic, minced	2
¾ cup	ketchup	175 mL
¼ cup	maple syrup	50 mL
1 tbsp	cider vinegar	15 mL
1 tsp	salt	5 mL
1 tsp	cracked black peppercorns	5 mL
½ tsp	dry mustard	2 mL

1. In a large pot of water, cook soaked beans until tender to the bite (you do not want them to be fully cooked), about 20 minutes. Drain and transfer to slow cooker stoneware. Add bacon, onion, garlic, ketchup, maple syrup, vinegar, salt, peppercorns and mustard. Stir well.

2. Cover and cook on Low for 6 hours or on High for 3 hours, until beans are meltingly tender. Stir well before serving.

Basic Beans

Loaded with nutrition and high in fiber, dried beans are one of our most healthful edibles, and the slow cooker excels at transforming them into potentially sublime fare. This recipe is also extraordinarily convenient. Put presoaked beans into the slow cooker before you go to bed, and in the morning they are ready for whatever recipe you intend to make.

Vegan Friendly

Makes approximately 2 cups (500 mL)

- Small to medium (2 to 3½ quart) slow cooker

1 cup	dried beans (see Tips, right)	250 mL
3 cups	water	750 mL
	Garlic, optional	
	Bay leaves, optional	
	Bouquet garni, optional	

1. **Long soak:** In a bowl, combine beans and water. Soak for at least 6 hours or overnight. Drain and rinse thoroughly with cold water. Beans are now ready for cooking.

   Quick soak: In a pot, combine beans and water. Cover and bring to a boil. Boil for 3 minutes. Turn off heat and soak for 1 hour. Drain and rinse thoroughly under cold water. Beans are now ready to cook.

2. **Cooking:** In slow cooker stoneware, combine 1 cup (250 mL) presoaked beans and 3 cups (750 mL) fresh cold water. If desired, season with garlic, bay leaves or a bouquet garni made from your favorite herbs tied together in cheesecloth. Cover and cook on Low for 10 to 12 hours or overnight, or on High for 5 to 6 hours, until beans are tender. If not using immediately, cover and refrigerate. In either case, drain and rinse before using.

Variation

Dried Lentils: These instructions also work for lentils, with the following changes: Do not presoak them, and reduce the cooking time to about 6 hours on Low.

Tips

This recipe may be doubled or tripled to suit the quantity of beans required for a recipe.

Soybeans and chickpeas take longer than other legumes to cook. They will likely take the full 12 hours on Low (about 6 hours on High).

Once cooked, legumes should be covered and stored in the refrigerator, where they will keep for 4 to 5 days. Cooked legumes can also be frozen, with liquid to cover, in an airtight container. They will keep frozen for up to 6 months.

Cranberry Pecan Pear Crumble

Desserts

Cranberry Pecan Pear Crumble

The combination of pears and cranberries adds a pleasant twist to this old favorite. Make it during those first chilly autumn days, when both fruits are plentiful and at their peak.

Tip

If you are halving this recipe, be sure to use a small (approx. 1½ to 2 quart) slow cooker.

Serves 8

- Lightly greased slow cooker stoneware
- Medium (approx. 4 quart) slow cooker

6	pears, peeled, cored and sliced	6
2 cups	cranberries	500 mL
¾ cup	granulated sugar	175 mL
	Grated zest of 1 orange	
2 tbsp	freshly squeezed orange juice	25 mL

Topping

1 cup	chopped pecans	250 mL
½ cup	whole wheat flour	125 mL
¼ cup	all-purpose flour	50 mL
½ cup	old-fashioned rolled oats	125 mL
½ cup	Demerara or other raw cane sugar	125 mL
½ tsp	ground cinnamon	2 mL
¼ cup	butter	50 mL
	Sweetened whipped cream or vanilla ice cream	

1. In prepared stoneware, combine pears, cranberries, sugar and orange zest and juice. Stir to combine.

2. **Topping:** In a bowl, combine pecans, whole wheat and all-purpose flours, rolled oats, sugar and cinnamon. Using a pastry blender, 2 knives or your fingers, cut in butter until mixture resembles coarse crumbs. Sprinkle evenly over fruit.

3. Place a clean tea towel, folded in half (so you will have 2 layers), over top of the stoneware to absorb moisture. Cover and cook on High for 3 to 4 hours, until fruit is hot, tender and juicy. Serve with whipped cream or vanilla ice cream.

Vegan Alternative

Substitute an equal quantity of non-hydrogenated margarine for the butter and drizzle with soy creamer instead of finishing with a dairy product.

Cider Baked Apples with Cranberry Apricot Filling

In the fall, when apples are in season, there is nothing quite like a warm baked apple to offset the first gusts of cold air. The combination of cranberries and apricots in the filling provides a fresh spin on this old favorite.

Serves 6

- Large (approx. 5 quart) oval slow cooker

½ cup	dried cranberries	125 mL
½ cup	chopped dried apricots	125 mL
½ cup	Demerara or other raw cane sugar	125 mL
¼ cup	toasted chopped almonds	50 mL
¼ cup	melted butter or non-hydrogenated margarine	50 mL
½ tsp	ground cinnamon	2 mL
½ tsp	ground ginger	2 mL
6	apples, cored	6
1 cup	apple cider	250 mL
	Table or whipped cream or soy creamer	

1. In a bowl, combine cranberries, apricots, sugar, almonds, butter, cinnamon and ginger. Using your fingers, pack filling into apples. Place in slow cooker stoneware, sprinkling excess filling over apples. Pour cider over top.

2. Cover and cook on Low for 6 hours or on High for 3 hours, until apples are tender. Transfer apples to individual serving dishes with a slotted spoon and spoon cooking juices over them. Pass table cream or soy creamer or top each apple with a dollop of whipped cream.

Tip

If you are halving this recipe, be sure to use a small (approx. 1½ to 3½ quart) slow cooker.

Entertaining Worthy

Vegetarian Friendly

Can Be Halved
see Tips, below

Tips

If you are halving this recipe, be sure to use a small (approx. 1½ to 3½ quart) slow cooker.

Not only does seedless raspberry jam obviously omit the pesky seeds, it also has a more intense flavor than its conventional cousin. If you don't have it, by all means substitute regular raspberry jam. The results will still be delicious.

Italian-Style Baked Apples

These boozy baked apples are nothing like what grandma used to make, but they certainly are tasty.

Serves 6

• Large (approx. 5 quart) oval slow cooker

⅔ cup	granulated sugar	150 mL
½ cup	butter, softened	125 mL
½ cup	seedless raspberry jam, divided (see Tips, left)	125 mL
6	firm apples, such as Granny Smith, cored	6
¼ cup	Marsala wine (sweet or dry)	50 mL
¼ cup	brandy or grappa	50 mL
	Vanilla ice cream or whipped cream	

1. Place sugar in a food processor. Process until very finely ground. Add butter and process until blended. Place about 1 tbsp (15 mL) of the jam in the bottom of the cavity in each apple. Set remainder of jam aside. Add butter mixture to cavity and spread any excess over top of the apples. Sprinkle Marsala over all. Place in slow cooker stoneware.

2. Cover and cook on Low for 5 hours or on High for 2½ hours, until apples are tender.

3. Transfer apples to individual serving dishes with a slotted spoon and keep warm. Transfer pan juices to a saucepan and bring to a boil. Add brandy and, standing well back, ignite, letting the flames burn off. Stir in remaining raspberry jam and return to a boil. Pour evenly over apples. Serve warm with a dollop of ice cream or whipped cream.

Vegan Alternative

Substitute non-hydrogenated margarine for the butter and drizzle the apples with soy creamer rather than topping with whipped cream or ice cream.

Granny's Apple Brown Betty

This is a great autumn dessert, especially if you've gone apple picking and are looking for ways to use up that big basket you harvested. I like to make this using slightly tart Granny Smith apples, but most other varieties work well, too. Make your own crumbs — Betties are another of those old-fashioned desserts that offer thrifty homemakers a vehicle for using up day-old bread.

Vegetarian Friendly

Can Be Halved
see Tips, below

Serves 8

- Lightly greased slow cooker stoneware.
- Small (approx. 3 quart) slow cooker (see Tips, right)

2 tsp	freshly grated lemon zest	10 mL
2 tbsp	freshly squeezed lemon juice	25 mL
1/4 cup	melted butter	50 mL
1 tsp	ground cinnamon	5 mL
Pinch	salt	Pinch
3 cups	fresh coarse bread crumbs (about half a large loaf) (see Tips, right)	750 mL
3/4 cup	packed brown sugar, preferably Demerara or other raw cane sugar	175 mL
8	apples, peeled and cut into 1/4-inch (1 cm) wedges	8
	Sweetened whipped cream or vanilla ice cream	

1. In a small bowl, combine lemon zest and juice. Set aside.

2. In a large bowl, combine melted butter, cinnamon and salt. Stir to combine. Add bread crumbs and brown sugar and stir well. Sprinkle one-third of mixture over bottom of prepared stoneware. Add half of the apples and sprinkle with half of the lemon mixture. Repeat, then finish with a layer of bread crumb mixture on top.

3. Place a clean tea towel, folded in half (so you have 2 layers), over top of stoneware to absorb moisture. Cover and cook on High for 3 hours, until bubbly and brown. Top with a dollop of sweetened whipped cream or ice cream.

Vegan Alternative

Substitute an equal quantity of non-hydrogenated margarine for the butter and drizzle with soy creamer instead of finishing with a dairy product.

Tips

If you are halving this recipe, be sure to use a small (approx. 1 1/2 to 2 quart) slow cooker.

If you are using a large oval cooker, double the quantity. Refrigerate leftovers and reheat.

Fresh bread crumbs are far superior to the ready-made kind, which can be very dry. They are easily made in a food processor by removing the crust, if desired, cutting the bread into manageable chunks, and then processing until the appropriate degree of fineness is achieved. Bread crumbs will keep, tightly covered, for 2 or 3 days in the refrigerator.

Tip

The cooking time will depend upon the number of ramekins you use. If you can squeeze 6 into your slow cooker, they will cook in about an hour. If you are only using 4, which will be fuller, expect the cooking time to be closer to 2 hours.

Madame Saint-Ange's Peruvian Cream

Published in 1927, La bonne cuisine de Madame E. Saint-Ange, *which contains over 1,000 recipes, became a bible of cooking for French housewives and inspired culinary superstars such as Julia Child. Here I have adapted her variation of* pots de crème, *which contains the delectable combination of chocolate, coffee, caramel and vanilla. Serve this with a dollop of sweetened whipped cream.*

Serves 4 to 6

- 4 to 6 tall ramekins or demitasse cups (see Tip, page 350)
- Large (minimum 5 quart) oval slow cooker

2 oz	bittersweet chocolate, coarsely chopped	60 g
¾ cup	whipping (35 %) cream	175 mL
¾ cup	whole milk	175 mL
1 tsp	instant coffee powder, preferably espresso	5 mL
¼ cup	granulated sugar	50 mL
2 tsp	corn syrup	10 mL
2	eggs	2
1	egg yolk	1
½ tsp	vanilla extract	2 mL
	Sweetened whipped cream	

1. In a saucepan over low heat, combine chocolate and whipping cream. Cook, stirring, until chocolate is melted. Add milk and coffee powder, whisking well, and heat until mixture reaches a simmer and coffee dissolves. Remove from heat.

2. Meanwhile, in a separate saucepan, combine sugar, corn syrup and 2 tbsp (25 mL) water. Cook over medium heat, swirling the pot until sugar dissolves. Reduce heat to low and cook, tilting the pot gently, if necessary, to prevent burning, until mixture turns a light golden color. Remove from heat. Add 2 tbsp (25 mL) hot water and return to element until caramel is syrupy. Remove from heat and set aside.

3. In a bowl, beat eggs, egg yolk and vanilla. Add ½ cup (125 mL) of the chocolate mixture, whisking to combine. Gradually add remainder, whisking to blend.

4. Place a fine-mesh sieve over a 4-cup (1 L) measuring cup or mixing bowl with a pouring spout and pour mixture through it. Stir in caramel. Pour into ramekins or demitasse cups and cover tightly with foil. Place in slow cooker stoneware and pour boiling water to come halfway up the side of the cups. Cook on High for 1 to 2 hours (see Tips, left), until custard firms up and centers just quiver. Let cool, then place in the refrigerator to chill thoroughly. Serve with a dollop of whipped cream.

Chile-Spiked Chocolate Pots

This is an updated version of the French classic pots de crème. *You won't taste the chile but it adds appealing depth to the chocolate. If they will fit in your slow cooker, make these in demitasse cups for a spectacular presentation.*

Tip

You may need to play with ramekins or cups to find 6 that will fit comfortably in your slow cooker. I use taller French porcelain ramekins, which fit nicely in my largest (7 quart) slow cooker, but many demitasse cups would also work well. The quantity really depends upon the combined configuration of your stoneware and the cups. If your slow cooker will only accommodate 4 ramekins, they will obviously be fuller, so expect the cooking time to be closer to 2 hours.

Serves 4 to 6

- 4 to 6 tall ramekins or demitasse cups (see Tip, left)
- Large (minimum 5 quart) oval slow cooker

3 oz	bittersweet chocolate, coarsely chopped	90 g
¾ cup	whipping (35%) cream	175 mL
¾ cup	whole milk	175 mL
¼ cup	granulated sugar	50 mL
2	eggs	2
1	egg yolk	1
2 tbsp	cocoa powder	25 mL
½ tsp	vanilla extract	2 mL
⅛ tsp	cayenne pepper	0.5 mL
Pinch	salt	Pinch
	Sweetened whipped cream	

1. In a saucepan over low heat, combine chocolate and whipping cream. Cook, stirring, until chocolate is melted. Add milk and sugar, whisking well, and heat until mixture reaches a simmer. Remove from heat.

2. In a bowl, beat eggs, egg yolk, cocoa powder, vanilla, cayenne and salt. Add ½ cup (125 mL) of the chocolate mixture, whisking to combine. Gradually add remainder, whisking to blend.

3. Place a fine-mesh sieve over a 4-cup (1 L) measuring cup or mixing bowl with a pouring spout and pour mixture through it. Pour into ramekins or demitasse cups and cover tightly with foil. Place in stoneware and pour in hot water to come halfway up the side of the cups. Cook on High for 1 hour, until center of custards quiver. Let cool, then place in the refrigerator to chill thoroughly. Serve with a dollop of whipped cream.

Butterscotch Pudding

Most people name chocolate as their favorite childhood pudding, but my fondest memories are of butterscotch pudding, which I helped my mother stir laboriously on the stovetop. This recipe captures those flavors but dramatically reduces the workload because most of the stirring is eliminated.

Serves 6 to 8

- 5- to 6-cup (1.25 to 1.5 L) baking dish, lightly greased
- Large (approx. 5 quart) oval slow cooker

¼ cup	butter	50 mL
1½ cups	Demerara or other raw cane sugar	375 mL
½ cup	all-purpose flour	125 mL
½ tsp	salt	2 mL
1 cup	whipping (35%) cream	250 mL
2	eggs	2
1 tsp	vanilla extract	5 mL
2 cups	milk	500 mL

1. In a saucepan over medium heat, melt butter and brown sugar. Stir in flour and salt and cook, stirring, for 2 minutes. Add cream and heat, stirring occasionally, just until mixture reaches the boiling point, about 5 minutes. Remove from heat and set aside.

2. In a bowl, whisk eggs and vanilla. Gradually whisk a small amount of the hot cream mixture into eggs until incorporated, then whisk mixture into saucepan. Whisk in milk, then pour into prepared baking dish. Whisk again. Cover with foil and secure with a string. Place dish in stoneware and add enough boiling water to come 1 inch (2.5 cm) up the side of the dish. Cover and cook on High for 3 hours, until edges are set but center is still jiggly. Stir well. Serve immediately or cover and keep warm until ready to serve. Stir well before serving.

Grandma's Tapioca Pudding

Tapioca is a form of cassava, a tropical plant, and it produces a thick, starchy pudding that is quintessential "nursery food." Most people use the smaller quick-cooking pearls, but I love the look and texture of the large ones, which you can purchase at Asian markets. Prepared in the slow cooker, tapioca pudding is extremely easy to make. Instead of constant stirring on the stovetop, all it requires is a couple of stirs during the cooking process to ensure that the pearls are equally distributed throughout the pudding. Serve this with fresh berries or enjoy it on its own.

Serves 6

- Lightly greased slow cooker stoneware
- Small (maximum 3½ quart) slow cooker

½ cup	tapioca pearls	125 mL
3 cups	milk	750 mL
½ cup	granulated sugar	125 mL
2	eggs	2
2 tsp	finely grated lemon zest	10 mL
1 tsp	vanilla extract	5 mL
Pinch	salt	Pinch
	Fresh berries, optional	

1. In a bowl, combine tapioca pearls with cold water to cover. Stir well and set aside for 20 minutes. Drain, discarding any excess liquid. Transfer to prepared slow cooker stoneware.

2. In a blender, combine milk, sugar, eggs, lemon zest, vanilla and salt. Blend until smooth. Stir into tapioca. Cover and cook on High for 2 to 2½ hours, stirring occasionally, until thickened and set. Stir well. Serve warm or cover and chill overnight. Top with fresh berries, if using.

Apple Blackberry Crisp

There is something quintessentially comforting about a baked fruit dessert. This one adds an additional nutritional hit with a topping of whole-grain oats. Served with a scoop of vanilla ice cream (my preferred accompaniment), it's a little on the rich side, so I like to keep the servings smallish. Extras keep well and can be reheated in the microwave for another meal.

Vegetarian
Friendly

Serves 8

- Lightly greased slow cooker stoneware
- Medium (approx. 4 quart) slow cooker

4	large apples, peeled, cored and sliced	4
2 cups	blackberries	500 mL
2 tbsp	freshly squeezed lemon juice	25 mL
²⁄₃ cup	granulated sugar	150 mL
½ tsp	freshly grated nutmeg	2 mL

Topping

¾ cup	old-fashioned rolled oats	175 mL
½ cup	packed brown sugar	125 mL
½ cup	all-purpose or whole wheat flour	125 mL
¼ tsp	salt	2 mL
½ cup	cold butter, cubed	125 mL
	Sweetened whipped cream or vanilla ice cream	

1. In prepared stoneware, combine apples, blackberries, lemon juice, granulated sugar and nutmeg. Stir to combine.

2. **Topping:** In a bowl, combine oats, brown sugar, flour and salt. Using a pastry blender, 2 knives or your fingers, cut in butter until mixture resembles coarse crumbs. Sprinkle evenly over fruit.

3. Place a clean tea towel, folded in half (so you will have 2 layers), over top of the stoneware to absorb moisture. Cover and cook on High for 2 to 3 hours, until crisp is hot and bubbly and top is browned. Serve with whipped cream or vanilla ice cream.

Vegan Alternative

Substitute an equal quantity of non-hydrogenated margarine for the butter and drizzle with soy creamer instead of finishing with a dairy product.

Entertaining Worthy

Vegetarian Friendly

Can Be Halved
see Tip, below

Tip

If you are halving this recipe, be sure to use a small (approx. 1½ to 3½ quart) slow cooker.

Poached Pears in Chocolate Sauce

Nothing could be simpler than these pears poached in a simple sugar syrup enhanced with vanilla and a hint of cinnamon. The fruit is delicious on its own, but if, like me, you enjoy gilding the lily, add the chocolate sauce, which is very easy to make.

Serves 6 to 8

- Medium to large (3½ to 5 quart) slow cooker

	Finely grated zest of 1 lemon	
2 tbsp	freshly squeezed lemon juice	25 mL
4	large firm pears, such as Bosc or Bartlett, peeled, cored and cut into quarters on the vertical	4
½ cup	granulated sugar	125 mL
1	piece (2 inches/5 cm) cinnamon stick	1
1 tsp	vanilla extract	5 mL

Chocolate Sauce

½ cup	whipping (35%) cream	125 mL
4 oz	bittersweet chocolate, chopped	125 g

1. In a large bowl, combine 4 cups (1 L) water and lemon juice. After preparing the pears immediately drop them into the lemon juice solution. (This will prevent the fruit from turning brown.)

2. In slow cooker stoneware, combine 2 cups (500 mL) water, sugar, cinnamon stick, vanilla and lemon zest. Stir well. Drain pears and add to stoneware. Cover and cook on Low for 6 hours or on High for 3 hours, until pears are tender. Transfer pears and liquid to a large bowl. Cover and chill thoroughly.

3. **Chocolate Sauce:** When you're ready to serve, combine cream and chocolate in a saucepan or microwave-safe bowl. Cook over low heat, stirring constantly, until melted, or microwave on High for 1½ minutes, then stir well.

4. To serve, using a slotted spoon, transfer pears to a plate and top with chocolate sauce.

Poached Quince

Quinces are a fabulous winter fruit that are made for the slow cooker because they demand cooking. Raw, the quince is a tough, fibrous ball. Softened by slow cooking, it turns a beautiful shade of pink and melts in your mouth, releasing a panoply of complex flavors.

Entertaining Worthy

Vegan Friendly

Serves 4 to 6

- Small to medium (2 to 4 quart) slow cooker (see Tips, right)

½ cup	water	125 mL
½ cup	agave nectar (see Tip, right)	125 mL
	Zest of 1 orange	
4	quinces (about 2 lbs/1 kg), peeled, cored and sliced	4
	Whipped cream, mascarpone or soy creamer	
	Toasted chopped walnuts, optional	

1. In slow cooker stoneware, combine water, agave nectar and orange zest. Add quinces and stir well. Cover and cook on Low for about 8 hours, until quinces are tender and turn pink. To serve, top with whipped cream or a dollop of mascarpone or drizzle with soy creamer. Sprinkle with walnuts, if using.

Tip

I like to use agave nectar to poach the quince because, unlike granulated sugar, it is a natural product. It also has a very mild flavor that doesn't interfere with the complexity of the fruit. Agave nectar is available in natural foods stores, but if you can't find it, use an equal quantity of granulated sugar instead.

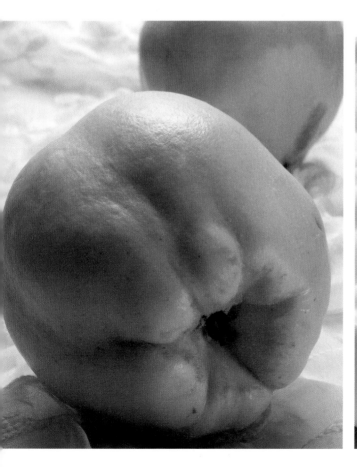

Tip

I prefer to use currants rather than raisins in this pudding as they have a firmer texture.

Make Ahead

Complete Steps 1 and 2. Cover and refrigerate overnight. When you're ready to cook, complete the recipe.

Mom's Bread-and-Butter Pudding

This is an old favorite from my childhood — rich, heavy and, if consumed in small quantities, marvelously satisfying. In the days when thrift was a virtue, mothers managed the food budget by making dishes such as bread pudding, which used up day-old bread and eggs that were heading toward their best-before date.

Serves 8

- 8-cup (2 L) baking or soufflé dish, lightly greased
- Large (minimum 5 quart) oval slow cooker

6	slices white bread, about ½ inch (1 cm) thick	6
¼ cup	softened butter (approx.)	50 mL
½ cup	currants or raisins	125 mL
3 cups	milk	750 mL
½ cup	packed brown sugar, preferably raw cane such as Demerara	125 mL
Pinch	salt	Pinch
4	eggs	4
2	egg yolks	2
1 tsp	vanilla extract	5 mL
2 tbsp	granulated sugar	25 mL

1. Butter bread on both sides and cut into ½-inch (1 cm) cubes. Place in prepared baking dish. Add currants and toss.

2. In a saucepan, combine milk, brown sugar and salt. Heat over low heat, stirring, until bubbles form around the edges and sugar is dissolved. Remove from heat. Meanwhile, in a small bowl, beat eggs, egg yolks and vanilla. Beat in a small amount of heated milk, then transfer to saucepan and whisk well. Pour mixture through a sieve over bread and stir well. Cover with plastic wrap and, using your hands, push the bread down so it is submerged in the liquid. Set aside for 10 minutes or cover and refrigerate overnight, pushing the bread down into the liquid once or twice.

3. Cover dish with foil, leaving room for pudding to expand, and tie tightly at the rim with a string. Place dish in slow cooker stoneware and add enough boiling water to come 1 inch (2.5 cm) up the sides. Cover and cook on High for 3 to 4 hours, until puffed and set.

4. Meanwhile, preheat broiler. Remove foil and sprinkle granulated sugar evenly over top of pudding. Place under broiler until sugar glazes, about 2 minutes. Serve warm.

Variation

Rum & Raisin Bread Pudding: Use raisins instead of currants and substitute ¼ cup (50 mL) dark rum for the vanilla.

Chocolate Bread-and-Butter Pudding

If you're looking for a rich, decadent dessert to satisfy self-indulgent longings, look no further. Finished with a dollop of vanilla ice cream, this will help you achieve a state of nirvana.

Vegetarian Friendly

Serves 8

- 8-cup (2 L) baking dish, lightly greased
- Large (minimum 5 quart) slow cooker

7	slices white bread, about ½-inch (1 cm) thick, trimmed of crusts	7
2 tbsp	softened butter (approx.)	25 mL
½ cup	seedless raspberry jam (see Tip, right)	125 mL
1½ cups	half-and-half (10%) cream	375 mL
8 oz	bittersweet chocolate	250 g
½ cup	granulated sugar	125 mL
1 tsp	vanilla extract	5 mL
Pinch	salt	Pinch
3	eggs	3
2 tbsp	Demerara or other raw cane sugar	25 mL
	Vanilla ice cream or sweetened whipped cream	

1. Butter bread on one side only and spread with jam. Cut into ½-inch (1 cm) cubes and set aside.

2. In a saucepan over low heat, combine cream, chocolate, sugar, vanilla and salt. Cook, stirring constantly, until chocolate has completely melted. Remove from heat.

3. In a bowl, whisk eggs. Whisk in chocolate mixture until thoroughly blended.

4. Pour one-third of chocolate mixture into prepared dish. Add half the bread, jam side down, overlapping as necessary. Repeat. Pour remaining chocolate evenly over top. Place a piece of plastic wrap over top of pudding and push down gently with your hand to ensure bread cubes are well coated with chocolate mixture. Let stand for at least 20 minutes or refrigerate overnight, pushing the bread down into the liquid once or twice. Remove plastic wrap.

5. Cover dish with foil and tie tightly with string. Place dish in slow cooker stoneware and add enough boiling water to come 1 inch (2.5 cm) up the sides. Cover and cook on High for 3 to 4 hours, until pudding is puffed and set and a toothpick inserted in the center comes out clean. Remove dish from stoneware and let cool slightly. When you're ready to serve, preheat broiler. Sprinkle sugar evenly over top of pudding. Place under broiler until slightly caramelized.

Tip

Not only does seedless raspberry jam omit the pesky seeds, it also has a more intense flavor than its conventional cousin. If you don't have it, by all means substitute raspberry jam with seeds. The results will still be delicious.

Make Ahead

Complete Steps 1 through 4. Cover and refrigerate overnight. When you're ready to cook, complete the recipe.

Eliza's Bread Pudding

This old-fashioned dessert is very easy to make and quite delicious. I adapted it from Eliza Acton's recipe for bread pudding circa 1845, with some contemporary twists. It's so simple that it lends itself nicely to variations.

Make Ahead

Complete Steps 1 and 2. Cover and refrigerate overnight. When you're ready to cook, stir well and complete the recipe.

Serves 6

- 8-cup (2 L) pudding basin or bowl, lightly greased
- Large (minimum 5 quart) oval slow cooker

2 cups	milk	500 mL
½ cup	granulated sugar	125 mL
Pinch	salt	Pinch
2 cups	packed fresh bread crumbs (about half a loaf)	500 mL
¼ cup	butter, cubed and softened	50 mL
3	eggs	3
1 tsp	vanilla extract	5 mL
	Finely grated zest of 1 lemon	
¼ cup	raisins	50 mL

1. In a large saucepan over medium heat, bring milk, sugar and salt to a simmer. Remove from heat. Add bread crumbs and butter and stir until butter melts. Set aside for 15 minutes.

2. In a separate bowl, beat eggs with vanilla and lemon zest. Stir in raisins. Add to bread crumb mixture and stir well. Transfer to prepared basin.

3. Cover with foil and tie tightly with string. Place dish in slow cooker stoneware and add enough boiling water to come 1 inch (2.5 cm) up the sides. Cover and cook on High for 2½ hours, until a toothpick inserted in center of pudding comes out clean.

Variations

Orange-Studded Bread Pudding: Substitute 2 tbsp (25 mL) brandy, orange-flavored liqueur or Grand Marnier for the vanilla and 2 tbsp (25 mL) candied orange peel for the raisins.

Cherry-Studded Bread Pudding: Substitute 1 tsp (5 mL) almond extract for the vanilla and ¼ cup (50 mL) dried cherries for the raisins.

Scottish Oat Pudding with Brandy Butter

This is an adaptation of an old Scottish recipe known as clootie dumpling because in the past it was steamed in a "clout," or cloth. It is extremely easy to make and quite yummy — everyone always eats more than they should. Interestingly, varying the fruit changes the flavor of the dish dramatically, although all suggestions are equally delicious.

Serves 6

- 3- to 4-cup (750 mL to 1 L) pudding basin or bowl, lightly greased
- Large (minimum 5 quart) oval slow cooker

½ cup	rolled oats	125 mL
¾ cup	whole wheat flour (see Tip, right)	175 mL
¼ cup	Demerara or other raw cane sugar	50 mL
1 tsp	baking powder	5 mL
1 tsp	ground cinnamon	5 mL
¼ tsp	freshly grated nutmeg	1 mL
¼ tsp	ground ginger	1 mL
¼ cup	cold butter, cubed	50 mL
1	egg, beaten	1
2 tbsp	golden syrup (see Tips, page 372)	25 mL
¼ cup	buttermilk	50 mL
⅔ cup	raisins, currants, dried cherries or cranberries	150 mL

Brandy Butter

6 tbsp	softened butter	90 mL
¼ cup	confectioner's (icing) sugar, sifted	50 mL
2 tbsp	brandy	25 mL
1 tsp	freshly squeezed lemon juice	5 mL
	Freshly grated nutmeg	

1. In a food processor, process rolled oats until floury. Add flour, sugar, baking powder, cinnamon, nutmeg and ginger and pulse to blend. Add butter and pulse until mealy.

2. In a bowl, combine egg, syrup and buttermilk. Add to dry ingredients and pulse just until blended. Fold in raisins.

3. Spoon batter into prepared pan. Cover tightly with foil and secure with a string. Place in slow cooker stoneware and pour in enough boiling water to come 1 inch (2.5 mL) up the sides of the dish. Cover and cook on High for 3 hours, until a tester inserted in the center comes out clean. Unmold and serve with Brandy Butter.

4. **Brandy Butter:** In a warm bowl, beat butter until creamy. Add sugar, brandy, lemon juice and nutmeg to taste. Mix well. Use your hands to form into a ball. Place in refrigerator until hard. Serve cold over hot pudding.

Tip

I like to use whole wheat flour in this recipe because it is more nutritious, but if you prefer, substitute an equal quantity of all-purpose.

Orange Sponge

This is a simple, old-fashioned dessert that still charms. The egg whites separate into a cake layer, leaving a lovely orange custard on the bottom.

Serves 4 to 6

- 4-cup (1 L) baking dish, greased
- Large (minimum 5 quart) oval slow cooker

½ cup	granulated sugar	125 mL
2 tbsp	butter	25 mL
	Zest of 2 oranges	
3	eggs, separated	3
¼ cup	all-purpose flour	50 mL
⅔ cup	milk	150 mL
½ cup	freshly squeezed orange juice	125 mL
1 tbsp	orange-flavored liqueur such as Cointreau, optional	15 mL
Pinch	salt	Pinch

1. In a bowl, using an electric mixer if desired, beat sugar, butter and orange zest until creamy. Add egg yolks, one at a time, beating until incorporated. Alternately, beat in flour and milk, making 2 additions of each. Beat in orange juice and liqueur, if using.

2. In a separate bowl, beat egg whites and salt until stiff peaks form. Gently fold into flour mixture to make a smooth batter. Spoon into prepared dish. Cover with foil and secure with string. Place dish in slow cooker stoneware and pour in enough boiling water to come 1 inch (2.5 cm) up the sides of the dish. Cover and cook on High for 2½ hours, until a toothpick inserted in the center of the pudding comes out clean. Serve immediately.

Blueberry Rhubarb Sponge Cake

This yummy dessert is very much like a cobbler, but the addition of eggs to the batter produces a topping that resembles sponge cake. Make it with your favorite fruits in season (see Variations, below) and be sure to finish it with a dollop of vanilla ice cream.

Tip

If you are halving this recipe, be sure to use a small (approx. 1½ to 3½ quart) slow cooker.

Serves 6 to 8

- Lightly greased slow cooker stoneware
- Medium to large (3½ to 5 quart) oval slow cooker

2 cups	blueberries, thawed if frozen	500 mL
2 cups	rhubarb, cut into 1-inch (2.5 cm) chunks, thawed if frozen	500 mL
1¼ cups	granulated sugar, divided	300 mL
1 tbsp	cornstarch	15 mL
	Finely grated zest and juice of 1 orange	
1 cup	all-purpose flour	250 mL
1½ tsp	baking powder	7 mL
½ tsp	salt	2 mL
2	eggs	2
1 cup	granulated sugar	250 mL
1 tbsp	melted butter	15 mL
	Vanilla ice cream, optional	

1. In prepared slow cooker stoneware, mix together blueberries, rhubarb, ¼ cup (50 mL) of the sugar, cornstarch and orange zest and juice.

2. In a bowl, combine flour, baking powder and salt. In a separate bowl, whisk eggs, remaining cup (250 mL) of sugar, 2 tbsp (25 mL) water and butter. Add dry ingredients and stir just to combine. Drop over fruit and spread as evenly as you can.

3. Place a clean tea towel, folded in half (so you will have 2 layers), over top of the stoneware to absorb moisture. Cover and cook on High for 2½ to 3 hours, until a toothpick inserted in the center of the crust comes out clean. Serve warm with vanilla ice cream, if using.

Variations

Strawberry Rhubarb Sponge Cake: Substitute 3 cups (750 mL) sliced strawberries for the blueberries.

Blueberry Peach Sponge Cake: Substitute 3 cups (750 mL) thinly sliced peaches for the rhubarb and the zest and juice of 1 lemon for the orange. Add 2 tbsp (25 mL) water and increase the amount of sugar in the fruit to suit your taste.

Coconut Rice Pudding with Flambéed Bananas

It is hard to believe that something this easy to make can taste so delicious. Whenever I make this, temptation strikes — I fantasize about not sharing it and eating the whole thing myself.

Serves 4

- Lightly greased slow cooker stoneware
- Small to medium (2 to 3½ quart) slow cooker

¾ cup	short-grain brown rice or Arborio rice	175 mL
1	can (14 oz/400 mL) coconut milk	1
1 cup	water	250 mL
½ cup	Demerara or other raw cane sugar	125 mL
1 tsp	almond extract	5 mL
Pinch	salt	Pinch

Banana Topping

3 tbsp	butter	45 mL
3 tbsp	Demerara or other raw cane sugar	45 mL
4	bananas, sliced	4
¼ cup	amaretto liqueur	50 mL
2 tbsp	toasted shredded coconut (see Tip, right)	25 mL

1. In prepared slow cooker stoneware, combine rice, coconut milk, water, sugar, almond extract and salt. Cover and cook on High for 3 to 4 hours, until rice is tender. Uncover and stir well. Serve hot or transfer to a bowl, cover tightly and chill for up to 2 days.

2. **Banana Topping:** In a skillet over medium heat, combine butter and sugar. Cook, stirring, until butter melts and mixture is smooth. Add bananas and cook, stirring, until tender, about 5 minutes. Sprinkle amaretto evenly over top and, standing well back, ignite. Allow liqueur to burn off. To serve, spoon pudding into bowls, top with bananas and garnish with toasted coconut.

Vegan Alternative

Substitute an equal quantity of non-hydrogenated margarine for the butter.

Tip

To toast coconut, spread on a baking sheet and place in a preheated 350°F (180°C) oven, stirring once or twice, for 7 to 8 minutes.

New York–Style Cheesecake

So-called Philadelphia-style cream cheese was invented in upstate New York in the late 19th century, paving the way for the development of home-grown cheesecakes. According to New York food authority Arthur Schwartz, they are a spin on cakes traditionally made from fresh curd cheeses in Eastern Europe. This is an adaptation of George Geary's version from his book 125 Best Cheesecake Recipes. *Like many recipes, George's does not include strawberry sauce — in my opinion, an integral part of the package.*

Tips

If using a springform pan, ensure that water doesn't seep into the cake by wrapping the bottom of the pan in one large, seamless piece of foil that extends up the sides and over the top. Cover the top with a single piece of foil that extends down the sides and secure with a string.

I like the hint of acid that a dash of balsamic vinegar adds to the strawberries, but this is purely a matter of taste. I also like an additional bit of nip, so I often stir in some crushed grains of paradise or freshly ground black pepper, to taste, when making the sugar syrup that is boiled with the strawberries.

Serves 8 to 10

- 7-inch (17.5 cm) 6-cup (1.5 L) soufflé dish, lined with greased heavy-duty foil, or 7-inch (17.5 cm) well-greased springform pan (see Tips, left)
- Large (minimum 5 quart) oval slow cooker

Crust

1 cup	graham cracker crumbs	250 mL
3 tbsp	melted butter	45 mL

Cheesecake

2	packages (each 8 oz/250 g) cream cheese, softened	2
¾ cup	granulated sugar	175 mL
2 tbsp	all-purpose flour	25 mL
1 tbsp	finely grated lemon or orange zest or combination of both	15 mL
2	eggs	2
1 tsp	vanilla extract	5 mL
3 tbsp	whipping (35%) cream	45 mL

Strawberry Sauce, optional

¼ cup	granulated sugar	50 mL
¼ cup	water	50 mL
2 cups	halved hulled strawberries, thawed if frozen	500 mL
1 tsp	balsamic vinegar, optional (see Tips, left)	5 mL

1. **Crust:** In a bowl, combine graham cracker crumbs and butter. Press mixture into the bottom of prepared dish. Place in freezer until ready to use.

2. **Cheesecake:** In a food processor, combine cream cheese and sugar and process until smooth. Add flour, zest, eggs, vanilla and cream and process until smooth. Spoon mixture over crust. Cover dish tightly with foil and secure with a string. Place dish in stoneware and pour in enough boiling water to come 1 inch (2.5 cm) up the sides of dish. Cover and cook on High for 3 to 4 hours, until edges are set and center is just slightly jiggly. Chill thoroughly before serving.

3. **Strawberry Sauce:** In a saucepan, combine sugar and water. Bring to a boil and cook for 1 minute. Add strawberries, return to a boil and cook until strawberries begin to lose their juice, about 4 minutes. Remove from heat and stir in vinegar, if using. Let cool and spoon over chilled cake.

Orange-Laced Rhubarb Ginger Pudding Cake

It's hard to believe that this light and flavorful dessert, which is basically a traditional English steamed pudding, is so easy to make in the slow cooker. Serve this with a dollop of vanilla ice cream or on its own. Either way, it's delicious.

Tips

An English pudding basin is actually a simple rimmed bowl, most often white, that comes in various sizes. The rim is an asset because it enables you to make a seal with foil, which can be well secured with string or rubber band.

If you prefer, cook this pudding in 6 individual ramekins, each about ³⁄₄ cup (175 mL). Divide marmalade mixture equally among them and check for doneness after 2 hours.

I prefer to use half whole wheat flour when making this dessert as it adds nutrients and pleasing texture. If you don't have any on hand, feel free to substitute all-purpose flour.

Serves 6 to 8

- 6-cup (1.5 L) pudding basin, lightly greased (see Tips, left)
- Large (minimum 5 quart) oval slow cooker

³⁄₄ cup	all-purpose flour	175 mL
³⁄₄ cup	whole wheat flour (see Tips, left)	175 mL
¹⁄₂ cup	granulated sugar	125 mL
1¹⁄₂ tsp	baking powder	7 mL
¹⁄₂ tsp	salt	2 mL
¹⁄₂ cup	butter, softened	125 mL
2	eggs	2
	Grated zest and juice of 1 orange	
2 cups	sliced (¹⁄₂ inch/1 cm) rhubarb	500 mL
2	balls stem ginger, chopped	2
¹⁄₄ cup	stem ginger syrup	50 mL
2 tbsp	orange marmalade	25 mL

1. In a food processor, combine all-purpose and whole wheat flours, sugar, baking powder and salt. Pulse to blend. Add butter, eggs and orange zest and juice and pulse until batter just begins to form a ball. Add rhubarb and stem ginger and pulse to blend.

2. In a small bowl, beat ginger syrup and marmalade until smooth. Place in bottom of prepared dish. Pour batter over top. Cover basin tightly with foil and secure with a string. Place in slow cooker stoneware and pour in enough boiling water to come 1 inch (2.5 cm) up the sides. Cover and cook on High for 3 to 4 hours, until a toothpick inserted in center of pudding comes out clean.

Chocolate Pudding Cake

It just doesn't get any better than this old-fashioned dessert. A rich, dark chocolate cake comes with its own luscious chocolate sauce — all baked in the same dish. Since I often can't resist gilding the lily, I like to serve this with a big scoop of vanilla or chocolate ripple ice cream. Yum!

Entertaining Worthy

Vegetarian Friendly

Serves 6

- 8-cup (2 L) baking dish, lightly greased
- Large (minimum 5 quart) oval slow cooker

Sauce

1 cup	packed brown sugar	250 mL
2 tbsp	cocoa powder	25 mL
1 cup	boiling water	250 mL
2 tbsp	liqueur (see Tips, right)	25 mL

Cake

1 cup	all-purpose flour	250 mL
1/2 cup	granulated sugar	125 mL
1/3 cup	cocoa powder, sifted	75 mL
1 tbsp	baking powder	15 mL
1 cup	milk	250 mL
3 tbsp	melted butter	45 mL
2	eggs, beaten	2
1 tsp	vanilla extract	5 mL
1/2 cup	chopped toasted blanched hazelnuts or almonds, optional (see Tips, right)	125 mL
	Ice cream, optional	

1. **Sauce:** In a bowl, combine brown sugar, cocoa powder, boiling water and liqueur. Stir well and pour into prepared dish.

2. **Cake:** In a separate bowl, combine flour, granulated sugar, cocoa powder and baking powder. Stir to blend. Add milk, butter, eggs and vanilla and mix just until blended. Fold in nuts, if using. Pour gently over sauce.

3. Cover dish with foil and secure with a string. Place dish in slow cooker stoneware and pour in enough boiling water to come 1 inch (2.5 cm) up the sides of the dish. Cover and cook on High for 2 1/2 hours, until a toothpick inserted in the center of the cake comes out clean. Serve hot, with sauce spooned over the cake and a dollop of ice cream, if using.

Variation

Double Chocolate Pudding Cake: Substitute 1/2 cup (125 mL) chocolate chips for the nuts and use a chocolate or coffee-flavored liqueur or brandy in the sauce.

Tips

I recommend using a liqueur that complements the flavors of the nuts — Frangelico, if you're using hazelnuts, or amaretto, if using almonds. Plain brandy will work well with either.

To blanch and toast hazelnuts: Bring 2 cups (500 mL) water to a boil in a large saucepan. Add 2 tbsp (25 mL) baking soda. (The water will foam up, so skim off the foam periodically.) Add nuts and boil for 5 minutes. Drain in a colander and rinse thoroughly under cold running water. Pop the skins off using your fingers and discard skins. Place peeled nuts on a baking sheet in a preheated 350°F (180°C) oven, until lightly browned, about 8 minutes. Chop the nuts on a cutting board, using a sharp knife. The same techniques work for almonds, but omit baking soda from the blanching water.

Pear and Chocolate Pudding Cake

This Italian-inspired dessert, which is a cross between chocolate coconut pudding and a rich dark cake, is the perfect finish to any meal. I like to serve it warm with vanilla-flavored whipped cream or a dollop of vanilla ice cream, but it is also good cold.

Tips

I like to use firm pears such as Bosc or Bartlett in this recipe. If you shred them ahead of time, be sure to put them in a solution of 4 cups (1 L) water and 1 tbsp (25 mL) lemon juice to prevent oxidation. Drain thoroughly before using in recipe.

I prefer a cake-like texture, but if you want this dessert to be more like a custard, reduce the cooking time to about 1½ hours.

Serves 8

- 8-cup (2 L) baking dish, lightly greased
- Large (minimum 5 quart) oval slow cooker

8 oz	macaroons (about 18)	250 g
⅓ cup	cocoa powder	75 mL
¼ cup	granulated sugar	50 mL
2 tsp	finely grated lemon zest	10 mL
1 tsp	ground cinnamon	5 mL
4	eggs, separated	4
½ cup	whipping (35%) cream	125 mL
4	ripe pears, peeled, cored and shredded (see Tips, left)	4
Pinch	salt	Pinch

1. In a food processor fitted with a metal blade, pulse macaroons until finely ground. Add cocoa powder, sugar, lemon zest and cinnamon and pulse to blend. Add egg yolks and cream and process until smooth. Add pears and pulse to blend.

2. In a bowl, beat egg whites and salt until soft peaks form. Fold into pear mixture. Transfer to prepared baking dish. Cover dish with foil and secure with string or rubber band. Place dish in slow cooker stoneware and pour in enough boiling water to come 1 inch (2.5 cm) up the sides of the dish. Cover and cook on High for 2 hours, until firm and puffed (see Tips, right).

Upside-Down Pineapple Gingerbread

If you hanker for a good old-fashioned dessert, try this. Sweet, juicy pineapple on a bed of deep, dark gingerbread makes an ambrosial combination. All you need to add is a big dollop of vanilla ice cream.

Serves 8

- Lightly greased slow cooker stoneware
- Large (approx. 5 quart) oval slow cooker

¼ cup	melted butter	50 mL
½ cup	Demerara or other raw cane sugar	125 mL
2	cans (each 14 oz/398 mL) pineapple chunks, drained	2

Cake

½ cup	light (fancy) molasses	125 mL
½ cup	butter	125 mL
½ cup	Demerara or other raw cane sugar	125 mL
2¼ cups	all-purpose flour	550 mL
1 tbsp	ground ginger	15 mL
1 tsp	baking soda	5 mL
½ tsp	salt	2 mL
1	egg, beaten	1
⅔ cup	buttermilk	150 mL
	Vanilla ice cream or whipped cream	

1. In a small bowl, combine butter and brown sugar. Spread over bottom of prepared stoneware. Spread pineapple evenly over top.

2. **Cake:** In a saucepan over medium heat, combine molasses, butter and brown sugar until melted and smooth. Remove from heat and set aside.

3. In a bowl, combine flour, ginger, baking soda and salt. Make a well in the center. Add egg, buttermilk and cooled molasses mixture. Mix just until blended.

4. Place 2 tea towels, folded in half (so you have 4 layers), over top of stoneware to absorb moisture. Cover and cook on high for 2 to 2½ hours or until a toothpick inserted in center of cake comes out clean. Serve with ice cream or whipped cream.

Tip

I prefer to use half whole wheat flour when making this dessert as it adds nutrients and pleasing texture. If you don't have any on hand, feel free to substitute all-purpose flour.

Caramelized Apple Upside-Down Spice Cake

This old-fashioned favorite has terrific caramelized apple flavor, not only from the apples but also from the apple butter in the cake batter. It's great for a potluck or a party because people can help themselves from a warm slow cooker. A big scoop of vanilla ice cream is the perfect finish.

Serves 8

- Lightly greased slow cooker stoneware
- Large (approx. 5 quart) oval slow cooker

Topping

¼ cup	melted butter	50 mL
½ cup	Demerara or other raw cane sugar	125 mL
6 cups	sliced peeled apples (about 8 small)	1.5 L

Cake

1 cup	whole wheat flour (see Tip, left)	250 mL
1 cup	all-purpose flour	250 mL
2 tsp	baking soda	10 mL
1 tbsp	ground ginger	15 mL
1 tsp	ground cinnamon	5 mL
1 tsp	ground allspice	5 mL
½ tsp	ground cloves	2 mL
½ tsp	salt	2 mL
½ cup	Demerara or other raw cane sugar	125 mL
1	egg, beaten	1
1 cup	apple butter	250 mL
½ cup	buttermilk	125 mL
2 tbsp	molasses	25 mL
¼ cup	oil	50 mL
	Vanilla ice cream	

1. **Topping:** In a small bowl, combine butter and brown sugar. Spread over bottom of prepared stoneware. Arrange apples on top.

2. **Cake:** In a bowl, combine whole wheat and all-purpose flours, baking soda, ginger, cinnamon, allspice, cloves and salt. Mix well and make a well in the center.

3. In another bowl, whisk together sugar and egg, then whisk in apple butter, buttermilk, molasses and oil. Pour mixture into the well and mix just until combined. Pour batter over apples.

4. Place 2 tea towels, folded in half (so you have 4 layers), over top of stoneware to absorb moisture. Cover and cook on High for 2½ to 3 hours or until a toothpick inserted in center of cake comes out clean. When ready to serve, slice and invert onto a plate. Top with vanilla ice cream.

Gingery Orange Sticky Pudding

This is a variation on the theme of great English puddings. The combination of marmalade and rich sugarcane syrup, which melt together while cooking to create a lusciously sticky sauce, is enough to make anyone request seconds.

Tips

Golden syrup, which is made from the juice of sugarcane, is a British product that is increasingly available in North American supermarkets. If you can't find it, substitute pure maple syrup, which will add a pleasant bit of maple flavor to the pudding or, if you have it, the syrup from a jar of stem ginger. The latter will intensify the ginger flavor.

To unmold, loosen the pudding all around using a knife and invert onto a serving plate.

Serves 6

- 4- to 6-cup (1 to 1.5 L) pudding basin or bowl, lightly greased
- Large (minimum 5 quart) oval slow cooker

1½ cups	all-purpose flour	375 mL
2 tsp	baking powder	10 mL
2 tsp	ground ginger	10 mL
½ tsp	salt	2 mL
½ cup	softened butter	125 mL
1 cup	Demerara or other raw cane sugar	250 mL
3	eggs	3
1 tbsp	light (fancy) molasses	15 mL
⅓ cup	finely chopped candied ginger	75 mL
¼ cup	orange marmalade	50 mL
2 tbsp	golden syrup (see Tips, left)	25 mL
	Ice cream or whipped cream	

1. In a bowl, mix together flour, baking powder, ground ginger and salt.

2. In another bowl, beat butter and sugar until creamy. Add eggs and beat until incorporated. Beat in molasses. Add flour mixture and beat until just blended. Stir in candied ginger.

3. In a small bowl, combine marmalade and golden syrup. Mix well. Place mixture in bottom of prepared dish and spoon batter over top. Cover basin tightly with foil and secure with a string. Place in slow cooker stoneware and pour in enough boiling water to come 1 inch (2.5 cm) up the sides. Cover and cook on High for 3 to 4 hours, until a toothpick inserted in center of pudding comes out clean. Unmold (see Tips, left) and serve warm with ice cream or whipped cream.

Malva Pudding

Dark and richly delicious, malva pudding is comfort food South African style. My friend Debby de Groot, who is from Johannesburg, remembers her grandmother making it the old-fashioned way, tied up and boiled in a cloth, and when I shared this version with her it resurrected fond memories. If you're looking for a unique finish to a special meal or a variation on Christmas pudding, try this.

Entertaining Worthy

Vegetarian Friendly

Serves 6 to 8

- 4-cup (1 L) bowl or pudding basin, lightly greased
- Large (minimum 5 quart) oval slow cooker

1 cup	all-purpose flour	250 mL
½ cup	granulated sugar	125 mL
2 tsp	baking soda	10 mL
1 tsp	ground ginger	5 mL
¼ tsp	salt	1 mL
2	eggs	2
2 tbsp	apricot jam (see Tip, right)	25 mL
1 tsp	almond extract	5 mL
½ cup	milk	125 mL
2 tbsp	melted butter	25 mL
½ cup	chopped soft dates, such as Medjool	125 mL

Sauce

½ cup	whipping (35%) cream	125 mL
½ cup	Demerara or other raw cane sugar	125 mL
¼ cup	butter	50 mL
¼ cup	apricot brandy or brandy	50 mL
	Vanilla ice cream, optional	

Tip

If your jam is chunky, chop it before using. If it has been refrigerated, you may need to warm it to ensure easy blending.

1. In a bowl, combine flour, sugar, baking soda, ginger and salt. Make a well in the middle.

2. In a separate bowl, beat eggs, jam and almond extract. Add milk and butter and mix well. Pour into well and mix with dry ingredients just until blended. Stir in dates.

3. Spoon batter into prepared dish. Cover basin tightly with foil and secure with a string. Place in slow cooker stoneware and pour in enough boiling water to come 1 inch (2.5 cm) up the sides. Cover and cook on High for 3 hours, until a toothpick inserted in the center of the pudding comes out clean.

4. **Sauce:** Just before the pudding has finished cooking, in a saucepan over medium heat, combine cream, sugar and butter. Cook, stirring, until sugar dissolves and butter melts. Remove from heat and stir in brandy. Unmold cooked pudding and pierce in several places with a long skewer. Pour hot sauce slowly over the pudding and let stand until sauce is absorbed. Pour remainder of the sauce into a pitcher and pass at the table. If desired, accompany with vanilla ice cream.

Maple-Spiked Carrot Pudding with Candied Ginger

Vegetarian Friendly

If you are having trouble getting your kids to eat their vegetables, try this unconventional but surprisingly delicious dessert. While carrot pudding traditionally resembles a steamed version of carrot cake, this rendition most closely approximates Mom's mash. The addition of sweet ingredients such as maple syrup and candied ginger transforms the savory vegetable into a yummy dessert, particularly if you serve it with a scoop of vanilla ice cream.

Serves 6

- Lightly greased slow cooker stoneware
- Small (maximum 3½ quart) slow cooker

3	eggs	3
¼ cup	table (18%) or whipping (35%) cream	50 mL
¼ cup	maple syrup	50 mL
¼ cup	toasted chopped pecans	50 mL
2 tbsp	softened butter	25 mL
1 tsp	vanilla extract	5 mL
½ tsp	freshly grated nutmeg	2 mL
2 cups	mashed cooked carrots (about 4 large)	500 mL
½ cup	finely chopped candied ginger	125 mL
	Toasted chopped pecans, optional	
	Pouring cream or vanilla ice cream	

1. In a food processor, combine eggs, cream, maple syrup, pecans, butter, vanilla and nutmeg. Process until smooth. Add carrots and process until blended. Add ginger and pulse to combine.

2. Transfer to prepared slow cooker. Place a clean tea towel, folded in half (so you will have 2 layers), over top of stoneware to absorb moisture. Cover and cook on High for 3 hours, until pudding is set. Serve warm, garnished with additional toasted pecans, if using. Pass cream at the table or accompany with a dollop of ice cream.

Vegan Alternative

Substitute soy milk or creamer for the cream and non-hydrogenated margarine for the butter. Substitute soy creamer for the pouring cream.

Index

Library and Archives Canada Cataloguing in Publication

Finlayson, Judith
    Slow cooker comfort food : 275 soul-satisfying recipes / Judith Finlayson.

Includes index.
ISBN 978-0-7788-0224-2

1. Electric cookery, Slow. I. Title.

TX827.F56 2009   641.5'884   C2009-901914-0